Our Year
of War

Our Year of War

TWO BROTHERS, VIETNAM, AND A NATION DIVIDED

DANIEL P. BOLGER

Da Capo Press

Copyright © 2017 by Daniel P. Bolger

Da Capo Press
Hachette Book Group
1290 Avenue of the Americas, New York, NY 10104
www.dacapopress.com
@DaCapoPress; @DaCapoPR
Printed in the United States of America

First Edition: October 2017
Published by Da Capo Press, an imprint of Perseus Books, LLC,
a subsidiary of Hachette Book Group, Inc.

The Hachette Speakers Bureau provides a wide range of authors for speaking events.
To find out more, go to www.hachettespeakersbureau.com or call (866) 376-6591.
The publisher is not responsible for websites (or their content) that are not owned
by the publisher.

Editorial production by Christine Marra, Marrathon Production Services,
www.marrathoneditorial.org
Book design by Jane Raese
Set in 10.5-point ITC Century

ISBN 978-0-306-90326-7 (hardcover); ISBN 978-0-306-90324-3 (ebook)
LCCN: 2017953360

LSC-C
10 9 8 7 6 5 4 3 2 1

For the men and women on the Wall

Ex virtute honos

Contents

Maps

Preface

I knew Chuck and Tom Hagel long before I met them. In the terrible year of 1968, young men like them lived in my suburban neighborhood west of Chicago. When their time came to serve, they went. We'd look for their faces when the camera scanned the crowd on the USO *Bob Hope Christmas Special* on television. Their fathers, like mine, fought in World War II or Korea. Their mothers showed us snapshots of bright-green jungles, thin foreign people in black pajamas, and loose-limbed young men in faded fatigues, smiling into the camera, Schlitz beer cans in hand. When they came home, they didn't talk about it. They took jobs or went to college. They moved on. I never heard of PTSD. And I never met a draft dodger.

You could make a powerful case, and many have, that the four most formative eras in American history were the Revolution and founding, slavery and the Civil War, the Great Depression and World War II, and the sixties and Vietnam. Of those, the last is surely the most discussed and least well understood. We're probably too close to it to sort it out completely.

Still, I think I owe it to Chuck and Tom, and to all the Vietnam veterans, most notably the officers and sergeants who led me when I joined the U.S. Army in the 1970s, to try to figure out what the hell we did to our enemies and ourselves in Vietnam and at home. This book is my attempt, through the story of Chuck and Tom Hagel, to explain the lasting significance of the tumultuous events of the Vietnam War and 1960s America. I've worked hard to get it right. Wartime sergeants, like the Hagels and my own father, measure officer types by one hard standard: Do they know the real deal? I think I do. The Hagels certainly do.

Fifty years after Tet, Vietnam remains very much with us. I believe that many Americans, especially younger ones, do not realize the full import of this divisive war abroad and the contentious era at home, in particular the decisive events of 1968. We continue to repeat the same errors and miss the same opportunities. I know. I lived through just those bloody mistakes in Iraq and Afghanistan. We see our past, but we don't understand it, even when men like Chuck and Tom Hagel plead with us to do so. It's past time to come to terms with Vietnam and the sixties. That's why I wrote *Our Year of War*.

Daniel P. Bolger
Lieutenant General
U.S. Army, Retired

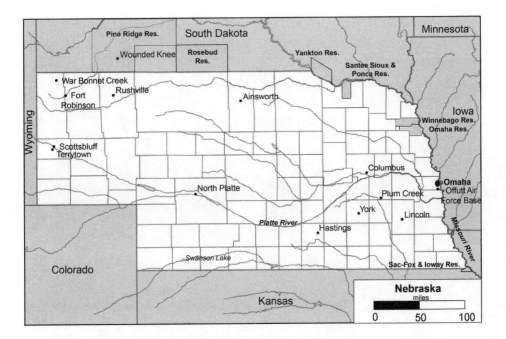

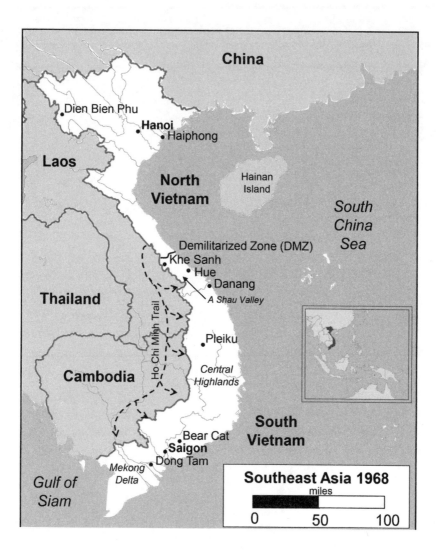

China

Dien Bien Phu

Hanoi

Haiphong

Laos

North
Vietnam

Hainan
Island

South
China
Sea

Demilitarized Zone (DMZ)

Khe Sanh

Hue

Thailand

Danang

A Shau Valley

Ho Chi Minh Trail

Pleiku

Central
Highlands

Cambodia

Bear Cat

South
Vietnam

Saigon

Dong Tam

Mekong
Delta

Gulf of
Siam

Southeast Asia 1968

miles

0   50   100

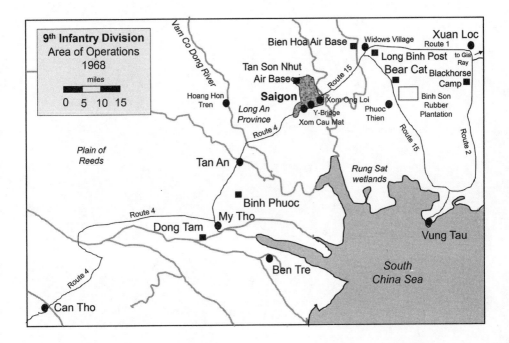

9th Infantry Division
Area of Operations
1968

miles

0   5   10   15

Vam Co Dong River

Bien Hoa Air Base

Widows Village

Xuan Loc

Route 1

Tan Son Nhut
Air Base

Long Binh Post

to Gia
Ray

Route 15

Bear Cat

Blackhorse
Camp

Hoang Hon
Tren

Saigon

Xom Ong Loi

Binh Son
Rubber
Plantation

Long An
Province

Route 4

Y-Bridge
Xom Cau Mat

Phuoc
Thien

Route 15

Route 2

Plain of
Reeds

Tan An

Rung Sat
wetlands

Binh Phuoc

Route 4

My Tho

Dong Tam

Vung Tau

Ben Tre

South
China Sea

Route 4

Can Tho

Light

A year ago, none of us could see victory.
There wasn't a prayer. Now we can see it clearly—
like light at the end of a tunnel.

GENERAL HENRI EUGÈNE NAVARRE
September 28, 1953[1]

Tom Hagel hated walking point. He disliked going first, breaking bush, knocking aside wet branches, stepping over fallen logs, slipping around leaning, mossy tree trunks, and all the while watching, listening, feeling, smelling, even tasting, seeking an enemy who knew exactly how to blend into the rotting woodwork. The Vietnamese jungle was greener than green, a riotous, enveloping ocean of foliage, the ground layer thick and tangled from the brown loam floor to a swaying mat of vegetation twice as high as Tom's angular, spare six-foot frame. It made for tough slogging. And that was before somebody took a shot at you.

Tom's head turned like a gun turret, slow and steady, listening and looking. He reached out, the long fingers on his left hand weaving through leaves and stems, just enough to push aside the abundant greenery. His right hand gripped the trigger region of his black M16 rifle. Eyes, ears, nose, and fingertips sought anything that did not belong there. An oddly broken branch. A Kalashnikov automatic rifle clicking from safe to fire. The sharp tang of human urine. A gleaming trip wire stretched like a garrote. Hagel had to stay alert for all of those telltale signs and dozens more. He had to do it despite the oppressive heat, the cloying humidity, and the pervading gloom. Not much sunshine filtered down through the soaring, thick tree canopy high above. In the fetid, tangled morass that choked the bottom of this rain forest, it was always dusk. Out there in the dim unending sea of vegetation, beyond sensing, lurked dangers past counting. Tom Hagel knew it only too well. There be monsters.

Yes, Tom Hagel hated walking point. But he was good at it. No—he was great at it. He kept his rifle company alive. He made sure they won their fights, because those sharp clashes usually started with him. Woe to the thing that did not belong. With one squeeze of his M16's trigger, Hagel would level it: rock and roll, full auto, punching out an entire magazine of twenty hot bullets as fast you could snap your fingers. And that would usually do it. The old sergeants, the ones who carried out this brutal business and lived to tell of it, said that he who shot first and in force gained the edge in a murderous jungle ambush. Tom Hagel was all about that edge.

Yet Tom Hagel hated doing it. He detested the war with all his heart. It wasn't just the dull ache of all combat soldiers in all wars, heartily sick of losing their friends, shaken by taking lives of strangers better left alone, and bone-tired from endless draining hours of hunting and being hunted. Tom Hagel's disgust went beyond that. He considered the Vietnam War an abomination, an awful deviant strain far removed from America's best instincts, a pointless bloody scrum on behalf of an utterly corrupt local ally. "It was wrong," he said later, with characteristic bluntness.[2] Still Tom Hagel walked point, and did it well.

He did it not for the flag, nor for the cause, such as it was, but for the other American soldiers who counted on him. It fell to this nineteen-year-old to balance the urgent pressure from his captain to move steadily onward and his own hard-earned wisdom to take care with each step. Slow is smooth and smooth is fast. That paradoxical phrase made no sense except to a battle-wary rifleman. Tom Hagel was one. The lives he saved would include his own, as well as those of his mates.

Those favored others started with the man right behind him. The green-clad, helmeted form stepped slowly, head down, checking his compass azimuth and consulting a folded, sweat-stained map sheet. That navigator wasn't just keeping the long file of riflemen on track. He was also guiding Tom Hagel. Well he should. It was his older brother, Chuck. Sometimes Chuck went first and Tom plotted the course. They formed a really effective point team. Two brothers in the same rifle platoon, trading off at the most exposed post of peril—if Hollywood showed it in a movie, cynical audiences would snort and object, certain that such a thing didn't happen anymore in modern warfare. The U.S. Army wouldn't allow it. America's mothers wouldn't accept it. There were policies and procedures and safeguards to prevent some poor family from losing two sons in a single flashing grenade blast. It could never occur. Except it did for almost a year, the bloodiest stretch of the war, the awful year 1968. Out front, brothers Tom and Chuck Hagel just kept trudging along.

Chuck didn't hate the war. He volunteered for it. He asked for the infantry, the most difficult, most dangerous, and most thankless of duties. Like Tom, Chuck grieved for lost comrades and found no pleasure in pulling the trigger. But he did it. "We had a job to do in Vietnam," he said later.[3] Chuck understood only too clearly that his brother had turned on the war effort. For his part, Tom knew Chuck still believed. Walking point together was their truce, their armistice, their way to set it aside day after day and night after night. Trying to stay alive rightly consumed their full attention.

Behind the intent brothers shuffled an extended conga line of sweating, stinking American soldiers. These dull-eyed, exhausted men had long ago learned to trust Tom and Chuck Hagel. They didn't care which one supported the war or which one did not. They just hoped that those two guys out front kept the rifle company on the right route, avoided the booby traps, and got the drop on the bad guys. It would have been nice to see the sun now and then. But as the American infantrymen picked their way through the dim bottom reaches of the Vietnam jungle, the veterans had long since given up on that. In the depths of this endless tunnel of smothering vines, twisted tendrils, and rain-slick fronds, only a few rookies still expected to see the light.

IN AN INSTANT the bulbs snapped on, brilliantly white, dazzling, bathing him. General William Childs Westmoreland had seen that kind of intense light on the tank ranges, when the massive armored brutes snapped on their big xenon beams and pinned their targets in pure, whiter than white illumination. Now it was all around him. The smothering luminous blaze seemed almost tangible, more than the warmth of the intense lamps, but almost a breath, a whisper in his face. Wasn't there something to that, the actual force of light? Perhaps it called up a random impression from some half-forgotten physics session from three decades ago, back at West Point. Maybe so.

The curtain of vibrant luminosity cut him off from the great room. It marked a boundary between him and them, those out there. Although the hall was well lit beyond the phalanx of television klieg lights, the crowd had receded into relative darkness. He could hear them though, a lot of them, their presence signaled by steady, vigorous clapping. That certainly had a physical pressure; a swelling wave approached him and then washed over him. It held for a bit, and that said something, too, something positive. In such a place, in such a time, he could be forgiven if for a moment he felt like the pope on the Vatican balcony, Lou Gehrig in his final bow at Yankee Stadium, or Caesar up there along the Rubicon River, addressing the XIII Legion.

But these were not loyal soldiers in the house. No, in the great gulp beyond the light barrier slouched the rough beast of the American press. The auditorium at the National Press Club brimmed with reporters, editors, and columnists, and even some of those aggressive television news people. More than a few thought ill of him. He knew that. In later years, his successors might hear vulgar catcalls or rude chants, but not yet, not in the America of November 21, 1967, when men still wore coats and ties to lunch, and applauded with customary respect when a famous general came to speak.

As the applause died away, he calmly touched the pages of his speech. This was his time, with the brilliant light shining on him like that of Valhalla. And so to work. "I would like to give you today," he began confidently, "a short progress report on some aspects of the war in Vietnam . . ."[4]

HE LOOKED THE PART. God knows he sure did. Tall, upright, shoulders squared, jaw thrust forward, he radiated purpose. The army called it bearing, and he had it. There wasn't an extra ounce on him. His handsome face was chiseled, his crew-cut hair still dark at the top, graying on the sides, and barely white at the temples. Bright brown eyes—regulation olive drab, even—glittered beneath dark, bushy eyebrows. When he looked at you, those eyes locked on like lasers. His handshake was so firm, so strong, so decisive, it sent a jolt up your forearm, like you'd grabbed a live electric cable.[5] If on some old movie lot David O. Selznick had dialed up central casting and barked, "Send over a general," this was the guy who would have shown up.

And that was a good thing. Westmoreland was America's top field commander, the four-star general at the top of U.S. Military Assistance Command, Vietnam, MACV in print, Mack-vee when spoken. Westmoreland was COMUSMACV to his multitudinous staff, Childs to his family back in South Carolina, Westy to his military peers (he had a few), the general to his troops, and the Man personified to those who opposed the war. By the autumn of 1967, many Americans did. But for the majority who still supported the ongoing war in Vietnam, Westmoreland was their general. He was the one leading our boys out there on the far side of the world. And he was up to it. Just look at him!

Many did, then and since. In 1968, biographer Ernest B. Furguson called his book *Westmoreland: The Inevitable General*. By 2011, West Point graduate, army officer, and Vietnam veteran Lewis S. Sorley went with *Westmoreland: The General Who Lost Vietnam*. Both titles rang true.[6] And both books left you with the feeling that this striking, impressive figure must have something missing on the inside, some "it" that good generals have and he lacked, all appearances aside. Between those two books stood the tragic American failure in Vietnam.

Westmoreland's record before Vietnam was a succession of achievements: Eagle Scout, First Captain—top cadet—at West Point, brilliant commander of the 34th Field Artillery Battalion and then hard-charging chief of staff of the 9th Infantry Division in World War II, dashing commander of the elite 187th Airborne Infantry Regimental Combat Team in Korea, a brigadier general by age thirty-eight, and then two, three, and four stars in quick succession, always in the spotlight. Major Otto Kerner, Westmoreland's immediate deputy in World War II, remembered the troops calling his commander "Superman," a reference to his tireless work ethic and "his deeds and capacity for deeds."[7]

Now came Vietnam. In Washington, President Lyndon Baines Johnson expected results from Westmoreland and his Americans. "I want 'em to get off their butts," urged LBJ, "and get out in those jungles and whip hell out of some Communists."[8] It wasn't exactly the approved format for a mission statement. But it sufficed.

Vietnam was Westmoreland's war. Ideally, he'd go north and smash the foe there, taking the enemy capital, Hanoi. That option never got serious consideration.[9] President Johnson and his inner circle feared Chinese intervention, like the surprise mass offensive that wrecked the attempt to unify the Korean peninsula in 1950. Only U.S. airpower would go north, and the bizarre on-again, off-again targeting directives from the White House ensured America's aerial offensive, although punishing, proved indecisive.[10] There'd be no victory from the skies. So be it. Sooner or later, Westmoreland knew, the NVA (North Vietnamese Army) must come south and the VC (Viet Cong) guerrillas were already there. Fine—good enough. Fight 'em where they were. Westmoreland believed he could win this war in South Vietnam.

The general executed with his customary energy and dedication. "The U.S. military strategy," he wrote later, "dictated by politicians, was essentially that of a war of attrition."[11] His job was to kill VC

and NVA, a difference with little practical distinction, as each passing month found more northerners in the south as both regulars and
guerrillas. Regardless, Westmoreland intended for his troops to find
the hostiles and kill them.

Starting in 1965, Westmoreland brought in large numbers of U.S.
troops to do the job. He explained his approach in his memoirs:

> Phase One: Commit those American and Allied [Australia, New
> Zealand, the Philippines, South Korea, and Thailand] forces neces-
> sary "to halt the losing trend" by the end of 1965.
>
> Phase Two: "During the first half of 1966," take the offensive
> with American and Allied forces in "high priority areas" to destroy
> enemy forces and reinstitute pacification programs.
>
> Phase Three: If the enemy persisted, he might be defeated and
> his forces and base areas destroyed during a period of a year to a
> year and a half following Phase II.[12]

Along with the 23,000 or so advisers and support units already
in country, Westmoreland estimated it would take 175,000 more U.S.
troops to get started, and then at least 100,000 more. But he warned
that based on what the VC and NVA did, additional forces might be
required. Notably, the strategy didn't count much on the ARVN (Army
of the Republic of Vietnam, the South Vietnamese). They would handle that pacification stuff, sweeping up the wreckage, restoring order
in South Vietnamese villages after the United States ran off the enemy battalions. In fact, when some asked if he wanted to command
South Vietnamese forces, as the Americans did in Korea, Westmoreland demurred.[13] Behind his rationalizations, the truth was obvious.
He didn't think the ARVN were up to the job. The Americans would
do it.

Running the timeline, it all amounted to a plan to win the war
with about 300,000 U.S. troops by the end of 1967. Later Westmoreland tried to walk it back, because he didn't exactly say when Phase
II would end and when Phase III would start. It was rather impre-
cise for a lifelong artilleryman. But back in Washington, Johnson

and his team heard what they wanted to hear. Give this general the tools—300,000 Americans—and he'll finish the job, probably by the end of 1967.

The American buildup went very rapidly. Protected by a steady flow of combat battalions, engineers, logisticians, and contractors erected a network of new bases, ports, roads, and air fields. By the end of 1965, there were already 184,310 U.S. troops on the ground. A year later, there were 385,300. By the end of 1967, 485,600 served in Vietnam, with about 40,000 more en route.[14] What the general wanted, the general got. And he wanted a lot. The U.S. passed the initial 300,000 estimate during 1966 and didn't even slow down. The pace of deployments developed momentum. The Americans were committed.

As U.S. troops surged into the country, the North also had to change course. Any idea of a war-winning push went out the window. Rather, the Hanoi leaders reverted to their long game. It was right out of the Mao Zedong guerrilla playbook:

Enemy advances, we retreat.
Enemy halts, we harass.
Enemy tires, we attack.
Enemy retreats, we pursue.[15]

The NVA and VC still fought, all right. But in most cases, they chose the time and place. By one reliable estimate circa 1967, the enemy initiated 88 percent of ground contacts.[16] Put another way, the opposition, not MACV units, held the initiative. The foe let the Americans chase and chase, walk and walk, search and search, and then . . . *enemy tires, we attack.*

Finding the elusive Cong stymied MACV. As an artillery officer, William Westmoreland understood well what to do in war, to include this kind of war: x (weight of explosives) divided by y (targets) equals z (kills). It was all about solving for y. The Americans tried and tried. Unable to pinpoint many targets, they went hard after those they did find. They bombed, brought in attack helicopters, shot artillery, and banged away with rifles and machine guns. But as one

MACV intelligence chief later put it: "The VC/NVA refused to defend any terrain feature. They would abandon even their base areas under a United States attack."[17] Sometimes the Americans got lucky. Now and then, a VC or NVA unit stumbled. But typically, if a fight occurred, it happened because the opposition wanted it.

By 1967, there had been fighting, lots of skirmishes and smashups in remote areas as Americans sought to find, fix, and finish NVA and VC units. The enemy backpedaled, with the NVA regulars withdrawing into the border wilderness fronting Laos and Cambodia and the VC in black pajamas melting into the village woodwork. American troops hunted NVA battalions, and caught them now and then. But the enemy units were bloodied, not destroyed. *Enemy advances, we retreat.*

U.S. firepower took its toll, all right. In a 1969 interview with Italian journalist Oriana Fallaci, the great NVA commander Vo Nguyen Giap admitted to 500,000 dead. Hanoi gutted through that horrific cost—for the North, this was total war, victory or death. But Giap also knew the United States had not embraced total war, not at all. For the Americans, each week brought what Giap termed "coffins going home," to the tune of 19,641 killed and nearly 134,000 wounded from 1965 through 1967.[18] Those were high prices to pay for limited success in a limited war.

Was that the master plan unfolding? Was that winning? In his Saigon headquarters, in between daily trips by helicopter all over the country, Westmoreland studied the comparative numbers. He did his artillery calculations—x divided by y equals z—and convinced himself that his troops were approaching, and might have even passed, the crossover point: the fabled juncture when we killed more of the hostiles than they could replace. Well, that all depended on the number of enemy. MACV, the Central Intelligence Agency, and various Washington agencies could never quite agree how many there were: 300,000? 400,000? 500,000?[19] How many were arriving each month in the South after marching down the Ho Chi Minh Trail? And how many were dead? Hanoi refused to tell. It sure wasn't obvious on the ground.

One of Westmoreland's best commanders reached his limit. He vented anonymously to CBS reporter Martin Fromson, who shared it with *New York Times* reporter R. W. "Johnny" Apple Jr. "I've destroyed a single division three times," the general said. "I've chased main force units all over the country and the impact was zilch." He also offered that "the war is unwinnable" and that "we've reached a stalemate and should find a dignified way out." He summarized: "Westy just doesn't get it."

Confronted with Johnny Apple's damning article, Westmoreland dismissed it as a journalistic fabrication. "No general of mine would ever have said that," he wrote in a message back to Washington.[20] Four decades passed before this unknown soldier identified himself: Major General Frederick C. Weyand, a man who led the 25th Infantry Division and then II Field Force, the corps-level contingent shielding Saigon. Weyand later rose to four stars, commanded MACV in its final days, and served as the U.S. Army chief of staff. But he knew it wasn't working and said so.

Like Fred Weyand and a lot of others in country, the great minds in Washington, DC, smelled failure. Korea had been bad enough. That whole thing ended up as a fumbling, embarrassing effort for the superpower that had just crushed the Germans and Japanese so handily five years before. Instead of an abject surrender by foes literally with hats in hand, Korea resulted in a tie at best, with the enemy holding fast to half the country and laughing at us across the most fortified "demilitarized zone" on earth. Yet, by 1967, confronted with the morass of Vietnam, such an unhappy outcome would have been taken and banked by President Johnson and his coterie.

LBJ's administration leaders on the Potomac, the McGeorge Bundy and Robert McNamara types, the ones David Halberstam labeled the "best and the brightest," the peerless Ivy Leaguers whom Southwest Texas State Teachers College graduate Johnson sometimes categorized as "you Harvards," well, they were headed for the tall grass. If you were looking for a Vietnam War cheerleader in Washington by late 1967, you'd have had little luck. The polling on the war had gone sour. Sure, a majority of the U.S. people still backed the effort, about 60 percent to 40 percent.[21] The trend looked bad, though, bending down. And that 40 percent opposed was getting noisy, gaining strength as 1967 was grinding on. There was a crossover point in America, too. It was getting closer by the day.

Thus Johnson turned to the one man who certainly still believed. At the president's direction, Westmoreland returned to America, put on his dress greens, and made the case for impending victory. He spoke to a joint session of Congress on April 28, 1967.[22] He made the rounds in Washington again in July. Finally, in the big one, on November 21, he went into the lion's den at the National Press Club. There he saw the light. He did his best to help others see it, too.

BASKING IN THE LUMINESCENCE, Westmoreland spoke confidently. His text was dense with qualifiers and heavy with policy-speak. It included laundry lists of achievements and a lot of numbers. But the money lines sure stood out. Reporters with notebooks wrote them down. Cameras rolled tape. The man was on the record, all right.

"I am absolutely certain," the general intoned, "that whereas in 1965 the enemy was winning, today he is certainly losing." He went on: "There are indications that the Viet Cong and even Hanoi know this." After reviewing various logistical and operational efforts, he offered that "we are making progress." Then in his boldest prediction, he offered not just a forecast, but an assurance: "With 1968, a new phase is now starting. We have reached an important point when the end begins to come into view." Westmoreland was talking about victory. He concluded: "It lies within our grasp—the enemy's hopes are bankrupt."[23] George Patton would have been shorter and earthier, but the message came through. We've got this. It's almost over, not quite two-plus years and 300,000 troops, but good enough. A win is a win.

In years after, many Americans thought the general referred to light at the end of the tunnel, the same fateful phrase once spoken by General Henri Eugène Navarre in the autumn of 1953, not long before France's catastrophic, war-ending defeat at Dien Bien Phu.

Despite contentions by some, Westmoreland never uttered those words aloud. No light and no tunnel were mentioned. But the image seemed to fit the moment.

Maybe the light at the end of the tunnel wasn't the dawn of victory glimpsed by Westy Westmoreland, hoped for by Lyndon Johnson, prayed for by so many Americans, in and out of uniform, all weary of this bloody rinse cycle of attrition. No, it wasn't sunrise up there in the tunnel mouth, but the glow of a smoldering pyre, a flame that, when it flared up, went rolling down the chute as an all-consuming fireball. It would burn them all.

CHAPTER 1

The Hole
in the Prairie

Hell, I even thought I was dead 'til I found out
that it was just that I was in Nebraska.
LITTLE BILL DAGGETT, *Unforgiven*[1]

In Vietnam, American soldiers filing out through the barbed wire around the firebase used to say they were headed into "Indian country." The nineteen-year-olds, with a few notable exceptions, were neither historians nor anthropologists, and thus they were not drawing some abstract academic analogy. No, the troops borrowed the term from hundreds of western movies and television shows. The GIs all knew the deal. Leaving the wire was like marching through the wooden palisades of some Hollywood frontier fort. Inside, we owned it. Out past that boundary lay the unseen enemies—the Indians.

So it had been in the Nebraska Territory. Before there was a Nebraska Territory, or a Nebraska state, or any United States, the Indians were there. They weren't just any Indians, either. They were the dangerous ones, the unbroken ones, the Great Plains warriors feared and respected most: the Arapaho, the Cheyenne, the Pawnee, and the fearsome Sioux. That last group of people called themselves Dakota, Lakota, and Nakota, but not Sioux. The name came from a

corrupted French term for "little snake," or more colloquially, an enemy, and a treacherous one at that. Whatever you called them, they
lived there on the broad grasslands, following the great buffalo herds
along the meandering shallow rivers that scarred the dry prairie. The
Indians called this region *Nbraske*, "flat water." [2] That's a pretty good
description of the Platte River that bisects the modern state from
east to west.

Today, trendy people, go-getters who live and work in New York
and Washington to the east or San Francisco and Los Angeles to the
west, refer to places like Nebraska as "flyover country," that expanse
of nothing between the parts of America that really matter (or think
they do). Before the Civil War, only birds and an odd balloon or two
flew over Nebraska, but those Americans who went there pushed
through as quickly as they could. Civilization, or what passed for it
in antebellum America, lay back east of St. Louis. The gold was out
west in California. And the Nebraska Territory, part of what nine-
teenth-century mapmakers helpfully designated the "Great American
Desert," well, the best idea there involved getting through it post-
haste in your Conestoga wagon with enough supplies and all your
bodily parts. Roaring grass fires, howling tornadoes, and marauding
Indians sometimes made that a very sporty proposition. Still, for the
Indians, and their numerous buffalo prey, the less settlers, the better.
Moving on through suited all parties.

After the Civil War, that changed. One of the laws pushed through
the Union Congress in 1862 encouraged settlement out west. The
Homestead Act granted land, typically a 160-acre plot, to any citizen "head of a family," male or female, over twenty-one years of age.
Union military veterans could also apply, even if they didn't have
a family or were not yet age twenty-one. Freed African American
slaves were included, too, by a later provision, although Confederates ("who had borne arms against the United States Government or
given aid and comfort to its enemies") were not. To gain permanent
ownership, the applicant had to engage in "actual settlement and cul-
tivation" for at least five years. [3] This act opened the Great Plains to
many, including waves of immigrants arriving from Europe.

With the homesteaders came the railroads, designed to link the eastern United States with the bustling boom towns of the Pacific coast. Coincidentally, the lattice of west-bound rails provided the means to sustain those who chose to take their chances on the prairie. Along with the Homestead Act, the Union Congress also passed Pacific Railroad Acts in 1862 and 1863, both of which granted land rights and federal financial backing for a transcontinental railroad line. In the Nebraska Territory, the Union Pacific commenced construction in earnest after the Civil War. The line passed through Omaha and paralleled the Platte River.[4] By March 1, 1867, the combined numbers of railway workers and sod-busting farmers provided enough population to allow Nebraska to gain statehood.

That year also saw a series of clashes with the Plains Indians. Those would go on for the next decade or so. History and Hollywood remember the one big battle, the Arapaho, Cheyenne, and Sioux victory over Lieutenant Colonel (brevet Major General) George A. Custer and the bulk of the 7th Cavalry Regiment on the Little Big Horn River on June 25–26, 1876. Yet that major engagement was atypical both in its scale and its results. The era's U.S. Army records reveal much more pedestrian data. From 1865 to 1898, the military counted 943 firefights. In these, 948 soldiers were killed and 1,058 were wounded. Indian losses, admittedly an estimate (and probably inflated by optimistic officers; some things never change), totaled 4,371 killed, 1,279 wounded, and 10,318 captured. This meant the usual encounter resulted in two soldiers killed or wounded, six Indian casualties, and eleven Indian prisoners.[5] An average year on the Great Plains, the entire United States between the Mississippi River and the eastern reaches of the Rocky Mountains, saw twenty-nine such skirmishes. If you blinked, you missed the "war," such as it was.

In the usual pattern in places like Nebraska, the soldiers followed the Indians here and there, rarely caught up, but over time wore them out. With wives and children exhausted, ponies tired, and braves despondent, one by one, the main chiefs accepted confinement to the great reservations: Pine Ridge, Rosebud, Spirit Lake, and Yankton. Most of the Indians survived.[6] But their way of life was gone.

Why did it end this way? The Indians were better fighters, man for man, than the young volunteer Regulars who chased them. The Indians moved faster. They shot well. They knew the prairies as their homes for centuries. They could subsist off the buffalo and stay ahead of the weather. And yet . . . and yet, in the end, it wasn't about that.

It wasn't about soldier versus brave. That was a symptom, not a cause. The fatal displacement wasn't done by advancing ranks of Regulars—there were far too few in uniform for that, 25,000 at best—but by the determined sod-busting of hundreds of thousands of plodding agrarians and herdsmen, drawn west to stake their homesteads: family farms without any elbow room for wandering warriors. The decisive penetration didn't come from cavalry troopers picking their way up creek beds, but from steel rails heading west, ever west, bearing commerce and passengers aplenty, none of them much interested in tenting on the prairie, nor all that interested in those who did. Even the slaughter of the buffalo reflected an urge for hides in America's teeming eastern cities, a tribute to modern weaponry, and the sad fact that the lumbering beasts reproduced too infrequently and grew up far too slowly to compete with the pitiless bark of thousands of repeating rifles, some in Indian hands by the 1870s.[7] Each 160-acre plot claimed, each rail line spiked down, and each buffalo killed wore away the life of the Plains Indians as surely as any shot from an army trapdoor Springfield rifle. The human wave from the east never let up. The Lakota called these numerous new arrivals *wasichus*, "uninvited visitors" who refused to leave.[8] They had that right.

The Plains Indians survived, penned and sullen, existing after a fashion on remote reservations. Six Indian reservations, all established in territorial days, remained in Nebraska. All were small, all underpopulated, all out of the way, and all well to the east, carved off the fringes of the state, home to a few thousand Indians hanging on by their fingernails. In the greatest stretch of Nebraska, the endless productive prairie, just the names endured, pinned to small towns and shallow rivers. Those fragments of Indian language mark the footsteps of ghosts.

This is what winning looks like in a people's war.[9] The side that prevails—the *wasichus*—moves in and never looks back. And the side that loses gets prodded, pushed, and squeezed by political, economic, cultural, military, and above all demographic pressures that do not stop. In later days, anguished national leaders pointed to Vietnam, and eventually Iraq and Afghanistan, too, and wondered if America could ever hope to win a war against insurgents. They might have done well to look at Nebraska. All that was left of the Indians was a hole.

LIEUTENANT GENERAL CURTIS EMERSON LEMAY looked at Nebraska. He didn't see the fading signs of the Indians. He wasn't concerned with them. What interested LeMay about Nebraska was what always interested him: winning America's wars. After the tremendous victories over Nazi Germany and imperial Japan in 1945, Americans all over the country, including those in Nebraska, figured the war was over. But LeMay was already thinking about the next one. That was his job.

Now the potential enemy was the Soviet Union. Along with atomic weapons, Russia had big bombers, too. After getting caught on the ground at Pearl Harbor on December 7, 1941, no American air force general was willing to do anything but assume the worst case. Hundreds of Soviet bombers with atomic bombs—that amounted to a hell of a threat. And those planes could arrive any hour on any day.

When LeMay took over the Strategic Air Command (SAC) on October 19, 1948, he took charge of America's nuclear bomber fleet, the country's Sunday punch. LeMay reported for duty at Andrews Air Force Base, ten miles from the center of Washington, DC, and less than a hundred miles from the Atlantic coast.[10] The Pentagon, the White House, the U.S. Capitol—all of those useful destinations for a SAC commander could be reached easily by air force limousine. Around SAC headquarters, Andrews featured nicely manicured lawns, a palatial officers' club, and a wonderful golf course. Any weekend, in less than two hours, you could motor to the beach to fish or frolic. Duty at Andrews was pleasant. Most generals loved it. Not LeMay.

Curtis LeMay saw SAC headquarters at Andrews as the Russians saw it: their top target, the one installation that, if allowed to carry out its primary task, could cause the Union of Soviet Socialist Republics (USSR) to cease to exist. And wasn't it handy that SAC planted its flag right near Washington, just a few minutes inland for a modern aircraft streaking in from the ocean? Hell, if war came, the base might not even survive the back blast from whatever array of nukes the Soviets unloaded on Washington proper. Andrews Air Force Base amounted to a staked goat, a sacrifice. LeMay had no intention of beginning World War III with his command post blown away.

Thus LeMay saw Nebraska in classic real estate terms: location, location, location. He wanted a place smack in the middle of the continental United States, as far as possible from the Atlantic and Pacific coasts and midway between the Canadian and Mexican borders. Those Russian bombers might get there someday. But they'd have to work for it.

Mapmakers pinpointed the exact center of the continental United States as 98° 35' longitude and 39° 50' latitude, an open field near Lebanon, Kansas, not far from the Nebraska border.[11] "X" marked the spot. Putting something out there in the middle of nowhere would take a lot of work, and a lot of time. LeMay demanded a solution way faster than that. He found one. If you went just 160 miles to the northeast, Nebraska offered a ready-made alternative: Offutt Air Force Base, just south of Omaha.[12] That would do.

The move to Offutt happened very quickly, weeks after LeMay assumed command. A plan had been in the works, but LeMay moved out in his usual way—immediately. By November 9, SAC had its command center up and running in Nebraska. The airmen set up in Administrative Building A, a three-story structure affiliated with the shuttered Glenn L. Martin bomber plant. During World War II, that massive factory complex churned out its own B-26 Marauder medium bombers and B-29 Superfortresses on license from Boeing. Among its 515 B-29s produced were *Enola Gay* and *Bockscar*, the mission aircraft for the atomic attacks on Hiroshima and Nagasaki.[13] In that sense, America's atomic bombers came home.

The move to Offutt turned out to be the first of many that made SAC the formidable nuclear-armed force it became, so powerful that it took the motto "Peace Is Our Profession." The message was stark. The Russians wouldn't dare attack. If they did, they'd be eradicated. LeMay commanded SAC for nearly nine years. When he took over, the organization comprised 450 piston-engine bombers with a war plan to deliver 133 atomic bombs on 70 Soviet targets. When LeMay left in June of 1957, the command fielded 1,655 jet bombers ready to drop 1,655 thermonuclear bombs, each one up to a thousand times more potent than the Hiroshima type, on 954 Soviet targets. After a maximum effort, all that would be left of the USSR would be what one officer called "a smoking, radiating ruin."[14]

And what of Offutt Air Force Base? Once the "go code" went out, its primary purpose would be fulfilled. It then became expendable. As LeMay departed in 1957, SAC moved into its purpose-built Building 500, complete with a three-story deep sub-basement command post. Of course, the advent of thermonuclear hydrogen bombs and intercontinental ballistic missiles, like the Russian rocket that launched *Sputnik* that year, meant Building 500's underground bunker wouldn't last long even with a near miss. Plus, those hostile missiles could arrive in thirty minutes. To prevent a bolt from the blue, SAC began to keep a relay of command jets aloft 24/7, code-named "Looking Glass." Even if Soviet warheads obliterated the Offutt rabbit hole, the SAC retaliatory codes would still go out through the Looking Glass.[15] Lewis Carroll was unavailable for comment.

The choice of Offutt Air Force Base as SAC headquarters elevated Omaha, Nebraska, and its quarter of a million residents from a lowly fortieth place among American population centers to number two on the USSR's hit parade, second only to the capital city of Washington, DC.[16] For the Soviet general staff, the death of the people of Omaha would amount to collateral damage, nothing personal, just business. It was a sword of Damocles ever present, if you thought about it. Most people in eastern Nebraska chose not to do so.

They also likely gave little consideration to another by-product of SAC's basing decision. Once SAC headquarters got up and running, Soviet foreign intelligence (KGB) and military intelligence (GRU) became very interested in Nebraska. For the entire Cold War, what happened in and around Offutt Air Force Base got plenty of attention.[17] Those poking about and asking questions rarely matched the ham-handed Boris and Natasha stereotypes. When assigned an objective, KGB and GRU officers consistently ran sophisticated agent networks to find out the information they needed. Consequently, both U.S. Air Force security entities and the Federal Bureau of Investigation stayed active in and around Nebraska, particularly Omaha.

So SAC came to Omaha. With the thunder of huge jet bombers coming and going, rattling windows and shaking roofs at all hours, the recognition that Omaha was now a USSR nuclear bull's-eye, and the suspicion that the next person who asked you for directions could well be working for Moscow, you might think locals in eastern Nebraska would have nothing but contempt for the man who inflicted all of this on them. This seemed especially likely when the laconic LeMay, curt indeed, answered a welcoming journalist's question about what it all meant. "It doesn't mean a damn thing to Omaha, and it doesn't mean a damn thing to me."[18] So there.

Nevertheless, they liked him. In so many ways, Curtis LeMay struck Nebraskans as one of their own. He reminded you of the guy who fixed your car: grease on rough hands, brow furrowed, wrench sticking out of a side pocket. Don't even think about skimping on paying the bill. He'd sock you. No small talk, no BS, just work. Whereas the regal General William C. Westmoreland looked like he belonged at a full-dress parade, Curtis LeMay matched the other kind of commander, the one you'd call up for a desperate battle, a death struggle. His square, determined face, often decorated with a protruding cigar, topped a football player's physique. Although only five feet, eight inches tall, he looked much bigger. He seemed solid, all muscle, and all aimed at getting things done. LeMay gave you the impression he'd smash right through a wall to go where he needed to go. He'd make things happen, this one.

LeMay made himself. His Ohio parents worked for a living, and although Curtis considered West Point, the U.S. Military Academy did not consider him. So he went to Ohio State University, worked at a local steel mill, majored in civil engineering, and gained his commission as a second lieutenant in 1928. He sought flight school and excelled in the air. Uniquely among the small U.S. Army Air Corps of the Depression era, LeMay qualified as a pilot and navigator, and could carry out the bombardier's duties, too. He also learned how to repair aircraft, tune the radios, and serve as a turret gunner. His hands were usually dirty. In 1937–38, he flew some of the first training runs with the big new Boeing B-17 Flying Fortress.[19] LeMay knew that aircraft cold. No man could outfly or outwork him.

LeMay was still a first lieutenant as late as 1940, as America prepared for war. He moved up quickly thereafter: captain in early 1940, major by 1941, lieutenant colonel and colonel within months in 1942, then one-star general by 1943. He earned his promotions in the deadly skies over occupied Europe. Never one for lectures or grandstanding, LeMay focused on flying. He drilled his air crews relentlessly. They learned to assemble quickly above the soup of foggy England, fly in tight formations, almost wingtip to wingtip, and use their onboard machine gun turrets to defend each other. Above all, they worked on bombing. In theory, the top-secret Norden bombsight allowed a B-17 to "put a bomb in a pickle barrel" from five miles up. But that presumed pickle barrel wasn't defended by skilled Luftwaffe fighter pilots. In reality, a bombardment group's lead bombardier did the aiming. The other guys, jokingly called "toggleers," flipped a switch once they saw the first plane unload. It made a ragged pattern on the ground. LeMay taught his group to stay tight in their combat box formation.[20] Close in the air, close on target—he preached it, taught it, and demanded it.

LeMay didn't send his crews out. He led them. He piloted the lead B-17. LeMay understood that it all came down to bombs on target. He taught his fliers to press on. Once they started the bombing run, neither flak bursts nor marauding Messerschmitt fighters could divert LeMay's airmen from their ominous task. His 305th Bombardment

Group never turned back. They made it to their targets every time, and regularly put twice as many bombs on their aim points as any other group. The crude bombsights and light bombs of 1943 lacked accuracy and hitting power. Able German defenders exacted a high price. But the 305th set the standard. By the fall, LeMay was leading the entire 3rd Air Division of seven groups.[21] He didn't look back.

Men died in the air over Germany: 37,500 Americans, 60,000 British and Commonwealth crewmen. People died on the ground, some 593,000. The Americans flew by day, tried to hit individual factories, and in so doing tore up complete German city blocks with high explosives. The British Royal Air Force flew by night and endeavored to burn out factories and workers' housing. Together, the Allies blew apart and broiled the enemy's aircraft plants and oil refineries. They paralyzed German rail and road networks. Twice—at Hamburg in July of 1943 and Dresden in February of 1945—British incendiary munitions and American high explosives hit hard enough, in sufficient volume, and in the right weather conditions to generate firestorms, self-sustaining vortexes that immolated entire cities. In ground combat, artilleryman William Westmoreland focused on killing enemy soldiers, the terrible arithmetic of attrition. Airman LeMay saw Westmoreland and raised him, following the path blazed by Sherman in Georgia and Sheridan in Virginia's Shenandoah Valley and tried all too often on the western plains. Whole societies made modern war. So entire societies must pay the price. "I'll tell you what war is about," LeMay said. "You've got to kill people, and when you've killed enough, they stop fighting."[22] By May of 1945, the Germans stopped.

Imperial Japan did not. When the sleek aluminum-bright Boeing B-29s finally arrived in numbers, they went to the Pacific theater to be used against Japan. Their unprecedented range allowed them to reach the Japanese home islands from China to the west and the hard-won island airfields of Guam, Saipan, and Tinian to the east. But the mighty Superfortresses proved ineffective. Many of Japan's industrial facilities were small and well dispersed, dependent on piecework handed out in urban neighborhoods. Tokyo alone hosted 45,000 of these microfactories. In the winter of 1944–45, low clouds and rain squalls obscured Japan's cities three weeks out of four. For the high-flying B-29 formations, weather up at 30,000 feet featured something unexpected, a 200-mile-an-hour wind sheer known as the jet stream.[23] The damn bombs went everywhere.

Enter Major General Curtis E. LeMay. When he took command of the B-29 force, he learned to fly the streamlined, ultramodern Superfortress, leading his men as usual. Right away, he realized that the standard methods developed in Europe didn't work for Japan. Determined to get the ineffective air campaign on track, LeMay asked his battlewise subordinates what they thought. He listened. He studied meteorological charts and bomb damage photos. And he looked hard at the gleaming B-29s. Just what could these things really do?

LeMay checked again with his intelligence officers. It appeared the Japanese didn't field many short-range antiaircraft guns. Their fighter planes were optimized to climb up and fight in the thin air. They had only a few radar sets, and no real night fighters. And the island country's production methods—the key industrial targets—relied on piece workers living in the densely packed streets of timber-framed houses. In the capital city of Tokyo, 98 percent of the structures were made of flammable wood. What if LeMay threw out the rule books from the U.S. air war over Germany? Strip down the B-29s. Leave behind most of the machine guns, most of the gunners, and the extra fuel tanks. Load up on incendiary bombs, like the British at Hamburg and Dresden. Go in low, under 10,000 feet. Maybe ease down to 5,000 feet. Go at night.

LeMay thought hard. He even conjured up a scene from the American Civil War. What might Major General Ambrose Burnside have told the mother of a dead Union soldier after Fredericksburg? We remember Burnside as a callous bumbler. In December of 1862, he took a gamble, pushing the Army of the Potomac up the heights into the teeth of Confederate guns. It failed utterly.[24] Was LeMay about to make the same kind of fatal mistake?

This time he could not pilot the lead plane. LeMay had been briefed on the atomic bomb. His flying days were over. So on March 9, he watched from a Guam runway as 334 B-29s took off into the setting sun, headed for Tokyo. Hours later, just after midnight in Japan, the American aircraft came in low, fast, and heavy with incendiaries. Twenty-seven B-29s didn't come back. But the others did gruesome execution, dumping enough munitions to kindle a massive fire tornado, Hamburg and Dresden squared. The howling gusts pulled victims into the raging inferno. When the fires finally burned out four days later, sixteen square miles of Tokyo were gone. So were 83,793 people.[25] Even with atomic weapons, neither Hiroshima nor Nagasaki equaled that apocalyptic toll.

Tokyo opened the fire-bombing campaign. LeMay's bombers kept it up. They gutted city after city, more than sixty in all, 178 square miles of desolation and 330,000 dead.[26] The two A-bombs in August punctuated a rain of horror that broke the proud Japanese. LeMay and his airmen had killed enough. The opponents stopped fighting.

In the Soviet Union after 1945, as the Cold War grew frigid; Russian leaders knew only too well the saga of the fire raids. They saw in Curtis LeMay a commander who would pull the atomic trigger, and they knew it because he already had. A man who could lay waste to Tokyo, Yokohama, and Nagoya could do the same to Moscow, Leningrad, and Kiev. Yes, SAC's nuclear arms provided a deterrent, an assurance that a Soviet attack would be answered by total destruction. Curtis LeMay gave deterrence a face, and a grimly determined one at that.

Long after World War II, it's easy to sit in a comfortable living room and paint Curtis LeMay as a heartless, knuckle-dragging monster, especially in light of his role in the Cold War, drilling his fliers to unleash Armageddon. And yet in our self-assured ex post facto moralizing we miss something important. Few men understood the horrors of war better than LeMay. Like others who had been there and done that, leaders who knew what it was like to shoot and be shot at—Grant, Sherman, Sheridan—LeMay understood that vicious as modern war was, it was better to get in, get on with it, and get it over. That's doubly true in a country where the citizens run the show. General of the Army George C. Marshall, the great strategist of World War II and veteran of World War I and the ugly Philippine

Insurrection, argued that "a democracy cannot fight a Seven Years War."[27] Amen. In LeMay's view, you did no favors by dragging it out. Use the big hammer. Finish it.

Curtis LeMay realized only too well how bad it could be. Like thousands of his airmen, LeMay made the long, cold, deadly runs over the targets. He'd watched bombers spinning down in flames, armless men tumbling through the thin air, comrades blown to dust in a single flak blast. LeMay knew the deal. He'd been there. He stood in quiet communion, sharing what went unsaid, as bomber crewmen came back from that first awful Tokyo raid silent, faces slack, eyes wide. Many had worn their oxygen masks, not needed below 10,000 feet, but only too necessary to block out the sickly sweet stench of roasting human flesh. Brown soot and a peppering of gritty flecks (wood? paper? *skin?*) coated the bottoms of their silver planes.[28]

And behind them? Below? Well, don't even think about it. That was the answer, maybe the only answer. Stay busy. Keep working. Focus on the next mission. And the next. Go at it every day. And when the war ended, keep going. Keep doing what had to be done. Handle the next problem: height of burst, aerial refueling, where to put SAC headquarters, how many B-52s to build.

What did LeMay think about it? What did his airmen think about it? Like most combat veterans, they tried not to do so. And they sure as hell didn't talk about it.

CHARLES DEAN HAGEL never talked about bombing Japan. He certainly took pride in his service. For a few years, he commanded American Legion Post 79 in Ainsworth, Nebraska, where he and his fellow veterans and their families gathered. They said the Pledge of Allegiance, carried the flag in local parades, and wore their distinctive Legion campaign caps. But late in the evening, after the wives took the children home to bed, when the blue haze of cigarette smoke lingered and the shots and beers went down one more time, the young men with old eyes said some things. The marine who'd hugged the black sand of Iwo Jima, the tank sergeant who'd pulled his stricken Sherman from a shell hole at Anzio, the submarine sailor who'd sweated out a depth charge attack in the Bungo Strait, and Hagel the B-24 tail gunner—well, they all talked a bit, usually about practical jokes, or stupid officers, or exotic sights. Never about the worst things. You didn't have to say them. These guys knew. So you drained the stale beers and stubbed out the smokes and headed home. And next Saturday night you'd do it again.

Charles Hagel was just eighteen when the Japanese bombed Pearl Harbor. His father, Charles Leo Hagel, known to all as Charlie, served in the Great War. So did Charlie's two brothers, both so badly wounded that they drew disability stipends and still lived at home with their mother, Bertha, and the Hagel patriarch, Herman Christian, who spoke English with the strong accent of his native Germany. Herman, another immigrant homesteader among many, settled in Rushville. The very name Hagel, German for hail, suggested an elemental force of nature. Sometimes, if pressed, the old man's temper erupted. But as a rule, Grandpa Herman kept it all well in hand. He epitomized the discipline of hard work. Herman drove a wagon for a living. Near the end of the Indian Wars, Grandpa Hagel often carried supplies north to Fort Robinson, Camp Sheridan, and the other U.S. Army posts rimming the Pine Ridge Reservation just across the state boundary in South Dakota.[29] Two counties east of his grandparents in Rushville, Charles Dean Hagel grew up in Ainsworth. There was no doubt that when the army called, he'd go. That's what Nebraskans did. That's what Hagels did.

Charles entered the U.S. Army Air Forces as a private. After stateside training, in 1942, he joined the 42nd Bombardment Squadron in Hawaii. They were a hard-luck outfit. At that point in the war, most of them were.

The 42nd flew B-17E Flying Fortresses. Caught on the ground at Hickam Field on December 7, 1941, the squadron suffered nine killed and twenty-two wounded, as well as the destruction of five of seven assigned bombers. The squadron's patch featured a snarling black panther leaping above a flaming Hawaiian torch.[30] These airmen had a score to settle.

The 42nd and its nine B-17s deployed south to New Caledonia and began operations on July 24, 1942. Missions in support of the Guadalcanal campaign kept the crews busy. They staged forward to Espiritu Santo in November and continued reconnaissance and bombing flights until February 7, 1943. In 363 combat sorties, the squadron lost eight aircraft and eight crews, seventy-two airmen in all, plus another pilot killed in action and two ground mechanics dead in a jeep mishap.[31] Hollywood made a wartime movie titled *They Were Expendable*. The 42nd lived it, and it didn't end after two hours. The remnant returned to Hawaii to regroup.

With but one plane left, the 42nd converted from the graceful, iconic B-17E to the blunt-nosed, slab-sided, high-winged, twin-tailed, unloved Consolidated B-24D Liberator. The Germans called the B-24 *dickewagon*, the "furniture van." It looked like one, and it handled like one, too, a flying semi-trailer truck laden with high explosives. But it had longer range than the B-17, and carried more bombs.[32] Charles Hagel would be back in the tail for most missions, although he sometimes flew up front as the radio operator. He'd be one of six enlisted crewmen working with four officers.

Except for the pilot and copilot, every other man joined Hagel as a gunner, to include the officers serving as navigator and bombardier. Eleven .50-caliber machine guns firing inch-and-a-half slugs protected the plane. Three pairs of these long, dull gray-black weapons were twinned in electric turrets—one Plexiglas bubble on top, one on the belly, and Hagel in the back. The other five .50 calibers poked out of the plane's nose and sides.[33] Whether in the motorized turrets or the single mounts, all the machine guns had to be aimed by hand. It helped to be young, to have good eyesight and fast reflexes.

In theory, all of this B-24 firepower meant an opposing airplane couldn't get close, especially when the Americans flew in tight formations. But in reality, Japanese interceptor squadrons soon figured out the holes in the defensive gunfire arcs. The enemy's single-seat, single-engine fighter planes proved fast, nimble, and tough to track for overmatched American gunners. Japanese Zero pilots swarmed in, determined to confuse and overwhelm the defending bomber

crews.[34] To coordinate shooting back at several speedy, twisting tor-
mentors at once—and to avoid punching bullets into the neighboring
friendly bombers—U.S. gunners used a clock technique to call out
hostiles, with the right wing as three, the tail as six, the left wing as
nine, and the nose as twelve. A favorite enemy tactic involved using
a Zero or two to distract the American gunners to one side, then
sending a bold fighter pilot, guns blazing, to dive right at the B-24
cockpit, the infamous "twelve o'clock high" position. Go straight for
the brain. Kill the guys flying the bomber. That usually did not turn
out well for Liberator airmen.

The 42nd trained with the new Liberator bombers in and around
Hawaii through most of 1943. These weren't milk runs. The B-24s
looked for lost U.S. planes, searched for Japanese submarines, and
bombed enemy-held Wake Island. During these months, three bombers crashed, with two complete crews erased and the third set of airmen injured but recovered. Among those missing, and subsequently
captured, was First Lieutenant Louis Zamperini, a former Olympic
athlete. His survival story became famous after the war.[35] In May of
1943, he was just another lost bombardier. Mission after mission, loss
or no loss, the pace did not slow up.

For bombing raids, missions followed a well-known routine. After
taking off and forming up, each crew experienced hours of droning
over-ocean flight. Bored gunners often dozed at their stations. Then
the target came into view. Things got very interesting very fast. For
thirty frantic minutes or so, ten young Americans, amped on pure
adrenaline, fired away at swooping, rolling Japanese Zero fighters
and hoped those black clouds of exploding antiaircraft shells didn't
do mortal damage. At the height of the mayhem, the B-24 steadied up
and settled into the death-grip bombing run, straight and true over the
aim point as flak fragments pounded on the hull. Now and then, a few
hot chunks ripped through, exposing unexpected patches of blue sky
where there should have been solid metal. When the bombs came
loose, the plane rose like an elevator starting up. Then, duty done,
each B-24 turned away, engines straining as each bomber worked to
regain its place in the squadron array. Enemy flak batteries, already

jumping on the next set of U.S. bombers, often tossed out a few parting shots. As fliers caught their breath, men looked around, counted friendly planes, and checked damage to men and machines. If any of the men aboard had been cut up or shot, young airmen wrestled in the freezing air to staunch the bleeding and keep the wounded alive. Battered bombers also needed attention; dead engine props had to be shut down, failed controls bypassed, and excess gear dumped out to reduce the stress on laboring motors. The sturdy Liberator could make it back with a hole in the wing or an engine out, or even worse, but the formation didn't wait for stragglers. If a B-24 fell back, that crew was on their own. Then came another long, lonely trip across the wide water, headed back to the landing strip. Sometimes bomber crews avoided all the perils and did everything right. Then some control wire snapped or a flap came unflapped and the four-engine B-24 cartwheeled into the water right off the end of the runway. Nothing was guaranteed.

Its Hawaiian defense stretch complete, the 42nd Bombardment Squadron and its twelve new B-24s staged forward to Funafuti in the Gilbert Islands on November 12, 1943. For two months, the 42nd flew into the heat of the action, backing up the marine landing on Tarawa and the army landing on Makin, and then the follow-on efforts in the Marshall Islands. In sixty-nine tough missions, three more bombers went down, with thirty men lost.[36] Charles Hagel found out how you made rank in the U.S. Army Air Forces. You stayed alive.

Another stint of retraining and replenishing in Hawaii followed, with more local search and surveillance operations. The crews traded in their remaining B-24D models for the latest J models, sporting a fully automated nose turret among other upgrades. By September of 1944, the squadron again entered combat, working from a forward airfield on Guam. The big, shiny B-29s also flew from that island, and nearby Saipan and Tinian, too. By now a sergeant, Charles Hagel and his crew flew reconnaissance and bombing runs against Iwo Jima and Okinawa. They dropped sea mines in Japanese home waters. Missions piled up: 96 in November, 124 in December, a similar number in January, and 115 in both February and March. U.S. aircraft still went down, with three more Liberators and more fellow airmen gone. As spring turned to summer, the unforgiving tempo continued. The squadron lost another two B-24s and more airmen in June of 1945.[37] No matter how many missions you flew, the next one might be the last. You never knew.

One more move followed. On July 2, 1945, the 42nd repositioned to Okinawa. Missions went against enemy airfields, ports, and railroad lines in Kyushu, the southernmost of the four Japanese home islands. Other raids struck military sites in southern Honshu, the largest island. Squadron bombers hit Japanese facilities in China and Korea, too.[38] These operations represented the opening rounds of preparatory strikes for the U.S. amphibious invasion of Kyushu itself, set for November 1, 1945. The Japanese fought back, but not like the old days. Their planes lacked fuel. Enemy ack-ack guns still banged away. But you could tell the shooting had gotten ragged, disorganized. The Japanese were barely keeping it together.

In July and early August, the 42nd bombed Japan in concert with Curtis LeMay's fleet of B-29s. A dozen years later, when that SAC officer referred to LeMay's plan to reduce the USSR to a smoking, radiating ruin, he might as well have been talking about Japan in the high summer of 1945. By August, even the radiation arrived right on schedule, courtesy of *Enola Gay* and *Bockscar*. The 42nd Bombardment Squadron's Liberator crews saw the ravaged cities, and smelled them, and added their share to the pain. Charles Hagel went through it all, looking down from his perch in the tail, peering through the smudged plastic bubble over his double machine guns, gagging in his oxygen mask from odors he hoped never to smell again. If some wise guy later insinuated that, unlike riflemen on the ground, airmen didn't really understand combat, Charles Hagel could have set him straight.

But then again, he didn't talk about it.

CHARLES HAGEL CAME HOME from the Pacific and went to work at the Cook Paint and Varnish Store in North Platte. Only a few decades before, just outside the town, the great showman, sometime army scout, and self-proclaimed hero of War Bonnet Creek, Buffalo Bill Cody maintained a ranch.[39] Charles Hagel's prospects were nowhere near as grandiose. He'd already had his adventures. In December 1945, Charles married Elizabeth "Betty" Dunn, one of six hard-working daughters of an Irish-Polish farm family with roots in the homestead era. In October of 1946, the couple's son Charles Timothy arrived, right on the baby boom timeline of that generation. The boy shared his first name with his father and paternal grandfather. They called him Tim, to avoid confusion with grandfather Charlie and father Charles.

With little Tim in hand, Charles and Betty moved back to Ainsworth. They'd be there for ten years. Charles took a position with the Hagel family lumberyard. Three more sons followed: Thomas Leo in November of 1948, Michael Patrick in 1950, and James Joseph in 1953. Family, the Catholic Church, school, and the American Legion defined the Hagels as they grew up among the thousand souls of dusty Ainsworth, a cattle town that proclaimed itself the "Middle of Nowhere."[40] Shadows of long-gone Indian braves stalked the low, windy sandhills and rustled the dry, waving prairie grass. And if you looked up in the cornflower blue dome of the sky, you could see the thin contrails of Curtis LeMay's jet bombers—some launched from Offutt Air Force Base—the younger, faster siblings of the B-24s dad Charles flew in the world war.

Boys experience life as it is. For Tim, Tom, and their brothers, Ainsworth felt just fine. Thoughtful journalist Myra MacPherson later characterized it as a "hard-scrabble childhood," and maybe it was. The Hagels worked from a young age. Beginning at age seven, Tim started his winter mornings by walking south to the Chicago and Northwestern railroad station. As a train rumbled by in the predawn gloom, somebody tossed out packs of *Omaha World-Herald* newspapers. Tim Hagel grabbed his share, clipped the binding wires, loaded them on his sled, then made deliveries around town.[41] In Ainsworth, children did that. Nobody thought it unfair or harsh.

Writer Carlyne Berens tagged the Hagel upbringing as a "Beaver Cleaver kind of world," echoing the popular 1957–63 television series.

Perhaps that fit, too. The brothers played war, rode horses, hunted snakes, and threw around the baseball and the football.[42] As Wally and Beaver did on many a TV show, the young Hagel boys "messed around." But Beaver grew up in suburbia, not on the open prairie. June didn't have to work outside the home. And Ward never went to the American Legion to say nothing much, nor did he ever take a drink, nor worry about his next paycheck.

In 1957, the same year so many American households met Beaver Cleaver, something went sideways in the Hagel family. For Charles, the occasional shots of liquor grew more frequent, maybe too frequent. Earning a living at the Ainsworth lumberyard became difficult, a "hostile workplace" in today's verbiage, although nobody in Nebraska would have considered such a description back then. Tom Hagel later described his dad's situation: "He was ill-treated by the man he worked for and refused to see it."[43] That unforgiving superior was Charles Dean Hagel's own father, Charlie. They just could not work together.

So the moves began. Charlie sent his son Charles to the family's other lumber store in Rushville in 1957. Handsome, engaging, with a winning smile, Charles had skills. "Dad could sell ice to Eskimos," his son Mike remembered. True enough, but in the end, Charles was about as popular as you'd expect the boss's son to be. He couldn't fit in. Frustrated, he cut ties with the family business.

More jobs and more moves followed in short order: Cox Lumber Company in Scottsbluff later in 1957, the same firm's place in nearby Terrytown in 1958, and then E.S. Clark Lumber Company in York in 1960. The boys switched schools year after year. The family moved in and out of houses, to include a six-month stint all packed into a basement efficiency apartment in York. Dad Charles struggled to keep his series of jobs. Mom Betty worked. "We didn't have anything," recalled the eldest Hagel son.[44]

In all of that shuttling around, Tim became Chuck. A Rushville football coach casually renamed him when he heard the eleven-year-old's full name. Determined to make the team, the boy went with it. He'd be Chuck Hagel from that day onward.

With their nomadic life, the four brothers grew close. Chuck was the natural leader, the one with the good grades, the top athlete. When playing army, "Chuck was always the general," brother Mike remembered. "The rest of us were privates." Brother Tom, always a quick study and a cut-up, rebelled a bit, frustrating his busy mother and upsetting his distracted father. But Tom respected Chuck.[45] Somehow, through it all, the oldest brother just kept doing things right.

In 1962, the family relocated to Columbus. Betty got a good job as a secretary at the Rural Electrification Association. Charles left the lumberyards behind and gave it a go at Gerhold Concrete Company. But he was drinking more. There were some binges and ugly interludes. For whatever reason, Charles took out his frustrations on Tom. Betty and even sixteen year-old Chuck tried to intervene. After each go-round, things would subside. But these seemed like truces at best. You never knew when to expect another bad day.

Christmas Eve of 1962 turned out to be one of them. Tom and his youngest brother, Jim, were horsing around. They knocked down the Christmas tree. Dad Charles didn't like it at all. He'd been drinking. He chased Tom through the house. Bitter words followed from all involved, the father and the sons. When the uproar subsided, Charles went upstairs to sleep it off. He never woke up.

The medical report read "heart attack." But an empty bottle of sleeping pills hinted at something darker.[46] Suicide? Who really knew? Still, as with so many old soldiers, you had to wonder. "Broken heart" would have been just as fair a verdict on Charles Hagel. His own father had given up on him, he couldn't keep a job anymore, the wife and sons he loved had been embarrassed by his drinking— and God knows what he saw or did out on all of those bombing missions in the Pacific. There wasn't enough whiskey on earth to wash all of that away.

It was a very sad Christmas that year. Betty Dunn Hagel, always made of sterner stuff, pulled the family together. She kept working, and made it clear that her sons needed to step up. They did. All four boys took a series of jobs, and not for spending money, either. Their salaries went toward the family's needs. Work, church, school—the

Hagels stuck to their familiar routines. But they didn't visit the American Legion post. Not anymore.

Chuck graduated from St. Bonaventure High School in 1964 as student council president and football stand-out. He earned a scholarship to Wayne State College. Tom managed to get "encouraged" out of the Catholic high school—too much comedy schtick and too many questions in theology class. He was so smart that he read encyclopedias for fun and cruised through public high school, skating along right above the bare minimums, but well on track to graduate in May of 1967. Mike and Jim hung in there, too. The four industrious brothers reflected the character and love of Betty Hagel. As Mike Hagel put it: "We are who we are because of that woman."[47]

Yet at every meal there was an empty chair at the table. Each passing year allowed the sons to put aside the memories of the rough days. Instead, they remembered Charles Dean Hagel the combat veteran, the patriot, the guy who worked hard, the parent who taught them all to love their country and go when called. The missing man, their father's hole, affected all four sons. They owed him, and each other, and their mom, and Nebraska, and the country.

Chuck Hagel didn't do all that much after high school. An injury ended the Wayne State football opportunity, and an attempt to try again at Kearney State flopped, too. He went to Minneapolis, Minnesota, and enrolled at the Brown Institute of Radio and Television, a technical school. He earned a certificate and in 1967 found work at KLMS, a radio station in Lincoln, Nebraska. He liked the job, but he knew he wasn't living up to his potential, not even close. "I couldn't stay disciplined or focused," he said. "Those were kind of lost years."[48] Restless, he didn't know what he wanted to do.

The Platte County draft board solved Chuck Hagel's problem. Alma Hasselbach had run the board for decades. She contacted Chuck and warned him to get enrolled in college or he'd soon be wearing a uniform. For a lot of young men in America in 1967, that amounted to a lethal threat. For Chuck Hagel, it seemed like an opportunity. Brother Tom, about to graduate from high school, thought it sounded good to him, too.[49] They could go in as a package deal, the brothers Hagel as a team, just as they'd been for years back home. What better way to honor their father, make their mother proud, and do their part for America?

So Chuck volunteered for the draft, and reported to the military induction office in Omaha in April. Brother Tom was right behind him, as soon as he graduated from high school in late May. Some people who heard what the Hagels did, especially years after the Vietnam War ended in misery, figured the brothers as rural rubes from what one reporter described as "a land of superpatriots." Yet both Chuck and Tom read widely growing up. Chuck subscribed to *Time* and *Newsweek* and the family dinner table often featured serious discussions of politics and history. Their parents were Republicans, like most in Nebraska, so Tom, of course, declared himself a Democrat.[50] Neither brother could or would claim to be an expert on the ongoing Vietnam conflict. Then again, in 1967 America, who was?

The two knew they were not volunteering for World War III. Like all sane Americans, they counted on SAC to keep that possibility remote. Anyway, nukes, B-52s, and missiles were not for them. SAC would stand its long watch without the Hagels.

No, Chuck and Tom thought they were signing up for their father's war, but smaller, like Korea. They had watched *Combat* on television and seen *The Sands of Iwo Jima* and *The Longest Day* at the movies. This Vietnam confrontation looked to be more of the same, with some new stuff like helicopters. Go over there, fight the uniformed enemy—they did call them NVA regulars, after all—and then come home, put on an American Legion campaign cap, and get on with life in Nebraska.

It never occurred to the Hagels, nor to many others, that Vietnam resembled World War II only in the sense that both were wars. What the two men from Nebraska faced would look a great deal more like those grim, ugly, fleeting clashes with the Cheyenne and Lakota. Like their fellow citizens watching at home, Chuck and Tom Hagel had a lot to learn. Their education began soon enough.

CHAPTER 2

This Man's Army

> None of the numbers mean much except one,
> which reads like craps: 11-Bravo.
>
> **PETER TAUBER**, *The Sunshine Soldiers*[1]

In the beginning was the drill sergeant, and the drill sergeant was with the army, and the drill sergeant was the army. Any U.S. Army recruit learns that in the first minute of the first hour of basic training. It's sometimes said that there are no atheists in the foxhole. Maybe so. In the foxhole of basic training, all become believers in the hard-won ways of the U.S. Army. And the drill sergeant makes them so.

Hollywood long ago rented a pew in this church. Whether dramas (*Sands of Iwo Jima, Take the High Ground, The D.I.*) or comedies (*Buck Privates, See Here Private Hargrove, Gomer Pyle USMC*), movies and television reveled in the inherent narrative tension of often unwilling civilians being turned into proud, disciplined soldiers.[2] The U.S. Army drill sergeant and his U.S. Marine Corps counterpart—and frankly, role model—the drill instructor (DI), standing tall in his "Smokey the Bear" 1911 campaign hat, dominated the center ring of the show. He was the star. With him calling the shots, well-worn tropes and clichés followed. Barbers cut thick heads of hair down to bare stubble. Drill sergeants violated the personal space of dazed recruits, shouting and cursing with gusto. Brilliant barracks lights flicked on at oh-four-hundred as an immaculately crisp drill sergeant banged away on a galvanized trash can. Ham-handed, lead-footed new troops, sweating it out in fresh, ill-fitted uniforms, fumbled to march in step and handle unfamiliar rifles. Individual screwups generated mass punishments. Men swung through arduous obstacle courses and banged away on hot rifle ranges. But by the end of the program, whether played straight or for laughs, the new soldiers marched by in serried ranks, good to go and ready to fight, no longer separate personalities, but interchangeable members of a team. And through it all, the drill sergeant set the pace. The Hagel brothers, like most volunteers and draftees of 1967, knew all of that, or thought they did.

With Tom Hagel wrapping up high school, Chuck went first. On April 26, 1967, induction orders in hand courtesy of the Platte County Selective Service Board, Chuck Hagel left Columbus, Nebraska, by bus. At the processing office in Omaha, Hagel met five other recruits. One of the others from Columbus, Joe Swierczek, sported long hair, a blue and white polka-dot shirt, and white bell-bottom trousers, quite appropriate as he played drums for a local rock band. The other four were more nondescript. By comparison, former athlete Hagel was older (age twenty-one), taller, almost six feet, barrel chested, with relatively short sandy hair, and looked you in the eye. Most importantly, he had a pronounceable last name. The duty sergeant who met the six men in Omaha gave Hagel the good news. You're in charge. Get these guys to dinner and breakfast. Be on the train tomorrow morning.[3] No trash-can banging, no in-your-face hollering, no Smokey the Bear hats—just one recruit dragging the others in his wake.

Hagel didn't know it yet, but he'd already gotten his first lesson in how the army really worked, the secret behind what the drill sergeants endeavored to teach you. Civilians without military experience often think the military is all about rapidly carrying out directives like a mindless robot. But because people are not automatons, and no disembodied verbiage makes otherwise sane humans willing to stand up in a hail of hot bullets, it's not about the orders. Soldiers may or may not follow orders. They *will* follow the example of those they trust. So the army looks for the exemplary ones. In picking potential leaders for the most deadly hunt of all, the army went with the older, bigger, faster, more alert ones. The younger, shorter, slower, less articulate people might demonstrate worthwhile talents over time. But they started their at-bat with a strike or two in the count.

Hagel and his five charges went where they were supposed to go and boarded the train for points south, to wit, El Paso, Texas. Then (and now) the military contracted travel to the lowest bidder, unless there was an emergency cooking. Getting six more recruits to Fort Bliss did not amount to a crisis. The sprawling post wasn't going anywhere. So the train chugged its slow way south, through Kansas, Oklahoma, and then across the endless stretch of Texas. At stops, more small groups of nervous, uncertain recruits boarded. The journey ended at an empty El Paso train station at 3 a.m., of course. Most good folks were abed, and most bad ones were just getting home. But for the U.S. Army, it was business time.

Now the drill sergeant arrived in all his theatric splendor. Campaign hat tilted low over his narrowed eyes, the senior drill sergeant "welcomed" his latest batch of greenhorns with the time-tested opening line: "You're all mine now!"[4] Indeed they were.

The drill sergeant bellowed and the tired, frightened young men lined up, literally scared into straight ranks, as they didn't yet know the rudiments of military drill. Their loud civilian clothes and unruly hair already felt wrong, and the drill sergeant made no secret that he thought so, too. He also offered that they were the worst batch of recruits he'd ever seen, that few if any could make it, or deserved to make it, in "this man's army." This tirade came suitably laced with an impressively original series of profanities. "And a new jarring gong of reality set in." Hagel recalled. "From that moment on, it was a different world."[5]

By the morning he met Chuck Hagel and two hundred other new soldiers, Sergeant First Class William Joyce had already served twenty-two years in the U.S. Army. He came from rural Alabama. "My only way out of there was the army," he said years later. Joyce missed World War II, but not Korea. At Fort Bliss, he headed the dozen drill sergeants training Chuck Hagel and the rest of his recruit company. Many of these young men were going to war, as Joyce well knew. "I'm going to teach you to be mean and tough," the drill sergeant said, "because if I fail, you get your head blown off in Vietnam."[6]

Joyce and his fellow drill sergeants had been carefully chosen. Although the army had had some form of mass basic training going back to the years prior to World War I, in the interwar years that languished. In the 1920s and 1930s, units ran their own little programs. An extensive system of large-scale pre-combat training started again with the 1940 draft and persisted well into the Cold War. It did the job, and few would call it easy. But it seemed rather . . . well, generic, GI (government issue) in the bad sense. Army initial entry training taught you how to march, mop the floor, and shoot a few rounds downrange, but the whole undertaking emphasized completing the busy schedule, learning skills. Building will to fight seemed like an afterthought. The clear implication was that unless you were going to the infantry, you'd never see most of this stuff again. Cooks and drivers and helicopter mechanics didn't really need to know how to fight, did they?

The marines thought they did. Tough, unforgiving, and unapologetic, Boot Camp made every marine a rifleman. Marines might then become cooks, clerks, or bottle washers, but all shared a visceral rifleman ethos. Unhappy with their service's mediocre approach, army generals argued for a more consciously marine-style version known as Basic Combat Training. That second word—"combat"—was in there for a reason. Basic Combat Training came to be in 1963, just in time for the Vietnam troop buildup. Army leaders studied the fabled Marine Corps methods at Parris Island, South Carolina. Selected army sergeants even attended the marine DI preparatory course. The soldiers didn't want to be marines. But they saw a lot of value in the way the corps turned diffident civilians into committed, disciplined military men. The army borrowed the techniques, the attitude—and the hat.[7]

Basic Combat Training lasted eight weeks. It aimed to break down scruffy civilians and rebuild them as confident soldiers, ready to proceed to Advanced Individual Training (which varied based on the soldier's assigned specialty), and then off to join actual units. The basic course included 352 hours of formal instruction and fifty-six days of 24/7 immersion in army discipline. Every eight weeks, Fort Bliss churned out 10,000 basic-trained privates. In addition to Bliss, by 1967 the army as a whole drew on centers at Forts Benning, Bragg, Campbell, Dix, Gordon, Jackson, Knox, Leonard Wood, Lewis, McClellan, Ord, Polk, Riley, and Sill to crank through up to 900,000 new troops a year.[8] It was mass production, not of B-52 bombers or 105mm cannon shells, but young soldiers. If you ever wanted to feel like an insignificant cog in a very large green machine, the U.S. Army was ready to oblige.

Fort Bliss added its own pleasures. It's hard to imagine a place less like Vietnam, with one exception: the temperature. The army got that right. "Oh, it was hot," said Hagel. Even at three o'clock on a mid-spring morning, it was a warm, dry 70°. Midday topped 90°, and over 100° in the direct, unbearably bright sunshine. As for the terrain, Hagel identified three basic varieties: "sand, desert, rocks."[9] Hagel and his fellow recruits soon grew intimately familiar with these characteristics, spending plenty of waking hours examining the Fort Bliss micro-terrain while in the "front leaning rest," that most unrestful army moniker for the "up" position in a push-up.

Drill Sergeant Joyce and his cadre ratified the decision of the administrative orderly back in Omaha. Starting that first lonely morning, Hagel found himself designated a recruit squad leader, complete with an armband marked with noncommissioned officer (NCO) chevrons. He was picked for the same reasons as always. He was a bit older, had some college, and looked athletic, tall and solid. Plus, Hagel didn't flinch when men yelled at him. His coaches, his father, hell, even the nuns at Catholic school had already done plenty of that. Hagel's rank was on an armband for a reason. It could go away as quickly as it arrived. It depended on how Hagel performed in each day's training. As in war, it was all graded. But unlike combat, failure did not equal death.

That first warm morning, with the sun not even risen, the eight weeks of Basic Combat Training stretched like an eternity. Yet there never seemed to be enough hours in the day, or night, to do all the things the drill sergeant demanded. For a soldier, especially a trainee at Fort Bliss, time could run as slowly as a limp Salvador Dalí clock or as quickly as a hummingbird's heartbeat. Hours could last for weeks, but if you lifted your head, bang, you were halfway through the day. The better soldiers—and Chuck Hagel turned out to be one—well, they figured it out. Do the job in front of you today, right here and now. Polish the brass. Clean the rifle. Pick up the cigarette butts. Run the mile. Deal with the immediate and focus there. Let tomorrow take care of itself.

The here and now of that first day kept everyone busy. Along with many other activities, the men moved into their new home. Trainee barracks at Fort Bliss were temporary buildings, built to last five years and house a platoon of thirty men. They were already twenty years old, and as the training program began, held forty souls.[10] Army experience told Drill Sergeant Joyce and his NCOs not to worry. A quarter of the men would soon drop behind—sick, lame, lazy, crazy—either recycled to the next session or out altogether. And the old barracks would be just fine. Recruits take very good care of buildings. They mop, dust, shine, scrub, polish, and paint with a vengeance. Every Saturday morning there'd be a white-glove inspection. Drill Sergeant Joyce would show the way for the company commander, an earnest lieutenant eager to be quit of Fort Bliss and off to Vietnam. In some ways, the sequence resembled a seeing-eye dog guiding a blind man. The officer missed things. Joyce saw all. "He was tough as hell," Hagel said.[11] Thanks to Joyce, when the officer departed, the bad items got fixed, pronto. That's how five-year barracks lasted two decades.

The first night, Chuck Hagel and his new platoon mates found out that the army had better things for its new troops to do than sleep. All

were exhausted, wrung out by a day filling out forms, drawing uniforms and field gear, and three times shoveling in some random food
in a steaming hot mess hall. Or was it steaming hot food in a random
mess hall? No matter. After each hurried meal, in-processing recom-
menced immediately: more forms to sign, more items issued, getting
yelled at, doing push-ups and getting yelled at some more, then more
push-ups. As the longest of long days ended, it fell to squad leader
Hagel to arrange an hourly schedule of fire watch. Soldiers in 1967
smoked a lot of cigarettes. A barracks built of old dry wood, in an
arid climate, coated with layers of paint and varnish—it practically
defined flammable tinder. The drill sergeants told stories of barracks
going up in a few minutes.

So fire watch must be done. One man was awake all night, on his
feet in full uniform, flashlight in hand. He walked the floor and made
sure the rest slept tight. Each hour, in accord with Hagel's slate, the
guy on fire watch woke up his backfill. Yes, it prevented immolation.
But the succession of sentinels, the office of the hours, also taught a
valuable coping skill. Over the eight weeks, men developed the capacity to rouse quickly, do things for a while, and just as quickly drop
down and crash back into sleep. War is all about getting rudely awak-
ened, functioning, and then shutting down and stocking up Zs. The
tossers and turners didn't last long in combat.

There was something else, too. Soldiers quickly learned who got
ready quickly and who dragged, the team players and the selfish
ones. Hagel paid attention to this, another increment in his education as a military leader. He himself set the standard. He pulled his
stint, and he was big enough to enforce the schedule. Drill sergeants
checked the barracks at odd hours of the night, but never seemed to
be around if a recalcitrant recruit needed some "motivation." It was
survival of the fittest. It might be 1967 outside Fort Bliss. But among
the double bunks at night, the Paleolithic epoch rolled on.[12] Big, alert
guys ruled. And Chuck Hagel was big and alert. From the outset, his
steely glance did the trick. As the eight weeks went on, he rarely had
to threaten and even more rarely had to act. So it passed, the evening
and the morning, the first day.

WORLD WAR II navy reserve officer Herman Wouk, in his wonderful novel *The Caine Mutiny*, explained it all rather succinctly: "The Navy is a master plan designed by geniuses for execution by idiots."[13] Substitute Army Basic Combat Training for the navy and you've got it. That's the worst case, of course. The drill sergeants were not idiots—far from it. And the recruits were not idiots either, although they started quite ignorant of military skills. With their considerable combined efforts, the drill sergeants and their budding privates took things to pretty high levels of achievement. But from the atmospherics of the drill sergeant persona to the constant pressures of harsh activity to the training itself—just the right mix of novelty and repetition—the entire eight-week tableau smacked of genius, all right. You can get people to do amazing things by working together. Fear jump-starts the engine of discipline. But by the end, the motor is inside. And the good ones power the whole unit. Hagel was a good one.

The eight weeks of Basic Combat Training featured three primary evaluations: the physical combat proficiency test, rifle marksmanship, and the individual proficiency test. Along with those relatively objective measurements, the men were assessed daily on physical fitness, uniform appearance, cleanliness of their equipment, and timeliness in carrying out duties. Chuck Hagel decided right away to "try to be the best guy."[14]

The first two weeks focused on individual skills. First, the rookie soldiers had to learn how to wear their uniforms: ever present metal dog tags on a neck chain, white drawers and T-shirt, green long-sleeve shirt, green trousers, green baseball cap, black cotton-web belt with brass buckle (for shining), green wool socks, and black combat boots (also for shining). Most struggled. Some, like Hagel, got it. Some did not. "I was in with a lot of kids who had never had any organization at all in their life," Hagel remembered. "They were drafted from Navajo reservations. We had Hispanic kids. In that part of the country, you threw them all in. We had kids who had quit school in seventh grade. We had some kids who'd never worn boots; hardly shoes. And it was a group that I had never ever quite experienced before. Tough group."[15] Drill Sergeant Joyce and his NCOs were tougher. Hagel was the company's role model, what "right" looked like. But he got no special deals, no privileges except the opportunity to stay ahead of the pack. He helped the guys who wanted helping. The quitters fell by the wayside.

Sergeants told the trainees that the most efficient way to move people from points A to B was marching in formation. Conflicting opinions were not solicited. And the drill sergeants loved marching: eyes front, arms swinging in time, booted feet striking the pavement in cadence, voices sounding off, "One, two, three, four." It looked like the ultimate physical manifestation of discipline, and felt like it, too, certainly for raw recruits struggling to fit into the mass. Attention (standing tall), parade rest (not at all a relaxing posture), right face, left face, the marching movements, the manual of arms—all of those used to be the army's battlefield tactics in the days of smoothbore muzzle-loading muskets, although they turned out to be almost universally fatal when tried in the face of accurate long-range rifles at places like Bull Run and Shiloh. Yet close-order drill persisted. It taught men to start, stop, and change direction on voice command. It imposed instant order. The army's wise heads, Wouk's geniuses, long ago put drill in place, and saw that it was good.

The army marched at quick time, 120 30-inch steps a minute. The army ran at double time, 180 36-inch steps a minute. Troops learned to march and run while wearing stiff boots, broken in the hard way. They wore steel helmets and web gear of utility belts and suspenders. From each soldier's webbing hung a bayonet and scabbard, a one-quart canteen, two ammunition pouches, a medical bandage packet, and a little butt pack the size of an overstuffed football, full of a rolled plastic poncho, a weapons cleaning kit, and other mandatory odds and ends. They also carried M14 rifles, 44.3 inches long and 10.7 pounds, beefed up versions of the World War II Garand M1.[16] Counting the rifle, the water, the helmet, and the other stuff, each man carried forty extra pounds—the equivalent of shouldering a four-year-old boy—on every march and run. The beast of burden feeling passed through your head every time the drill sergeants commanded (without even a hint of irony), "Saddle up." You got used to it, so much so that after the first two weeks, when you took off your equipment, you felt funny and light on your feet, like an astronaut loping along on the moon.

Recruits did not wear the full ensemble for the physical fitness test. At the end of the first week, the men stripped to their uniform shirts and trousers, doffed their caps, and ran through the five scored events. First, they did the 40-yard crawl (36 seconds to pass, 25 seconds for a maximum score). Next, the men swung like Tarzan, hand over hand, along the 13-rung horizontal ladder, turning at each end for as many iterations as possible (36 rungs pass, 76 rungs max). Then came the run, dodge, and jump a little pair of wooden rails and a shallow ditch to traverse in a figure eight (26.5 seconds to pass, 22 seconds max). A 30-yard grenade throw followed (3 hits pass, 5 hits max). Finally came the one-mile run (8.5 minutes pass, 6.5 minutes max).[17] Most of the raw troops made it through that initial trial, more or less. Almost all passed the test by week eight. Chuck Hagel did well from the outset. He kept his squad leader chevrons.

The rifle range occupied weeks three and four. The semiautomatic M14 shot one round with each trigger pull. It fired the standard 7.62mm NATO cartridge, and it had a decent kick against the shooter's soldier. Troops in Vietnam did not use it anymore, having long ago switched to the lighter, smaller M16 with its "rock and roll" full automatic setting. But Hagel and the trainees used the older weapon.[18] It went with their shiny brass belt buckles, the black leather boots, and the Korean War–era field gear. Fundamentals of marksmanship did not change. Hagel paid close attention to the drill sergeants' coaching. He qualified expert. Once more, he led the way.

Week six, bivouac week, found the men out overnight in the scrubby desert. By this juncture, the weaklings had either gotten stronger or fallen out. The soldiers set up two-man pup tents and ate canned C-rations. From their little camp, they sortied out for day and night tactical maneuvers and practice patrols.

Training included throwing live hand grenades, always exciting with rookies. M26 fragmentation grenades have a pin and a handle. When you pull the pin, the handle pops loose. Then you have four seconds to throw it to where it needs to be before it blows.[19] Sometimes, a nervous trainee dropped one. The drill sergeant then earned his pay, grabbing it and tossing it clear. None of that happened in Hagel's outfit.

On the night infiltration course, the men crawled under barbed wire as live machine gun rounds ripped overhead. If a soldier stood up, he'd get shot and likely killed. The guys all knew better now. They ran through it like pros, heads down, bellies flat on the sand, inching forward. It gave the troops some idea of what it might be like to be under fire.[20] Sure, it was canned and controlled. But it conveyed the right point. You could get killed doing these things. Stay alert. Stay alive.

After bivouac week, the trainees pushed into their individual proficiency test. This one got at the various key soldier skills. The first station subjected the troops to a sit-down multiple-choice test to examine knowledge of military customs, courtesy, and justice. A second station also used a written test to quiz army traditions, organization, and ranks. The group then moved outside and reclaimed their field gear and rifles. They'd need them. The third spot assessed manual of arms and close-order drill, beloved of the sergeants, but of tactical value only if the War of 1812 broke out again. At the fourth site, graders assessed hand-to-hand combat techniques. Location five focused on tactical movements, notably the high crawl, the low crawl, and the three-second rush. The sixth area tested battlefield first aid: clear the airway, stop the bleeding, protect the wound, and treat for shock. The soldiers then proceeded to site seven to demonstrate skills with gas masks and reacting to chemical threats. Number eight offered a guard duty practical exercise. As the men finished, all of the various subtasks were totaled.[21] Once more, Chuck Hagel stood first.

The eight-station test culminated the eight-week program. Most of the soldiers wondered what came after the graduation parade. The army placed each newly minted private in a designated role, known as an MOS (military occupational specialty). Some already knew their MOS. Those who had gone to recruiting offices and signed voluntary enlistment contracts for three or four years had it down in writing

before they'd ever gotten to Fort Bliss. Hagel, like all the other draftees, got his orders in the last week of Basic Combat Training. For
him, Advanced Individual Training would be at Fort Ord, California.
Hagel knew immediately what that meant. "I had the most famous of
all MOS's, 11-Bravo [11B]," he said, "which is the infantryman MOS. I
didn't fight that. I thought that if you're going to be in the Army, you
want to be a warrior."[22] The army agreed.

The army had more for Hagel, the best in his platoon and company. In the few free moments, when the other privates smoked,
joked, or goofed off, Hagel studied field manuals and polished his
boots. It paid off. After looking at all of the top scorers, the senior
drill sergeants and colonels in command designated Private Chuck
Hagel as the number one trainee of the 10,000-man cycle. He received
a promotion to private first class, a certificate of achievement, and
a trip to the El Paso chamber of commerce to accept the American
Spirit Honor Medal. Chuck Hagel would earn many distinctions in
uniform and afterward. But these mattered more than most. The guy
who couldn't get settled after high school had found his way. "I can
really do this," he told himself.

Sergeant First Class William Joyce escorted the army's newest
PFC (private first class) to the awards luncheon. Hagel had dealt
with Joyce every day at Fort Bliss, but strictly in the line of duty. As
they drove into El Paso, Joyce shared some advice. He told Hagel:
"You've got to be the best and give your best because people are
going to rely on you. They're going to depend on you if you go to Vietnam."[23] Hagel listened intently. Vietnam. Like the grunts in country
liked to say: there it is.

WHEN MANY YOUNG AMERICANS headed west for the Summer of
Love in San Francisco, Chuck Hagel did, too. Ignoring Scott McKen-
zie's song "San Francisco," Hagel didn't wear flowers in his close-
cropped hair. He didn't smoke dope, and he didn't join the "be in"
in Haight-Ashbury.[24] Instead, in that endless summer of 1967, he reported to Advanced Individual Training at Fort Ord, a hundred-odd

miles south of the hippies and the fun. A hundred thousand youth in the Bay Area made love, not war. Hagel worked on making war.

Advanced Individual Training took things to the next level. For eight weeks, Hagel and the other 11Bs learned about the key infantry weapons and how to use them. They popped fat 40mm grenades out of the tubular M79 "blooper" or "thumper," which looked for all the world like the army's real-life version of Elmer Fudd's cartoon break-action shotgun. They learned how to rip off belts of 7.62mm ammunition (four ball, one tracer) through the M60 machine gun, the "pig," developed by reverse engineering the German army's wicked MG422, scourge of the 1944 Normandy beaches. They still carried M14s, and did more shooting with them, but also got some time with M16 automatic rifles. Handling weapons, shooting them, and growing comfortable with them formed the core of the Fort Ord weeks.

One range stood out. Called "quick kill," this set of lanes lined up the new infantrymen, then confronted them with brief glimpses of man-shaped targets. E-silhouettes, a flat dark-green cardboard head and torso, represented a standing foe. F-silhouettes depicted a head and shoulders poking out of a trench or tunnel mouth. The Es and Fs popped up, some half seen behind barriers, others in shadows. The riflemen in training, moving upright as they'd be on foot patrol, turned and shot as fast as they could. It all taught the soldiers to fire reflexively at noises and flashes.[25] The drill sergeants warned the budding infantrymen. You won't see the Viet Cong. The jungle is too thick. Go with your instincts. Quick kill.

Other field exercises attempted to teach what to expect in Vietnam. Hagel and the others learned how to look for trip wires across trails. They searched mock Vietnamese villages, set up night ambushes, and ran reconnaissance patrols. Within the bounds of the possible, it rated as adequate, maybe even pretty good, preparation for war. But you had to recognize what didn't occur. Nobody shot back, no men in training suffered wounds, and the "enemy" consisted of detailed play-dead guys for the blank-fire phases or cardboard targets on the shooting ranges. It all lacked a lot. The army tried to fill that major deficiency by substituting physical exhaustion, insistent time standards, and intrusive grading. The entire enterprise bore the same relationship to real combat that shadow-boxing does to real boxing. Nobody punched back. Nobody bled. And in the end, that made all the difference.

In addition to the demanding combat exercises, there were still barracks inspections and marching and running and push-ups. But the drill sergeants, who gave no quarter on Fort Ord's training ranges, backed off some on the spit and polish. [26] This wasn't basic. Many of these guys in training would leave Ord and head right to Vietnam.

Hagel didn't get orders to Vietnam. Instead, he got an offer and a special assignment. The army asked Hagel to consider going to Officer Candidate School. Flattering, yes—but it also ensured three years of service in addition to what Hagel had already completed. He declined.[27]

The other opportunity, the special assignment, wasn't optional. Hagel and nine other enlisted men assembled at White Sands Missile Range, out in the New Mexico desert west of Fort Bliss. White Sands wasn't a training center, but a proving ground. The army tested rockets and even nuclear bombs out in that lonely expanse. What did that have to do with PFC Chuck Hagel?

He had been judged capable of learning fast and keeping a secret. For three months, Hagel and his fellow soldiers received intensive training on the FIM-43 Redeye shoulder-fired antiaircraft missile. The launcher looked like a World War II bazooka, a pipe with a sight and trigger handle mounted on it. With a round inside, the thing weighed just over eighteen pounds. The missile peeped out of the open muzzle, and its clear bubble nose shielded an infrared seeker. If you pointed a loaded Redeye launcher up into the sky, the missile searched for a heat source—say an enemy jet engine. When you felt a vibration in the handle, sort of like a buzzing cell phone today, the thing had locked on. Then you pressed the trigger and, racing out at nearly twice the speed of sound, the Redeye streaked up into the air and rammed into the hostile airplane's tailpipe. So went the concept.

In actual firings, the Redeye could be finicky. Its range was just under three miles, around 15,000 feet in altitude. So opposing planes had the option of flying higher. If the target turned fast, the way jet fighters do, the Redeye might lose its fix. Opposing aircraft could spoof it by dumping out flares. A lot depended on a missile-man willing to hang in there and track the bad guy until the Redeye lined up. Hagel and his nine teammates worked hard to get the hang of it.

They did so in silence. No phone calls were allowed. Mail arrived and went out, but authorities checked all of it. As the soldiers gained the ability to track and hit aerial targets, word came down. They'd all be going to Germany, via Fort Dix, New Jersey.[28] Hagel got a short leave first. He returned to Nebraska.

While Chuck perfected his craft with the secret weapon, brother Tom also missed the Summer of Love. As he and Chuck had agreed back in Nebraska, Tom started down the same path as his brother. He, too, went through Basic Combat Training at Fort Bliss. Although some clerk recommended Tom to be a cook, the younger Hagel received 11B as his MOS, and then headed to Fort Ord. Tom didn't rack up all the kudos Chuck earned, but the younger brother did just fine. He, too, met the drill sergeant's preferred standard—tall, smart, clear-eyed, articulate, and trustworthy. Belligerent NCOs didn't faze Tom. The drill sergeants noticed. Even with an iffy high school record and no college, Tom also merited Officer Candidate School. And he turned it down. His orders, like Chuck's, read Germany. But Tom heard that after six months in Europe, he'd likely get levied to Vietnam. Volunteer draftees tended to end up there, and Tom had no special-purpose Redeye qualification to keep him squared off against the Soviet air force.[29] Tom's timeline ran about two months behind that of his brother.

After seeing Betty, Mike, Jim, and the extended family, Chuck left for Fort Dix. When he got to the post in New Jersey, Sergeant First Class William Joyce's words came swimming back up. *People depend on you . . . if you go to Vietnam.* He thought about it. There'd be no "if." "The right thing," Hagel said, "was to go where the war was." Hagel went to the orderly room. He volunteered for Vietnam. That sure quieted the place.

The sergeant at the desk told the captain, who immediately came out of his adjoining office. They called a chaplain. Together, the Fort

Dix people tried to be sure Hagel was in his right mind. He was. When Tom got word of it, he volunteered, too.

When she got the phone call, mom Betty was none too happy. But she knew her sons. This is what they wanted, and she supported them. "Well," she said, "I hope you've made the right decision."[30] In the bitter fall of 1967, the Hagel brothers thought they had.

IN THE VIEW of millions of young Americans in 1967, Chuck and Tom Hagel had just screwed up—big time. To those opposed to the war, the entire U.S. Army and its soldiers, not to mention the rest of the U.S. Armed Forces, the Johnson administration, the Establishment (whoever they might actually be), and pretty much everyone over age thirty seemed too immoral to be trusted. The Vietnam War clearly represented the worst, most depraved thing in American history, probably world history, and possibly prehistory, too. That was not yet a majority opinion in the United States. But by 1967, to the bewilderment of General Westmoreland and the chagrin of President Johnson, it was getting there.

The anti-war youth surely had a point. All wars are bloody, confused, and wasteful. That's baked in the sordid cake. In a democratic republic, we tolerate short, decisive wars. Smaller is better. We'll put up with a big one, like World War I or World War II, if it looks like we're winning and it doesn't drag out. As a strategy, attrition never earned high marks in a West Point textbook, but Americans resorted to it in the trenches of the Argonne Forest in 1918 and the Anzio beachhead in 1944. It all depended on how it turned out. By 1967, the full-scale U.S. campaign in Vietnam had only been going on for two years, and though unwon, it did not yet seem unwinnable. Still, the indicators looked bad. Despite the optimistic calculations of Westmoreland and the desperate desires of LBJ, nobody could tell for sure when this thing would wrap up, or how many lives would be lost.

Confronted with an apparently no-win war, politically conscious American youth turned on the war with the assured vitriol of true believers. No Communist Party propagandist in Hanoi, Moscow, or Beijing could hope to outdo the things said in rallies, inked onto posters, and printed on paper. In the great October 21, 1967, march on the Pentagon, you saw and heard them all. "Hey, hey, LBJ, how many kids did you kill today?" "Bastard Johnson's doom comes soon!" "Out demons! Out!" "Ho, Ho, Ho Chi Minh, the NLF [National Liberation Front; the Viet Cong] is gonna win!" And finally, a few raised a plaintive cry, inverting the usual formula heard in unhappy under-developed countries. "Yankee come home." When former B-24 pilot Senator George McGovern ran for president in 1972, he borrowed a variant of that last one as the theme of his nomination acceptance speech: "Come home America."[31]

A few of those who marched for peace in Vietnam stuck with it for the rest of their lives. They became convinced, or maybe they started out that way, that war was indeed bad for children and other living things. These pacifists have marched against every American war, great and small, since Vietnam: the rest of the Cold War, El Salvador, Nicaragua, Lebanon, Grenada, Panama, Iraq I, Somalia, Haiti, Bosnia, Kosovo, Afghanistan, and Iraq II. You have to respect them. There's no easy money in peace activism, that's for sure.

But most of the young people who loudly objected to the war, and the multitudes who sympathized but didn't march, concentrated their objections to this particular war at this particular time. As they grew older and Vietnam receded into history, the majority of them found that national interests countenanced other wars at other times. Why?

Self-righteous posturing aside, it all came down to the draft. Young men didn't want to die. Who can blame them? College students figured out well before MACV that the body count strategy, such as it was, boded ill for the young Americans who made up the U.S. side of the equation. If the draft didn't exist, the widespread anti-war move-ment of the 1960s might have remained fervent but small, a few com-mitted pacifists hanging out on the fringes of U.S. politics, the same place they had resided in all previous wars. But taking in 300,000 young men a year and sending a lot of them to Vietnam, well, that sure got attention. It really riveted the interest of those who had the education, time, and money to take a hard look at their prospects in the care of the strange creature known as the Selective Service System.

Since its foundation on June 14, 1775, even before independence, the U.S. Army has traditionally been a volunteer force. The United States drafted soldiers for the Civil War (both North and South did it) and World War I. Established in 1940, before the United States entered World War II, the Selective Service System endeavored to strike the right balance between military requirements, wartime industrial and agricultural needs, and longtime social order. Required numbers were set in Washington. The actual picking, the selective part, occurred in local draft boards, committees of prominent local worthies. In 1967, there were about 3,700 such boards across the country. The one in Platte County contacted the Hagel brothers.

Then the selecting started. Although the United States committed wholeheartedly to both world wars, draft American-style never approached the relentless dragnets established by the French Revolution's draconic *levée en masse* of 1793–1814 or the drastic measures of the Soviet Union's Red Army in World War II. Even so, in the United States during World War II, conscription reached far and wide. In 1940–45, if a man met the right age category (eighteen to forty-five), proved mentally and physically qualified for service, and did not have some critical farm or factory job, he went.[32] As that had been the experience of most adult Americans in 1967, they thought the Vietnam draft ran the same way. If it had, draft resistance in the 1960s would likely have been a footnote to history. And win, lose, or draw, the Vietnam War would have been settled in a few years. When you send them all, the folks back home demand results.

But in Vietnam, we did not send them all. Even at the height of the war, the army didn't need them all. Some went. Most didn't. And that very arbitrariness created its own rack of tensions.

From 1964 to 1972, the U.S. draft pool of young males aged eighteen to twenty-six numbered 27 million. About a third of that amount (8.7 million) served in uniform over those years. And just above a third of them (3.3 million) served in or around Vietnam, to include men on naval vessels offshore, in Thailand and in Guam, a U.S. territory. Draftees supplied a third of all men in uniform during the war, and that number included the 10 percent of those, like the Hagel brothers, who requested to be drafted. The other two-thirds, the nonconscripts, were volunteers.[33]

Crunching the numbers, the arithmetic for the unwilling suggested that Uncle Sam only compulsorily enrolled one of nine young men eligible to put on a uniform. Two more joined on their own. And the other six? They never got asked. Or if they did, they found a preferred alternative.

Confronted with a summons from the draft board, American males faced a spectrum of possibilities. Indicative of the way things tended to go, only three of eighteen Selective Service categories (I-A, available; I-A-O, conscientious objector willing to serve as a noncombatant; and I-C, already serving) earned you a trip to Fort Bliss and maybe Vietnam.[34] The paths out were many.

At the far end of the range stood outright resistance. You could simply refuse to play and go to jail. Despite the impression that millions refused to go, the actual numbers fall far short. Todd Gitlin, a prominent student activist and historian of the period, estimated that from 1967 to 1972, about 200,000 faced accusations of draft-related misbehavior, to include up to 5,000 who burned or publicly repudiated their draft cards. Of these, 25,000 faced indictments. Courts convicted 8,750 and 4,000 of those men went to prison. Most earned parole in six to twelve months. A handful served four to five years.[35] While a few prominent figures went all the way—boxer Muhammad Ali comes to mind—not many chose this unpleasant course.

Those lacking the stomach for outright law-breaking sought avenues of avoidance. You could qualify as a nondeployable conscientious objector, a religious minister, or a divinity student. Belief in God took quite a jump in the 1960s, not all of it fueled by LSD or marijuana. A doctor might square you away for physical or mental reasons. A few hundred fled overseas. More headed north to Canada. Some 10,000 just went "underground," off the grid, easier to do in that pre-Internet age.[36]

The student deferment (category II-S) formed the most common way out. In some ways, it resembled the Civil War practice of paying a substitute. But in this case, if you could get into college and stay there, you were good. And the local draft board picked the next guy in line. The number of those who studied and studied, year after year, ran to around 750,000 annually.[37] Famous deferred students included President Bill Clinton, Vice President Dick Cheney, and President Donald Trump. "Everybody" did it, as long as the everybody you knew were middle class and clever.

For those willing to wear a uniform on their own terms, the National Guard and service reserves offered a useful option. While this did entail the initial entry regimen—Basic Combat Training and the like—it typically resulted in a weekend of duty a month and two weeks every summer, all near your home. By 1967, Guard and reserve units found their rosters full. Some even had waiting lists. Vice President Dan Quayle in Indiana and President George W. Bush in Texas met their obligations in this manner. Of course, at any time, these reserve component elements might be called up for federal service. Fortunately for those who tried this route, LBJ refused to call up the Guard and reserves for duty in Vietnam.[38] But in an irony typical of 1960s America, more than one war-averse army guardsman or reservist found himself in the street face to face with unruly peace protestors.

Another way to meet your military obligation and avoid slogging through a rice paddy involved joining the other armed services. This enabled the navy, air force, and coast guard to keep their forces full. The marines, heavily committed to the ground war in the northern part of South Vietnam, did not benefit too much from this type of voluntary enlistment. But they were smaller in strength and recruited hard among the adventurous types, to include poaching restless draftees awaiting call-up. In addition, the navy and air force flight units were fully engaged in combat, and damned dangerous work at that, with 3,720 fixed-wing aircraft and all too many flight crewmen, some 2,100, lost in the war. As for the rest of the navy, air force, and coast guard, they all kept substantial contingents active in and around Vietnam. In addition, some of those who joined the navy found themselves, M16 rifle in hand, on small, dangerous patrol boats plying Vietnam's coasts and rivers.[39] Senator John Kerry served in this capacity. Air force air security police also fought on the ground in country. So even if you became a sailor or an airman, depending on your assignment, things sometimes got quite interesting. It wasn't army 11B duty, but it wasn't safe, either.

It was also possible to sign up for the active-duty army and stay out of the line of fire. Enlistees had a lot of say over their MOS and some sway over their posting. But as you had to sign up for at least three years, sometimes four, the Vietnam option often played out anyway. Still, if you had to go to Vietnam, going as a clerk-typist or a headquarters intelligence analyst sure seemed less risky than humping a machine gun through the bush.

That said, many Americans embraced the opportunity to go to war. It's noteworthy that every uniformed woman assigned to Vietnam volunteered to be there. Plus, some young men wanted to fight. Airborne, ranger, special forces, infantry, armor/cavalry, aviation (helicopters), artillery, and engineer units all had their share of willing soldiers. Two-thirds who entered the theater arrived as voluntary enlistees.

As for draftees, if they volunteered, as did the Hagels, or just complied with the "Greetings" message, they almost always got the full-meal deal. They didn't have a contract, so they found themselves assigned in accord with the "needs of the service." And the army had many needs, but mostly in combat units and mostly in Vietnam. Branches like infantry, armor, and artillery featured relatively short stretches of Advanced Individual Training as compared to some year-long course in esoteric satellite signal work or the Chinese language. The best use of a draftee's two years amounted to basic, advanced, and then off to Southeast Asia. In the combat arms, 70 percent of the junior enlisted men units came via the draft. Even so, 77 percent of those killed were volunteers, either by enlistment or, like Chuck and Tom Hagel, by asking to be conscripted.[40]

Of course, along with the draftees and short-term volunteers, long-service officers and NCOs also went to Vietnam. General Colin

Powell went twice, once as a captain, then again as a major, a pretty typical pattern for army professionals.[41] Men like Sergeant First Class William Joyce might be disparaged as "lifers," or even loafers, by their younger troops in country. Some of the senior people found staff jobs on safe bases. But a lot of them did their duty. For these officers and NCOs, the draft amounted to a source of troops, not a personal matter.

So that's how the draft played out. Who actually served? The conventional wisdom suggests the most gifted Americans did not go. Thus the war devolved on the young, the destitute, the ill educated, and the nonwhite. As Myra McPherson acidly put it: "The 'best and the brightest' started the Vietnam War but they did not send their sons."[42] It adds one more twist of the knife, one more evil associated with this foul war.

Except it ain't exactly so.

With the war long over, we have pretty good demographics on who fought. We often hear that while the average age of a World War II conscript was twenty-seven, the typical Vietnam draftee was only nineteen. That's true, as far as it goes. But only a third of the men in country came through the draft. Casualty records tell a less told tale. Men killed in Vietnam averaged 22.8 years in age. In the entire war, 101 eighteen-year-olds died. Eleven percent of the dead were more than thirty years old, usually field-grade officers and senior NCOs.[43] The soldiers in Vietnam were younger than those who fought in Europe and the Pacific in 1941–45. But they weren't all fuzz-cheeked teenagers.

Matters of economic class also deserve scrutiny. In a 1992 study sponsored by faculty members at the Massachusetts Institute of Technology and West Point, the authors examined the hometowns of the 58,307 Americans killed in Vietnam. They found that, considering local affluence, 30 percent of the dead came from neighborhoods in the bottom third of society, 44 percent from the middle third, and 26 percent from the upper third. Three particularly well-off communities—Belmont, Massachusetts; Great Neck, New York; Chevy Chase, Maryland—sacrificed more men proportionately than the average losses in the rest of U.S. towns and counties. Yale University lost thirty-five graduates in the war, four of them from the Class of 1968, a rate right in line with the computed national average.[44] Many of the more fortunate Americans didn't go. But a lot did.

They weren't stupid, either. In the 1960s, 65 percent of American young men had completed high school. But nearly 80 percent of those in uniform finished high school first. That compared to 45 percent high school graduates in World War II. Proportionately, three times more college graduates served in Vietnam than in World War II. Some college men who served competed to be officers, but most didn't want the extra time in the army, so took their chances as draftees. If the latter, they, like the Hagels, tended to end up in the combat arms.[45] It made for a very literate, perceptive fighting force.

The military in Vietnam looked like America, too. Official roll-ups reflected a military 80 to 85 percent white, 10 to 12 percent black, and the remainder Hispanic or other groups. Casualties followed the same pattern: 86 percent white, 12.5 percent black, and the rest from other ethnicities. Some of the evidence for perceived higher rates of African American casualties came from the well-publicized 1965 actions. In that opening year of the major U.S. campaign in country, 23.5 percent of the enlisted dead were black.[46] In an America where de facto and de jure segregation still held sway, that solemn toll rightly raised flags. Over time, as the sad numbers mounted, the proportions settled into a much closer correlation with U.S. society. Yet the underlying disquiet never went away. It still hasn't. The numbers don't lie. But enough others did, sometimes for years. As a result, perceptions long ago eclipsed reality.

Thus the U.S. Army manned its battalions for the great war in Vietnam. Unlike Chuck and Tom Hagel, the vast majority of American young men didn't go anywhere near Vietnam. A lot of those who stayed home told themselves over and over they did not only the expedient thing, but the moral thing, the ethical thing, the righteous thing. "The unspeakable and inconfessible goal of the New Left on the campuses," observed shrewd social critic Tom Wolfe, "had been to transform the shame of the fearful into the guilt of the courageous."[47] By and large, the nonservers succeeded.

Of course, the earnest peace advocates turned out to be only too right about the war. It descended into a complete cock-up, an utter flop, with the long-suffering Vietnamese people battered and then abandoned to the pitiless communists as the final iniquity in an endless sequence of unredeemed betrayals. Mention that grim outcome, and the peaceniks bent their shaggy heads and mumbled into their tie-dyed T-shirts. But in the end, the smug had their day. The protestors got it right for the wrong reasons.

Those who served found themselves bogged in a bloody mess, a war gone wrong even if attempted for the right reasons. Decades later, all of that looks only too clear, as preordained as the plot of a Greek tragedy. But neither Chuck nor Tom Hagel, nor their fellow troops, nor Westmoreland, nor Johnson, nor the still-hopeful American citizenry knew any of that in the darkening autumn of 1967. A ravenous Moloch few saw coming would soon enough devour hearts and minds over there and back here. The terrible year 1968 loomed.

CHAPTER 3

Widows Village

Crack the sky. Shake the earth.

PRE-ATTACK MESSAGE FROM HANOI[1]

The flashes came from right behind, like lightning on the ground, erasing the night. Then the thunder boomed, close, really close, 122mm rockets and 82mm mortars and God knew what else. The explosions crumped and cracked, one right after the other, banging into the heart of the big U.S. Long Binh base complex. Nothing good was happening inside the fence back there. The place contained so many juicy targets: field force headquarters, three brigade command posts, the replacement barracks, the stockade (Long Binh Jail, Vietnam's own LBJ), multiple supply warehouses, fuel storage tanks, two field hospitals, a post exchange—a damn military department store, of all things, chock-full of color TVs, lawn chairs, and coffeemakers—plus 60,000 rear-echelon troops, and the entire conglomerate snuggled up next to a gigantic ammunition dump, like putting your house on the slope of Mount Vesuvius.[2] From outside the long fence line, you couldn't hear the sound of running boots and the frantic shouting as the Long Binh faithful ran for their lives like startled cockroaches in a suddenly lit kitchen. But you knew.

PFC Chuck Hagel sure did. In the strobing half-light of the successive impacts, he looked at his wristwatch, the one Private Jerry

Duvall gave to him back at Fort Dix, when the Nebraskan volunteered for this good deal. Duvall said his brother wore the timepiece for a year in Vietnam and never got a scratch.[3] It looked like the watch's juju would get a workout this time. Three a.m. "Oh-three-hundred" in army lingo. The witching hour, all right. In Vietnam, nothing positive ever happened at 3 a.m.

It didn't do any good to look over your shoulder at the sound and light show. That problem cooking off back there belonged to the poor bastards inside Long Binh Post. Hagel and the rest of Company B had their orders. They had been told to watch the dark jungle right in front of them, to scan the trees and underbrush fronting either side of the black gap in the vegetation that marked Highway 15.[4] The bombardment of Long Binh base sure seemed like preparatory fire. Any minute, an enemy infantry assault wave might come boiling out of the tree line, like some crazy banzai charge from a World War II movie. Sweaty hands tense on their plastic and metal M16 rifles, Hagel and the other riflemen stood by.

Unlike most Americans in country, Hagel and his fellow troops were awake, ready, and almost in the right position. To their backs, the Tet Offensive had just kicked off. At Long Binh, and across the country, the onslaught didn't come out of the jungle, but from the inside, right from the guts of South Vietnam's towns and cities—and there was a message in that, for sure. Tet was massive. It was desperate. It was decisive. And in the end, it cost America the war. But at 3 a.m. on Wednesday, January 31, 1968, nobody knew that yet.

WELL, ACTUALLY VO NGUYEN GIAP and the rest of the North Vietnamese army general staff knew it. So did Ho Chi Minh and his politburo. They called the plan *Tong Cong Kich-Tong Khai Nghia* (General Offensive–General Uprising). By simultaneously going after 120-plus key urban sites during the annual weeklong truce marking the Tet Lunar New Year holiday period, akin to hitting America during the stretch from Christmas to New Year's Day, the North expected to set off a countrywide rebellion in favor of the communists. The Hanoi leadership thought they'd win the war in a single stroke.[5]

The Tet operation arose because the NVA needed very much to change the war's trajectory. Political rhetoric aside, the North was getting pounded, and attrition, dead Vietnamese, did matter. The U.S. aerial bombing of the North might be randomly turned on and off, inconsistent in its choice of targets, and baffling in its focus. Just what in hell were these capitalist war mongers up to? But where the bombs struck, they struck hard. And in the south, the unstoppable flail of U.S. firepower took an immense toll. The NVA and VC ran and hid, but not all the time, and not well enough. If this continued, maybe the terrible arithmetic would eventually add up for Westmoreland and MACV. Ho Chi Minh dare not go there. So this situation must change. The communists had to recast the battlefield. That required taking the initiative, an attack on the grandest possible scale. In the spring of 1967, probably around May, the decision makers in Hanoi directed plans for what would become the Tet Offensive.

The North understood Westmoreland's American-led attrition strategy and used it against the United States and its South Vietnamese allies. For the last few months of 1967, NVA regiments forced major engagements in the sparsely populated north and northwestern border regions of South Vietnam. Eager to kill their enemy at remote places like Con Thien, Dak To, and Khe Sanh, Westmoreland's MACV battalions went hard after the NVA. By early 1968, half of all U.S. combat battalions had shifted to the north and northwest, following the bait. The marine combat base at Khe Sanh became a focal point. The Americans thought they were taking out NVA soldiers faster than Hanoi could replace them, the long-sought crossover point. Yet for the NVA generals, MACV had done exactly as intended, leaving the hapless ARVN shielding their country's major population centers to the south and along the coast. North Vietnam suffered heavy casualties. But as Giap stated: "The life or death of a hundred, a thousand, or tens of thousands of human beings, even if they are our own compatriots, represents very little."[6] The NVA had the aggressive Americans and the ineffectual ARVN right where they wanted them. The communists called this "preparing the battlefield."

With MACV and the ARVN in their places, some 84,000 Viet Cong, heavily reinforced by NVA cadres and selected units, drew the main tasks. The rest of the NVA (more than 400,000 strong), both in country and just outside, in Laos and Cambodia, waited to reinforce success. Stealthy VC assault detachments infiltrated into the vicinity of their carefully chosen urban objectives: 5 of 6 autonomous cities, 36 of 44 provincial capitals, 72 of 245 district centers, and numerous locations inside the national capital of Saigon, including the brand new American embassy, MACV headquarters, and the huge U.S. Army base at Long Binh. During January, the VC reconnoitered their many Tet targets. They rehearsed. They prepositioned key weapons and explosives. And then they waited for the order to go.[7]

The men in Hanoi overreached. Like able military men everywhere, they looked for opportunities. But their assumptions stretched well beyond any sober wartime calculus. The communists believed the ARVN would fold up, quit, or maybe even turn coat. Worse, they trusted that the collapse of Saigon's military would trigger a huge groundswell of politically motivated southerners, welcoming the VC and NVA as liberators and offering hearty assistance. Worst of all, they then leaped to the conclusion that this mass movement would take arms and, led by VC main force battalions and NVA regiments, drive the Americans into the sea, a supersized countrywide Dien Bien Phu. So the communists hoped.

But hope is not a method, as experienced U.S. Army planners are wont to say. The wide-ranging VC attacks—yes, those could well happen, and might do a lot of damage. But finishing the 800,000-man ARVN? Rousing the sullen southern population? Running off 500,000 well-armed, well-trained Americans? Maybe a few too many May Day pep rallies, or too many ceremonial toasts, or too many puffs of the pungent local marijuana—no, those outcomes sure looked unlikely. The best the NVA might do, to borrow from General Erich Ludendorff and the German army in 1918, would be to punch a hole and see what happened next.[8] And by the way, it didn't work out too well for the guys from Berlin.

One thing the Hanoi leadership did not intend at all was to cause some kind of domestic upheaval in America. The NVA general staff, Giap in particular, denigrated the influence of the peace movement in the United States. The North Vietnamese appreciated the sentiments and warmly welcomed various dissident delegations. But the Hanoi inner circle thought President Lyndon Johnson unlikely to knuckle under to throngs of hippies chanting outside the White House. It never occurred to those up north that a much bigger slice of American opinion-leaders and unhappy citizens, lulled by Westmoreland's assurances of military progress, might react very strongly to the shock of the Tet Offensive. As NVA lieutenant general Tran Do noted, any such development would be, as he understated it, "a fortunate result."[9]

CHUCK HAGEL AND the other men of Company B expected trouble. The Tet holiday cease-fire started at 6 p.m. on Monday, January 29. Liberal leave for South Vietnamese soldiers allowed them to go home for family meals. Local street celebrations occurred in hamlets, towns, and cities. Firecracker strings popped and sparklers lit the night as all of Vietnam welcomed the Year of the Monkey.

Monkey business followed. Somebody in the NVA, or more likely jumpy VC part-timers, got their days mixed up. American units up north reported eight attacks, and not the usual hit and run shenanigans, either. At thirty-five minutes after midnight, VC mortarmen plunked six rounds just outside a South Vietnamese navy site at Nha Trang; a battalion-sized ground assault followed. An hour later, two enemy battalions attacked into the center of Ban Me Thuot, the provincial capital. Another hostile battalion pushed into the little district capital of Tan Canh. About 2 a.m., three VC main force battalions assaulted the provincial capital buildings in Kontum. An hour after, another ground column assailed the district capital at Hoi An, just south of coastal Da Nang, South Vietnam's second-largest city. In Da Nang proper, VC infiltrators struck the local AVN corps headquarters.

At 4:10 a.m., two VC battalions took the government radio station compound at Qui Nhon. A half hour later, a major attack struck the highlands provincial center at Pleiku.[10]

Those details, of course, never made it down to PFC Hagel and his guys. Across most of South Vietnam, U.S. and ARVN commanders read intelligence reports that some more concerted enemy strikes might be imminent. Naturally, the intel guys, nervous neddies all, predicted ten out of every three attacks that might hit you. Commanders did more or less to get ready. The Americans sure as hell weren't on some kind of Tet holiday. And the ARVN cancelled the Tet furlough for South Vietnamese troops, although in their usual lackadaisical fashion, some units obeyed, some did not, and most got it about half right.

But in the Saigon area, the word got out. Way up the chain at II Field Force headquarters at Long Binh, Major General Fred Weyand, reporter Johnny Apple's unnamed critic of the attrition strategy, repositioned his American battalions to protect key sites around Saigon. Weyand had plenty of combat experience, to include service in the forbidding China-Burma-India theater in World War II, infantry battalion command in Korea, and two years in charge of the 25th Infantry Division in Vietnam, fighting from just north of Saigon out to the Cambodian border. Weyand read the tea leaves well. The enemy was up to something. So Weyand moved his pieces around to block the bad guys. Westmoreland and many of the rest of the MACV staff would later claim they saw it coming, too. If so, they sure didn't do much to get ready.[11] But Weyand did.

Thus Chuck Hagel, Company B, and the rest of the 2nd Battalion (Mechanized), 47th Infantry found itself fronting the jungle southeast of the barrier fence around Long Binh Post. On the maps at II Field Force headquarters, a blue rectangle marked the 2-47th's lonely position. Inside the field force command post, ducking pieces of the ceiling lights raining down, dutiful sergeants marked red squares all around, reported locations of various elements of the "Bien Hoa" VC Sapper Company, 238th VC Local Force Company, U-1 VC Local Force Battalion, 274th VC Main Force Regiment, 275th VC Main Force

Regiment—a division-scale attack.[12] Nobody had ever seen anything like this. It promised to be a very interesting day around Long Binh. And it had started early.

CHUCK HAGEL WAS right there. He'd come a long way from that well-lit office at Fort Dix, New Jersey, to a hot, humid defensive line in the small hours of the morning just outside Long Binh Post. His journey took him from Fort Dix to a five-day leave in Nebraska, to the Oakland Army Terminal in California, to Travis Air Force Base, to a contracted jet airliner over the Pacific, to the hot tarmac of Tan Son Nhut Air Base, to a ride on a green school bus with mesh over the windows—keeps the hand grenades out—that stopped for a few days at the 90th Replacement Battalion at Long Binh Post, one of the unhappy recipients of VC ire early on the morning of January 31, 1968. From the crowded tents of the 90th, Hagel boarded a sandbagged 5-ton cargo truck and, escorted by armed vehicles, rode in a long road convoy headed south on Highway 15. The convoy's destination was Camp Martin Cox at Bear Cat, home of the 9th Infantry Division, the Old Reliables, Westmoreland's World War II outfit. A stint followed at the Reliable Academy, five days of intense jungle school, the "inside tips" on Vietnam tactics not covered at Fort Bliss and Fort Ord. Finally, after about ten days of all of those draining preliminaries, Hagel arrived at Company B, 2-47th Infantry. The company issued him an M16 rifle, helmet, flak jacket, and other field gear. The battalion sergeant major welcomed Hagel and the other new guys. Remarks by the company commander and the first sergeant came next. Then came chow and some fitful sleep on a cot inside a tent. At five the next morning, a week or so before Christmas, the rifle company, Hagel among them, moved out on a weeklong operation.[13]

This long, tiring picaresque didn't always make sense at the PFC level. For the U.S. Army it constituted business as usual. To the institutional army, Chuck Hagel equaled MOS 11B10. His arrival in country on December 4, 1967, filled a hole. And Company B, 2-47th Infantry had one.

Hagel arrived in the same way his father Charles Dean Hagel showed up in Hawaii in 1942 and the way his brother Tom entered Vietnam on February 7, 1968—as an individual replacement. The U.S. Army formed units stateside and then sent them to war. When they took losses, like the 42nd Bombardment Squadron did in 1942, the system sent replacements, such as Charles Dean Hagel. In World War II, units and men fought for the duration. With few exceptions, nobody went home early except the severely wounded. When people got sick, or hurt, or died, the army sent in replacement soldiers, like feeding fresh bullets into a machine gun.[14] It all had a certain logic in Washington.

The army used the same system in the Korean War. At first, entire regiments and battalions deployed. But Korea was a limited war, and keeping troops in for the duration did not wash with hometown America. After a year or so, as the squalid Asian conflict settled into a static trench confrontation and casualty numbers dropped, soldiers were allowed to serve about a year and then go home, to be back-filled by individual replacements.[15] As another limited war, Vietnam seemed tailor-made for this same method: units first, then individual replacements, soldier by soldier.

When units entered Vietnam in strength starting in 1965, MACV smoothly established man-by-man rotations, set as twelve months for soldiers and, drawing on some arcane USMC arithmetic, thirteen months for marines. Experienced in World War II and Korea, Westmoreland never considered any other approach: "The one year tour gave a man a goal. That was good for morale."[16] So he thought.

Thus units trained and deployed together, like the 1st Cavalry Division from Fort Benning, Georgia; the 101st Airborne Division from Fort Campbell, Kentucky; and the 9th Infantry Division from Fort Riley, Kansas. Within a year after arrival, it all went to pieces. The division flags stayed in Vietnam, but the wholesale shuffling of people began and never let up. It resembled trading a finely forged steel sword for a glued-together collection of metal shards. All the leadership in the world couldn't retemper that blade. The best you got might be a blunt instrument.

Sending troops into Vietnam one by one, as individual replacements, may have satisfied the adjutant general officers and the efficiency experts surrounding Secretary of Defense Robert S. McNamara. Reams of thick studies proved again and again how training two-year draftees for several months in the United States and then sending them to spend a year in Vietnam constituted optimum use of manpower.[17] All the number crunchers agreed.

Frontline officers and NCOs did not. Men are not machine gun bullets, nor are they widgets or screws to be shuffled from drawer to drawer around the globe. People fight for the guys on either side of them. They willingly obey leaders they know and trust. Other armies—the British, the Canadians, the French, the Australians, all veterans of many wars in the more unpleasant corners of the world—have long deployed by battalions. The United States could have done so. Instead, we settled for war one soldier at a time. And somehow, even so, with a half million men in theater, units in Vietnam remained understrength, short on NCOs, and replete with individuals mismatched to their training, square pegs in round holes. MACV daily awaited their share of "the invisible horde of people," as described by Lieutenant General Lesley J. McNair as far back as 1944, "going here and there but seemingly never arriving."[18] When steady men like the Hagel brothers showed up, they went right to work.

Chuck Hagel later commented on what he experienced in country. "We were terribly understrength at every level," he said. "As I recall, we were even rotating cooks and clerks into the field to fill some of those gaps." He went on: "You had guys rotating in and out daily. You would break the continuity of leadership. You'd break the continuity of confidence, of teamwork." Soldiers near the end of their year, "short-timers," avoided risks. They sought duty at the base camp. That meant others went out on more patrols, filling the gaps. Young soldiers like Chuck and Tom Hagel stepped up for the senior NCOs who were wounded or not assigned. "It was a very bad policy," concluded Chuck.[19]

You could make a case, and some wiser officers and NCOs did, that units in Vietnam fought most effectively in the first few months after deployment. Once the first year ended and the cohesive original organizations came apart—exactly what happened to the 9th Infantry Division in December 1967—things rarely went as well.[20] Good leaders, even great leaders, inspirational figures like George Washington or George Patton, would be hard-pressed to pull together a mass of individuals. To do so under fire in a frontless war against guerrilla enemies? Well, forget it.

The younger professional officers and NCOs in Vietnam saw the problem only too clearly. Men like General Colin Powell (captain and major in country) and H. Norman Schwarzkopf (major and lieutenant colonel at the time) insisted on unit deployments and unit rotations in the Iraq War of 1990–91. Unit swap-outs were the rule in Haiti in 1994–96, Bosnia starting in 1995, and Kosovo in 1999. U.S. Army vice chief of staff General Jack Keane (captain in Vietnam) ensured the unit approach in 2003 as it became evident the dual Iraq and Afghanistan campaigns required a long-term commitment.[21] We may not be happy with the course of those indecisive wars, but our units held together year in and year out. So we got that right. Wars must be fought by units, by formed teams, not by a gaggle of strangers. Vietnam taught that hard lesson in blood. Some of it belonged to Chuck and Tom Hagel.

CHUCK HAGEL MET his enemy on a day before Christmas of 1967. He and the rest of the riflemen had been out for days. The army referred to the mission as route security, code-named "Riley" and "Akron" and "Santa Fe," keeping Route 1 and Route 15 open to traffic.[22] The troops called these efforts "roadrunner operations" or "thunder runs." Most U.S. units searched and searched to find the opposition. But if you spent enough time going up and down the major roads, the VC found you.

Hagel's 2-47th Infantry wasn't elite. Not marines, not special forces, not paratroopers, not airmobile heliborne troopers, the 2-47th amounted to just another American infantry battalion, typical of them all. Indeed, for the 1994 movie *Forrest Gump*, when Vietnam veteran Winston Groom and screenwriter Eric Roth chose a unit for their fictional protagonist Forrest and his friends Bubba Blue and Lieutenant Dan, they selected Company A, 2nd Battalion, 47th Infantry.[23] The movie got many details right enough for Hollywood, but missed a big one.

The real 2-47th brought something extra to the fight, and that capability made them ideal for roadrunning. In Vietnam, most U.S. Army and Marine infantry walked, even though often they went into action by helicopter. But 2-47th relied on the M113A1 armored personnel carrier (APC). This 12-ton tracked vehicle looked like the world's largest shoe box, sixteen feet long, nine feet wide, seven feet tall. Behind its sloped flat bow squatted a 215-horsepower diesel engine. The vehicle's aluminum armor ranged from a half inch to an inch-and-a-half thick, better than nothing, but not by much. An M113 could shrug off fragments and rifle bullets, although the heavier stuff punched right through. A heavy armored ramp on the back let eleven men get on or off. When the ramp dropped, those inside ran off like troops leaving a landing craft on D-Day. The APC driver sat to the left front; a track commander handled a long .50-caliber machine gun centered in a little turret on top. Both men could keep their helmeted heads up (not very safe) or slam the hatch and peer out through a ring of thick glass vision blocks and try to drive that way (also not very safe). The 2-47th called their vehicles "one-one-threes" or "tracks."

Having four M113s per platoon made 2-47th "mechanized," one of only ten such U.S. outfits among the 117 maneuver battalions in all of MACV; there were also ten armored cavalry squadrons (with tanks) and four tank battalions (two army, two marine). The 9th Infantry Division owned two mechanized infantry battalions, and used them to keep major highways open—and as quick reaction forces when trouble erupted unexpectedly. Heliborne troops flew only in good weather and arrived with hand weapons and the ammunition they carried on their persons. Helicopters were fast as hell, over a hundred miles an hour, but unarmored. On a hot landing zone, with the VC machine gunners blazing away, you could lose a lot of helicopters very quickly, and the survival rate in chopper crashes wasn't good.

M113s only moved at twenty-five miles an hour on good roads (not many in Vietnam), but they carried a lot of ammunition, those powerful .50 calibers on top, and a rack of riflemen aboard, and ran in all weather. Most importantly, M113s mounted long-range amplified radios, the lifelines to medical evacuation, resupply, reinforcements, artillery, and air support. If hit, M113 APCs could be towed out, and likely repaired. Nobody towed off a UH-1D Huey helicopter except to blow it up.

Looking at the 2-47th, it seemed like Hagel belonged there, even though he'd had very little mechanized training before he showed up in country. His father, Charles, had certainly fought out on the far side of the Pacific, and now son Chuck was there, too. The .50 caliber, "a tremendous, effective machine gun" in Hagel's words, just happened to be the same heavy weapon his father once used to defend B-24 Liberator bombers. In another coincidence, 2-47th Infantry, like Charles Dean Hagel's 42nd Bombardment Squadron, used the black panther as the unit symbol. If you believed in fate, or karma, or the Lord moving in mysterious ways, you noticed such things. Chuck Hagel did.[24]

While a good number of senior officers, paratroopers like Westmoreland for example, thought the M113s almost as good as tanks, the men who fought aboard the aluminum-hulled APCs had no such illusions. Mines and VC rocket-propelled grenades (RPGs) posed significant threats. One solid hit and the track would rip apart or even flip over; sometimes the diesel fuel started on fire. Once heated up, aluminum burned, too. Tracks sometimes burned down to a pile of steaming silver slag. With this in mind, men rode on top when moving from point A to point B. "You didn't find it particularly healthy to be on those armored personnel carriers," Hagel found out. "There's no point in losing six or seven men to one rocket. So it's better to lose a driver and a machine gunner," said Hagel. "If you're going to lose men, lose two, not seven." Even a new guy like Hagel learned that hard equation very quickly. If the unit expected contact, or deployed to clear a road, the riflemen got out and moved through the brush on either side, about a hundred yards out. Men on foot with mine detectors and sharp eyes—engineers if available—walked in front to check the route itself for buried munitions. It took an hour to move a mile like that.[25] But it cleared the road and kept Americans alive.

So it might have been Santa Fe, or Riley, or Akron, or a mission without a formal name on Route 1, somewhere between Saigon and Xuan Loc. After a week or so in country, Hagel knew the drill. As a PFC rifleman, he followed the man in front of him. The Americans moved slowly through the thick greenery. They could hear the tracks trundling along on the roadway, but if the troops looked over their shoulders, the heavy vegetation made it hard to see more than distant dark outlines. The soldiers had been doing this on other stretches of highway both day and night over the last ten days. Some other platoons had glancing contacts, pop shots, an old mine—French era—unearthed. But so far today, nothing.

Supposedly, December counted as the dry season near Saigon. The humidity ran around 80 percent, an uncomfortable match for the 88° temperature. The taller trees shaded the rest, dimming an already dull day. Imagine walking through an abandoned greenhouse run riot—in a sauna—and you've got it. Under the gray, overcast sky, sweating, steel helmet bobbing on your wet head, you just tried to stay alert.

The guerrilla enemy loved days like this. A U.S. unit droning along, midday, nothing much going on. It looked like they were pretty worn out. Flip to that page in the Mao Zedong hymnal, and sing along . . . *enemy tires, we attack.*

The flat crack of an AK-47 sounded—first one, then three, then plenty, all from the front. After you heard it enough, you always recognized an AK. Those hot little 7.62mm slugs had a voice all their own. "The bullets were whizzing through the underbrush and trees," Hagel wrote later. "You could hear and see them tearing the leaves a few feet over your head." The rounds zipped as they broke the sound barrier near your ears. American drill sergeants like William Joyce always preached "shoot low." A marksman can always adjust up on to target, watching puffs of dirt or bark or whatever. But high rounds just launch out into the atmosphere. Thankfully, most VC shooters didn't get that class. PFC Hagel was learning the difference between hearing fire (common in country), receiving fire (less often), and receiving effective fire (uh-oh).

Some of the VC got it right. "The guy in front of me was hit," said Hagel, "then the guy next to me, square in the chest." For a nanosecond, in that weird slowed-down sense of time common to firefights, Hagel thought he was next. But "the training kicked in."[26]

The U.S. riflemen curled near tree trunks and snuggled behind mounds of moist dirt. They shot back. A few M16s rattled on full automatic. Individual shots rang out, one after another, a metallic snap, snap, snap characteristic of the M16's high-velocity 5.56mm bullets. Hagel pulled the trigger, facing outboard, not toward the road and the tracks. He couldn't see any enemy. He didn't know yet that you never saw them. You heard them, or glimpsed muzzle flashes, maybe. But in modern battle to be seen is to be shot. And that wasn't good. So people on both sides tried very hard not to be seen. In the jungle, that was almost always the story.

The M60 pig started snorting, its .75-inch-long 7.62mm bullets banging away. The experienced machine gunner ran through a belt, not the neat six- to nine-round bursts taught at Fort Ord, but a long rip, maybe a hundred rounds in one whack. Then, from out on the highway, one of the M113s opened up with its .50 caliber, pumping inch-and-a-half-long slugs through the greenery just in front of the beleaguered column of U.S. riflemen. That was enough for the enemy. They pulled away. The shaken Americans dealt with two wounded.

This kind of glancing encounter happened often enough to be unremarkable, and Hagel would see his share and then some. The official 2-47th summary of the multiweek operation reads like a shopping list, with about as much drama. The battalion claimed "a confirmed body count of 300 VC/NVA," a nice, round number. If any VC died in Hagel's little skirmish, nobody found them. But then again, they always dragged off the bodies, right? In addition to the enemy casualties, 2-47th captured "100 pounds of salt, 11 pounds of documents, 3 RPG-2 [rocket-propelled grenade launchers], 200 rounds of AK-47 ammo, one 81mm mortar, and eight 81mm mortar rounds."[27] At that rate, the war of attrition might have wrapped up by 2067, give or take a few decades.

Thus the VC introduced themselves to Chuck Hagel. The troops called them "Victor Charlie" in the military phonetic alphabet, and "Charlie" day to day. When the enemy got serious, they called them "Mr. Charles." That's who showed up for Tet.

ONCE THE VC STRUCK in force along the perimeter of Long Binh Post, it took a while to figure out exactly what to do with 2-47th. Military school instructors counsel "tactical patience," taking time to "develop the situation" before committing forces. Maybe the people under attack at Long Binh were doing that. The military police units and ad hoc gaggles of headquarters guys had their hands full with energetic VC. Sorting out how best to use a mechanized infantry battalion had to wait.

At 3:35 a.m., battalion told Company B to prepare to move. Hagel's commander, Captain Robert G. Keats, had only been in charge for a week. But the quick-thinking West Pointer knew what to do. He brought in the two ambush patrols, teams of four men out in the jungle to snare VC snoopers and provide early warning. The men began to roll up their concertina wire, circles of razor-sharp barbed wire that could be expanded or folded up just like an accordion. The track commanders stayed up on the .50-caliber machine guns and the riflemen continued to man their fighting holes. Nothing had come out of the jungle yet. But the VC clearly had stepped it up this time. So maybe they were baiting the Americans to move too soon. Then they could rush the fence.

At 5:20, just before dawn grayed the sky, orders came by radio. Normally, the captain received a coded message. But this time, Lieutenant Colonel John B. Tower spoke in the clear, addressing all companies simultaneously. Company A and the battalion headquarters had to clear the village of Ho Nai, just north of Long Binh. Company C was told to go into the center of Bien Hoa city, near the U.S. airfield, to defend the ARVN III Corps headquarters. Company B drew the short straw—clean out the ammunition dump. And do it without getting blown into the stratosphere.

When one of the company commanders asked about filling foxholes and pouring out sandbags, Tower cut him short. Leave it all. Move now.

Keats did not hesitate. He ordered Company B to go. "We left—we left ponchos," said Hagel. "We left everything right on the ground. And we grabbed guns and were on those APCs and down that road." It was 5:35, twenty minutes before dawn. The first hint of morning twilight lightened the eastern horizon.

Captain John E. Gross, commanding Company C, described the scene:

> As we turned right onto Highway 15, an unbelievable spectacle stretched before us. Having been struck by mortars or rockets, the fuel tanks at the air base, as well as several buildings throughout Bien Hoa, were burning brightly. Flames illuminated the clouds, forming an eerie glow; flares hung in the sky and helicopter gunships crossed back and forth firing red streams of tracers into the city.[28]

By 6 a.m., Hagel's company, assembled into a long column of twenty-two M113s, pulled out on the road, en route to the Long Binh ammunition facility. Riflemen rode atop the tracks. They had to be careful, as the base's defenders were trading bullets with various known and suspected VC. Of course, you couldn't see any bad guys. But they were there. Random bullets zipped by and skittered off the pavement of Route 15.

The Company B tracks drove hard for the ammunition dump's gate. The lead platoon reached it at 6:38 a.m. Men jumped off the lead vehicles, running for the dirt-covered ammo storage bunkers. Where were the VC? Where were their timed charges? The racket of gunfire rose in intensity, most of it from the arriving Americans. The big .50 calibers hammered away. In a James Bond movie, the hero confidently located the right wire, snipped, and stopped the insanity.

But that busy morning at Long Binh, nobody found any painfully obvious ticking time bomb with big red digits clicking down. The VC
didn't roll that way.

Company B's brave riflemen did identify a few bulky khaki back-
packs, ripped out the time fuses, and flung the detritus far outside the
compound. While frantic soldiers searched for more, the clock ran
out. Evidently, VC sappers had placed enough charges, focused on
explosives arrayed out in the open. A pallet of 175mm artillery propel-
lant went first. Three others followed, then more. The immense concussions, fire, and smoke boiled up "like a nuclear mushroom cloud,"
said Hagel.[29] A nearby Long Binh headquarters soldier said, "We could
see the shock wave coming through the foliage. Everybody ducked as
it passed over, stirring up a tremendous amount of dust in its wake."

Hagel's vehicle was just outside the fence when the eruption
cooked off. The two tracks in front of Hagel's M113 had dropped their
infantry already—a lucky thing. When the ammunition went up, that
pair of APCs were "essentially as vaporized as you can be," said Hagel. Amazingly, all four men in the wreckage survived, though badly
wounded. Smacked by the blast, Hagel's APC leapt off the ground
and slid into a ditch. Some aboard were burned, but nothing serious.
It was only 7:39 a.m.[30]

Well, that was a hell of a start. The ammunition dump was toast.
Sympathetic detonations and fires continued throughout that day
and well into the next. No more could be done there. But the stretch
of government housing across Route 316 seemed to be lousy with VC.
If the ammo stocks couldn't be saved, they could be avenged.

Company B's tracks turned toward Widows Village for the next
round with Mr. Charles.

THE SAIGON GOVERNMENT had built the little community as a model
town for the wives and children of those ARVN soldiers killed in action. It appeared to be a Vietnamese version of suburban tract housing, eight rows of twenty identical little homes, stretched about a
thousand yards along the roadway. The widows staked out concertina

wire—thank you, America—to delineate their garden plots. Maybe seven hundred people lived there.

In the days before Tet, ruthless VC elements infiltrated the village. They killed the troublemakers and cowed the rest. For Mr. Charles, attacking into Long Binh Post from Widows Village amounted to win-win. If the great offensive worked, all well. If the Americans counter-attacked, they'd be compelled to smash through some of the most loyal South Vietnamese in so doing. It was insidious, but you had to tip your hat to the opposition's chutzpah. They played at the big money tables, all right.

The VC battalion commander's orders for Tet instructed him to attack across Highway 316, smack into the II Field Force Headquarters on the northwest edge of Long Binh Post. Had that attack succeeded, Major General Weyand might have really had his hands full. But the VC officer lacked initiative. He'd been told to wait until several hundred rockets pummeled the U.S. base. When he only counted ninety, the VC commander chose to hold his position. His machine gunners opened fire, and so did a few snipers. But most of the enemy battalion just sat there.[31]

Lieutenant Colonel Tower, by now up in a bubble-top OH-23 helicopter (very much like the kind used in the movie and TV show *M*A*S*H*), saw the opportunity. He ordered in both Company B and the battalion's scout platoon. Part of Company B went first, with Chuck Hagel's platoon trailing a ways back. First Lieutenant Henry L. S. Jezek brought his four 1st Platoon tracks on line and started working from southwest to northeast. He put an M113 on each narrow street and fanned out his rifle squads to check the silent houses.

House clearing is one of the most difficult infantry tasks. The men checked each little building. If they suspected anything dangerous inside, the riflemen led with a fragmentation grenade, just as they taught you to do at Fort Ord. Of course, these structures stood on concrete slab foundations. If you tossed in an M26 grenade, you had better stand back or eat a faceful of your own frag. It took about an hour to clear the first third of the village. The VC lay low.

Then they didn't.

In an instant, Mr. Charles opened up with AK-47s, a lot of them, a steady ripple of the all too familiar sharp cracks, some marked by the foe's green tracers. (Americans used red tracers.) An RPD machine gun joined in. That thing was an AK-47 on steroids, firing the same deadly Russian-designed short 7.62mm slugs. Its gunner shot high. You could see the tracers winging overhead.

Stunned by the fusillade, the Americans ducked and flinched. Riflemen scrambled behind the little buildings. A few crouched in the lee of the idling M113s. AK bullets pinged off the broad track fronts. One green tracer ricocheted straight up.

In seconds, U.S. troops began to fire back. They couldn't see much. But they shot anyway, aiming in the direction of the VC shooting. The U.S. M16s snapped away. An M60 pig fired, too, snorting out a belt of ammunition, one red tracer for every four unseen 7.2mm bullets. Shooting low—thank you, drill sergeants—the Americans tore up the bottom corners of a few suspicious houses. At this juncture, close was good enough.

Then a VC rocket-propelled grenade streaked out, headed right for an M113 halted right near Highway 316. In the little turret, Corporal Robert A. Huie saw the thing coming—they flew slow enough to watch, but fast enough to get you—and he cut loose with the .50-caliber machine gun, aiming at the source of the smoke trail. The projectile hit in a shower of sparks, rocking the track. Huie didn't let up. His .50 kept right on pounding.

Another RPG lashed out. The second rocket warhead burst right on the turret gunshield, killing Huie. His long machine gun swung around, unmanned.

Lieutenant Jezek ran to the stricken track. Along with Huie, clearly dead, Privates Donald Matchee and John Corrilla also lay dazed inside the stricken M113. They had severe wounds. An AK round smacked Jezek hard on his right side, then another RPG blew up near his head. The lieutenant went down in a heap. Somebody dragged him behind the disabled track. The cacophony of shooting kept right on going.

Seeing the platoon leader bowled over, Sergeant First Class William Nelson Butler took charge. He knew he had one dead, one APC immobilized, and three badly wounded. Matchee and Corrilla both barely hung in there. Jezek look bad, too. His head lacerations bled freely, as such injuries often do. These guys needed medical evacuation, a dust-off helicopter.[32] And the VC weren't letting up.

With their hands full, Butler and his men fought to hold their position, banging away at Mr. Charles. Butler's platoon, three good tracks and a dozen sound riflemen, anchored themselves on a woodpile near Highway 316, right on the east side of the housing area. They faced an aroused VC battalion. The platoon awaited the arrival of the rest of the company, including PFC Hagel, and the scouts.

In this kind of situation, the stationary U.S. platoon usually called in artillery to pin and beat up the enemy force, lest they break contact and escape. Overhead, Lieutenant Colonel Tower wouldn't allow any artillery fires. He worried about the South Vietnamese civilians potentially still hiding in Widows Village—and in fact, there were a few. Sergeant First Class Butler's men hadn't seen any locals, innocent or not. More ominously, one American grenadier actually sighted a fleeting armed figure and pumped out a 40mm round, scoring a direct hit. If the VC had the guts to show themselves, that couldn't be good.[33] Butler's men kept up the fire. So did the VC.

But in the clear light of midmorning, as the VC machine gunners and AK-47 guys kept at it, Mr. Charles began to slip away, right out of the guerrilla playbook. *Enemy advances, we retreat.* Overhead in his little OH-23 helicopter, Lieutenant Colonel John Tower saw the hostiles exfiltrating by threes and fours, hopscotching away from house to house, creeping down the drainage ditches, and crawling behind the folds of red dirt. Tower had been to this rodeo before. If only he could have used the big howitzers to flail the Cong. But how many widows and children was Tower willing to sacrifice? None, if he could help it. Still determined to catch the withdrawing VC battalion, Tower urged his other units into the fight.

The rest of Company B was way behind. PFC Chuck Hagel and the rest had gotten entangled with some stubborn VC shooters en route to Widows Village. At 10:15 a.m., during the firefight, Captain Keats reported nine wounded in action. It took a while to clean that up. PFC

Hagel did his part.[34] Nothing was easy. It all took longer than anyone wanted. Every movement got somebody else hurt.

Meanwhile, about the same time, First Lieutenant Brice H. Barnes and his eight scout platoon tracks rolled in to link up with Sergeant First Class Butler's guys. In most battalions, the scouts comprised the top lieutenant, the sharpest sergeants, and the best junior soldiers, all in an oversized combat platoon with extra radios. In conventional warfare, scouts went out front to locate the opponents first. In Vietnam, the scouts served almost like an extra rifle company, handy for the battalion commander to use to make a difference. That sure held for the pugnacious Barnes and his guys in 2-47th.

More help came at 10:35 a.m., when Company B, 4-39th Infantry arrived. They descended into an open, dusty dirt patch just southwest of Widows Village, brought in by a flight of UH-1D Huey helicopters. The VC lit up the landing zone, dirt puffs and green tracers and holes punched in the Hueys. But the choppers made it in and out okay, and so the fresh rifle company did, too. Somebody up higher had shifted the 4-39th riflemen from a different battalion area, seventeen miles away. When air mobility worked, it was a wonderful thing.

The 4-39th captain, Barnes, and Butler got together behind an M113. They agreed on a simple plan—the foot troops to the west, scouts in the center, Butler's men to the east. When the rest of Company B arrived, they'd fill in behind and "mop up," a rather innocuous term for the dangerous work of winkling out any VC die-hards. The U.S. ground attack commenced about 11:45 a.m.

The tracks led, .50 calibers shooting up each house. The M113 gunners didn't spare the ammunition, either. Riflemen followed, popping off 5.56mm rounds at known, likely, and suspected VC, which is to say every muzzle flash, dust devil, and suggestion of movement. M79 grenadiers blooped their deadly 40mm eggs behind buildings and into ditches. The U.S. line advanced methodically, chewing its way north. The echoing din and dry dirt clouds were tremendous, a manmade storm front rolling slowly north through Widows Village. Several houses started on fire, adding smoke billows to the already acrid midday air.

Overhead, Lieutenant Colonel Tower watched the attack from his usual perch. How those battalion commanders relished their ringside seats a thousand feet up! From that altitude, it all seemed like a board game. See the big picture. Move the pieces around. Coordinate supporting arms. The guys on the ground, sweating and struggling, hated the sky-box micromanaging, except when the flying commanders brought in needed help. This time, Tower delivered.

The lieutenant colonel scared up two new AH-1G Cobra gunships. With real humans doing the aiming, Tower trusted the helicopter guys to look before they fired inside Widows Village. The aviators would be a lot more accurate than a pattern of artillery shells fired off a map estimate and arcing in from miles away. Tower warned his men on the ground to halt in place. Then he cleared the helicopters to go after the VC holed up in the north end of the streets.

Both armed helicopters passed overhead as their crews sized up the situation. Then they swung wide, lining up, one behind the other. The lead bird dropped its nose and went to work. The Cobra unleashed a brace of seven 2.75-inch folding-fin rockets, tearing up the VC-held houses. He pulled away. Then the second Cobra slid down, rocketing the same shattered, smoking buildings. As the trail helicopter rose up and clattered off, the lead AH-1G came back around, aligned its nose turret, and gave the hostiles some mini-gun (from six 7.62mm gatling-style rotating barrels) for good measure. A throaty rasp, some kind of god-awful chainsaw, ripped the air. The second bird then followed suit—more chainsaw, then silence. A cloud of reddish dust bloomed over the beaten zone.

When the Cobras finished up, declaring "Winchester" (out of ammunition), a follow-on pair of UH-1C Huey Hogs appeared, repeating the pounding with more rockets and machine gun bullets. The two rounds of gunship strikes finished off the VC, minus the stragglers, the stubborn, and the stupid.[35] Hunting them down fell to the rest of Company B, including Hagel. It took most of the afternoon.

Scout lieutenant Brice Barnes earned the Distinguished Service Cross after dodging fire all day, culminating in a rare face-to-face shootout with an especially doughty VC. Company B, the scouts, and the 4-39th Infantry together claimed seventy-seven enemy killed and ten prisoners taken—very impressive, but also an indication that hundreds of men from the VC battalion got away. The intel people at battalion confirmed that supposition just before sunset. To take Widows Village, the Americans lost three killed (two scouts and Corporal Huie) and sixteen wounded (twelve from Company B, three scouts, and one from 4-39th). At least two local civilians, hiding out in the ruins of Widows Village, got killed, too. The ARVN's model settlement had been thoroughly trashed. But after a very long, very dicey twenty-four hours, Long Binh Post was safe.[36] The Americans called it a victory.

Chuck Hagel knew it had been a hell of a fight. More action followed for the next few days. "We took tremendous hits," he said. Many were leaders. To add to the pain, two days later, the riflemen moved forward through a different ramshackle hamlet, looking for VC. Hagel was near Captain Robert Keats. "We were in a cemetery one morning," said Hagel, "and a sniper shot him right between the eyes, and he was right next to me."[37] After evacuating their fallen captain, the company kept going. The war didn't let up.

TOM HAGEL LANDED in Vietnam two weeks before the Tet Offensive. He didn't linger at Long Binh. He had hoped to serve with brother Chuck in country, and got pretty close when the clerks at the 90th Replacement Battalion sent him, too, to the 9th Infantry Division at Bear Cat. Like Chuck, he sharpened his battle skills in five days of jungle training at the Reliable Academy. In those relatively routine last days of January, nobody there had any idea of the storm about to break over Vietnam.

During his week or so at Bear Cat, Tom sewed on the 9th's Octofoil shoulder patch, the eight-pointed red and blue flower surrounding a white circle, all mounted on a round, olive-drab background. In medieval heraldry, the white circle designated the ninth son—the division—surrounded by his eight brothers, red for artillery, blue for infantry, and not coincidentally America's national colors.[38] Irreverent young soldiers called the patch "flower power" and the "psychedelic cookie." And both Hagels wore it. By army measures, they didn't live in the same house, or even the same street. But they were in the same town of 16,000 souls. They shared the patch.

That wasn't by request, nor by design, but by the routine machinations of army accounting, the individual replacement system puttering along, the widgets and screws drill. The 9th had first deployed to Vietnam in December of 1966 and January of 1967. With the first year up, the division needed a huge infusion of soldiers to backfill the departing original deployers.[39] Losses in Tet only turned that crank faster.

Nobody had time to ease Tom Hagel into the war. He reported to the 3rd Squadron, 5th Cavalry just as the Tet Offensive cooked off. The 3-5th had sustained significant casualties before, during, and just after Tet, with eighty-two men—pretty much an entire troop—lost right about the time Tom Hagel made it to Vietnam.[40] The squadron needed men.

This unit employed M48 tanks, M113 armored personnel carriers, and dismounted soldiers, too. In keeping with the cavalry tradition, the battalion-size outfit was designated a "squadron," the companies were "troops," and the men proudly called themselves "troopers." The frontier Regulars at long-ago Fort Robinson, Nebraska, would have recognized the nomenclature immediately, and indeed, the original 5th Cavalry had carried the day back in 1876 in a scrap with the Cheyenne at War Bonnet Creek, Nebraska. Great-grandfather Herman Hagel used to resupply the old-time 5th Cavalry. Now son Tom served in the Vietnam-era version. Much like the mechanized 2-47th Infantry, 3-5th acted as a reaction force when things went haywire. The Tet Offensive surely qualified.

To chase down and finish off troublesome pockets of VC infiltrators, the 3-5th "Bastard Cav" was on loan to the biggest separate armored organization in country, the powerful 11th Armored Cavalry Regiment. PFC Tom Hagel went right out on operations near Bien Hoa Air Base. He took a minute to jot a note to his brother, courtesy of the army post office:

Dear Chuckles,

Well, by now I'm sure you're wondering what the hell happened
to me. I am in what amounts to a recon squad and securing force.
When we move to the DMZ [demilitarized zone; the border with
North Vietnam], I'll really be busy. I'd just as soon be with the 2/47
as here. The CO [commanding officer] is a real prick. Well, take it
easy and I don't know when I'll be seeing you next.[41]

It's unclear to which particular prick Tom Hagel referred, as he
had a troop, squadron, and regimental commander, and one, two, or
all three certainly might have qualified for the epithet. In any event,
as Tom warned Chuck, the squadron's activities around Saigon soon
wrapped up. On February 16, 1968, Tom's Headquarters Troop scout
platoon, Troop A and a platoon of Troop C left Blackhorse Camp en
route to New Port, Saigon.[42] The Bastard Cav was about to get a new
daddy. They were headed north.

GENERAL WILLIAM C. WESTMORELAND got his first whiff of the full
import of Tet when he went to the courtyard of the U.S. embassy.
Dead VC, shattered masonry, and expended cartridges lay here
and there. Blood stained the walkways. Nineteen enemy sappers
breached into the compound. But they never entered the chancery
building. It was over after a few awful hours.

Now came Westmoreland. Impeccably attired in his clean green
jungle fatigues, four silver stars on his cap, upright and forceful, the
MACV general inspected the site. A gaggle of cameramen and reporters trailed in his wake. Then, at about the same time on the morning
of January 31 that 2-47th waded into Widows Village, Westmoreland
turned to address the accompanying press.

The commander summarized the embassy incursion, being careful to note that all the VC were dead and the chancery remained intact. "In summary, the enemy's well-laid plans went afoul," he stated.
It was factual as far as it went.

He continued: "The enemy very deceitfully has taken advantage of the Tet truce in order to create maximum consternation in South Vietnam, particularly in the populated areas."[43] You could say that, all right, with more than a hundred separate assaults throughout Vietnam. It took days to clear out the attackers in Saigon. It was the same in the Mekong Delta and the Central Highlands. Up north was even worse, which was why Tom Hagel and 3-5th Cavalry were headed that way. A marine regiment remained encircled at Khe Sanh. The fighting inside Hue city went on for weeks, with the Viet Cong flag flying over the old imperial citadel right to the end.

Just in and around Saigon, the list went on and on: Bien Hoa Air Base, Tan Son Nhut Air Base, South Vietnam's Independence Palace, the national radio station, several ARVN command posts, and even MACV headquarters. Westmoreland had to duck rockets whistling into his command post and then dodge bullets on the harrowing ride to the embassy. Hell, if MACV headquarters and the U.S. embassy weren't safe, what was?

Stalwart as ever on the trashed embassy lawn, Westmoreland emphasized his bottom line. "The enemy exposed himself and he suffered great casualties."[44] So there you had it. We killed them by the gross. Therefore, we won.

As a victory announcement delivered over the background racket of gunfire and explosions around Saigon, it rang hollow, perhaps even delusional. The fact that the NVA and VC could pull off a massive surprise offensive, when supposedly beaten to their knees and on the verge of quitting, riveted attention back in America. North Vietnam might have taken horrendous losses, but they didn't shy from more, and there was zero indication that Ho Chi Minh and his politburo might throw in the towel. Even as the opening round of Tet attacks died down, NVA and VC elements kept right on fighting. And young Americans kept right on dying. Crossover point be damned. If this was winning, a redefinition of goals seemed overdue.

As television networks beamed back burning cities and crashed helicopters, and U.S. casualties mounted—the average American only tracked our side of the MACV ledger—a groundswell of shock and dismay rolled across America, the ammunition blast wave at Long Binh magnified to a continental scale. Pole-axed by the unsettling public reaction, generals and Johnson administration officials blamed the press. A good number of reporters certainly sexed it up and painted the canvas darkly. But in the United States, the press is a mirror, and despite the fonder hopes of some agenda-driven editors, only rarely a prism. Journalists reflect what we already know. As anchorman Walter Cronkite of CBS said, off the air for the moment: "What the hell is going on? I thought we were winning the war."[45] Uncle Walter, as he often did, spoke for Mr. and Mrs. America.

Many military men, including Westmoreland, compared Tet to Adolf Hitler's last-ditch Ardennes counteroffensive, a desperate attempt to win a lost war.[46] Yet in December of 1944, no objective person could argue that the Allies were not winning, and decisively so. The great Battle of the Bulge caused a setback, not a reset. Even as German panzers tried one last lunge, you knew how that war would end up.

Westmoreland believed that the Tet Offensive validated his attrition strategy. Driven by the bloodletting of 1965–67, the enemy came out of the shadows, stood up, and fought. And died. According to MACV counting, through February 11, the Tet Offensive cost the North's forces 32,000 killed and 5,800 captured. American losses were 1,001 killed, and the oft-maligned ARVN lost 1,081. Hanoi's general offensive went off on schedule, achieving a high degree of surprise. But to the astonishment of many, maybe even themselves, ARVN troops held. The popular general uprising fizzled completely. Pushed out front by NVA officers, Viet Cong guerrillas in particular bore the brunt of the beating. To Westmoreland, it smelled like a victory.[47] Then and now, most military observers agreed.

But war is more than trading shots with the other uniformed foe.

In Vietnam and America in 1968, Tet cast into question all of the progress claimed to date. The numbers, always the numbers, the metrics of death, us versus them, trends and forecasts, ratios and percentages—they went on and on. The old NFL adage applied. Statistics are for losers. Getting stunned by a massive countrywide surprise offensive sure didn't feel like victory. That other crossover point—U.S. public support for the war—was fast approaching. A half million Americans in uniform in Vietnam, Chuck and Tom Hagel among them, were about to find out what it meant to be on the losing side.

CHAPTER 4

The Butcher of the Delta

LUDENDORFF: The English soldiers fight like lions!
HOFFMAN: True. But don't we know that they are lions
led by donkeys.

ALAN CLARK, *The Donkeys*[1]

He knew what they called him. It rolled right off. In fact, he took pride in it. Asked about his reputation, he remarked that "there was a definite group that thought, as I mentioned, that I was Attila the Hun." He went on: "This guy [himself] was a barbarian or something because I'd get out there and just kick hell out of these people—not our people, but the enemy."[2] Nobody, but nobody, killed Cong like Julian Johnson Ewell.

Lieutenant General Ulysses S. Grant, "Grant the Butcher," locked in a blood-soaked embrace with the Army of Northern Virginia in 1864–65, recoiled from the sobriquet, and probably didn't deserve it. Going against General Robert E. Lee and his tough, veteran Confederates pit strength on strength. Maneuvering didn't work—Lee was always a step ahead, and just as determined. Only killing, slow and ugly, Abe Lincoln's terrible arithmetic, sorted it out.[3] Grant had been a butcher, but he never asked, nor sought, to be one.

Field Marshal Douglas Haig, the "Butcher of the Somme," mired in the sanguine trench struggle with the Imperial German Army in 1916–18, denied the title altogether, and he had done (and not done) just enough to earn it. On the Western Front, caught under the deadly hammering of Krupp artillery and Spandau machine guns, the British Expeditionary Force labored for years seeking a way out of the morass. Refining assault waves, tweaking barrage timetables, adding numbers—none of it availed. After enough slaughter, and some new weapons called tanks, the Germans slowly fell apart.[4] Haig, too, had been a butcher, and he rationalized it to his last days.

And Ewell? He sought the role, embraced it. He'd prepared his entire life to command a U.S. Army division in combat. He didn't care what the troops or the news media or some swivel-chair whiz kid in Washington had to say. As Chuck and Tom Hagel and so many others soon found out, Ewell was all about killing Cong.

You'd never mistake Ewell for Westmoreland. The latter looked like a general should, tall and bold, stalwart in mien and stature. For his part, Ewell reminded you of an insurance adjuster come to appraise your crumpled fender. He wore the black, horn-rimmed glasses —a tribute to Buddy Holly, and by 1968 about as out of date—issued by the thoroughly unfashionable army medical supply system. His head leaned forward a bit on a stalk of a neck. He was pasty faced, loose limbed, and somewhat awkward when he moved. His voice seemed a bit high pitched, especially when he got angry, as he often did. As one officer wrote of him: "He lacks command presence."[5] But he more than made up for it with brains and guts. Julian J. Ewell had both in spades.

He also had a prominent martial name. In 1968, a few years after the centenary of the American Civil War, some observers noticed. Although he came from a military family, Julian J. Ewell never claimed any relationship to Confederate Lieutenant General Richard Stoddert Ewell, corps commander in Lee's Army of North Virginia. That officer, "Old Bald Head," didn't look the part, either. The Civil War Ewell had his moments, but his men learned that he wasn't a closer.

In battle, most notably at the climactic clash at Gettysburg in 1863, Ewell played it safe. He held back.[6] Not so Julian J. Ewell. He never hesitated—not once, not at all.

Young Julian may not have claimed Old Bald Head, but he certainly was born into the army in 1915, two years before the United States joined the Great War. His father, Lieutenant Colonel George W. Ewell, taught military science at Oklahoma Agricultural and Mechanical College (today Oklahoma State University) in Stillwater. His mother, Jamie Offutt Ewell of Kentucky, came from the same extended family as Jarvis J. Offutt, the World War I pilot who gave his life in France and his name to the Strategic Air Command's headquarters base near Omaha, Nebraska.[7] In addition, Julian and his parents lived in Panama, California, Pennsylvania, and Washington, DC, all courtesy of the U.S. Army. It all clearly influenced Julian's choice of profession.

He took a long route to the colors. After an initial term at the New Mexico Military Institute, he attended Duke University in North Carolina for two years. He made it to West Point in 1935 and graduated in 1939, a second lieutenant of infantry at age twenty-four, two years older than most of his classmates.[8] As the son of a long-serving officer, well aware of the rhythms of the army, he felt like he was already behind. That nagging idea motivated him his entire life, to Vietnam and beyond.

He had an opportunity right away, and he took it. With World War II raging overseas, America reluctantly prepared for war. The draft commenced in 1940, and the army worked to modernize its moribund force structure. Having seen the brilliant exploits of Nazi German paratroopers and glidermen in the Netherlands and Belgium during the blitzkrieg of 1940, the U.S. Army established its own airborne element. Eager to contribute and ever hungry for a challenge, Lieutenant Ewell joined the new 501st Parachute Infantry Battalion at Fort Benning, Georgia.

Tough and willing to experiment, Ewell and his fellow paratroopers figured out how to organize, train, and carry out mass parachute jumps. Their parachutes weren't the slow, steerable flying wings used today at public sport parachuting. The army used the T-4 parachute, a round hemispheric canopy twenty-eight feet in diameter. Mounted on a man's back, the T-4 featured a strong cord snapped onto a metal wire inside the transport aircraft, typically a twin-engine C-47 Skytrain, the military version of the popular DC-3. Called a static line, the cord stayed hooked securely to the plane as the jumper went out the door. The cord pulled open the backpack, and the 'chute blossomed out with a strong jerk, which paratroopers called the opening shock. The parachutes dropped men quickly, about five hundred feet in twenty seconds or so. Landings were abrupt and hard. Ewell and the others learned to bend their legs, turn into the wind if possible, and above all, to keep their feet and knees together.[9] A lot of ankles and knees paid for that hard-won practical knowledge. Old men, unless in great physical condition, need not apply.

A few months after America declared war, when a delegation of new airborne generals and colonels came to Fort Benning for a demonstration and a practice jump, Ewell acted as jumpmaster, sending the senior guys out the door of the C-47. His stick (group of jumpers) included a patrician artillery colonel named Maxwell Davenport Taylor. Ever interested in talent that could be helpful to the army and himself, Taylor took note of the all-business Ewell.[10] That tough young West Pointer had potential.

On November 15, 1942, Colonel Howard R. "Skeets" Johnson activated the 501st Parachute Infantry Regiment at Camp Toccoa, Georgia, and Ewell took command of the 3rd Battalion. Just three years out of West Point, he held a lieutenant colonel's billet, commanding six hundred paratroopers. When the 501st jumped into the darkness over Normandy to initiate the great invasion on June 6, 1944, Ewell found himself with few followers, about forty in all. Most of his paratroopers had been scattered all over the flooded, marshy stretches west of Utah Beach. Well, U.S. Army paratroopers had long been taught to find who they could and start going after Germans. Ewell and his men did so. His bunch included his 101st Airborne Division commander, Maxwell Taylor. Once again, Taylor noticed this gangly young battalion commander who refused to quit.

Once the Normandy operation wrapped up, the 501st Parachute Infantry Regiment returned to England to stage for the next mission. It came on September 17, 1944. The Americans and the British 1st Airborne Division jumped to take a series of bridges leading to the Rhine River. The idea was to get a crossing and force the end of the war. While the daylight drop went well, the operation failed. German tanks counterattacked violently, and British armored forces struggled to link up. The British paratroopers sixty miles north at Arnhem were cut up and forced to pull out. Many didn't make it.

Neither did Skeets Johnson. On October 8, a German mortar shell killed the charismatic 501st commander. Major General Maxwell Taylor appointed twenty-nine-year-old Julian J. Ewell to take over.[11] Johnson had been a larger than life, inspirational commander. He led the regiment on runs and in battle, and carried an M3 "Grease Gun" automatic weapon. He used it, too. Now he was gone.

Ewell had big jump boots to fill. It wasn't his style to be a "personality," so he wasn't. The regiment lost 662 paratroopers, more than a quarter of its strength, in seventy-two days of combat in the cold, dank woods on the border of the Netherlands. The survivors were withdrawn to camps near Rheims, France, to bring in replacements, retrain, reequip, and rest.

The Germans ended that interlude on December 16, 1944, with their powerful Ardennes counteroffensive. Both American airborne divisions were thrown in to blunt the German panzer attacks. The 82nd Airborne Division went to Werbomont and relative obscurity, although the paratroopers fought with distinction. Ewell and the rest of the 101st Airborne Division ended up in Bastogne, surrounded, hard pressed, and soon enough famous.

Ewell lived up to every expectation from his subordinates and his superiors. The 501st led the U.S. truck movement into Bastogne, getting there late on December 18, right ahead of the Germans. Recognizing the unforgiving minute, Ewell didn't wait for formal orders. After a quick look at the terrain and a glance at the black horizon, already alight with nearby artillery explosions, Ewell led his men out into the frozen fields. His 501st took up positions facing due east, right in the path of Panzer Lehr, the German main effort.

Snow, ice, and bone-chilling cold made it perilous. Day after day, night after night, led by tanks, the Germans surged forward again and again. Fighting was vicious and bloody. But the Americans did not back up. Tireless, courageous, and smart, Ewell roamed the thinly held front lines hour after hour, day and night. He arranged and rearranged the 501st defenses against the successive German attacks. It all cost 580 men, but Ewell's regiment held. He was badly wounded in the foot on January 9, 1945. That merited the Purple Heart. Maxwell Taylor ensured that Ewell also received the Distinguished Service Cross, second only to the Medal of Honor.[12] Well he should. Ewell earned it.

After less than six years in uniform, Ewell had proven himself. Compared even to known high performers like Westmoreland, Ewell had shown the right stuff. Had he been advanced to general right then, or soon after, the army would have benefited greatly. But left to sit for two decades, restless and frustrated, watching those he considered less able move upward, Ewell stewed. His already acerbic outlook curdled even more. He watched others advance well ahead of him: William Westmoreland, Creighton Abram, Reuben Tucker, John "Mike" Michaelis, and his classmate Harry W. O. Kinnard. And through it all, Ewell marked time.

Maxwell Taylor tried to help him. He put Ewell on his staff in Berlin after the war, helped him get command of the 9th Infantry Regiment in Korea during the last months of the war, and arranged for him to take charge of cadets at West Point. When Taylor came back on active duty under President John F. Kennedy, he sent for Ewell and kept him in his outer office. Finally, in 1963 Ewell pinned on his first star. Making brigadier general at twenty-four years in service matched the usual pace of U.S. Army promotion. But for Ewell, it was far behind the rest of the great colonels of World War II.

From 1965 until 1968, Ewell served in Germany and in stateside posts. Nobody in Vietnam asked for the old 501st commander. Finally, in the wake of the Tet Offensive, Westmoreland gave Ewell a chance. He didn't offer Ewell the 101st Airborne, the one the 501st veteran really wanted. Instead, Ewell received orders to the 9th Infantry Division—Westy's World War II division—south of Saigon. Things down there did not look good. Well, as the acid-tongued Fleet Admiral Ernest J. King supposedly said after Pearl Harbor: "When they get in trouble they send for the sonsabitches."[13] On February 25, 1968, they did.

WHAT DID EWELL INHERIT?

Stated briefly: a mess. The Mekong Delta and the area south of Saigon amounted to South Vietnam's overcrowded, flooded basement. Because the area's farmers grew rice, the staple crop for the entire country, both sides wanted to control the Delta. The Viet Cong movement originated in Kien Hoa Province, and by February of 1968, the best estimates showed only 38 percent of the northern Mekong Delta under Saigon's authority. The southern reaches were probably worse, but it was hard to tell. ARVN's optimistic reporting rarely passed the smell test. One number wasn't disputed. Only 84 percent of the required rice harvest made it into Saigon's economy.[14] The rest fed the Viet Cong or rotted in the water-logged paddies.

The unhappy Delta formed the rickety foundation of the shaky, war-weakened South Vietnamese state. That old soldier Julius Caesar once wrote that all Gaul was divided into three parts.[15] For ARVN, South Vietnam split into four: the north (I Corps), the Central Highlands (II Corps), the Saigon region (III Corps), and the Mekong Delta (IV Corps). There were provinces and districts and such, but they didn't matter too much. The four corps tactical zones did.

Each had its own character. The north, with a population of 3 million in five provinces, abutted Laos and North Vietnam. Most of the people lived in and around the coast, to include the key cities of Quang Tri, Hue, Da Nang, and Chu Lai. The ARVN I Corps (two divisions) tried to secure the populace. For MACV, III Marine Amphibious Force employed two U.S. reinforced marine divisions (1st and 3rd) and the 23rd Infantry Division (Americal). The NVA dominated, and some of the war's biggest conventional battles, Khe Sanh and Hue city, occurred up north. Westmoreland moved half his maneuver battalions into this area, which he saw as decisive in his quest to find and attrit NVA regiments.

The Central Highlands, with 3 million more people in twelve provinces, bordered Laos and Cambodia. Again, most people lived on the coast, with a number inland around the cities of Pleiku and Ban Me Thuot. ARVN's II Corps (two divisions) attempted to hold the villages. The U.S. I Field Force included the 4th Infantry Division, the 173rd Airborne Brigade, and the Republic of Korea forces (two divisions and a brigade of ROK marines). As up north, the Americans sought to engage NVA and VC Main Force units.

The Saigon region, with 4.7 million people in eleven provinces and the capital zone, also fronted on Cambodia. The ARVN III Corps (three divisions) worked on pacifying the towns and hamlets. The U.S. II Field Force included the 1st Infantry Division and 25th Infantry Division, both between Cambodia and Saigon to the northeast and northwest respectively. The 11th Armored Cavalry Regiment and 199th Light Infantry Brigade also served in this area, as did two-thirds of the 9th Infantry Division, the Australian/New Zealand Task Force, and the Thailand forces. The U.S. units nearest Cambodia sought NVA organizations; the rest tangled with the VC.

Finally, the Mekong Delta population totaled 6.5 million in sixteen provinces. ARVN's IV Corps (three divisions) tried to keep order in the Delta in the face of a strong, long-standing VC insurgency. One brigade of the 9th Infantry Division, part of a unique army-navy riverine task force, served in the Delta. The United States had largely ceded the fight in IV Corps to the ARVN. Said another way, the VC had pretty free rein down there.

For emergencies, the South Vietnamese relied on their airborne, marine, and ranger units to shift around the country as required to meet emergencies. Westmoreland at MACV used the 1st Cavalry Division (Airmobile, which is to say heliborne) and the 101st Airborne Division (soon to convert to the airmobile configuration, too). For Tet, both of these divisions had brigades in multiple regions, with most of the 1st Cav up north and two-thirds of the 101st near Saigon.[16] Although all American maneuver battalions were quite mobile by both air and ground, they tended to stay in or near their assigned areas. The northward shift of 3-5th Bastard Cav, including PFC Tom Hagel, was unusual in that regard.

Thus the U.S. Army outfits in country came in two major flavors: regional (most of them) and national (1st Cavalry and 101st Airborne). Accordingly, Ewell's 9th Infantry Division, a regional division, most closely matched the 1st, 4th, and 25th infantry divisions, each with a few armored/mechanized units. The stitched-together 23rd Infantry Division ("Americal," a World War II nickname), which wise guys called Metrecal after the bland diet drink powder, had been assembled in country from orphan brigades and late-arriving units. All of the U.S. Army divisions fielded three brigades and nine or more maneuver battalions (walking "leg" infantry, mechanized infantry, armor, or cavalry). In both theory and practice, battalions moved between brigades as the mission required. As a highly mobile mechanized battalion, 2-47th switched brigades a lot.

Even though battalions include regimental designations, like Chuck Hagel's 2nd Battalion, 47th Infantry, the numbers amounted to a historical name. In World War II, three such battalions made a regiment, and almost always fought together as an integrated whole. Korea saw the same practice. But a pre-Vietnam conversion junked the World War II regiments. Battalions gave up any semblance of regimental affiliation. Battalions could be, and were, swapped between brigades like Lego pieces. Ewell's 9th Infantry Division included 6-31st, 2-39th, 3-39th, 4-39th, 2-47th, 3-47th, 4-47th, 2-60th, 3-60th, and 5-60th.[17]

The 9th's line-up fielded two mechanized battalions (including 2-47th), five leg infantry, and three riverine infantry outfits. As far as paratrooper Ewell saw it, he had five useful maneuver battalions and five with issues. The division had already sent 3-5th Cavalry (with tanks, APCs, and Tom Hagel) away and gained the 6th Battalion, 31st Infantry in return, a good deal, as the new battalion had just formed at Fort Lewis, Washington, and so came as a cohesive, well-trained team, admittedly having practiced searching mock Vietnamese villages in snow drifts. But the two mechanized battalions, while handy for road clearing and immensely useful in and around Saigon during Tet, really did not seem to have much utility in the marshy Mekong Delta. Ewell wrote later that he assessed mechanized units to be "more of a hindrance than a help" and "more and more difficult to employ," especially in the May to October wet season when monsoon rains soaked the already soggy ground. He sent one mechanized battalion to the 1st Infantry Division and received a leg infantry outfit in return. Only 2-47th kept their tracks, and by Ewell's direction: "We finally had to keep them partially unhorsed in order to force them into learning to conduct effective offensive small-unit foot operations."[18] There's a lot of vitriol behind that sentence. Ewell didn't trust 2-47th, and that caused him to lean especially hard on the battalion. And Ewell sure knew how to lean hard.

The riverine battalions also seemed less than effective. Ewell's 2nd Brigade had, since June of 1967, affiliated with the U.S. Navy's Task Force 117 to form the Mobile Riverine Force. At first, the armored gunboats, motorized landing craft, and barge artillery caught the VC by surprise. But the advantage didn't last. Viet Cong leaders figured out where the boats could go and put themselves elsewhere. "However, after about six months," Ewell's division chief of staff wrote later, "the Viet Cong in the upper Delta had pretty much learned to cope with the Riverine Force and, in fact, were beginning to establish ambushes along the waterways."[19] Yet due to the navy's commitment, the Mobile Riverine Force remained active past its use-by date. Ewell and plenty of others wondered why the marines didn't pick up this amphibious role. But the Marine Corps units came ashore as the first U.S. ground combat battalions back in 1965, way up north on the coast. And the marines liked to keep their guys together, under their own generals. So the 9th and the navy were stuck with the riverine mission. Ewell didn't like it. He had to figure out how to make it work.

MAKING IT WORK—MECHANIZED, leg, or riverine—meant finding, fixing, fighting, and finishing the elusive Viet Cong. Ewell had no doubt about his core task: killing VC. In an operational document, Ewell's staff summarized their commander's thinking this way: "The simplest and most relevant statistical index of combat effectiveness was the average number of Viet Cong losses inflicted daily by the unit in question."[20] Stack 'em up. That was the gist of it.

That wasn't easy in the face of an experienced guerrilla foe. As Ewell put it: "You didn't have any great tactical battles, like the Bulge [1944 German Ardennes counteroffensive], it was just a question of grinding these people down." He went on: "The only way you could get them out of there was to beat on them until they were so weak that they just didn't dare come into the populated areas."[21] That was what the new commanding general wanted his division to do.

Before he took command of the 9th Infantry Division, Ewell made a close study of the American tactics used in Vietnam. He had heard plenty about the pluses and minuses of "search and destroy" operations. In the purest form, the term meant looking for NVA/VC units and finishing them off, killing Cong in accord with Westmoreland's attrition strategy. But by late 1967, search and destroy carried connotations of rogue U.S. units rampaging through the countryside burning villages and slaying civilians. Exaggerated or not, the phrase became toxic back in the United States. So MACV changed the name to "search and clear." Whatever you called them, in Ewell's view, "the tactics were pretty well chosen and did the job."[22] So he started there.

The basic American method long predated Vietnam. Ewell knew it well from World War II. Send a bullet, not a man.[23] Industrialized and technologically advanced, the United States relied on its mass of quality weaponry to make up for lack of numbers and to keep young Americans alive. Thus Charles Dean Hagel, Curtis LeMay, and thousands of others did their business in 1941–45, death from above, war from the air. Their dangerous bombing missions spared hundreds of thousands of U.S. soldiers and marines from the carnage of an opposed landing on the Japanese home islands. Under the lash of American high explosives, the Japanese, as well as the Germans, and eventually the North Koreans and North Vietnamese, experienced horrors aplenty. But we saved our people. That was hard war indeed.

Rather than throw people at the enemy, Americans used prodigious firepower, an endless, destructive torrent of bombs and shells. Close was good enough, and more was better. At Anzio, Italy, in 1944, it took about 200 artillery rounds to kill one German. By Korea in 1953, it took 300 artillery projectiles to account for one Chinese communist soldier. By Vietnam, the estimate ran to 340 howitzer shells to get a single Viet Cong guerrilla. In the 25th Infantry Division in early 1967, it took an average of 896 rounds to kill one opposing soldier. [24] The profligate outputs amazed even veterans of the worst battering matches in World War II. A quarter century after Vietnam, U.S. information technologies would enable widespread use of precise smart munitions, one shot, one kill. But those armaments were in their infancy in Vietnam. In 1968, we had plenty of dumb and lethal ammunition, and the enemy didn't. Better to fire away than to lose our guys.

The predilection for firepower led to the second characteristic of U.S. tactics in country: "maneuver and fire." This varied from the practice of "fire and maneuver" taught in both world wars and Korea. In the standard version of fire and maneuver, at the small-unit level, American infantry relied on a base of fire, usually machine guns or Browning automatic rifles, to suppress the enemy with a high volume of bullets while the rest of the riflemen maneuvered, which is to say advanced by alternate rushes, ducking from cover to cover and crawling when necessary, as it often was. Attacks culminated in an infantry assault, man to man, with grenades, bayonets, and gut-shots in the heart of the hostile position.

In Vietnam, dense vegetation often made it very tough to get right on top of the VC. In addition, close combat negated U.S. firepower, as the explosive radii of 105mm artillery shells and 500-pound bombs proved indiscriminate on the ground. Clever VC commanders taught their men to "hug" the Americans to frustrate the supporting U.S. gunners and pilots. When the Americans tried to back away to use howitzers and air strikes, the VC broke off and escaped. So the more enterprising U.S. colonels reversed the usual formula and taught their men to maneuver up to the enemy, make contact, then try to hold the bad guys in place by rifle and machine gun fire. When the big stuff rolled in, the Americans ducked their heads and brought down the scunion.[25] There was no classic infantry assault, just a sweep of the shattered wreckage of the VC position, policing up any prisoners, tending to the foe's wounded, and counting the enemy dead.

Of course, reliance on supporting air and artillery firepower and stopping when in contact gave the VC yet another immediate option to engage or leave. Even the best American artillery fires, prearranged and ready to go, took a few minutes to begin impacting on the ground; as an area weapon, the big shells had to be "walked" onto a furtive foe half seen at best in the scrub brush. And artillery came in relatively quickly. Helicopters and jet fighter-bombers took even longer to come on station. As no U.S. squad, platoon, or company had unlimited bullets, after the initial high-volume exchange, the firefight often petered out a bit. All too often, the VC and NVA used that breather to get away.[26] This came atop the already preponderant enemy capacity to avoid or accept battle in the first place.

To take away that hostile initiative, the Americans preached "pile on." Colonel George S. Patton III, son and namesake of the World War II great, commanded the 11th Armored Cavalry Regiment from July of 1968 to April of 1969. He explained piling on as "literally throwing forces together from all directions in order to first encircle or fix, then compress and finally destroy the enemy."[27] It sounded good, but rarely worked out. Even with tanks, tracks, helicopters, and a cascade of artillery, rockets, and bombs, the Americans were just too slow and too ham-handed to pull it off. The trap never quite closed, and a lot, if not most, of the enemy always seemed to wriggle free.

The 2-47th firefight on January 31, 1968, at Widows Village showed these tactical ideas in execution. Having figured out they had enemy in the houses, the Americans, including PFC Chuck Hagel, searched for their hidden opponents, covered by their track-mounted .50-caliber heavy machine guns. When the VC made contact—they opened up first, as usual—the Americans responded with all they had. No artillery was permitted, and that was a deviation from the typical solution, but armed helicopters participated with both rockets and machine guns. Company B/4-39th Infantry landed by helicopter to pile on. And despite a good number left dead, most of the VC got away.

Why?

Ewell though he knew the answer. By his reckoning, he had the big guns and attack helicopters to kill VC. What he needed were more riflemen—more beaters—to find his prey.

When Ewell ran the numbers for his new division, the result stunned him. At any particular time, of 16,000 or so troops assigned, about 1,000, including Chuck Hagel, were actually out in the bush hunting Charlie. Some of the rest guarded base camps, protected construction sites, defended a petroleum tank farm, and secured a radio relay site. Although the army filled divisions to 102 percent of their authorized strength, most rifle companies ran with about 65 to 70 men in the field, less than half their paper strength of 164. The other infantrymen existed on the rolls, but were not out on patrol. These 11Bs filled headquarters billets, attended unit schools (including training for young NCOs), recovered from wounds and illness (malaria and immersion foot predominated in the 9th Infantry Division), and came and went from rest and recreation (R&R) leave. At any one time, about a sixth of each company (one-twelfth in, one-twelfth out) processed to and from Vietnam, yet another curse of the individual replacement system.[28] Each base camp sucked in 11B manpower like a stellar black hole pulling in matter and light itself.

And what of those brave few who did go out? Chuck and Tom Hagel could have told Ewell the way it went, but the restless general found out for himself. The units took turns, as would be expected in a lengthy war characterized by days and days of routine, unopposed patrolling. While one company walked out in the woods, the other rifle companies operated from a firebase, flying out every other day on airmobile missions. Every night, each company sent out an ambush patrol.[29] The battalions kept a schedule, sharing the burden. Given the hot, humid weather and lack of worthwhile targeting intelligence, it made sense.

Ewell didn't agree. For him, to get the VC required "excruciating pressure" 24/7, day patrols and night ambushes. He couldn't get more men. So he elected to make those he had work harder, much harder, as both Hagel brothers would find out. He thought he increased "paddy strength" by demanding to see daily roll-ups at rifle company level.[30] Well, he certainly increased reporting. But hounding from a major general, even one as insistent as Ewell, didn't change the institutional inertia of individual replacements, R&R, base camp defense, and individual one-year tours.[31] The numbers went up some, but never enough to suit Ewell.

The division commander did more. He reorganized the leg battalions to add a fourth rifle company, then demanded that each lieutenant colonel keep three of four companies in the field day and night. The VC still refused contact almost 90 percent of the time. To his endless consternation, Ewell couldn't change that. But he could increase the number of his own units finding the VC 10 percent of the time, a brute force solution for sure. By flooding the zone with patrols, Ewell generated more contacts.[32] And that led to more kills.

Ewell ordered day and night "constant pressure," with few standdowns. One of the reasons the major general didn't care for Chuck Hagel's 2-47th involved their M113s, which required regular maintenance to keep running. So he made them work without tracks on many occasions. The mechanized infantry battalions only had three rifle companies. Ewell kept at least two in the bush, and it galled him to think a third of the battalion wasn't out there.[33] It ensured that 2-47th stayed in the commanding general's doghouse.

As helicopters also needed a lot of maintenance, Ewell went after them, too. He recognized that airmobile insertions, like Company B/4-39th at Widows Village, and helicopter gunship attacks, also seen in that engagement, both greatly increased the effectiveness of combat actions, doubling or even tripling enemy casualties inflicted. So aviation mattered. To get more flying time out of his helicopters, Ewell insisted on night maintenance work in lit hangers—the threat of VC mortar barrages notwithstanding—more tools, more spare parts, and, of course, direct reports to him on progress or lack thereof. By his hounding, Ewell squeezed an extra 30 percent of flying hours out of the division's fleet of Hueys, Cobras, and OH-23s.[34] The division's aviators contributed their share to the constant pressure mantra.

He preached it. He enforced it. "You operated twenty-four hours a day, seven days a week, every day, and you just kept grinding the enemy down."[35] Aboard his command chopper, Ewell ranged far and wide, day and night, making a lot of it happen exactly as he prescribed.

He also prevailed on II Field Force to reduce his area of operations and thus allow him to focus his effort. The 9th Infantry Division got rid of Bien Hoa and Long Khanh east of Saigon and shifted fully to the upper Mekong Delta. The division kept Long An (334,000 people) and Dinh Tuong (548,000) and added Kien Hoa (531,000) and Go Cong (173,000). This permitted Ewell to hand over the Bear Cat base to the Thais and move the division headquarters to Dong Tam, squarely in Dinh Tuong Province, and previously held only by the riverine 2nd Brigade and the sedentary ARVN.[36] Why did Ewell go there? In the new commanding general's estimate, that's where the VC had been most active. And he was all about hunting VC.

The commanding general also put paid to the escapades of the vaunted Mobile Riverine Force. Before Ewell's time, the army-navy contingent managed six operations a month, way below anything that the new commander would tolerate. Plus, the VC avoided the slow-moving armored watercraft or, worse, nailed them on terms favorable to the enemy. So the 2nd Brigade got new orders. "It was put into Kien Hoa Province—a real Viet Cong bastion," said Ewell, "taken off its boats, and buckled down to work."[37] There were still some riverine missions, but for the most part, the three battalions of 2nd Brigade worked on foot, slogging through the rice paddies and marshes.

To keep track of all of these tactical actions, Ewell insisted on regular, detailed reports, and woe to those who did not measure up. The general's investment in statistics bordered on mania. He looked hard at the kill ratio, "a very good measure of skill." Ewell put his finger right on the key question: how many U.S. soldiers killed did it take to kill X number of communists? Well, that sure cut to the chase. What was a dead American worth? Ewell proposed to settle on a value.

He then developed criteria, rating unit performance by kill ratio: one to fifty, highly skilled; one to twenty-five, fairly good; one to fifteen, low but acceptable, good for ARVN; one to ten was the historical U.S. average; one to six was the historical ARVN average. "We wouldn't wipe our shoes with one to ten in the Ninth," concluded Ewell. He claimed to run at one to eighty, with up to one to a hundred at times.[38] It was amazing what a determined man could wring out of the division.

And wring it he did. Everything came down to killing VC. Captain Ronald Bartek, a West Pointer, remembered an early briefing with the new division commander: "He wanted to begin killing '4,000 of these little bastards a month' [Ewell's words] and then by the following month wanted to kill 6,000." To a struggling commander, Ewell barked: "Jack up that body count or you're gone, colonel."[39]

This driven man drew his fair share of detractors in 1968 and in the years to follow. One perceptive officer wrote that "he is a superb Division commander—for the infantry or armored infantry war in Europe in the 1940s. He fights in Vietnam using the methods that would have made him a successful and popular commander with his superiors and with the public in World War II."[40] Many made that charge, less eloquently but no less forcefully, and it matches nicely with the old saw that generals always fight the last war. But it misses Ewell's true achievement.

Very much a creature of America's Vietnam War, Julian J. Ewell figured out how to get the most out of his division. Some generals— George Casey of the 1st Cavalry Division and Keith Ware of the 1st Infantry Division, both killed while in command—were more beloved. Ewell wasn't. Others—Olinto Barsanti of the 101st Airborne Division and Bill DePuy of the 1st Infantry Division—were tough on subordinate colonels. Ewell was tougher. And a few—Lew Walt of the 3rd Marine Division and Fred Weyand of the 25th Infantry Division— showed a lot of tactical acumen. Ewell outdid even them in the narrow sphere of killing Cong. He, above all division commanders who served in country, understood exactly what Westmoreland wanted. And Ewell sure delivered it. There was only one problem. He showed up three years too late.

ABOUT THE SAME TIME Julian J. Ewell began wrestling with his tactical situation in the upper Mekong Delta, General William C. Westmoreland decided to follow up what he saw as the successful pummeling administered to his NVA/VC opponents in their failed Tet Offensive. Working closely with the Joint Chiefs of Staff, the MACV commander sought to exploit his perceived gains. He asked for another 108,000 troops, with a marine regiment and a brigade from the 82nd Airborne to deploy immediately, a down payment on the big reinforcement to come. He actually had ideas of invading Laos to cut the Ho Chi Minh Trail.[41]

The Joint Chiefs, running out of draftees, saw the MACV request as their chance to replenish America's strategic reserve, the troops held in the homeland for other emergencies. A week before Tet erupted, the North Koreans had gone off the rails, sparking firefights in the demilitarized zone, seizing the surveillance ship USS *Pueblo* and its eighty-two sailors, and launching a special forces raid to kill South Korea's president. In Europe, the Soviet army continued to build up its armored regiments in and around Czechoslovakia, where a reforming government's days seemed numbered, with unknown repercussions for NATO. Israel, Egypt, and Syria remained locked in a simmering conflict that threatened to go hot at any time. The Cubans stirred the pot in the Caribbean and Latin America. And who knew what the election year of 1968 might bring to America's restive inner cities and college campuses. So the Joint Chiefs saw Westmoreland's request and added to it, topping out at 206,000. This would require President Lyndon Johnson to call up the National Guard and the service reserves. It would fully commit the nation.

To what?

More war? Ultimate victory? Was that even possible? At what cost? Outgoing secretary of defense Robert McNamara, heartsick over doing just enough to get the United States into Vietnam, nothing to guarantee victory, and not near enough to get us out, offered his opinion. No. That's it. Stop bombing the North. Negotiate. Turn it over to Saigon's troops. Pull out.[42]

His successor—shrewd Washington attorney, presidential counselor, and consummate DC insider Clark Clifford—probed the Joint Chiefs for answers. His account is damning indeed:

> How long will it take? They didn't know. How many more troops would it take? They didn't know. Would 206,000 answer the demand? They didn't know. Might there be more? Yes, there might be more. So when it was all over, I said, "What is the plan to win the war in Vietnam?" Well, the only plan is that ultimately the attrition will wear down the North Vietnamese and they will have had enough. Is there any indication that we have reached that point? No, there isn't.[43]

With both the old and new secretary of defense skeptical, LBJ did what he did best. He equivocated. He sent the marines and paratroopers, 10,500 in all, to meet Westmoreland's immediate request.[44] But he well understood that this was the moment of decision.

Johnson summoned the wise men, the best and brightest from Vietnam, the Cold War, Korea, and World War II. Generals Omar Bradley, Matthew Ridgway, and Maxwell Taylor (Ewell's World War II commander) came together to offer their judicious counsel. It's noteworthy that LBJ didn't ask Curtis LeMay, although the retired air force four-star was certainly available. LeMay's notoriously blunt brand of strategic thinking apparently wasn't welcome. In any event, the approved trio of generals, well spoken and housebroken, joined the other luminaries: Dean Acheson, George Ball, McGeorge Bundy, Arthur Dean, Douglas Dillon, Supreme Court Justice Abe Fortas, Arthur Goldberg, Averell Harriman, Henry Cabot Lodge Jr., Robert Murphy, and Cyrus Vance. New secretary of defense Clark Clifford participated, too.[45] The wise men would tell LBJ what to do. Then he'd do it. And this, too, would pass.

Out on the far side of the world, Westmoreland waited. Up north, at beleaguered Khe Sanh Combat Base, marines fought and died. So did the NVA. So did soldiers on both sides all across South Vietnam. In the northeastern reaches of the Mekong Delta, Ewell and the 9th Infantry Division hunted Cong. The war hung in the balance, awaiting the word of Lyndon Baines Johnson.

AT THE PFC LEVEL, none of this mattered much. Not yet. Up north with the marines, Tom Hagel and 3-5th Cavalry stayed busy, and not in a good way. "They were hard core NVA up there," he remembered. "Everybody was just getting blown away constantly."[46]

Hagel wasn't speaking idly. In two weeks spent supporting the 7th Marine Regiment near Dong Ha and other areas north of Quang Tri city, Troop A lost two killed, Troop C lost three more, and one man from the Headquarters Troop was killed, too. The NVA wounded nineteen troopers. It amounted to a platoon gone, a rude introduction to the new area. The marines suffered two wounded in action. In return, the Americans believed they killed four NVA and wounded an unknown number. The marines dropped five tons of bombs and assessed four "structures" and eight sampans destroyed.[47] Who could know for sure?

East of Saigon, PFC Chuck Hagel continued operations, too. After losing Captain Keats on February 2, Company B/2-47th worked through some other neighborhoods around Long Binh Post and in other hot spots around Saigon. Nervous MACV logistics and headquarters people saw a lot of VC in the weeks after Tet. Some were there. Most were not. Hagel and the other riflemen spent many days looking for Charlie, and finding him now and again.[48] Once things settled down in Saigon, the company returned to Bear Cat to fix their worn-out M113s, bring in new guys, and then resume the route security mission. Routes 1 and 15 hadn't gotten any better since Tet.

In between dealing with the Tet Offensive and its aftermath, both brothers endeavored to link up. For two junior soldiers in a war zone, that was easier said than done. They talked very briefly on the telephone and swapped notes via the army post office.

Tom thought he had heard somewhere that two brothers couldn't be sent to the same theater of war at the same time. He guessed that if he was in country, maybe Chuck could go home. Of course, he never asked Chuck, who had no intention of leaving. But the younger brother figured why not try it. Some barracks lawyer convinced Tom that the Red Cross would sort it out. When Tom tracked down a Red Cross representative, the person gave him the penguin salute, arms up and flapping—never heard of it.[49]

But Tom had read a lot, and his memory served him pretty well. He was indeed on to something. There was a protocol, the so-called Sullivans Rule, that said something about brothers or sisters serving together in the same unit. It stemmed back to the sinking of the light cruiser USS *Juneau*, torpedoed by the Japanese on November 13, 1942, following a fierce night naval clash off Guadalcanal. Sailors George, Frank, Joe, Matt, and Al Sullivan of Waterloo, Iowa, had asked to serve together. They died together, too. Their sacrifice became a rallying cry on the home front in World War II and resulted in posters, a movie, and a destroyer named USS *The Sullivans*.[50] It was a noble and heart-rending episode.

And the U.S. Congress, overseeing a military composed of citizens in uniform, had no intention of letting it happen again. In 1948, congressional legislation established the Sole Survivor Policy, which most people knew as the Sullivans Rule. It provided that if one child had been killed, gone missing, or declared captured, any sole survivor could apply to be discharged from the armed forces or excused from the draft if not already in the ranks. The policy did not require the services to separate siblings in units, nor did it compel them to release sole survivors automatically. An individual had to apply. In addition, any potential sole survivor might waive eligibility.[51] Unless or until one died in Vietnam, neither Hagel brother qualified.

But with one door closed, another opened. Nothing prevented the brothers from serving together voluntarily. So both soldiers made application to serve together. Chuck applied for 3-5th Cavalry. Tom asked for 2-47th Infantry. The documents got typed up by bored base camp clerks. Signed off, the forms vanished into the gaping maw of the U.S. Army Adjutant General Corps. As Chuck recalled: "And we decided that I would put a transfer request in to go where he is, and he would put a transfer request to come to where I am, knowing full well the way this all works, we would never ever see each other, but maybe once during the time we were there in Vietnam, we might run across each other."[52] The Hagel brothers gave it a shot, then kept right on going, as did the war.

In mid-February, just in to the battalion tent city at Bear Cat following another ambush patrol, a sergeant handed Hagel orders for the 25th Infantry Division. So maybe that was the plan—get him and Tom together in another unit. The sergeant offered zero explanation, only instruction in the unmistakable army style: "Pack your bag. Grab your rifle. Get your ass on that fucking truck." Hagel complied. The truck loaded up with other men, then headed out the gate.

Unexpectedly, just past the exit, the vehicle stopped with a screech. A military police soldier, "MP" on his shoulder brassard, just like stateside, walked to the back of the truck. The MP looked down at a clipboard. Then he spoke.

"Is there a Private Charles Hagel on the truck?"

No answer. Hagel wondered, "What now?"

The MP grimaced. "Are you so dumb, soldier, that you don't know what your name is?"

This time, Hagel acknowledged.

"Get down here, Private Hagel," said the MP. "The captain wants to see you. Bring your bags."

The captain told him to get back to his platoon.[53] He headed out on operations shortly thereafter. Chuck Hagel never did go to the 25th Infantry Division, and as for what became of the orders, who can say? The ways of army administration can be mysterious indeed.

Without fanfare, the big green machine ground its cogs and spat out one more unanticipated event. As March of 1968 began, PFC Chuck Hagel found himself, as usual, out on foot patrol, screening for the column of tracks, clearing yet another stretch of roadway. Around midmorning, as the men finished one segment of their route, they formed a roadside perimeter to take a break. A sergeant motioned to the PFC.

"Hagel, come on back here. There's a chopper coming in to pick you up and take you back to base camp," he said. Hagel didn't get it.

"Well, why is that?" asked the PFC.

"Well, I don't know. They didn't tell me," the sergeant answered. "They said get Hagel out of the field. Bring him back to base camp." "They" said a lot of things in the army, especially to a PFC, and to sergeants too, evidently.

Hagel connected some dots. "Well, sergeant, is this about my brothers or something there that I need to know about?" He thought of Tom up north, but Mike and Jimmy back home also crossed his mind. Things happen to young men all the time, and not just in wars.

The sergeant shrugged. "If I knew, I'd tell you," he said, "but you don't need to know that. Your instructions are to get on that chopper, it's going to be here in an hour, and get the hell out of here." Okay then. Like the good PFC he was, Hagel got on the Huey when it briefly touched down.

In a few minutes, the helicopter landed on the dusty helipad and Hagel clambered out, more than a little disoriented to be back in Camp Martin Cox while his unit stayed out on patrol. Nobody met him. He didn't know what else to do, so he went to his tent. Using excellent PFC logic, he figured if they needed him, they would send for him. Trust in "they."

Nothing happened.

Just before the evening meal, Hagel decided he had waited long enough. He went to the company orderly room. The clerk looked up. Hagel asked why he had been flown back from his platoon. "We don't know," the office soldier said.

"Do I have orders to leave?" Hagel asked. He wondered if the 25th Infantry Division assignment had come back into play.

"Well, I don't know." Nobody seemed to have a clue. Yet Hagel was right there. Somebody summoned him, and thought enough to send a Huey.

At a time like this, a good infantry soldier's thoughts turn to the fundamentals, i.e., food. Lacking any other instructions, Hagel went to the mess hall to eat. There he ran smack into First Sergeant Martin M. Garcia of Killeen, Texas. "And he was not a particularly [*sic*] favorite of mine or I don't think anybody's," Hagel noted. A hard-bitten, busy first sergeant rarely had anything good to say to a PFC.

But that night, Garcia had the word.

"By the way, Hagel," he said, "your brother's coming down. He's been transferred to your unit."

"When's he going to arrive?" asked Hagel.

"He'll be here tomorrow morning," answered Garcia. At eight the next morning, Tom Hagel showed up, duffle bag in hand. If he ever heard of the Sullivan brothers, First Sergeant Garcia did not let it affect assignments in Company B. As promised, the first sergeant put Tom into Chuck's platoon. And the platoon sergeant figured what the hell and assigned Tom to Chuck's squad.[54] They served together from that time onward.

THE HAGELS FOUND OUT that the 2-47th scout platoon also included two brothers, big men from Michigan with bright red hair and matching handlebar mustaches. It seemed like someone somewhere up the chain decided to honor these kinds of requests. A week or so back— hard to remember, the days and nights ran together—Chuck Hagel had mentioned his request to serve with his brother to a visiting general. Had it been Ewell, full of energy as he grabbed hold of the 9th Infantry Division? Chuck Hagel definitely met the new division commander later, and saw him often, out and about, "a very hands on general."[55] Ewell very much wanted to keep his infantry soldiers happy and out fighting. If the Hagels asked to serve together, that worked for Ewell. And it kept riflemen in the field, chasing VC.

Back in Columbus, Nebraska, Betty Hagel and sons Mike and Jimmy waited for every letter from Vietnam. Mike realized that Tom had done a good amount of hunting, so that boded well as far as protecting Chuck, who didn't do much with firearms before the army.[56] Betty said, "I was just glad they were together. That they would be company for each other." Aside from the odd snatches of televised "bang-bang" on the nightly news, the raw details of infantry combat in Vietnam remained opaque on the home front. It was just as well.

The prospect of losing a son, let alone both, lurked somewhere back in Betty Hagel's mind. But she dared not think about it. As she remembered: "If I had seen an Army officer walk up the front steps, I would have probably run out the back door as fast as I could."[57] Like Charlie in the Delta, she could run, but she couldn't hide.

CHAPTER 5

Blast

Something strange happens when a man is hit.

JAMES JONES, *WWII*[1]

The Hagel brothers walked point. Major General Julian J. Ewell could talk all he wanted about sending out more hunters, finders, beaters, whatever. In concrete terms, that meant groups of young riflemen walking through villages, rice paddies, or jungles, looking for the Viet Cong. And where those men walked, somebody had to go first. For Company B, 2-47th Infantry, Chuck and Tom Hagel were those somebodies.

According to the Infantry School at Fort Benning, the point element consisted of an eleven-man rifle squad led by a staff sergeant. Under that NCO, two sergeants ("buck" sergeants) each led five-man fire teams. Along with the sergeant in charge, each fire team included an M79 grenadier and three riflemen. One soldier carried a flimsy little aluminum fold-up bipod to make his M16 an "automatic rifle." It was a leftover from another era, as any M16 became "full auto" by a simple flip of the selector switch, easily thumbed on the left side of the rifle, just up and back from the trigger. Anyway, the field manual told you to send the point about two hundred yards forward of the following troops. The book even provided a neat little diagram. [2]

War doesn't follow the book. It never did. Forget about sergeants and grenadiers and the rest of the panoply. In their habitually understrength 2nd Platoon, leading their equally undermanned Company B, the Hagels, both PFCs, were the entire point. And as for being two football fields out front, well, in the dense jungle near Bear Cat, that would be the equivalent of the far side of the moon. The point team stayed about ten yards ahead and you could barely see them, just some waving fronds and an occasional flash of a sweat-stained green fatigue shirt. They needed to be just far enough out to absorb the first shot. And, of course, the VC opened the show 88 percent of the time.[3] For point men, it was not healthy to dwell on that particular number.

The first brother looked for trip wires, buried mines, flashes of movement, and physical evidence of the VC: footprints, trash, maybe broken branches that indicated something wicked this way came. The point man also broke brush, often with a machete. Picking the way, hacking a good bit, a hundred yards an hour, head on a swivel, a smart point man took his time. Stands of tough bamboo, replete with rough edges, flayed arms exposed in rolled-up sleeves. The high heat and humidity slowed him down. So did his exhaustion—with night ambushes and alerts, riflemen rarely got more than a few hours of uninterrupted sleep. There had been method to the madness imposed by the frantic pace of Basic Combat Training back at Fort Bliss. If nothing else, it offered a preview of what to expect. But it didn't make it any easier.

The second brother, the "slack" man, stayed back about three yards, maybe less. He held the compass, and used it to keep the point man, and thus the platoon, going in the right direction. That's one reason the second guy had to stay close: to give directions. Talking was kept to a whisper, and preferably not done at all. A gesture sufficed. A good point and slack duo could run for hours without a word. The Hagels were very good.

Some platoons used a separate pace man to measure distance.[4] With the Hagels, the slack man kept the pace. A good slack man knew how many steps it took him to move a hundred yards. For a six-footer like Tom about sixty-two would do it. Chuck, an inch or so shorter, needed a few steps more. Each time the slack man hit a hundred yards, he tied a knot on a cord. The second brother also consulted a paper map with the route legs marked—segment by segment, direction and distance through the bush, all the way to an oval blob, the objective, the neck of the woods where Charlie supposedly hung out. The Hagels knew each leg of the route, direction and distance.

Behind the brothers, the lieutenant and platoon sergeant also glanced at their maps, checked their compasses, and kept their own pace counts. Even though they trusted the brothers, the platoon's leadership double-checked the pair. The NCO knew his stuff. The rookie officer—well, the jokes about second lieutenants and maps reflected only too many actual goofs. As Chuck Hagel commented afterward: "Some of the officers couldn't read maps very well."[5] The Hagels could and did.

That morning of March 28, 1968, the brothers led a long file of Americans, the entire field strength of Company B. Those pleasant little drawings in the field manual depicted echelons, vees, wedges, and orderly open columns with entire squads pushed out forward, trailing, right, and left to clear the way and push off curious enemies. With less than sixty men—Major General Ewell would not approve at all, but there it was—incredibly tangled undergrowth, and a wary, elusive foe, the company commander, as usual, chucked the Fort Benning school solution. In this endless green bamboo thicket, the captain put out no flankers, judging it better to have clear shooting lanes port and starboard rather than a few more guys on either side seeking trip wires and swinging machetes. For early warning, the captain counted on the Hagels in the lead and a "drag" duo at the very end of the file, ten yards back. The tail-end man spun around every ten steps or so. Sometimes he walked backward for a minute or so.

Except for the point and drag teams, everybody else followed the man to his front, the classic ranger file, maybe a yard between each man. The Infantry School instructors said that this kind of follow the leader formation emphasized speed over security. In the primordial underbrush near Bear Cat, the file enjoyed no pretense of speed. But by going so cussedly cross-country, Company B confounded preset hostile ambushes. Even Charlie couldn't tippy-toe through this stuff without raising a racket. If the VC came from the side, as they often did, they'd be heard. Then the formula became right face or left face and cut loose.[6]

In the long, long row, each sweating soldier carried the usual burden: his M16 rifle (about eight pounds with a magazine loaded), a steel helmet with lime green cloth cover, web gear (a belt with suspenders), two full one-quart canteens (emptier by the hour), a first-aid pouch with sterile bandage pack, belt-mounted ammunition pouches crammed with twenty-round magazines (the army recommended ten and the soldiers doubled that), two baseball-sized M26 fragmentation (frag) grenades, and a rucksack packed with more ammunition (two hundred linked rounds for the M60 pig machine gun and C4 plastic explosive), an entrenching tool ("e-tool," a little fold-up shovel), a nylon poncho liner (lighter-than-air quilted blanket), rifle cleaning kit (the M16 was touchy), a spare pair of socks (critical to change out to keep feet in good shape), a bit of shaving gear, a toothbrush, the ever popular canned C-rations, and for most, some cigarettes wrapped to stay dry. A few men—short-timers and nervous ones—wore the heavy flak jackets, but most used those only when operating with the tracks. In the bush, you took your chances. You already carried way too much.

While American manufacturers took out every smidgen of excess weight, water and ammunition weighed what they weighed. The field manual estimated it all added up to 78.18 pounds, almost double the amount toted in Basic Combat Training.[7] In that regard, the Benning book got it about right. Of course, slight, short Charlie Cong carried much less. The Hagels and their mates struggled along with the equivalent of a Viet Cong wrapped around each tired American. Fleet and nimble they were not.

As they labored ahead, the primeval vegetation hemmed them in. "You couldn't see the sun," Chuck Hagel remembered. "It was like you were inside all the time."[8] Gloom, heat, humidity, sleep deprivation, and routine generated tunnel vision. Slowly, slowly, a football field of distance an hour, the troops rustled along, picking their way through the "wait a minute" vines and the dripping leaves. Other than a few leaders and the men at point and drag, the troops droned, heads bobbing, one nylon and leather jungle boot in front of the other. If this constituted hunting, it depended on pursuing some pretty dumb, cooperative, inert beasts. The VC were anything but that.

Company B's patrol sought a new, particularly dangerous enemy force. The analysts at division G-2, the intelligence staffers, guessed that the opposition brought in some necessary reinforcements— probably true NVA, really from the North—to rebuild after the savaging suffered in Tet. The intel people wanted to locate the VC K-34 Artillery Battalion, an outfit armed with 120mm mortars (3.5-mile range) and 122mm rockets (5-mile range), big, dangerous weapons that caused a lot of mayhem during Tet. A month ago to the day, the VC bombarded Camp Martin Cox itself, dumping rockets and mortar shells all over the Bear Cat base and killing six soldiers and patients in the 9th Medical Battalion area.[9] That had to stop.

Thus 2-47th went out without its tracks, looking for the VC shooters, Black Panthers on the prowl in the jungle. It briefed well up at division headquarters. But the daily grind of patrols and nightly ambushes, done "unhorsed" at Ewell's direction, pulled the battalion one way, keyed on a slippery hostile unit. At the same time, roadrunner missions aboard the M113s, tied to routes 1 and 15, compelled 2-47th to do a very different kind of task. In both cases, whether used for the mission or not, the tracks demanded constant repairs and upkeep. Companies alternated between the dismounted search for the K-34 Artillery Battalion and mounted road security operations. Neither went well. Lieutenant Colonel John Tower felt the heat. Even Chuck Hagel noticed that "there was an additional pressure put on the senior guys."[10] It rolled downhill fast.

One early success only whetted Ewell's voracious appetite up at division. On March 3, 1968, a patrol from Company B had followed up on the typically vague intelligence and, wonder of wonders, found a massive tunnel network only a few miles from Bear Cat. Not one VC turned up. They'd vanished before the Americans got there. They were good at that.

At the tunnel complex's entrance port, a medium-sized tree blocked the way. But when you gave the trunk a yank, not even that forcefully, the roots popped loose in a shower of dirt. A passageway opened. Behind it, packed earthen corridors yawned six feet high and showed soot from lanterns. The corridors ran seven levels down, and looked to be some kind of VC hospital. Playing fast and loose with the Geneva Conventions—what else was new—the enemy filled several warrens with mounds of weapons, some dating back to the French era, and some so newly arrived from the USSR and China that they hadn't been unpacked. Sergeant First Class William Nelson Butler, late of Widows Village, and still working without a lieutenant due to Tet casualties, later said, "We searched the complex and never found the bottom." For years, American soldiers had laughed at the 25th Infantry Division, which sited its base camp right on top of the intricate, deep Cu Chi tunnels. Well, that was one way to find Charlie.[11] Now this underground lair squatted only miles from the 9th Infantry Division's massive Camp Martin Cox. How long had it been there? Nobody knew. But at least the Americans had a grip on it now.

Very impressive, said the division commander. But it wasn't the VC K-34 Artillery Battalion. Finding buried treasure was swell. Killing VC would be much better. Ewell applied the screws to brigade, battalion, company, platoon, squad, right down to Chuck and Tom Hagel. When would 2-47th bag some Cong?

If they could be found, they could be killed. But where was Charlie? The intel guys sifted radio intercepts, reviewed tips from village snitches, sorted through soiled captured documents, and plotted historical patterns of VC activity. Clean men in well-lit, pleasant huts measured the ranges of enemy 120mm mortars and 122mm rockets. Pins got stuck into maps. Nicely typed orders went down the line, laying out sequences and schemes. It all made perfect sense at division and maybe brigade. But below that? It devolved into more hot, draining walking around, looking for Charlie.

"The intelligence sharing with the guys further down was nonexistent," Chuck Hagel said. "I don't think even a lot of our senior sergeants were told much. I don't know how far down the officer corps got [intelligence] on what was going on," he surmised. "Of course we were never told everything."[12] Maybe the higher-ups knew. But like the VC, they weren't telling.

So on the morning of March 28, Company B waded into the bamboo and greenery fringing the old French Michelin Company's Binh Son rubber plantation. After a draining morning of slashing brush, stepping and halting, sweating and sighing, all the Americans had to show for their toil was an uninteresting nest of eight long-abandoned VC bunkers. The written logs at the various command posts all read the same: NSTR. Nothing significant to report. The Hagels hacked on.

ABOUT NOON, the Americans had about ten yards to go to reach a shallow stream, a "blue line," as the soldiers called it, based on how it appeared on a standard military map. Once he sent the point element and then the lead platoon across, the company commander could halt the company, form a tight security perimeter, and fill canteens. Water sure sounded good. Maybe guys might want to gulp down a can of Cs, although in the enervating heat, the desire to drink pushed aside most thoughts of eating. As Rudyard Kipling once wrote of the British regulars slogging through tropical India: "If you wish to talk of slaughter you will do your work on water."[13] Amen, Gunga Din.

In Vietnam, creek water, no matter how clean it looked, swarmed with nasty microbes. It had to be purified with halazone tablets. The additive gave the water a very strong chlorine tang, like gulping a mouthful from the local public swimming pool. But thirsty riflemen could live with that.[14] Canteens nearly empty, the men smelled the stream before they saw it.

With the little watercourse a few steps away in the convoluted foliage, the captain stopped the column—time to swap out the point. The Hagels had been at it all morning. Another pair got the nod. The two chosen riflemen jostled past the brothers. Chuck and Tom Hagel stood in place, perspiration shining on their faces, to let the file pass them. When they saw their squad come by, they'd fall in.

Up front, barely seen, the new point team moved out. No machete noises now—it sounded like they'd found a narrow trail, some broken bush, maybe from animals, or local farmers, that led right to the brook. If you looked up, right and left, perpendicular to the approaching American file, you could see the break in the tall trees, a dirty gray-yellow sky. In a month or two, monsoon rains would fill up the calf-deep rivulet to chest height. Today, though, the stream ran slow and shallow, more evident on the map than the ground. But the gap in the treetops marked its course.

A hundred yards back, at the distant end of the snaking file of sweating Americans, the drag man turned around, rotating like a weather vane in a breeze. But there was no breeze. Man, that stream, that welcome water, couldn't come too soon. No words could be heard, simply the cracking of brush and the soft, wet swishing of overloaded men breasting through dense foliage. A little bit more, a few minutes to go—just lean into it. The two in the lead should be about at the blue line now.

Wham!

The point man, Corporal John T. Summers III, blew back like a rag doll. So did the slack man, and Chuck Hagel, and Tom Hagel, and another dozen soldiers, the entire lead squad and most of the next bowled onto their backsides by a giant's hot hand. A thin curtain of gray dust rose and hung over the trickling waterway.

Shouldn't have used that damn trail . . .

One AK opened up on auto. Crack-crack-crack-crack. Others joined in, filling the air with metallic hammering. No RPD machine gun yet, but the Americans had men down, and nobody could see anything. Twigs and leaves and bamboo slivers clipped off as the insistent AK slugs whizzed by. Some zipped past at ear level—not good at all.

A few Americans shot back, not many, not enough. The AK-47 shots all came from up ahead. And the U.S. riflemen at that end were down and dazed. How does a single file sort that out? This could be why the Infantry School manual warned about using this long, strung-out formation due to "limited firepower to front and rear."[15] Too true. In the book, decisive little arrows showed how to swing around to the side and bring up machine guns and riflemen. In this undergrowth, you had to be kidding.

The captain and his NCOs did what they could, angling up a few able men. After a very long minute or two, a pig, an M60 machine gun in the hands of a confident gunner, ran through a belt, tearing holes in the low bushes up near the bad guy side of the stream. On the radio, the captain called for artillery. Something went awry—seemed like it often did when push came to shove. No artillery rounds fell. Mercifully, while the Americans floundered, Charlie slipped away. These U.S. troops sure weren't going anywhere for quite a while.

The AKs had stopped for a few minutes before the platoon sergeants ordered the Americans to cease fire. The hot, dim jungle settled. Breathing hard, hyperalert, the riflemen faced outward, every other man turned right or left. Was Charlie gone? Would he be back?

You could hear leaves rustling. Guys snapped new magazines into their M16 rifles. Radios hummed with indistinct chatter. And groaning.

Not a sound came from the crumpled John Summers. The eighteen-year-old African American, a regular army volunteer, sure had been a good point man, quiet and steady. After taking the full impact of hundreds of red hot ball bearings (BBs) from a set of Claymore mines—stolen from Americans, or Chinese knock-offs, who knew or cared—Summers was gone. It didn't look like there'd be an open casket back in Baltimore, Maryland.[16]

Tom Hagel stumbled to his feet and glanced behind him. Brother Chuck, eyes wide, lay on his back. Every time Chuck breathed out, a bit of blood bubbled up from his shrapnel-peppered chest. Tom grabbed Chuck's compression bandage from his brother's web gear. The younger brother slapped it on the gurgling wound and pressed down. Blood seeped out on the edges. Specialist 5 Phillip Rogers, the company's trusted senior medic, and thus "Doc" to all, materialized beside a drooping nipa palm. Rogers handed Tom two more field dressings. Then the medic moved forward to treat others.[17]

Tom mashed down on his brother's chest. Stop the bleeding. That's what they taught you back at Fort Bliss. He tied off the first bandage.

Then he bore down and tied off another. Then for good measure, he leaned on Chuck's chest and applied a third. That army training, the hours of doing it and doing it with a drill sergeant right in your ear, paid off.

As Tom staunched Chuck's bleeding, he noticed a twinge in his left arm. The elbow was a bloody mess. His shoulder also showed red leaks. More of those blazing BBs, it appeared. The VC must have rigged up a half dozen Claymores, right at head level in trees, facing that trace of a crossing site. "The reason we got blown up," Tom said, "is that we walked on the trail."[18] Take a shortcut, pay the price. Both Hagels knew better. But the captain took a risk. And the bill came due immediately.

From the side, a hand, another medic, passed Tom another bandage. He tied it off on his own elbow. Next to him, Chuck sat up. He wasn't okay, but given the state of the others, he was at least conscious and mobile and, in a pinch, able to shoot back. The Hagel brothers rolled over and faced outboard with their rifles—one left, one right.

At the front end of the ragged file, Doc Rogers and the other medics worked on the casualties. To ease pain, delay the onset of shock, and quiet the wounded, no small thing with VC in the neighborhood, Rogers jabbed those worse off with a 5cc morphine syrette, a tiny toothpaste-style tube with a needle and the drug inside. If a man received such a shot, the medic who gave it hung the little injector on the fatigue shirt collar. It kept men from getting too much morphine.[19] The medical corpsmen also started intravenous drips. They wrapped gauze and bandages, plugging gushing holes, blocking horrific cuts, and tying off the heavy packings.

As the French army first taught it in the Napoleonic Wars, Doc Rogers did triage, the separation into thirds. Poor Summers was dead, and thankfully, nobody else looked "expectant," which is to say, so far gone that working on them wasted medics' time and precious medical supplies. Another bunch would make it, but required treatment sometime soon. Both Hagels fell into this group, although Chuck certainly needed a good going over with an X-ray machine, then cleaning up and stitches. Finally, there were those whom the medics could coax into surviving, in some cases just barely, until they could be evacuated. Those who showed up alive at a field hospital usually made it. During the Vietnam War, the army said their doctors and nurses saved 98 percent of them.[20] It sure was a comforting statistic—if evacuated.

That was a big "if." On that dank, bathtub-warm midday, Company B had penetrated into the deep jungle, with a full verdant canopy soaring overhead. No medevac helicopters could land in this tangled wilderness. In certain situations, the soldiers might pool their C4 plastic explosives and blow down trees to clear a circle. But jungle this thick defied a few blocks of C4. Making a landing zone in such a godforsaken place required something like an M121 Daisy Cutter, a 10,000-pound megabomb trundled off the back ramp of a C-130 Hercules transport plane. That thing could blow out a 150-foot clearing. In March of 1968, though, the M121 ordnance still lingered in testing.[21] So that wasn't going to happen.

When the first medevac chopper arrived overhead, clattering above the treetops, the UH-1 Huey pilots offered to use their onboard hoist to lower Stokes litters.[22] As some men had exposed bones and missing arms and legs, that seemed like a decent compromise. The badly wounded would never make it being lugged out for six hours on slippery, jouncing stretchers. Plus, given the number of immobile casualties, more than half of Company B would be carrying stricken buddies. Defending the column would be pretty problematic. The VC lived to tear up that kind of vulnerable target.

So out by hoist it must be. Summers and the rest had already paid full price to buy this crack of a creek bed. Looking up, soldiers could see the bottom of the Huey hanging overhead. While their mates pulled security facing outward, about ten of Company B's fit and near-fit soldiers went at it with machetes, knives, and the edges of e-tools. As well as they could, the men cut away enough underbrush to widen that patch where the trail met the blue line. From that wet, muddy bottom of the green chimney, the wounded would ascend.

Doc Rogers nodded his head. He had ten to go out, including Summers. The dust-off aviators never wanted to pull out the deceased.

But as Rogers pointed out, as an enlisted medic, he couldn't formally declare anybody dead. Only a physician could do so. Rogers let Summers go last, as he was past caring, and it got him safely out of the jungle and off the hands of the beaten-up company. The captain got on the radio. Lower away.

Down through the greenery came a wobbling Stokes litter, a stretcher inside a wire-mesh basket braced by a tubular metal frame seven feet long, two feet wide, and eight inches deep. The chopper's downdraft spun the thing like a slow propeller. Doc Rogers and the platoon medics guided it down and strapped in the first wounded soldier, a man with a reddened bandage-swathed stump for a right leg. As Tom Hagel remembered, the bright blood looked "like Campbell's tomato soup."[23] It took about twenty minutes from the first appearance of the device until the laden basket cleared the treetops. At tremendous hazard, the Huey hovered stationary overhead. Thankfully, the VC did nothing.

So the Stokes litter lifts began. The effort took a lot longer than anyone expected. The army rated the Huey to haul six litter patients, but not the basket types, and not in the drenching humidity and shimmering heat in the jungle southeast of Bear Cat, Vietnam.[24] Airborne medics, essential to stabilize the patients, used up vital weight, too. Straining their engines and gulping fuel to do so, each helicopter loitered overhead, pulled out one man, then headed back to Long Binh Post to the helipad at the 24th Evacuation Hospital.[25] The tenth, eternally silent Summers, left about 5:45, just before sunset.

SPENDING THE ENTIRE AFTERNOON pulling out casualties reduced the options for the company commander. He might have had his troops rip out more of the overgrown plants and bushes to spread into a legitimate perimeter, clear fields of fire, scratch out some soggy foxholes, and settle in Company B for a night defense. But that presumed Company B to be fresh, alert, and fully manned, rather than drained, dazed, and short on numbers. The catastrophic bloodying at the brook stunned the Americans into a dull stupor. Instead, the soldiers lapsed into the same old, same old inculcated as far back as basic training. They focused only on the here and now. They pulled static security, watching for Charlie, as the wire baskets slowly fell and rose. Their universe closed in to the next ten yards, the next ten minutes. Hold this ground. Send up the Stokes litters. Get our wounded out.

So now, too many hours later, that was complete. Now what? To stay in an unprepared thicket invited the VC to finish off the work the Claymores started. True, nobody had seen Charlie all day—who ever did—and nobody had heard from him since the shoot-out after the explosion. But it was like swimming in the ocean. Just because you didn't see the sharks, it didn't mean they didn't see you. The VC were out there. They loved the night, too.

With the sun going down, the Americans had to get moving. Few relished the prospect of chopping a route out from the fatal stream-bed. The captain well understood, thanks to the day's painful tute-lage, not to try the morning's already slashed path. Charlie surely had rigged that up already.[26] Company B faced a long night trek to reach a decent-sized opening along Route 15.

Like a few more of those less seriously cut up, both Hagels re-mained with the company. Categorized as walking wounded, they had to get out under their own power. As the brothers and the rest of the riflemen stood up and got ready to go, the company commander sought Tom and Chuck.

"Can you guys make it?" the officer asked.

Both Hagels said they could. The captain stood there, hesitating. He spoke again.

"Can you get back on point and lead us out?"[27]

So there it was. A superpower at war, a half million men in coun-try, the famous 9th Infantry Division charging hither and yon apply-ing Major General Julian J. Ewell's patented "excruciating pressure" to the enemy, and it came to this. Forty-odd smoked, scared infantry-men counted on a nineteen-year-old and a twenty-one-year-old—both bloodied up, neither in the army an entire year yet—to get them out to safety.

The U.S. Army put itself in this mess. The official table of organization depicted Company B as having 164 soldiers, including 6 officers and 50 NCOs.[28] Units came to Vietnam that way. But after arrival as a cohesive unit, a year later, the individual replacement system took hold—the insidious widgets and screws drill—and the numbers went haywire. The paper total, the "aggregate," in adjutant general lingo, ran right around 164, full strength. But, of course, once you deducted the sixth joining up or departing, the sixth headed out or returning from R&R, the men recovering from minor wounds, the guys at division sniper school or the like, the men fixing the M113s (a unique drain on mechanized outfits), and the sick, lame, and lazy, somehow 164 at the base camp became 60 out in the bush. And then the VC voted with hot metal, as they did to Company B around midday on March 28, 1968.

On top of the overall short-handed roster, the lack of experienced sergeants hurt more. During Vietnam, the army's best NCOs came into country as each division and separate brigade deployed. After a year, when the formed units disintegrated, the veteran sergeants left Vietnam. As they did, some backfill sergeants came out from the training centers, stateside outfits, European divisions, and other nooks and crannies of the service.[29] Even so, the figures never quite matched up.

Juggling the books, the army had no choice but to tap the first batch again. By 1968, the initial wave of sergeants, the 1965–66 Vietnam deployers, were just starting to get orders for round two in Vietnam. Some of the senior sergeants, veterans of World War II and Korea, had enough, and exercised their right to retire at or after twenty years of service. Other older men, especially in the infantry, bore wounds and injuries that disqualified them for grueling duties in a rifle company. Plus, more new units had been added to the rolls, and each of them required a replacement rack of NCOs, too.[30] The green machine found itself staring at a yawning gap between sergeants needed and NCOs available.

As MACV strength rose, the army brought in enlisted volunteers and draftees by the hundreds of thousands, by definition all "privates and second lieutenants" in the words of General Creighton Abrams, MACV deputy commander in early 1968. The army didn't have a proportionate number of solid sergeants, and no way to get them unless President Johnson mobilized the entire National Guard and Army Reserve. He did not. As for growing the NCOs over time, well, it took five years to develop a buck sergeant, ten to create a squad leader, and fifteen to make a platoon sergeant. They just weren't there, and they would never be there, unless the war lasted two decades.[31] That wasn't much of a plan.

So like so many others in country, Company B played short. The unit had some fine NCOs: First Sergeant Martin M. Garcia, Sergeant First Class William N. Butler, Sergeant First Class Lawrence E. Pugh, Sergeant First Class William E. Smith, Specialist 5 Phillip Rogers. As Chuck Hagel stated: "The senior sergeants were the reassuring, calming guys. And in many cases, many cases, these were the guys that didn't fall apart."[32] Under fire, the privates and the young officers watched the steady older sergeants. As they went, so went the company.

But a rifle platoon had at most a single experienced sergeant first class or staff sergeant, maybe one buck sergeant with some time, and all the rest young guys.[33] With or without enough veteran sergeants, though, squads still must be led. Somebody had to take charge. As a result, the old imperative took over. Again, the prescience of Basic Combat Training applied. The smart, strong, large, and alert rose to take charge, to lead the way in the field. Both Hagel brothers fit that description. The two were acting NCOs almost from the day Tom arrived, "the fighting Hagel brothers," as the younger one put it.[34] They could be trusted.

Moreover, they wanted to be trusted. They sought point and slack duties. As Chuck said, he "always felt a little better" with him and Tom in the lead. Fellow Company B soldier Edward E. "Gene" Bacon, with two years of college under his belt, explained why. Chuck came across as "very articulate, very bright" and "commanded real respect from the officers right away." Tom, too, stood out. He made the other soldiers laugh. Exceptionally well read and perceptive, he asked the right questions before and during missions. And he never forgot anything.[35]

To THESE TWO, the captain entrusted the fate of the truncated ranks of Company B. Tom Hagel knew the company had to "chop our way out—*every step of the way* [italics in original]." With the light fading, Chuck led on what he later called "the path of most resistance," right through the heaviest vegetation. Better bamboo than booby traps. Tom pulled slack, compass in hand.

Chuck whanged away with the machete. Before each cut, he scanned the darkening shrubbery. Tom hung close in the dusk.

About twenty-five yards from the start, Tom spat out urgent words in a low tone: "Stop. Don't move." Chuck immediately froze in place, no answer, fist up. Tom raised his fist, too, and the gesture rippled down the file, right out of the Fort Benning infantry manual. Halt.

There. There it gleamed in the fading light, a gossamer filament. Trip wire? Looked like it. So the VC had in fact been right nearby, the hungry sharks skimming just past where you could see them. They left this piece of death behind.

Tom traced the taut string to a can nailed to the crotch of a thin softwood tree trunk. From the can's open mouth, like an evil chick ready to hatch, poked the top of an American M26 hand grenade.[36] Very sporting of us to supply both sides. If Tom pulled the wire, the pinless grenade would slide out, its handle would pop off, and four seconds later, goodbye Hagel brothers.

Tom studied the thing like a surgeon sizing up an especially tricky open abdomen. With trip wires, a point man had three choices, all perilous. He could cut the wire, which left the grenade in its hole, harmless. Sometimes, though, Mr. Charles rigged the lines so that releasing tension blew the device. It might be possible to avoid the snare, and swing wide of it. But the VC liked to use more than one. Any attempted bypass could run into more booby traps, and thus be equally deadly. Finally, and most tricky of all, a soldier might attempt to remove the grenade and keep the handle down, then toss it far aside to blow in the distance. In this twilight stretch of jungle, with low-hanging branches all around, such a throw might very well bounce back in your face.

Tom went with cutting the cord.

Nothing.

He and Chuck then sidestepped quietly away.[37] The file followed. Like they used to say at Fort Bliss: "Pay attention, soldier." The life you save may be your own . . . and your brother's.

NOT LONG BEFORE MIDNIGHT, one by one, the company's riflemen emerged from the rough green treeline into the cleared area along Route 15. Along the highway, America's big Rome plows had clear-cut the jungle. Out among the stumps and deadfall, the battered riflemen looped into a wide circle. Men took a knee and exhaled. It had been a wearing night march through the swaddling, steaming vegetation, darker than dark. For most of the long row of exhausted soldiers, as Tom noted, "All you could do was hold to the back strap of the one in front."[38] But the Hagels got it done. Company B made it.

Within a half hour or so, helicopters fluttered down onto the makeshift pickup zone. A night lift was unusual, but the company had taken quite a beating. Fortunately, one of Ewell's many initiatives required helicopter crews to fly more night missions. Two decades later, army aviators used purpose-designed night-vision goggles for such tasks. In 1968, they took risks by relying on onboard lighting, ambient horizon glow, sticking to familiar routes, and taking it slow.[39] Lucky for Company B, the aviators capably dealt with the cleared shoulder of Route 15. The Hagels and the rest flew back to Bear Cat.

The company's mission amounted to a failure, redeemed only by the successful extraction of all those hit. In a war impelled by a strategy of attrition, carried out by young Americans on individual one-year deployments directed by but a few veteran front-line leaders and opposed by a guerrilla foe who opened almost nine of ten engagements, Company B's vexing day matched far too many similar experiences. Yes, the U.S. infantry drove off the VC and held the field, a traditional mark of victory in conventional wars. But once the stricken departed, so did Company B.[40] If that was winning . . .

On the 9th Infantry Division scoreboard, the stark numbers spoke for themselves: one U.S. killed, fourteen U.S. wounded, VC body count zero. The dispassionate analysts at division G-2 rated the VC K-34 Artillery Battalion as "combat effective" and not located with any precision beyond somewhere in southeast Bien Hoa Province. But to throw the beat-up 2-47th a bone, and perhaps spare Lieutenant Colonel Tower the considerable wrath of Ewell, the intel staffers found that "the measure of success" for the March 28 firefight and related operations lay in this finding: "The enemy had not been able to renew his offensive attacks against Saigon despite rumors and intelligence reports that such attacks had been planned."[41] Five weeks later, events in greater Saigon put paid to that hopeful supposition.

At his level, Chuck Hagel harbored no illusions. In a multipage letter home, he excoriated Tower's "asinine policies," mentioned the enemy's use of "ingenious homemade booby traps, constructed with our material," and wrote that it resulted in fifteen men wounded. He didn't mention Summers, killed in action.[42] In World War II, some lieutenant might well have censored every one of those burning lines out of Hagel's missive. But by Vietnam, that no longer happened. It wasn't the whole story, but it was all Betty Hagel was going to get, and probably more than she wanted.

WITHIN AN HOUR of landing at Bear Cat, the brothers arrived at the 50th Medical Company's clearing station, and then found themselves packed into another bird, headed to the 24th Evac at Long Binh.[43] They got there well after midnight.

The 24th Evac had already seen the rest of Company B. Some kept right on going, heading for Japan. A few stayed over, as doctors and nurses worked to keep them going long enough to fly out. The Hagels showed up in the receiving area, two filthy, bloodstained, bone-tired, gaunt, hungry young men in a well-lit facility. To the over-worked medical people, some of them female Nurse Corps officers, the brothers must have resembled hoboes in jungle fatigues.

Under the bright lights of the treatment suite and the knowing gaze of the experts, the clumsy, messy field dressings on Chuck and Tom stood out as amateur efforts, kindergarten finger-painting in-truding into the studio of master artists. Without a word of judgment, the medical people went to work. The blood-crusted, sweat-stained wrappings went away to be burned.

Cleaning up took a few hours. Both men got washed thoroughly, not as pleasant as it sounds. Infantrymen accumulate a lot of grime. Hospitals don't approve. So hot water and scrubbing took a while.

The doctors—real physicians, not the brave but much less well-trained field medics—dug a lot of ball bearings out of both men. Because Chuck's scatter pattern hit him smack over the heart and lungs, the diggers left a few in there, nestled between the ribs. "And so it's interesting when I get chest x-rays," Chuck noted later.[44]

To be sure nothing became infected by the ubiquitous tropical germs of Vietnam, the brothers both stayed a few blessed days. The price of admission for this hotel ran pretty high. But it had its pluses: food, rest, the presence of women (admittedly mostly officers). The leaders at 24th Evac understood that riflemen had it tough. If two nights under clean sheets helped, all to the good.

This is when Chuck found time to write his family his long letter about the incident. Author Myra MacPherson read it years later, and referred to the way both Hagels explained their experiences to their worried mother Betty and brothers Mike and Jimmy as *The Hardy Boys Go to Vietnam*.[45] While few could dispute MacPherson's deep insight into the Vietnam generation as a whole and the brothers Ha-gel in particular, she owed the guys a bit more credit. Chuck to a great extent, and Tom for sure, had plenty to write about some rather disturbing aspects of the war. Where they pulled up short involved all references to their own personal experiences. Some of it reflected their upbringing. Young men from small towns in Nebraska didn't trash-talk or beat their chests. Things happened, you stated them plainly, and you moved on. In addition, both Chuck and Tom were looking out for their single mom, already carrying a hell of a burden.

What else could they do? No civilian would ever understand the real deal. And if you loved them, you made sure they did not:

> It's time now for another episode in "Surprise Surprise."
> I hope you haven't received anything from the Army as
> yet. [She had not.] But (oh yes, light a Camel, get a cup of
> hot coffee, and then sit down) your two sons have earned
> a distinguished medal, the Purple Heart. Now please stay
> calm.[46]

Hagel went on to explain that he received "a pellet" in his chest "which was no problem" and Tom got "a pellet" in his elbow "which was easily popped out." Those statements were true, but greatly understated the number and impact of scalding ball bearings that slammed into each man. Chuck went on: "So No Problems. No sweat!" And then he invoked "the Good Lord, the Saints, Dad" for their evident efforts to keep the brothers safe.[47] It was one way to describe the outcome.

Both brothers, then and now, downplayed their injuries. "Our wounds were no big deal," said Chuck later. "There was nothing that was life-threatening." But Tom, ever thoughtful when he had time, remembered the rest of the awful scene: streaks of blood swirling in the stream, bright red swathes smeared on spring green leaves, the abject confusion, soldiers too stunned to talk, others unable to stop moaning, the men down, some without legs, a few without faces, the one who didn't make it, and then that long, slow walk out through darker woods than Dante Alighieri ever imagined on the lip of hell. "It was one of the most terrible times," said Tom.[48]

Tom got at the deeper meaning of the wounding, one seen a quarter century earlier by another rifleman in a jungle war, Corporal James Jones of Company F, 2nd Battalion, 27th Infantry Regiment, 25th Infantry Division. Later the acclaimed author of the novels *From Here to Eternity* and *The Thin Red Line*, Jones thought hard about what it meant to get hit by the enemy. "They had crossed this strange line," he wrote of the wounded.[49] They knew something that those not struck would never know.

The infantryman's war in Vietnam, like the way into Dante's pit of hell, passed through descending circles: arrival in country, first live patrol, first contact with the enemy, first wounded friendly seen, first wounded foe encountered, first dead GI right there, first dead VC observed, first time shooting back, first prisoner taken, first enemy shot close enough to recognize him as a man, and first time wounded. There was only one more step. Those who took it, like John Summers of Baltimore—well, they never reported back.

That was the line Jones mentioned. Now the Hagels had stuck their toes across, and pulled them right back. But for a few minutes, they'd been there. For a lot of men, even those "lightly" wounded like the Hagels, once was enough. A good number of them never really went back to the war. They found ways out, some acceptable, some less so. It's easy to get the curious types, the bravado boys, to go to the first firefight. But the second, or the twenty-second, or the one after Charlie put a hole in your hide? No way. Yet Chuck and Tom went back.

Why?

The brothers returned to Company B because they figured out one of the dirty big secrets of the army. For all the laws, regulations, and orders, for the enlistment contracts sworn in front of the flag and the mandatory "greetings" of Selective Service, for the many articles in the Uniform Code of Military Justice, for all the bluster of generals and colonels and sergeants major, in the end, Americans in Vietnam who stayed at it, who kept going out to hunt Charlie, *chose* to do their duty. They chose it every day in country. They were not compelled, and could not be.

If you asked the Hagels (and people did, even in 1968), they'd say they did it for the country, or to honor their father, or to protect America. Yes, Old Glory gets you into the induction station. Out in the lethal greenwood southeast of Bear Cat, though, abstract patriotism doesn't go too far.

Soldiers don't fight for the grand old flag. They fight for each other. America shrinks to the men to the right and left willing to shoulder a rifle and go at it. They keep each other going. Chuck and Tom sure did.

Think about it. Does the threat of court-martial motivate a man to go out on patrol? Hardly. The worst army stockade offers three hots and a cot, and nobody stays there more than a few years, if that, just for shirking. As for officers or sergeants intimidating guys, or threatening to shoot them, well hell, the privates far outnumber the leaders. And every rifleman has his own loaded weapon. It almost never came to that, despite the fondest hopes of overwrought Hollywood screenwriters.

The low field strength of a rifle company in Vietnam, or in the world wars, Korea, Afghanistan, or Iraq for that matter, reflected those few, those tough few, willing to keep going. The faint hearts flaked off along the way, and the army let them. It was just as well. On patrol, nobody wants to hear that the man next in line doesn't care to fire his M16 today. Good men kept going. Chuck and Tom Hagel were such men.

So was John Summers.

IN THE WELL-KEPT WARD of the 24th Evac, the brothers had some time to catch up on the wider world. Like most soldiers in country, they relied on the *Stars and Stripes*, a semi-official daily newspaper that mixed accounts by uniformed military public affairs writers with wire service clippings and other articles drawn from the press in the United States. Because the *Stars and Stripes* sometimes went its own way, the generals didn't care for it. But the troops did. As Chuck said, "I don't know if there were really any other newspapers that we ever looked at or saw."[50]

The brothers paged through a stack of back issues. One caught their eye. The March 7, 1968, edition featured a big black front-page headline: "Youth Slain as Wallace Visit Ignites Violence in Omaha." A big photo showed Alabama governor George Wallace getting pelted by debris.[51]

What was George Wallace doing in Omaha? And why did his visit result in a riot? That kind of stuff didn't happen in Nebraska. Something had gone very wrong back home.

CHAPTER 6

Killshots

The war in Vietnam is but a symptom of
a far deeper malady within the American spirit,
and if we ignore this sobering reality . . .

DR. MARTIN LUTHER KING JR.
"A Time to Break the Silence"[1]

George Wallace flew with LeMay. In later days, when political pundits questioned how and why the presidential candidate selected the general as his running mate, it came back to that simple fact. Curtis LeMay commanded the Twentieth Air Force in the great 1945 fire-bombing campaign against the cities of imperial Japan. And Staff Sergeant George Corley Wallace Jr. flew as a flight engineer and gunner on a B-29 named *Li'l Yutz*.[2] Like Charles Dean Hagel, Wallace had been in on the fiery finale. He idolized the grim-visaged general who set the pace in those desperate times. When Wallace thought of a leader, he thought of LeMay. For the campaign of 1968, there could be no better choice to join Wallace's ticket as a candidate for vice president.

For the rest of his days, Wallace proudly touted his war record. Yet we don't remember George Wallace as a staff sergeant on a B-29 bomber crew. What we know instead is a man who began his tenure of office as governor in Montgomery, Alabama, bellowing:

"Segregation now, segregation tomorrow, segregation forever." Even as Wallace said those words in 1963, and stood in the doorway at the University of Alabama a few months later in a vain attempt to block racial integration, he was way behind the mood of the country.[3] Fellow southerners Harry S. Truman of Missouri, Dwight D. Eisenhower of Kansas and Texas, and Lyndon B. Johnson of Texas saw the future. Wallace stood in the door, but he looked only backward, to a past steeped in America's original sin of slavery.

By 1968, the angry little man from Alabama wanted to be president himself. Neither his own Democrats nor the opposition Republicans would have him. So he struck out on his own as the standard-bearer of the American Independent Party, which amounted to George Wallace and those who thought like him. In the tormented, fractured America of 1968, there were millions. Enough to elect Wallace? Probably not—even Wallace understood that.[4] But there were enough to get attention, maybe even force the 1968 election into the House of Representatives. The peace marchers and the civil rights activists had their day and their say. Wallace and his ilk demanded to be heard, too.

By Wallace's calculations, made with the care of an experienced B-29 flight engineer juggling fuel rates, his crooked road to the White House ran through the Corn Belt, notably Nebraska. Most of America saw that prairie state as farmland, Alabama with less cotton, more corn, and a folksy twang rather than a mellifluous drawl. But George Wallace saw Nebraska, Omaha especially, as the place he intended to make a point. Like the cagey old lawyer he was, he chose his venue with care. Wallace wasn't coming back to see Lincoln, where he met his bomber crew, or Offutt Air Force Base, where his former commander Curtis LeMay once ran the show in the house that SAC built. No, Wallace went to Omaha for one reason. He knew that North Omaha was a very restive African American neighborhood. And he aimed to do what he did best—stir the pot.

THERE WERE BLACK PEOPLE in Nebraska. They had been there from the beginning, with the first free African American arriving in Omaha in 1854, the year the city was incorporated. In 1968, African Americans amounted to a true minority, about 39,000, a bare 2.7 percent of the 1.4 million Nebraskans. Two-thirds of those black Nebraskans lived in Omaha, about 9 percent of the city's populace. Almost all of them resided in North Omaha.[5] It was de facto segregation, never done by law, but by practice. Officially Jim Crow never made it to the free soil of Nebraska. But Mr. Crow was alive and well in Omaha.

To hear the white citizens talk, African Americans lived in North Omaha because they just did. Why, some of white people's best friends were black. They came to visit all the time. Sure they did. They just happened to bring along mops and brooms and lawnmowers. But as for working with black people, going to church with black families, socializing with black folks, well, that pretty much happened . . . never. The city's cemetery was integrated, which boded well for the next life.[6] There was that.

In this life, before the 1960s, Omaha had endured one particularly vicious race riot. An enraged white mob attacked the Douglas County courthouse and lynched an African American man accused of rape. Somebody—rioters, police, soldiers—killed two white miscreants. Seven police officers suffered wounds. An unknown number of white and black people went to local hospitals for injuries. Black homes and businesses had been burnt.[7] After 1919, African Americans stayed in North Omaha: separate, but as in the southern states, hardly equal.

The realtors steered black families to North Omaha. Schools, churches, and businesses developed accordingly. African Americans in 1950s Omaha might aspire to a brand of genteel poverty, as long as they knew "their place." Americans celebrated jazz musicians like Louis Armstrong and baseball greats like Jackie Robinson. But look at pictures of American police officers, judges, astronauts, college alumni, or business executives from the era. Every face is white. A century after the violent emancipation of the American Civil War, that didn't cut it anymore.

One son of Omaha, Malcolm Little, took the name Malcolm X. He advocated violence to secure civil rights for African Americans, separate and truly equal by revolution.[8] Although he moderated his views prior to his assassination in 1965, a figure like Malcolm X terrified men like George Wallace. What if black Americans didn't know their place? What if they decided they wanted white America's share, and decided to go after it lock, stock, and barrel?

Fortunately for the people of Nebraska and America, black and white, the influence of firebrands like Malcolm X remained marginal. The civil rights movement took its lead, instead, from Doctor Martin Luther King Jr., a Baptist minister dedicated to advancing the cause of African Americans within the law when he could, by agitation when he must, but consistently by nonviolent means. King brought his soaring rhetoric to the Salem Baptist Church in North Omaha in 1958.[9] Like that other Baptist named John, King prepared the way for big things to come.

A brutal, bloody 1965 riot in the Watts district of Los Angeles marked a new wave of racial unrest in America. Chicago and Cleveland burned in the hot summer of 1966, with a hundred more cities to follow the next year.[10] Omaha did not escape.

On July 4, 1966, temperatures reached 103°. That evening, a thousand-plus young men gathered at North Twenty-fourth and Lake Streets in North Omaha. When about a hundred Omaha Police Department officers showed up to disperse the crowd, trouble erupted. Rowdies trashed two police cruisers, then went on a rampage up and down the streets. Men tossed Molotov cocktails into vacant buildings and looted storefronts. Damage cost owners millions of dollars. Governor Frank Morrison rolled in six companies of the Nebraska National Guard. When he later visited shot-up North Omaha, he called it "unfit for human habitation."[11] Morrison blamed the violence on unremediated poverty.

Omaha mayor Axel Vergman "Al" Sorenson disagreed. He attributed the entire situation to outside agitators, notably the Black Panthers, a violent nationalist organization in the tradition of Malcolm X at his most radical. It's unclear how big a part, if any, the Panthers played in the riot. But by August, Black Panthers guarded some key buildings in North Omaha.[12] That got attention in Washington.

To those concerned with American national security, Omaha wasn't just a city in Nebraska. The Strategic Air Command's headquarters at Offutt Air Force Base controlled the bulk of the country's nuclear deterrent force. A riot in Cleveland was a problem for the state of Ohio. A riot in Omaha threatened America's ability to keep the Soviet Union at bay. So the Federal Bureau of Investigation (FBI) paid very close attention to matters in Omaha.

Long-time FBI director J. Edgar Hoover, an institution unto himself in Washington, made his reputation busting gangsters in the 1930s, Nazi saboteurs in the 1940s, and Soviet spies in the 1950s. That last bunch remained only too active, and in Hoover's view, the red tentacles extended into the anti-war movement, such as the Students for a Democratic Society (SDS), and to disaffected African Americans like the Black Panthers. It only made sense, at least to Hoover. If the Moscow leadership wanted an uprising, an American equivalent of the Bolshevik revolution, why not allocate some expertise and money to the disaffected? The Soviet Union's active KGB foreign intelligence officers, joined by the GRU's military intelligence operatives, did just enough to convince Hoover he had it right.[13] That attribution of some kind of master plot gave comfort to Hoover and those of similar mind, but it didn't match reality. In truth, Soviet intelligence people dealing with the various disparate American underground groups, including the SDS and Black Panthers, resembled ants atop a log rushing down whitewater rapids. The ants thought they were steering. Evidently, so did the FBI.

A far better understanding of the real problem behind the racial tension roiling Omaha could be found in a fifty-eight-minute documentary entitled *A Time for Burning*. Director William C. Jersey of San Francisco chronicled the efforts of the white Augustana Lutheran Church to reach out to embittered, embattled African Americans in North Omaha. In a telling comment, one minister quoted a parishioner: "This one lady said to me, 'pastor,' she said, 'I want them to have everything I have, I want God to bless them as much as he blesses me, but,' she says, 'pastor, I just can't be in the same room with them, it just bothers me.'"[14]

That's why George Wallace came to Omaha in 1968.

WALLACE ARRIVED IN Omaha on Sunday, March 3, 1968. About fifteen hundred supporters met him at the airport. In a follow-on press conference, Wallace stated that riots reflected the work of "militants, activists, communists, and revolutionaries" and that in his judgment "leaders and sympathizers of militant civil rights organizations are communists."[15] Expecting trouble, Mayor Al Sorenson assigned four uniformed police officers to Wallace, who also brought his own security team. The police added both uniformed and off-duty officers to the rally set for Monday night at the Omaha Civic Auditorium.

When it came time for the gathering, the house was rocking. A thousand Wallace supporters occupied folding chairs on the auditorium's main floor. Thousands more filled the balcony. Into this scene marched fifty young protestors, most of them black men, carrying anti-Wallace signs. The Wallace people let in the demonstrators and ensured they found a place in front. The Alabama governor relished the upcoming confrontation. Wallace delayed his speech for an hour as the crowd shouted at the interlopers. The protestors held their positions but did not reply. That seemed to upset many of the Wallace faithful. The rain of insults continued, more and more vicious, and full of vile epithets heard today only in certain unsavory rap songs. It was like letting a pressure cooker build up steam. Both sides knew it, too.

When Wallace came out, the crowd responded with an enthusiastic wave of applause. The governor raised his arms for quiet, then began his address. Down to his front, the fifty objectors waved their signs, but Wallace kept right on going. His American Independent Party needed 750 signatures to get on the Nebraska ballot for president. It looked like Wallace would get them.

He got more than he bargained for. Ignored and frustrated, their chants unheeded, some of the protestors tore up their signs and began throwing the pieces, to include the wooden sticks, at the podium. That did it.

On the dais, Wallace stopped speaking. He covered his face. His guards stepped up to shield him. Young African American reporter David Rice, representing the rather sketchy underground publications *Asterisk* and *Buffalo Chip*, tried to quell the rain of debris. For his troubles, he earned a faceful of mace from an undercover police officer. Other police began to usher the protestors out of the hall. Enraged Wallace enthusiasts swung their metal folding chairs, whacking the greatly outnumbered young men as the police tried to get them outside.[16]

Within an hour, North Omaha rose up. Looting became widespread, with a dozen plate-glass storefronts shattered and ten shops aflame. Two city buses had windows knocked out. The night rang with gunfire, sirens, and tinkling glass. Caught by surprise, the Omaha Police Department scrambled to get officers into the neighborhood.

Inside one darkened pawnshop, off-duty police officer James Frank Abbott confronted Howard L. "Butch" Stevenson, age sixteen. Stevenson appeared suddenly, hopping in through a smashed front window. Abbott hollered, "Hold it." Stevenson kept right on going. The officer pumped out one 12-gauge shotgun shell at point-blank range. Hot pellets punched fatal holes in young Stevenson's torso. The looter was unarmed.[17]

Stevenson's death kept the kettle bubbling the next day. Students at Horace Mann Junior High (95 percent African American) smashed windows and set fire to shrubbery and grass as police stood by. At Central High School, police officers broke up a demonstration, arresting several students, including star basketball player Dwaine Dillard. On March 9, Central had to play short-handed for the state championship in a final game moved at the last minute to more tranquil Lincoln. Central lost, another casualty of the unrest.[18]

This time, the National Guard never left their armories. The fires burned out. The police tallied one dead, thirteen injured (two of them Wallace backers), and nine arrests.[19] For his part, George Wallace got his signatures and his media exposure and scuttled off.

The FBI Omaha Field Office dutifully reported its version of the unrest.[20] That unhappy summary went directly to President Lyndon B. Johnson. Already wrestling with the quagmire in Vietnam, LBJ faced the front end of yet another long, hot summer on top of the urban horrors of 1965, 1966, and 1967. Wallace reminded him of the political threat from the reactionary right. Others in his own Democratic Party outflanked him to his left. Johnson lamented: "I sometimes felt that I was living in a continuous nightmare."[21] He was. And so were the rest of those he routinely addressed as his fellow Americans.

LYNDON JOHNSON RESPECTED the experts. He didn't always listen to them, but he had long ago determined that the most difficult policy decisions worked best when underwritten by the opinion of a blue-ribbon panel. Even as LBJ's hand-picked wise men contemplated the way ahead in Vietnam, the bad news from Omaha had the president reaching back to the last set of recommendations he'd gotten from a previous line-up of great American minds. The findings landed on Johnson's desk on February 29, 1968, a few days before Omaha blew up again.

The president had been expecting it, and knew the report would not be good. In the summer of 1967, as Detroit and Newark smoldered, LBJ tapped Governor Otto Kerner Jr. of Illinois to form the National Advisory Commission on Civil Disorders. In World War II, Kerner proved himself as a major in the 34th Field Artillery Battalion under the command of then-Lieutenant Colonel William C. Westmoreland. Now he stepped forward to try to figure out why America's cities burned every summer. Ten other prominent Americans joined the effort. The Kerner Commission represented a nice balance of America's sensible center, balancing white and black members, Democrats and Republicans, labor and industry, and city, state, and federal levels. The fringe nuts, the George Wallace people and the ghetto rabble-rousers, did not receive invitations.

The group's verdict proved stark. "Our nation is moving toward two societies, one black, one white—separate and unequal."[22] The only answer appeared to be a massive commitment of government resources to remedy the problem. Anything less than an urban Manhattan Project, an inner-city Apollo moonshot program, promised more of the same for decades.

For LBJ, it amounted to another kick in the teeth. If Tet upended the president's war in Vietnam, the Kerner Commission's pessimistic conclusion reflected abject failure in the war on poverty. Like the damn North Vietnamese, poverty looked to have the upper hand. And as in Vietnam, the underlying conditions played America false. Johnson's 1964 Civil Rights Act and 1965 Voting Rights Act finished de jure racial segregation. The administration's Great Society—Head Start for little children, Medicare for seniors, Medicaid for the poor, decent housing for the cities—seemingly struck at de facto racial divides. But as in Vietnam, the metrics all represented U.S. resources going in. What came out? Watts 1965. Chicago 1966. Detroit 1967. And now Omaha 1968. Laws and spending couldn't change hearts and minds in middle America, any more than bombs and bullets could do so in Southeast Asia.

In his very public turn against the war on April 4, 1967, Martin Luther King Jr. had warned that the fixation on Vietnam forestalled necessary reckoning at home.[23] He spoke as America's best self, the national superego telling us what we should be. And George Wallace surely croaked as the country's rotten id, demanding a return to a past that never really was. In the middle stood LBJ, U.S. ego personified, a man who consistently projected strength, yet harbored an inner character fissure as big as the jagged channel of the Pedernales River near his south central Texas roots. All the bills came due that grim March of 1968.

ON MARCH 10, the *New York Times* exposed the military's 206,000 troop request. The fine print mentioned ideas about ground incursions on the Ho Chi Minh Trail and the need to mobilize the national guardsmen and service reservists. Half of the requested troops would go to Vietnam, with the rest slated to meet U.S. worries about other hot spots like Korea, NATO's central front, and the Middle East. Nobody read any of that. All they saw were those huge black screaming headlines: "Westmoreland Requests 206,000 More Men, Stirring Debate in Administration."[24] More. More. More.

On March 12, the Democrats of New Hampshire cast 42 percent of their votes for a little-known Minnesota senator named Eugene McCarthy. LBJ won—of course he did, he was the sitting president, the architect of the massive 1964 Democratic Party landslide. But this guy McCarthy, backed by hundreds of earnest door-knocking young men and women shorn of long hair and love beads, "clean for Gene," made his point. McCarthy ran explicitly as "not Johnson," and implicitly on getting the United States out of Vietnam.[25] McCarthy was his own man, a quixotic figure in every way.

Yet in the returns coming from New Hampshire, LBJ saw not the Minnesotan, but the smiling countenance of Senator Robert F. Kennedy of New York. The dead JFK, and now the very live RFK, hovered just out of reach, dogging Johnson, rebuking him, mocking him. The debonair Harvards would have done it right. The Harvards would have done it better. They'd have wrapped up Vietnam, soothed the stewing black ghettos, and gotten a U.S. flag on the moon already, and likely put one on Mars to boot.

The day after New Hampshire, RFK told reporters: "I am now reassessing my position."[26] Of course he was. Johnson felt vindicated— he'd long expected Bobby Kennedy to jump into the race—but that offered nothing to help him meet the upcoming challenge to his presidency. Wallace loomed to the right, Kennedy to the left, and out on the other end, the Republicans turned to the wily Richard M. Nixon, back from the political graveyard.

The polls, notably the respected Gallup survey, also augured peril. In 1967, as MACV sought the casualty crossover point, us versus them, Americans continually backed the war about 60/40, with some erosion over the year. After Tet, war support briefly spiked as the citizens rallied around the flag. But by mid-March, that surge dissipated. About 40 percent, the doves, wanted peace. Another 60 percent, the hawks, wanted to "win," whatever that meant. And more than 60 percent, both hawks and doves, thought LBJ had bungled the whole shebang.[27] Any way you cut it, Johnson and his administration were slowly sinking.

By mid-month the president knew he had to act. He waited on the wise men to tell him the right answer, but he sensed what was coming. New secretary of defense Clark Clifford already had LBJ's ear. Clifford convinced the president that the Westmoreland strategy was bankrupt. The MACV commander had to go. On March 22, without fanfare, Johnson announced that Westmoreland would report back to Washington in June to take over as U.S. Army chief of staff.[28] Announced as a promotion, the press reported it as a relief, not a good thing in military circles. LBJ let it ride.

On March 25–26, the wise men gathered to report out. They told Johnson what he expected. Get out. The interim steps would be a bombing halt up north, negotiations, and "Vietnamization," turning the war over to ARVN, the exceedingly unexpected heroes of the Tet Offensive.[29] But those measures all amounted to temporizing, making the best of a bad bargain. Essentially, the United States had failed. Now it remained to be seen what might be salvaged.

On March 31, 1968, Johnson went on television to announce the change in strategy. He looked like he'd been horsewhipped. "Tonight" he intoned, "I want to speak to you of peace in Vietnam and Southeast Asia." He then calmly and slowly reviewed his stillborn prior peace initiatives, each rebuffed by Hanoi. But this time, the United States would act "unilaterally, and at once." "We are reducing," he said, "substantially reducing—the present level of hostilities." He explained the bombing halt. There would be no big troop influx, nor any ground attacks into Laos or Cambodia, and certainly not any thrusts into North Vietnam. He emphasized that America had "no intention of widening this war."

Johnson stated that he anticipated these U.S. actions would allow for peace talks, and he named the U.S. envoy, Averell Harriman, one of the wise men. The president mentioned a few more forces already tapped to deploy, including a small call-up of reserves. He also noted that even a war held to the new limits required additional taxes, never popular, especially in an election year. Finally, he turned to his own role. He saw resolving Vietnam as his key duty: "Accordingly, I shall not seek, and I will not accept, the nomination of my party for another term as your President."[30] Not only was America quitting, albeit in slow motion—Johnson, too, had thrown in the towel.

Four days later, it got worse.

DOCTOR MARTIN LUTHER KING JR. enjoyed the rare distinction of being tracked and vilified by both the Soviet KGB and the American FBI.[31] These rival organizations kept tabs on King. They didn't quite understand all he meant to America, especially black America. But they sure knew he was important.

So did James Earl Ray, a white petty criminal and drifter born in Alton, Illinois. Ray had once volunteered for the George Wallace campaign in North Hollywood, in Los Angeles, California. He didn't like African Americans. And he hated King. So on April 4, 1968, he killed him.[32]

Ray got away cleanly from Memphis, Tennessee, and he remained on the run for two months. The FBI's inability to say immediately who shot King, and the lengthy manhunt that followed, satisfied few across America. Many anguished African Americans suspected all manner of conspiracies, and the well-known antipathy of the FBI, George Wallace, and way too many white Americans offered fertile ground for speculation. President Lyndon Johnson and the other white American leaders said all the right things. Even George Wallace called the shooting a "senseless, regrettable, and tragic act."[33] But in restive inner cities, people weren't listening anymore.

Within hours of King's death, unrest spread across southwest Memphis. Baltimore, Chicago, and Washington followed suit, as did over a hundred other cities. State governors mobilized more than 50,000 guardsmen. The regular army sent in more than 23,000 soldiers.[34] America burned.

North Omaha went up, too. It didn't rate any regular army troops, but the Nebraska National Guard took to the streets. Nobody died, although there were injuries and property damage. The already beaten-up Twenty-fourth Street business corridor lost more stores. Up and down the thoroughfare, seemingly in every other building, plywood replaced plate glass. Burnt storefronts marked the path of the looters.[35] Twice in two months—when would it end?

Across the nation, the great riots of April 1968 cost 31 dead and 3,129 injured. Police arrested 16,268 suspects and fire departments responded to over 2,000 conflagrations. Along with Baltimore, Chicago, Memphis, Omaha, and Washington, the biggest disturbances occurred in Cincinnati, Detroit, Kansas City, Louisville, New York City, Pittsburgh, and Wilmington, Delaware.[36] Bad as things got—and they got very bad—this awful wave ended the grim annual cycle of inner-city riots that marred the 1960s. There'd be exceptions: Omaha in 1969, for one. The country's underlying racial distress had been suppressed, not resolved. And there were other societal demons, way too many, still unsatisfied.

In the halls of power in Washington and in divided, damaged cities across America, anxious civil authorities prepared for the worst. On the campaign trail, Bobby Kennedy called for understanding among all Americans. George Wallace demanded a crackdown on the affluent white hippies and belligerent black urban rioters. And Richard Nixon? He planned "to restore order and respect for law in this country."[37] He didn't mention race. But most Americans, black or white, got the message.

AFRICAN AMERICAN SOLDIERS in Vietnam got the message, and they didn't need to hear it from Richard Nixon, either. The United States might not be able to appoint a single black cabinet secretary, nor find a black federal district court judge, nor select even one black Apollo astronaut. But by God, those Selective Service draft boards sure made their numbers, right in accord with the population percentages. If you looked around any firebase in Vietnam, that became obvious. Thanks to de facto segregation—and not just in Omaha, Nebraska, either—most American communities might not look like America in a racial sense. But the army in Vietnam sure did.

The army even had a role in LBJ's Great Society, doing something for equal opportunity. In 1966, Secretary of Defense Robert McNamara introduced Project 100,000, designed to "rehabilitate" those he labeled the "subterranean poor." When measured on standardized tests—admittedly geared for those with the advantage of a good education—most Project 100,000 candidates hailed from the bottom third of the available manpower pool. Some were accepted from the bottom 10 percent of all recruits. By dropping the standards, to include waiving minor legal infractions, underprivileged youth could put on a uniform, get some discipline, and learn a skill, such as automotive repair or electronics maintenance. It amounted to the Job Corps with a GI haircut. Had America's army been at peace, or just pulling Cold War duties in West Germany and South Korea, that might have worked out. But with the Vietnam War going full tilt, it sent a lot of these marginal youths right into the line of fire. Of 354,000 inducted under this policy, 41 percent were African American. A post-war study rated the program as "less than successful" and noted that military service "doesn't appear to be the panacea for struggling youth."[38]

Chuck Hagel, an acting NCO by April of 1968, described the results of such assignments. He recalled: "You were having drafted into the Army guys that had their options. Either go to jail in Texas or New York or New Jersey or whenever, or go into the Army. So you didn't have the model soldier in the Army in 1968. And it showed."[39] The excesses of Project 100,000 gave credence to the often cited beliefs that the poor and the black fought the war while the wealthy and white stood aside. It wasn't so. But well-intentioned do-gooding like Project 100,000 led directly to these perceptions. Young African Americans in Vietnam drew their own conclusions about the war and "the Man."

The assassination of Martin Luther King Jr. shook Americans in uniform no less than those at home. Most soldiers, white and black, found it shocking, another indicator that the country was going mad back on the other side of the Pacific. Chuck Hagel remembered how it hit him and his fellow soldiers: "Everyone was silent."[40]

But even as these understandable reactions rippled across the force, it's important to keep in mind that MACV's battalions daily exhibited a casual degree of racism unthinkable in the U.S. military fifty years later. Many vehicles and bunkers flew Confederate flags, and few white men thought anything of it. Not often, but enough, the word "nigger" served as just another noun. Even certain sergeants and officers, not all from the south, either, resorted to the slur in speaking to or about African American troops. The majority, the decent leaders, didn't use the term or permit it. The less aware kept right on blabbing. And those who thought themselves slick split the difference, eschewing the insult in public and employing it when they guessed the black soldiers were out of earshot.[41] But combat troops have excellent hearing.

All too often, the official army didn't seem to notice that one in eight U.S. troops was African American. Photographs in field manuals and on instructional posters consistently displayed white males demonstrating the proper use of weapons and equipment. Soldiers of color usually didn't make an appearance, and if they did, their placement was clearly subordinate. Supply sergeants and those running the little post exchange huts hardly ever stocked magazines, hair care products, and hygiene items of interest to young black men. Even the USO shows rarely featured black entertainers—plenty of Joey Heatherton and Wayne Newton, not enough Lola Falana or James Brown, and certainly no Jimi Hendrix.[42] It all added up. It all grated.

There was more for those inclined to look, and after King's death, many young African Americans did. A lot of "dark green" troops appeared to get tagged for more than their share of work details: digging trenches, filling sandbags, and burning human waste. A notable fraction of "light green" soldiers seemed to end up shuffling papers in the headquarters. The officers would say such assignment choices reflected education, and maybe they did.[43] That simply rubbed jagged salt in a raw gash.

When frustrated African Americans looked up the chain of command, the number of black officers amounted to a fraction, a mere

4 percent of the entire U.S. Army officer corps, and almost all them lieutenants and captains.[44] There were higher-ranking officers of color like Major Colin Powell (G-3 for the Americal Division). There were even senior leaders like Brigadier General Frederic E. Davison, who commanded the 199th Light Infantry Brigade in Saigon during Tet. But there weren't many.

A good number of African American soldiers took the news about King very hard. Right on its heels came press reports, then letters from home, and phone calls for a few, all emphasizing neighborhoods in turmoil. In 2-47th Infantry, the body of John Summers, killed in action in the firefight on March 28, made it back to his hometown of Baltimore in the shadow of columns of smoke. His funeral became one more in the sequence of seven men killed in the riots of April 6–11, 1968.[45]

At Bear Cat, 2-47th felt the backlash. As Chuck Hagel explained, in Company B "there's no question that the King assassination set off a real powder keg that had been simmering under the surface." Over the previous months, thoughtless officers and NCOs had allowed troops to self-segregate into black tents and white tents. The company's few senior sergeants, both black and white, cautioned against it. But the company had been busy with field operations since Tet, and seen three different captains in command in just over three months. After losing the competent Captain Robert G. Keats at Tet, the replacement struggled. He let the privates do as they wished, not usually a good idea in a rifle company. When the news broke about King's death, the company's African American soldiers refused to go out on a mission. Some loudly defied the white officer. The rest apparently agreed.[46]

A young lieutenant from Chicago thought otherwise. Jerome "Skip" Johnson, age twenty-three, went through Officer Candidate School, earning a commission as an armor officer. With 3-5th Cavalry detached almost two months earlier, the 9th Infantry Division didn't have tanks anymore, so a personnel officer assigned Johnson to 2-47th Infantry, mechanized on their M-113 tracks and thus close enough. Johnson served as a platoon leader and, due to the endemic officer shortage, also acted as company executive officer, second in command to the captain. Johnson knew his business. Chuck Hagel considered him "steady, careful, never excitable—and in combat, that's who you want leading."[47]

With the white captain flummoxed, it fell to Skip Johnson to sort it out. His older brother had been killed in country in 1967. His home city of Chicago burned in 1966 and ignited again after King's killing. America had asked a lot of Johnson, and given him damn little in return. Even his officer's rank, something honored even on the West Side of Chicago in 1968, wore heavy on his collar in those days after King's death.

Skip Johnson did not hesitate. He went to the tents that housed the African American soldiers. Every face turned his way. He didn't say much—just enough. "We are all Americans," he said. "We're going to live together, we're going to take care of each other, we're fighting together, we're going to get each other's backs. Let's get it done." He went to leave, but then stopped, turned back, and stood there.

"This is not just an order from your commanding officer," he said. "This is from me, Jerome Johnson. You will deal with me personally on this."[48]

That ended it—for now.

IT'S UNLIKELY THE FLINTY OLD MEN in Hanoi knew of the confrontation in the tents of 2-47th Infantry. At their level, the U.S. mechanized infantry battalion might have rated a dot on a map. The internal doings of one of about 120 such American outfits didn't rise to the top. In the wake of the Tet Offensive, the northern politburo had bigger fish to fry.

In the short run, Tet and its blood-soaked aftermath—most notably at Khe Sanh and in Hue city, but also in the Central Highlands, the towns and jungles around Saigon, and in the rice paddies of the northern Mekong Delta—exacted a horrendous price for minimal gain. Not one liberated town center had been held. In the weeks after the initial wave of attacks, the NVA sent more than 80,000 new troops south to refill their depleted ranks. Tet had torn the guts out of the VC. After the great offensive, northerners predominated, even in many nominally local guerrilla units.[49] In a military sense, the North's Tet Offensive failed. Both sides knew it.

And yet, the NVA generals also recognized that the comparative body count, while slanted dramatically against the communist cause, only went so far in determining the long-term result. General Westmoreland might have proclaimed victory, but clearly his Washington leadership did not agree.[50] They sent few reinforcements. They announced Westmoreland's departure. Then, in a development that surprised even the North Vietnamese, President Johnson altered the U.S. strategy: no wider war, a unilateral bombing halt, and a plea for negotiations. Finally, in an example of the supposedly inevitable consequences of the class struggle between haves and have-nots so beloved of Marxist-Leninist true believers, some alienated loser killed Martin Luther King Jr. America's cities burned. So much for a U.S. triumph.

Even the 9th Infantry Division staff, thoroughly and rightly averse to commenting on U.S. domestic politics, saw it. In their operational summary of the post-Tet situation, an unnamed intelligence officer soberly wrote: "The Viet Cong offensive failed militarily, but it must be viewed as a psychological success."[51] Hanoi's inner circle smiled.

Although crippled by Tet casualties, the North Vietnamese knew what to do. Pursuant to the American request, peace talks in Paris would start on May 10. The NVA generals wanted to put their markers on the table, to continue the political struggle from the barrel of a gun. The solution came right from the guerrilla creed. *Enemy tires, we attack.*

CHAPTER 7

Heat

It might feel safer inside as long as nothing happens, but you
couldn't hope for a pleasant death if anything did happen
shut up in a blazing steel room that was rapidly becoming
white-hot and filled with an infernal symphony of fireworks as
your own ammunition caught fire and added to the horror.

STEPHEN BAGNALL, *The Attack*[1]

The rains came late that year. Usually, the rain blew in with May.
As long as the dry season persisted around Saigon, the skies
stayed relatively clear, and U.S. helicopters and jet fighter-
bombers flew freely.[2] Drier ground allowed MACV rifle units to keep
hunting Charlie. For a mechanized battalion like 2-47th Infantry, every day without the wet monsoon offered another opportunity to get
the 12-ton M113s off the roads and trails to find the enemy. The Viet
Cong K-34 Artillery Battalion remained unlocated, of course. They
knew how not to be seen.

The NVA and their VC auxiliaries would move in early May, rain or
no rain. The opening of the peace talks in Paris set that timing. In the
weeks before the planned attack, the enemy went to ground, even
underground. North Vietnamese Army doctrine taught their officers
one slow, four quicks. Slow preparation came first, followed by quick
advance, quick assault, quick clearance, and quick withdrawal.[3] April
1968 was for preparation.

Waiting for the NVA to act did not work for Major General Julian J. Ewell. He hounded the 9th Infantry Division's battalions to get out and get after their elusive enemy. While he had a strong personal regard for Lieutenant Colonel John Tower, whom Ewell regarded as a fighter, the division commander considered the 2nd Battalion (Mechanized), 47th Infantry an asset of limited utility.[4] The 2-47th could keep roads open, escort supply truck convoys, and, in emergencies like Tet, move quickly to the sound of the guns. Yet except for the clashes during Tet, 2-47th did not register much of a body count. And once the wet monsoon blew in, the constraints of weather on M113 mobility guaranteed even less production. As an old paratrooper determined to find and kill Cong, Ewell preferred walking infantry inserted by helicopter. He disliked the slow, predictable riverine guys. But he hated the mech.

So 2-47th stayed not just busy, but hyperbusy, as if a frenetic pace of activity could make up for lack of results. The costly firefight on March 28 came from this push. With the internal dissension over the King assassination resolved, operations continued day and night. When pressed, the American intelligence analysts kept pointing to the Binh Son rubber plantation and its environs, right on the doorstep of the 9th Infantry Division's Camp Martin Cox at Bear Cat, as the most likely place to find the VC. For his part, Charlie stubbornly refused to be found.

JUST AFTER NOON on April 22, the village chief of Phuoc Thien reported that the VC had moved into his village, just west of Route 15 and about five miles south of Bear Cat. He contacted the 9th Infantry Division headquarters and demanded help. Normally, such bleatings were ignored unless the local South Vietnamese official had a really good reputation. This guy did not. But it had been a long time between contacts, and the 2-47th battalion commander was desperate to placate Ewell. So Lieutenant Colonel John Tower gave the order to Company B. Search and clear the cluster of buildings that made up Phuoc Thien.

Company B's captain received the mission. He had 3rd Platoon twenty-five miles to the east, way out on Route 1 past Xuan Loc, protecting the engineer rock quarry and signal relay site at Gia Ray. The other two rifle platoons operated much closer to Bear Cat.[5] Either would do. The company commander tagged 2nd Platoon.

Chuck and Tom Hagel were with 2nd Platoon when the call came. The Americans had been guarding a bridge, one of the mundane tasks allotted to 2-47th. While keeping the bridge intact secured a key U.S. supply line and permitted the South Vietnamese to get to and from the farmer's market, it offered almost no possibility of meeting the enemy, especially in daylight. The U.S. troops were bored. The radio message to go search a VC-held hamlet got the men interested, particularly the new guys. But most of these missions came to naught. In daytime, right near Highway 15? This smelled like a wild goose chase. So guessed the old-timers.

Those wary veterans now included Chuck and Tom Hagel. Their lacerations from the March 28 engagement had healed enough. Chuck served as a squad leader. He'd lead some of the riflemen that would dismount from the track once they got to the village. As usual, the infantry rode on top of the boxy armored personnel carrier. With all the ammunition packed inside, one hostile land mine would pulp anyone below the deck. So the riflemen sat on the armored vehicle's flat roof, hanging on to antenna mounts and tie-down rails.[6] Nobody expected trouble, but you never knew. Because he and his brother remained reliable navigators, Chuck's squad would lead the way.

Tom was Chuck's track commander, standing in the M113's little open-topped turret to man the M113's .50-caliber machine gun. On his head, Tom wore a small combat vehicle crewman helmet with built-in earphones and a mike. By flipping a switch, Tom could talk to his driver in a private intercom or switch to the radio to talk across the platoon or higher. When Chuck and the other soldiers hopped off, Tom and the other track commanders intended to stay mounted, covering the movements of those on the ground.

It took the platoon of four M113s about a half hour to reach Phuoc Thien. The run down Route 15 crossed through a washed-out, ashen dead zone, stark tree trunks and bare branches without a hint of green on them. The cleared area came thanks to a lot of sprayed defoliant chemicals, the infamous Agent Orange, as well as some Agent Blue and White, too. U.S. Air Force C-123 "Ranch Hand" propeller planes dusted the stuff all along both sides of the roadway, weed killer applied thousands of gallons at a time. In the dry season, it worked, and created what Tom Hagel later described as a "moonscape." Once the monsoon rains came, the chemicals washed away, the greenery rose resurgent, and the spray planes had to go back to work.[7] Agent Orange's long-term effects on the Vietnamese farmers who lived in it, not to mention the U.S. soldiers who walked through it, remained to be seen. But even in 1968, just looking at the desiccated mess, you knew planeloads of toxic chemicals could not be good for all things great and small. As the Americans approached, Phuoc Thien and its immediate set of trees and fields stood out of the gray background like some lunar colony, a spot of color and greenery in the prevailing defoliated wasteland.

The four tracks slowed to turn into the place. From his vantage point up in the lead M113 turret, Tom Hagel noticed the burnt-out French villa near the village entrance. It had been a nice place once. But now only a blackened shell stood there, a mute monument to France's colonial regime.[8] Nobody had time for history lessons.

The tracks rolled into the center of the hamlet in a row, one behind the other. Ideally, Americans established a cordon before searching such a settlement. That required outposts to block each of the key egress routes.[9] To encircle this aggregation of a couple dozen dingy houses, huts, and sheds would have tied up all of Company B. And even then, a determined guerrilla—in other words, a standard-issue VC—might easily find gaps in the cordon, typically by slipping out through a tunnel or working slowly through heavy vegetation, clandestine paths the locals knew well and the Americans did not. Pressed for time and bristling with firepower, the U.S. mech platoon just plunged right into town. The M113s spread out as best they could, with the .50 caliber gunners like Tom scanning the thinned, defoliated woods. Nothing.

No VC fire greeted the tracks. Rather, the bewildered South Vietnamese inhabitants stopped whatever they'd been doing and stood there, no doubt wondering why these four U.S. armored personnel carriers clanked onto their central dirt road. That village chief? Well, nobody could find him. Like many in the corrupt Saigon government, he did not live among "his" people. Now it fell to twenty-five Americans to figure out if Charlie was really here, had ever been here, or seemed likely to return.

Chuck Hagel and his five riflemen slipped off the track. The men shook themselves out. The machine gunner carried his long black M60 pig and, criss-crossing his body like some Hollywood bandit, two belts of gleaming 7.62mm rounds, two hundred each.[10] Another man had the M79 grenade launcher. The rest, including Chuck, carried M16 rifles. Two other squads also dismounted. Sergeant First Class William E. Smith took charge. The platoon didn't have an officer (again). The company had lost another lieutenant a week ago. So Smith, an eighteen-year veteran, ran things by himself, as good platoon sergeants do.

Searching a *ville* took time. Soldiers had to enter every structure. One man covered, weapon at the ready, while his partner checked out each place. Even at midday, the hovels were dim inside. Pawing through civilian clothing, bedding, pots and pans, and rice jars hardly endeared the Americans to the Vietnamese. Every turned cloth smelled pungent. Flies buzzed lazily here and there. The abject poverty just stared you in the face. These people had nearly nothing, and now big men from the far side of the world insisted on rooting among what little they had.

The small, slight Vietnamese, to a man and woman, regardless of age, wore faded black pajama trousers. Certain of the people, perhaps the fashionable sorts, sported white or pastel-colored shirts. Most of the older ones wore matching black tops. Sometimes "experts" announced that the VC uniform consisted of black pajamas, which is another way of saying the opposition didn't have a uniform. It would be like telling a security patrol in America to look for the guy wearing a T-shirt and blue jeans.

As usual, only women, children, and old men sullenly eyed the inquisitive Americans. No young men hung around. Maybe they all had jobs in Saigon. Well, they had jobs, all right . . . Tom summarized later: "You never knew who your friends were, or if you had any at all."[11]

Trying to figure out what you saw made the search doubly difficult. If you found a big ceramic jar of rice, did that serve to feed the family? Or had the VC made them keep it? If a military item turned up, even an innocuous thing like a canteen cover, did that reflect a VC quartermaster's work, a stolen ARVN-issue item, or a child's souvenir? A paper map might feature pencil marks identifying property limits or cultivated fields. Or maybe those light etchings demonstrated carefully gathered intelligence about U.S. and ARVN locations and movements. Everything had dual uses. Everybody seemed to have two faces. Most of these quiet civilians looked to have hedged their bets. In the old game of with us or against us, they'd checked both boxes.

Many of the homes had what U.S. intelligence officers referred to as "bunkers." These were really just holes in the ground with a plywood cover and a rug on top. Used to having Americans comb through their belongings, smart Vietnamese never left rice or anything remotely military in the family hidey-hole. That allowed them to shrug and claim the dugout strictly as a prudent safety measure, what with the constant fighting in the region. Naturally, any shrewd VC guerrilla could move in and move out as suited him. As Chuck Hagel summarized: "They were very inventive."[12]

Now and then, the rummaging unearthed a real VC tunnel. Those tended to go right out of town. If one of them turned up, then the fun started. The Americans had some smaller soldiers—tunnel rats—picked and trained to crawl into the tight spaces, .45 automatic pistol in one hand, flashlight in the other. Alternatively, you could just toss in a hand grenade or three and call it a day.[13] This afternoon in Phuoc Thien, Chuck Hagel and the other riflemen found no tunnels.

Soldiers also checked out pigpens and chicken coops. The VC liked to squirrel away weapons and ammunition in unpleasant, slimy, smelly spots. So all had to be examined. The U.S. riflemen poked around. Nothing appeared out of the ordinary.

One final location got attention. In soggy areas, the Vietnamese interred their dead in stone crypts, about six inches of which protruded above ground. A big slab topped each tomb. Hard experience taught the Americans to look inside. Soldiers hefted the heavy rectangular lids. The VC often stashed AK-47s, RPD machine guns, PRG launchers, and ammunition in grave sites. But not this time. Annoyed villagers "said we were desecrating graves," Tom Hagel remembered.[14] It was one of the few times that day when the locals said anything. The older ones learned long ago that when the Americans came calling, go with the poker face. Anything else might get you taken away.

Americans took away two kinds of Vietnamese. Clearly, if the platoon met resistance, prisoners of war went out for interrogation. In the lull after Tet, the entire 9th Infantry Division took only 203 battlefield prisoners. But they took ten times as many "detainees," people in civil dress scooped up on sweeps. These needed to be screened as possible bad guys. Of 2,303 detained, only 853 were eventually classed as innocent civilians and released.[15] The other 1,500 or so went into long-term captivity as VC or NVA.

Because the hostiles hid in plain sight, any VC or likely VC was nabbed, and that meant a younger man with a weapon (even a single AK bullet), or military web gear, or a bellicose stare. A military-age male, anything from twelve to fifty or so, who couldn't account for his daily activities usually became a detainee. Women also found themselves apprehended if they possessed military gear or communist documents; the VC included many female members, including fighters and leaders. When in doubt, Americans picked up anybody at all shady. Better safe than sorry.

The Hagels' platoon didn't take anyone captive. The search found no VC material, either. It took all afternoon, right into the dusk. But the Americans came up empty. With night coming on quickly, the platoon needed to get out of Phuoc Thien and get back on its bridge site. Sergeant First Class Smith ordered his men to mount up.[16]

Chuck Hagel and his guys scrambled aboard. Chuck sat just behind and left of his brother Tom, still in the turret. That let Chuck, as squad leader, pull up the radio handset through the open cargo hatch.

The radios were on the track's left side, just below where Chuck sat. Once all his men were on top and set, Chuck Hagel notified Smith by radio: good to go.

At that, Smith's track gunned its diesel engine and the 12-ton aluminum box spun about like the Batmobile—very nifty. The tracked M113 could turn two ways. For wide moves, the driver up front on the left side yanked on a lever to brake the tread in the direction of the turn. Pull the right lever, and the right tread slowly halted while the left one kept churning. And the track swung about like a garbage scow, fast or slow, depending on how far down the driver pushed the acceleration pedal. But for tight spots, like Vietnamese villages, the driver had the option to use two little curved handles hanging from a sideways fixture just above the normal driving levers. Those smaller handles allowed pivot steering. Pull on the right one, and the right side stopped instantly as the left side kept going.[17] That's how an M113 turned on a dime.

All four tracks quickly slewed into position, one behind the other, a 180-degree reversal in how they entered the *ville*. Tom and Chuck Hagel now had the fourth track to head out. A light wave of dust settled. The lead track spouted some exhaust, hard to see in the near darkness. But even over the radios and rumbling motors, you could hear it. With a squeak, the first M113 headed out.

The second one allowed about ten yards, then followed. After a short delay, another ten yards, and number three rumbled forward. Finally, the Hagels' track jolted a bit and crawled forward, slowly creeping out of the hamlet. Behind them, a few cooking fires twinkled in the cloud of dirt raised by the departing American vehicles. Well, so far—

Ka-whang!

The dusk lit white, a bolt of hot ground lightning, a flashbulb the size of a house. The explosion shot up the left side of the Hagels' M113, tossing the 12-ton sideways like a toy. Then came the yammering of RPD machine guns and AKs, green tracers reaching out of the dark village. And for every bullet you saw, there were four you did not. Those VC nobody found? Well, here they were.

For Chuck. the tracer display played out in near silence. No Americans shot back. Chuck Hagel's left eardrum had been perforated. So had the right one, although not as badly. His entire left side felt like he'd been roasted on a spit. Bright flames climbed up the side of the track. Along with Chuck and the radio rack, the explosion blew right under the APC's 95-gallon tank of diesel fuel. Diesel didn't explode, but it burned just fine. And the M113 was full of ammunition.[18]

Chuck couldn't hear much, but he quickly took charge. Get the guys off this thing before the ammo goes. The other riflemen slid off okay. One had finally started shooting back. Then the pig gunner joined in, a healthy dose of red tracers back at Charlie.

What about Tom? What of the driver? That land mine—and it was a mine, a 500-pounder, maybe a former U.S. Air Force bomb repurposed by the ingenious Mr. Charles—knocked them out. The driver, up on the left but a bit away from the detonation, stirred some, then woozily crawled out of his hatch, seemingly oblivious to the green tracers zipping overhead. Thank God Charlie shot high.

Tom Hagel didn't move.[19] Chuck grabbed him under the arms and pulled up. The intercom wire popped loose. Chuck tossed his brother bodily off the track then fell on him. Not exactly proper first-aid technique, but staying low was a good idea right now.

Chuck pulled off Tom's crewman's helmet, working the earphones loose. Even in the dark, the firelight showed blood trickling from Tom's ears and nose. Trouble, for sure.

About then, the welcome hammering of .50 calibers announced the return of the other three M113s. That drove Charlie away. As the firefight petered out, strong hands grabbed both Chuck and Tom and bundled them into another track. Someone—a medic, maybe—rubbed some kind of ointment on Chuck. Tom was alive but not moving and not conscious.[20]

As the platoon cross-loaded their men into the three intact vehicles and the stricken track burned, with bullets cooking off like deadly firecrackers, it occurred to a few Americans that the Vietnamese settlement had just done duty as a shooting gallery. All of the mayhem couldn't have been a happy thing in the *ville*. But Sergeant

First Class Smith and the other U.S. NCOs didn't have time to deal with that. Smith focused on pulling out his guys, getting out onto the open highway, bringing in a medevac chopper for Tom Hagel and Chuck, too. Tom lay still as death.

When they finally flew out, Tom remembered almost nothing: noises, lights, people talking that he couldn't hear. Chuck, in extreme pain from his raw skin, later mentioned hearing Linda Ronstadt and the Stone Poneys, maybe while waiting in the other squad's M113, maybe even on the medevac helicopter, singing about traveling to the beat of a different drum.[21] Linda sure got that right. This one beat damn hard.

TWO BROTHERS, THREE weeks, four Purple Hearts, all in a period of allegedly low-intensity enemy activity—what the hell. At this rate, the Hagels didn't look like a good bet to see Nebraska again. Being a good soldier in Vietnam put you at risk. And the brothers were fine soldiers, acting NCOs. They lived in a degree of danger unimaginable to those back home. And just like drill sergeant William Joyce told Chuck way back at Fort Bliss, people counted on both brothers.

Blown eardrums healed. So did second- and first-degree burns. Both men, Tom more than Chuck, also endured an unseen wound, what later medical researchers termed traumatic brain injury. It's what happens when the brain slams a few too many times against the unyielding skull bone. Boxers get it, as the sad later lives of Joe Louis and Muhammad Ali taught many. Football players suffer also, as did Chicago Bear Dave Duerson and San Diego Charger Junior Seau. Combat soldiers face this peril, too. If you sustain too many concussions one after the other, the brain gets permanently damaged. Over time, paranoia, depression, homicidal urges, and suicidal tendencies can result. By luck, rather than design, both Hagels benefited from the exact right treatment—a break, a chance for their bruised brains to repair battered cells before getting scrambled again.[22] For almost two weeks after the mine blew, both men did only light duties around Bear Cat.

Chuck's burns, mostly severe first degree with some second-degree blistering, kept him swathed in bandages "like a mullah."[23] He had salve to apply, easy to do in base camp. Doing that out on missions looked to be pretty tough. But at least for a while, that wasn't an issue.

The April 22 explosion didn't move the ball, at least as far as Major General Ewell reckoned matters. The division scoreboard showed "negligible contact" at the cost of two wounded in action, one M113 "damaged" (burned to aluminum slag), and no VC body count. To Sergeant First Class Smith's credit, he refused to game the system and claim phantom dead opponents. But the 2-47th Infantry battalion commander couldn't let this go on. On May 4, 1968, Captain James B. Craig, an officer with a superb combat record in the 101st Airborne Division, took charge of Company B. He was the outfit's fourth commander in a bit more than three months.[24]

Days later, Mr. Charles reintroduced himself as only he could.

THEY BLEW THE SIREN for this one. The horn wailed, loud and long, warbling out from the green metal speaker mounted high on the thin wood pole over the 2-47th motor pool. Men scrambled to their M113s, like Spitfire pilots running to the flight line to meet a Luftwaffe raid on London. Lieutenant Colonel John Tower had insisted on this procedure, just in case the battalion was in the Bear Cat base camp when something really bad cropped up. At 12:20 p.m. on May 9, 1968, it did.

Company A wasn't there; they had the routine task twenty-five miles to the east at Gia Ray, of defending the engineer rock quarry and the radio site. Aware the battalion had to roll short one company, Companies B and C gathered up every man they could. Specialist 4 Jimmy Dye, a squad leader in 3rd Platoon, recalled: "All the tracks in the motor pool was up and runnin' and people was jumpin' on 'em." Dye had a fever, but he went. Cooks and clerks came at the double, gripping rarely fired rifles.[25] Chuck and Tom Hagel went, too. Light duty was over. That screaming siren meant all hands on deck.

The urgent order to assemble and head out immediately came directly from Major General Ewell himself. The irascible division commander thought little of his mech guys, but even he recognized that nothing matched an M113 outfit for firepower and speed in an emergency. Just such a situation had boiled up in south Saigon.

At 4 a.m. on May 5, those pesky VC battalions supposedly defeated in the Tet Offensive in January–February rose from the dead, thanks to a huge influx of North Vietnamese regulars. All the usual suspects emerged: the Phu Loi II Battalion, 2nd Independent Battalion, 5th Nha Be Battalion, 265th Battalion, 506th Battalion, even the slippery K-34 Artillery Battalion. That last bunch rained rockets and mortar rounds on Tan Son Nhut Air Base, to include the MACV headquarters compound. Two battalions (5th Nha Be and 506th) went after the Y-bridge, a key interchange in south Saigon. A third battalion (Phu Loi II) supported that effort, moving to block Highway 232 east of the Y-bridge.[26] It wasn't as big as Tet—a lot fewer communist troops, fewer targets, and a lot less follow-through. But it was big enough, especially in South Vietnam's capital city. Troops called this major enemy push Phase II, the Second Wave, the May Offensive, May Tet, Little Tet, and most often, Mini-Tet.[27]

For a day or so, MACV tried to let the ARVN deal with the attacks around Saigon. The South Vietnamese couldn't pull it off. Even with substantial U.S. supporting fires, South Vietnam's best troops—airborne, marines, and rangers—proved unequal to the challenge.[28] So Americans went to work. Before 2-47th cranked up the siren, II Field Force had already sent two battalions (1-5th Mech Infantry and 3-4th Cavalry) from the 25th Infantry Division to sort out an attempted perimeter breach at Tan Son Nhut Air Base. Ewell's 9th Infantry Division rolled an entire brigade-plus into south Saigon—5-60th Mech Infantry, 3-39th Infantry, 6-31st Infantry in the urban zone, and 4-39th Infantry into the arc of VC-infested villages southwest of the city.[29] It wasn't enough. Despite all of that troop strength, artillery, helicopter gunships, and air strikes, the enemy held on to the neighborhoods seized. The call went out to 2-47th: pile on.

Captain Craig and Company B led, each M113's bow decorated with a snarling black panther. It was time to live up to the nickname. In a cloud of rusty red dust—the dry season lingered—the long column of tracks left Bear Cat, en route to the Route 232-230 intersection in south Saigon. Over the radio, the commander received his orders. The good guys had the Phu Loi II Battalion pinned in Xom Ong Doi, a pro-government Catholic district of small shops and shabby houses, as well as a large number of temporary shacks inhabited by refugees driven into town by combat in the countryside. To the west stood the understrength 5th Battalion, Republic of Vietnam Marine Division, an outfit maybe the size of a U.S. rifle company. South of Xom Ong Doi, two companies of 6-31st Infantry tried to block VC exfiltration. A wide waterway made exit to the east unlikely. Craig's Company B and the rest of 2-47th were supposed to seal off the north. Once that happened, U.S. firepower could pound away, to be followed by a sweep of what was left of the VC . . . and Xom Ong Doi.[30]

When they neared the objective area about 1:30 p.m., the Americans slowed. The dirty dark-green M113s passed groups of civilians, maybe two hundred in all. The people trudged east, away from the fighting. Women and children and a few old men walked by slowly. The American vehicles' throaty diesel engine noises blocked the sound, but looking at facial expressions, many Vietnamese were crying. A lot of the females, even the elderly ones, balanced bundles on their heads. Children lugged bags of clothing and brass pots tied by strings. These folks wanted out, and they were heading there. Company B was going in.

Black smoke towered like a thunderhead over Xom Ong Doi. Somebody had been busy making a mess. Now it fell to Captain Craig's Company B to slam the door to the north. Route 232 beckoned. To the right of the idling tracks, a single line of dilapidated market stands and small sheds to the north fronted a canal. To the south loomed quite a few two-story buildings, some of stone and brick dating back to the French era. Between the aging colonial structures, one-story hovels filled the gaps. The four-lane road between the canal-side shacks and the taller buildings stood as empty as a street in a Hollywood western, high noon indeed.[31]

The word went down the column. Dismount. Get the riflemen out and forward. Second Platoon led, with both Hagels out on the ground, Chuck with his squad, Tom as a fire team leader. This time, they did not go first. Sergeant First Class Smith pushed another squad up. The M113s followed, one to the right, another echeloned to the left, freeing two .50 caliber gunners to fire as necessary.

A point team of two riflemen moved out, shaded to the south side, toward the old French buildings. Behind them, one squad picked along, sliding from doorway to doorway right near the walls. Nobody messed with the flimsy wood, canvas, and sheet metal shanties on the north side, near the canal. No cover there—bullets would rip right through that light stuff. And for God's sake, stay out of the road. The veterans, those like Chuck Hagel who'd fought at Widows Village, knew that deal. They warned the rookies.[32]

Trailing the foot troops came the four tracks, creeping up at walking speed. A squad of riflemen followed each of the lead tracks, with a drag team of two soldiers behind the fourth one. The rest of Company B followed, riflemen on the road surface, gunners and drivers mounted.

Nobody saw any more civilians, at least no live ones. Here and there, a stiff corpse sprawled against a building. Bloated dark-gray pigs and limp, tattered ducks littered the road on the canal side. Slain chickens dotted the cracked pavement, feathers moving, but nothing else. You smelled all of them before you saw them. And they smelled bad in a way only dead things can.

It reminded Tom Hagel of a "World War II style of fighting," like Aachen or Manila. Both Hagels knew this would be intense. Although 2-47th occasionally patrolled just outside this end of Saigon, the troops had never been in or around congested Xom Ong Doi. One thing for sure—nobody wanted to be on the tracks, sure magnets for trouble and trundling along exactly where not to be, in that open street.[33] Guys scrunched down in their bulky flak vests. Take it slow. Stay ready.

Up in the cupola of the first M113, Specialist 4 Philip Streuding watched with his hands on the grips of the M2HB .50-caliber machine gun. He saw the point duo gingerly approach an overturned jeep. Two South Vietnamese national policemen, the ones the Americans called "White Mice" after the color of their helmets and gloves, lay facedown on the street. Back in the column, Specialist 4 Dye saw "a guy in a ditch who looked like he'd been hacked to death with a machete."[34] Wafting in the hot, humid air, the stench from all the remains, human and animal, made Americans gag. Even the old-timers felt it.

At 2:20 p.m., the point team crossed carefully to the far side of the Route 320 intersection. So far, so good.

Then it wasn't.

Cracking and barking with a purpose, dozens of AK-47s opened up. The point man and slack man, Specialist 4 George W. Darnell and Private First Class Larry G. Caldwell, both collapsed to the stained pavement. Caldwell came from Omaha, Nebraska.[35] He wouldn't see it again.

Streuding opened up, working the big .50 caliber up and down the building that he thought held the VC guerrillas who'd shot the two soldiers. Plaster and underlying brick flew away in chunks. In one doorway, a 55-gallon drum of gasoline exploded in an orange fireball. Right out of the movies, a few guys thought. Then the riflemen kept right on shooting.

As Streuding fired, the gunner in the next track back began to tear up other suspicious buildings. They taught you back at Fort Ord to engage known, likely, and suspected targets. This afternoon, that amounted to pretty much everything.

As the lead element exchanged fire, VC all along the column also opened fire. Shadows flitted in doorways and second-story windows. Other VC crouched on the rooftops. AK-47s and RPD machine guns stuttered away. Nobody fired RPGs. They were too close; the warheads wouldn't even arm. The enemy couldn't be more than ten yards away, sometimes closer. But you still couldn't really see them—you hardly ever did. But you saw movement. And muzzle flashes. Lots of those.

Company B's tracks pivoted left. Dismounted U.S. soldiers sought cover near doorposts, ditches, wall corners, and on the sheltered sides of the stationary tracks. All of that training back in the States, and all of the hard-won field experience—this is why it mattered. Officers and NCOs didn't have to say or do anything. The American rifle company convulsed with fire, a wounded, cornered carnivore lashing back. Riflemen, pig gunners, and M79 grenadiers banged away. As Jimmy Dye said, "You're not thinking, you're just reacting."[36]

Captain Craig had slid behind his track on the north, the canal side. AK rounds pinged off the exposed flank of the M113. With one radio, Craig talked to his embattled platoons. With the other he reported to Tower, circling overhead in a bubble-top chopper. Over him orbited the brigade commander. And another layer up, Ewell watched. It sounded like even Major General Fred Weyand from II Field Force was up there somewhere. And they were all on his communications net, "helping."[37] Good Lord.

Fortunately, the artillery had their own radio frequencies, and spectating great men didn't talk on them. On his own initiative, forward observer Lieutenant Paul H. Bowman called in artillery, starting a way out. He opened with a white phosphorus round to mark. The projectile smacked in just south and west of the front of Company B's column. A brilliant white cloud rose up. Good enough—Bowman told the battery to fire for effect.[38] Bowman sure hoped those South Vietnamese marines had their heads down.

Company B's soldiers ducked as the artillery began blowing into the south side of the row of old French buildings. Unwilling to endure the pounding, the VC backed off. Their shooting died away, and by twos and threes, the guerrillas began slithering south, squirreling themselves into the center of the ramshackle hootches of Xom Ong Doi. They'd have to be blown out or dug out, probably both. But for now, Charlie had had enough.[39]

About an hour into the fight, as the VC tried to pull away to the south, Company B started to take fire from the north, across the canal. A keyed-up pig gunner shot right back, zipping through a belt of 7.62mm ball and tracers, and joined by some riflemen. It took a few minutes of back and forth on the radio, and tossing out colored smoke grenades, to figure out that those were probably ARVN over there, although some Americans thought they saw NVA uniforms. Anyway, Craig made his men cease fire.[40]

Specialist 5 Phillip Rogers and his medics had already been carrying out their usual heroic work. He did what he could for poor Darnell and Caldwell, but they were too far gone. Doc Rogers and the rest of the medics helped the other eleven wounded men.[41] For a change, that number did not include Chuck and Tom Hagel. It had been a vicious close-quarters firefight, but this time, both brothers came through fine.

Company B's street clash attracted plenty of attention from the high-ranking gallery in the helicopters overhead. Tower exerted his authority to clear the command net, and to their credit, the higher-ranking officers backed off, hopefully a bit chastened. Seeing the good done by Bowman's artillery fire mission, the 2-47th commander worked to get helicopter gunships into action. He also requested fighter-bombers. The proper headquarters acknowledged Tower's transmissions. Then . . . nothing.[42]

These steps, calling in helicopter gunships and close air support, amounted to standard U.S. tactics out in the countryside. Inside populous Saigon, even days into Mini-Tet, the use of such violent means generated lengthy consultations with Saigon city officials, ARVN generals, MACV staff types, and even senior figures at the U.S. embassy. On a good day, South Vietnam couldn't locate most of its own police elements and ARVN units, let alone thousands of random civilians. The cross-canal dust-up typified the confusion. Firepower looked sure to kill friendlies. How much of that could be tolerated? The big guys debated. Minutes ticked away: ten, twenty, thirty, forty. Americans on the ground bled. Some died.

Ewell had already permitted artillery. He owned it, and he cleared its use. The notoriously impatient division commander also got tired of waiting and soon unleashed his armed helicopters, too. But to get air force jets took MACV approval. The general ensured John Tower got the word. It would be hours before the heavy stuff arrived.[43]

That meant 2-47th had to use its own resources. Accordingly, while arranging the big hammers and awaiting the pleasure of the high command, Tower told Company C to move up to close off the north side between Company B and the river. Once that defensive array was set, then 2-47th could really bring in the firepower and powder the VC stuck in the noose.[44]

Old soldiers recognize that friction, confusion, and misunderstandings characterize combat, especially in close quarters. Bad things happen. Late on the afternoon of May 9, one of those problems occurred. Tired, keyed-up, and trying to hear over a roaring engine and rampant explosions, the Company C commander misunderstood his orders. Lieutenant Colonel Tower wanted him to block, facing south. That captain heard attack south. He did.

It did not turn out well at all.

Company C's tracks faced south, came on line, and charged into a grassy field on the northeast quarter of Xom Ong Doi. Some bogged down. Others backed away. American riflemen piled out of the stuck vehicles, trying to work their way toward the buildings. Offered this opportunity, the VC opened up with a vengeance: RPD machine guns, AK-47s, and rocket-propelled grenades. Out on that wet grass, the RPG gunners had plenty of range. The fat rockets slammed into the aluminum tracks.

A squad or so of fast-moving Company C soldiers sprinted through the gunfire and somehow made it into the first row of structures in Xom Ong Doi. Others pulled back to the tracks, crouched down behind the inert aluminum boxes as bullets ricocheted off the bows and sides. Casualties piled up—two dead, twenty-two wounded, an entire platoon knocked out, and more to come if something didn't change.[45]

Right on time, right overhead, a team of two UH-1C Huey gunships clattered past, top cover for the floundering rifle company. The choppers' rasping mini-guns quelled the VC fire. Then the aviators switched to rockets. Pods of flashing 2.75-inch munitions blew off sheet metal roofs and started fires in the rows of huts that made up Xom Ong Doi. Under this pummeling, the VC finally quit shooting.

One rocket went awry. It slammed into a stalled Company C M113, killing two American soldiers and wounding a third. As their mates attempted to recover the stricken troops, U.S. artillery landed in their midst. More confusion—maybe a mistake by the distant howitzer crews, or transposed numbers, or perhaps misreading the military map, where an inch on paper equaled ten football fields of jumbled shacks and smoking buildings. Who could be sure at this point? Thankfully, the errant 105mm rounds did no additional damage. Company C consolidated its position, some tracks out in the open grassy field, anchored by the squad with a foothold in the town. They lost two more killed and another wounded in so doing. [46] It had been expensive, but the Americans now held that stretch of the ring.

To their west, Company B also settled in, holding on to their dearly won string of shot-up houses and stores along Route 232. Track machine gunners and individual soldiers with M16s traded shots with VC marksmen. Radio reports titled these hostiles as "snipers," the common way to refer to any lone enemy banging away.[47] Had any of the VC been real trained snipers, Company B's casualty list would have been much longer. And it was already long enough.

With both companies in position, the lengthy discussions about close air support finally wrapped up. Emphasizing the mounting U.S. infantry losses in Xom Ong Doi, Major General Ewell prevailed. That released the aerial hounds. At about 5:45 p.m. on the battalion command radio net, a warning went out. The air force jets were inbound. Captain Jim Craig told the men of Company B to take cover.

Two F-4 Phantoms roared overhead, confirming the designated target, and low enough that as they streaked past, the riflemen on the ground could see the two bright orange circles of their jet engines. It had been more than three hours since Lieutenant Colonel Tower asked for them. Better late than never. They did the job, and then a second set of screaming Phantom fighter-bombers overdid it. The two pairs of aircraft dropped high-explosive 250-pound Snakeye bombs and unloaded napalm canisters—snakes and nape, shake 'em and bake 'em. Xom Ong Loi, already smoldering, erupted in awful black clouds and raging fires. Each set of jets then strafed the streets of Xom Ong Loi, punching 20mm slugs all through the shantytown.[48] That pretty much did it for Charlie.

As the jets pulled away and the sun set, an angry red disk behind the roiling dark smoke clouds, a stray piece of hot metal whirred into Company B. It hit Doc Rogers right on the shoulder. The steady African American medic smiled broadly, thinking he'd gotten his "million dollar wound" and with it, hopefully, a ticket home to North Babylon, New York. He was the last American in Company B medically evacuated from the great fight on May 9.[49]

FOR THE COST of eight killed and thirty-six wounded, plus three M113s trashed, 2-47th Infantry set its part of the cordon. When they swept the blackened wreckage of Xom Ong Loi after daylight on May 10, the battalion claimed 202 VC dead. But only 16 VC bodies turned up. The 2-47th picked up one confused, unarmed VC prisoner. Where did the rest of the Phu Loi II Battalion go? Who knew?

Far more disturbing, U.S. riflemen found thirty-six South Vietnamese marine family members, all dead in their wrecked homes. It wasn't clear who got them—vengeful VC with AKs, American artillery and air, or both. A few dozen more dazed, shell-shocked Vietnamese civilians, some injured, came out on Route 232. The Americans sent them east, out of the beaten zone.[50]

After a day of unopposed searches and reorganization, to include taking aboard a lot of ammunition to replace the thousands of rounds so liberally expended on May 9, Captain Craig received new orders. At first light on May 11, Company B shifted to control of 3-39th Infantry for unfinished business more to the west on Route 232, past the Y-bridge. That big highway span crossed the canal, and at the outset of Mini-Tet, a VC assault team had blown a hole in the bridge deck. Most of two VC battalions (5th Nha Be and 506th) tried to take the big edifice, but couldn't hold it. They pulled back and remained hunkered down in Xom Cau Mat, pretty much the same kind of place as the pulverized Xom Ong Loi. The leg infantry of 3-39th had the place surrounded but needed some oomph to finish the job. Company C of

2-47th was too beat up. So Company B, a bit less bloodied and with more operational M113s, got the job.[51]

Craig ordered his men into action. They moved mounted to the big Y-bridge, an incongruously modern sight, seemingly transplanted intact from the Los Angeles freeway. Once west of the overpass, the riflemen dismounted, Chuck and Tom Hagel among them. Again, Route 232 stretched due west, devoid of movement. Left of the Americans, to the south, ran storefronts and houses, the now familiar mix of old French two-story buildings and newer single-floor structures. To the right, north, squatted another row of sheds and huts, with the canal bank just behind them. Different day, same story.

The men of 5-60th Mech and some doughty South Vietnamese national police—a bolder section of White Mice than usually seen—held the west. The scheme called for 3-39th to push up from the south, with a 6-31st rifle company attached to block the north exits. Craig's Company B drew the mission of forcing a defended dead-end street to the east.[52] If not taken, the remnants of both VC battalions would probably escape that way. It fell to Captain Craig and his men, including Chuck and Tom Hagel, to prevent that.

About 2 p.m., the company started south on the dead-end street. Craig, who'd been wounded twice in his previous service in Vietnam with the 101st Airborne Division, didn't like the look of things. His wife served in country as an army officer, too, a nurse at 3rd Field Hospital at Tan Son Nhut. Craig wanted to visit her, but not on a stretcher.[53]

The Americans did not mess around. They knew the VC were there and waiting. It sure would have been smart to level the street with bombs, but the Saigon city fathers had again prevailed, and that wasn't yet permitted on May 11. Every day required a renegotiation between the Americans and their South Vietnamese allies. So this would be done the hard way.

Chuck Hagel noted that in these "urban areas where the VC had gotten in" the opposition "had worked and changed their tactics." Inside the city, the enemy hadn't had time to set up booby traps or bury mines. So the guerrillas depended on direct fire, the old school.[54] In

Xom Cau Mat, Mr. Charles sought belt-to-belt contact, at least long enough so that the unengaged portion of the VC unit could escape and evade.

The two lead tracks, almost abreast, went first, with no point team in front of them. Behind the hulking M113s walked the riflemen, bent slightly forward, stepping methodically from doorway to doorway. The lead .50 caliber gunners "reconned by fire," which is to say that they opened up on anything that didn't look right. Not much looked right. The big U.S. machine guns chugged away.

The VC replied right away. In the two-lane (if that) side street, the cracks and snaps and snorting machine guns echoed and reechoed. One .50-caliber round hit a 55-gallon drum full of gasoline and it blew, bright and yellow. The shower of hot debris started a junked Renault car afire. The lead track passed right through the flames.

Riflemen aimed at fleeting VC on the rooftops. Some guys later alleged they saw khaki uniformed hostiles, but if so, not for long. Americans fired at muzzle flashes, dust puffs, and any movement, known or guessed. As Tom Hagel later explained: "You had to watch every window, and every door, and if you saw something, shoot."[55] American riflemen stayed low. Men passed ammunition from the stopped tracks. The Company B soldiers ran through a lot of bullets that afternoon.

About ten minutes into the firefight, a guerrilla nailed Captain Jim Craig, drilling a hole through his right lung, and thereby causing the dreaded sucking chest wound. Every breath bubbled up bloody froth on the company commander's chest. If not treated soon, the buildup of blood in his chest cavity would suffocate the officer. With Doc Rogers gone, another medic took over. A few men carried Craig back to Route 320. Within a half hour, a medevac chopper took him and a few other wounded away.[56] They all survived, and Craig saw his wife, too. At least that worked out okay.

The company executive officer, Lieutenant Skip Johnson, took charge. He never got too excited. Even the raucous fusillade all around him didn't rattle the young officer. Coolly sizing up the situation, Johnson halted the advance and told the lead APCs to back off about twenty yards. With fourteen more wounded, Johnson decided it was time to let the artillery, helicopters, and jet fighters go to work. They did.[57]

For the rest of the afternoon, helicopters and fighter-bombers traded runs over the trapped foe. Once night fell, U.S. Army artillery took over. Xom Cau Mat burned, the red glow of flames masked by the endless, stinking smoke. That sick-sweet odor of roasting flesh sullied the night breeze every time another clutch of 105mm howitzer shells impacted.[58] Maybe this is what Sergeant Charles Dean Hagel saw and smelt from his tail turret over Japan in that final terrible summer of 1945. If so, no wonder he never wanted to experience it again.

At daybreak on May 12, Company B sent a platoon south to check out a smashed-up set of houses south and east of the dead-end street. A firefight developed. Again the Americans resorted to supporting arms. The artillery settled things.

Unfortunately, 3-39th troops under fire also brought in artillery. One round fell well out of the predicted sheaf, blowing right on the dead-end street where Lieutenant Johnson was assembling his men to sweep south. Specialist 4 Antony P. Palumbo and PFC Philip M. Wooten both fell, as did two others. Palumbo died, but Wooten hung on long enough to see his brother, a soldier also serving in country, although not in 2-47th. Lieutenant Johnson got on the radio and told 3-39th's artillery observers to cease fire.

Eager to finish off the VC, and no doubt feeling the usual heat from Ewell at division, the 3-39th lieutenant colonel overruled Johnson. The senior commander demanded a repeat of the artillery fire mission. It was too bad about the stray projectile, but the 3-39th commander insisted. When his artillery forward observer officer refused, the lieutenant colonel fired him. Not that it mattered—during all the confusion, the VC stopped shooting.[59] As usual, Charlie found a way out.

THE FIGHTING ON May 12 ended Mini-Tet, although follow-on sweeps continued for a week. The 9th Infantry Division counted 39 Americans

General William C. Westmoreland greets President Lyndon B. Johnson on the runway at Cam Ranh Bay, South Vietnam, on October 26, 1966. Westmoreland commanded in the field while Johnson determined strategy from Washington. Both men misunderstood the war. (U.S. Department of Defense)

On August 4, 1898, Omaha, Nebraska, celebrated "Indian Day" with a major parade. A U.S. Army soldier from Fort Crook took this picture. (U.S. Department of Defense)

General Curtis E. LeMay commanded the Strategic Air Command from 1948 until 1957. Tough, smart, and blunt-spoken, LeMay flew lead on some of the most dangerous missions in World War II. He had one focus—winning wars. To frustrate Soviet Union bomber commanders, LeMay moved Strategic Air Command headquarters to Omaha, Nebraska, smack in the middle of the continental United States. (U.S. Department of Defense)

Private Charles Dean Hagel of the 42nd Bombardment Squadron posed for this picture early in his World War II service. Hagel's jaunty cap tilt typified the aggressive spirit of the U.S. Army Air Forces. (U.S. Senator Chuck Hagel Archives, University of Nebraska at Omaha)

The B-24J Liberator wasn't as famous as the iconic B-17 Flying Fortress, but the United States produced more than 19,000 and used them in every theater of World War II. On his missions in the Pacific, Sergeant Charles Dean Hagel manned the vulnerable tail gun turret. (U.S. Department of Defense)

Four generations of Hagel men pose in the early 1950s. From left to right stand great-grandfather and U.S. Army supply contractor Herman, grandfather and World War I veteran Charles Leo, father and World War II veteran Charles Dean, and young Tom, Mike, and Chuck. Son Jim is not pictured. (U.S. Senator Chuck Hagel Archives, University of Nebraska at Omaha)

Charles Dean Hagel is buried in Columbus, Nebraska. His death on Christmas Day of 1962 shook the Hagel family. (U.S. Senator Chuck Hagel Archives, University of Nebraska at Omaha)

With her husband's untimely death, it fell to Betty Dunn Hagel to pull the family together. She did. In November 1964, she posed with her sons Tom, Chuck, Mike, and Jim. (U.S. Senator Chuck Hagel Archives, University of Nebraska at Omaha)

In 1967, Chuck and Tom Hagel began their U.S. Army training by meeting their drill sergeant, a no-nonsense noncommissioned officer distinguished by his imposing "Smokey the Bear" campaign hat. Pictured here, Staff Sergeant John Arthur Hooker served as a drill sergeant at Fort Polk, Louisiana, in 1967. He later joined the 9th Infantry Division and was killed in action in Vietnam on March 10, 1968, at the age of twenty-nine. Hooker epitomized the professional NCO corps, the "backbone of the Army" who trained new soldiers and then led them in combat. (U.S. Department of Defense)

On the first day of U.S. Army Basic Combat Training at Fort Bliss, Texas, new recruits Chuck and Tom Hagel reported to the "reception center." There they shed civilian clothes and most of their hair. Thousands of young men did likewise in 1967. In this photo from Fort Ord, California, the body language speaks for itself. (U.S. Department of Defense)

Both Hagel brothers learned that strenuous exercise characterized the daily regimen of Basic Training. Here, army trainees carry out rifle calisthenics at Fort Campbell, Kentucky, in 1968. (U.S. Department of Defense)

Chuck Hagel arrived in Vietnam about six weeks ahead of brother Tom. Here, he displays his M16 rifle, the standard infantry weapon for Americans in country. He also has an egg-shaped M26 fragmentation grenade on his upper left shoulder. Chuck was assigned to Company B, 2nd Battalion, 47th Infantry, a mechanized outfit that went into action aboard boxy M113 tracked armored personnel carriers. The M113s provided speed and firepower, and Chuck's unit served as the preferred American reaction force whenever things went wrong. (U.S. Senator Chuck Hagel Archives, University of Nebraska at Omaha)

The battalion operations officer's M113 track of 2-47th Infantry displays the battalion's black panther emblem on its front. In an interesting coincidence, Charles Dean Hagel's 42nd Bombardment Squadron used the same image during World War II. So did African American radicals in Omaha in 1968–70. Behind the soldier lighting a cigarette can be seen the M2HB .50-caliber heavy machine gun, capable of shooting a lethal stream of 1.5-inch-long bullets out to about a mile. (U.S. Department of Defense)

This mushroom cloud is not an atomic blast, but what nearby soldiers saw when the huge U.S. Army ammunition dump at Long Binh Post exploded on the morning of January 31, 1968, during the opening hours of the great Tet Offensive. Chuck Hagel and his unit were right near ground zero. As a U.S. senator and secretary of defense, Chuck hung a similar picture in his office. (U.S. Department of Defense)

Soldiers and M113 armored personnel carriers of 2-47th Infantry deploy for action to clear Viet Cong defenders from Widows Village on January 31, 1968. Although the Americans secured the wreckage of the village that same day, fighting in the local area went on for days. (U.S. Department of Defense)

As the Tet Offensive began, Tom Hagel reported for duty with the scout platoon of 3rd Squadron, 5th Cavalry. Tom and his unit fought around Saigon, then moved up north to counter enemy regular troops menacing U.S. firebases near the demilitarized zone. The squadron took significant casualties and inflicted even more in a series of sharp engagements. (U.S. Department of Defense)

World War II paratrooper Major General Julian J. Ewell (center) took command of the 9th Infantry Division in February of 1968. Here, Ewell listens to 1st Brigade commander Colonel John Geraci. Colonel Ira A. Hunt Jr., the division chief of staff, stands to the right. Smart, aggressive, and uncompromising, Ewell bent his considerable energy to one end—killing Viet Cong. (U.S. Department of Defense)

In 1967, an F-100 Super Sabre fighter-bomber unleashes a clutch of 2.75-inch rockets on a Viet Cong position in the jungle. Note the drifting mist, rocket smoke, and the wild trajectories of some of the projectiles. In Vietnam, American close air support had a devastating impact on the foe, but it was a big hammer, not a precision implement. (U.S. Department of Defense)

In March of 1968, Tom Hagel joined Chuck in Company B, 2-47th Infantry. Chuck would be wounded twice, Tom three times. Each saved the other's life. (U.S. Senator Chuck Hagel Archives, University of Nebraska at Omaha)

Patrolling in the deep jungle of Vietnam was debilitating and deadly. This 1969 photograph depicts a scene that would be only too familiar to both Hagel brothers. (U.S. Department of Defense)

In Vietnam, a 9th Infantry Division soldier reads the *Stars and Stripes*, which brought news from home, good and bad. Note that this issue refers to protests. Both Chuck and Tom Hagel read the *Stars and Stripes* in country. Most U.S. troops did. (U.S. Department of Defense)

In the late 1960s, U.S. Army active duty soldiers and national guardsmen often deployed to quell civil unrest in America's inner cities. Here, troops get organized in Washington, DC, in April of 1968. Omaha, Nebraska, witnessed all too many similar scenes. The Nebraska Army National Guard moved in to restore order on July 4, 1966, when racial tensions boiled over. The National Guard returned to Omaha in April 1968 and again in June 1969. (U.S. Department of Defense)

First Lieutenant Jerome "Skip" Johnson of Chicago, Illinois, served in Company B, 2-47th Infantry in 1968. He started as a platoon leader, then rose to be executive officer (second in command) and finally company commander. In April of 1968, Chuck and Tom Hagel watched Johnson quell a potential racial confrontation in the wake of the assassination of Dr. Martin Luther King Jr. (U.S. Department of Defense)

Three U.S. Air Force C-123 Provider aircraft spray Agent Orange and other defoliant chemicals on swathes of the Vietnamese jungle. The potent liquid killed the plant life but also produced lingering unwelcome effects on all exposed, including American troops. The 9th Infantry Division's area of operations around Bear Cat received multiple applications of these powerful toxins. After the war, both Chuck and Tom Hagel worked to help those affected by Agent Orange. (U.S. Department of Defense)

U.S. Army armored personnel carriers shared the road with Vietnamese civilians. In 1968, these three tracked vehicles of the 5th Battalion, 60th Infantry—
the other mechanized outfit alongside the Hagel brothers' 2-47th Infantry in
the 9th Infantry Division—wait to move near the city of My Tho in the Mekong
Delta. The nearest vehicle is an M577 command post carrier, notable for a
"second story" to permit soldiers to work inside while standing up. The M113 to
the left has an ammunition box on top, its ramp up, and the small troop access
door open. The M113 broadside in the center of the scene carries a 106mm
recoilless rifle, a useful bunker buster. (U.S. Department of Defense)

Chuck and Tom Hagel, both acting NCOs, take a break atop an M113 armored
personnel carrier. The brothers wear berets given to them by Royal Thai Army
soldiers working with the U.S. 9th Infantry Division. The M60 machine gun
between the Hagels was known as the "pig" for its loud snorting sound as it
ripped through 7.62mm ammunition belts like those draped over Tom. Whether
mounted on tracked vehicles or carried on foot patrol, the M60 could deliver
effective fire out to about a half mile. At close range, it was especially lethal.
(U.S. Senator Chuck Hagel Archives, University of Nebraska at Omaha)

In May 1968, south Saigon became a war zone during the enemy offensive known as Mini-Tet. This overhead view shows a column of U.S. M113s waiting to move out. Two M48 tanks (lower right) are part of the task force. The 2nd Battalion, 47th Infantry, including Chuck and Tom Hagel, went into action in this area on May 9, 1968. (U.S. Department of Defense)

As a wounded soldier on the ramp awaits evacuation, riflemen of 2-47th Infantry shelter inside an M113 near the critical Y-bridge in Saigon during the May 1968 Mini-Tet fighting. (U.S. Department of Defense)

With their helicopter on the ground, a UH-1D Huey flight crew looks up as U.S. Air Force fighter-bombers pound south Saigon during Mini-Tet. The enemy intentionally dug into civilian neighborhoods. (U.S. Department of Defense)

A UH-1D Huey helicopter brings in a rifle squad in Vietnam. Spurred by pugnacious Major General Julian J. Ewell, 2-47th Infantry spent much of the summer of 1968 landing by helicopter right atop enemy positions. It was an effective tactic, but costly. (U.S. Department of Defense)

Lieutenant Colonel Frederick Van Deusen commanded 2-47th Infantry during the busy summer of 1968. He was General William C. Westmoreland's brother-in-law. On July 3, 1968, a Viet Cong guerrilla downed the commander's helicopter, killing him and six others. Tom Hagel shot the enemy soldier who took down Van Deusen's chopper. (U.S. Department of Defense)

Chuck and Tom Hagel enjoyed their leave in Hawaii in the summer of 1968. The five days with their family went by way too fast. (U.S. Senator Chuck Hagel Archives, University of Nebraska at Omaha)

Tom and Chuck Hagel relax with drinks at their place in North Omaha in the summer of 1969. Not long after this photo was taken, the brothers came to blows over Vietnam. (U.S. Senator Chuck Hagel Archives, University of Nebraska at Omaha)

In the late summer of 1968, 2-47th Infantry occupied the firebase at Binh Phuoc. The M113 tracks parked in the northeast corner, at the upper right in this 1970 aerial photograph. Six howitzers from an artillery battery fired from the south end of the cramped compound. This is where both Chuck and Tom Hagel served their final weeks in country. (U.S. Department of Defense)

Secretary of Defense Chuck Hagel shares a joke with U.S. soldiers at the Kabul Military Training Center in Afghanistan on March 10, 2013. (U.S. Department of Defense)

Secretary of Defense Chuck Hagel walks through a U.S. military cemetery in Manila, the Philippines, on August 20, 2013. In Vietnam, he and brother Tom wondered who spoke up for the average rifleman. As a U.S. senator and then the secretary of defense, Chuck Hagel did so. (U.S. Department of Defense)

killed in action and 265 wounded in action, a battalion's field strength lost. In return, the division chalked up 976 NVA/VC killed, 10 prisoners taken, and 253 civilians detained. In the Ewell calculus, the division achieved a 25 to 1 ratio of dead enemy to dead Americans. The general saw it and found it good, and he publicly praised the battle in south Saigon as "one of the biggest allied victories of the war." [60]

Up at MACV, General Westmoreland agreed. Almost at the end of his fifty-four long months in country, the general found time to announce yet one more sterling success. Mini-Tet had been repulsed, "more nuisance than threat," with 40,000 more North Vietnamese killed.[61] That count pretty much matched the final toll assessed for the countrywide Tet Offensive back in January and February. Few bought it.

For the umpteenth time, MACV's numbers did not add up. Most of Mini-Tet happened in Saigon. Ewell, aggressive as hell and not averse to choosing the higher-end figures when filling in the ledger on dead foes, only accounted for one-fortieth of MACV's total estimate of enemy fatalities. While there had been sharp encounters in the U.S. marine area near the Laos border and in Central Highlands as well, "the enemy accomplished nothing more in the north than mortar and rocket attacks," in Westmoreland's words.[62] Even allowing for a coincident major operation by the 101st Airborne Division under way up north in the forbidding A Shau Valley, where and how did all those other tens of thousands of North Vietnamese die?

The ones killed in Saigon also raised questions. The 9th Infantry Division's battalions fought hard in the streets near the Y-bridge. In both Xom Ong Doi and Xom Cau Mat, combat proceeded at short range inside some of the tighter cordons achieved in the war. Post-action searches and tabulations were extensive. Yet the Americans only recovered 238 enemy rifles and pistols and forty-two mortars, RPG launchers, and machine guns. Moreover, the Phu Loi II Battalion, 5th Nha Be Battalion, and 506th Battalion all somehow survived the battle intact, passing like ghosts right through the formidable American encirclements.[63] Skeptical journalists in Saigon and antiwar voices in America took note.

Customary rationalizations ensued. Perhaps a great many weapons vanished in the general devastation, certainly possible given the 23,450 rounds of artillery used, not to mention the high volume of helicopter rockets, aerial bombs, and napalm pumped into the embattled pockets of resistance.[64] U.S. intelligence analysts also observed that the NVA/VC had an excellent battlefield recovery program, ruthlessly policing up key gear. Maybe so. It sure seemed to be a convenient corollary to the standard shibboleth about Charlie dragging off his side's bodies with an efficiency that would be the envy of any U.S. graves registration outfit. Or maybe less than half of the hostile dead carried arms. That would be quite a hazardous way to go to war, but it was possible.

Such dubious accounting led invariably to other suspicions. South Vietnamese authorities and U.S. embassy personnel estimated the number of civilian casualties in south Saigon as anywhere from three hundred to three thousand, depending on who you asked. The 9th Infantry Division's medical teams treated "many thousands" of civilians after the Saigon fighting, and MACV estimated that a quarter million residents of the city lost their dwellings, with 150,000 homes utterly destroyed. As a final gesture, designed to curb disease, the 9th Infantry Division sprayed insect-killing DDT (already known to have distressing side effects) all over what American officers termed "the entire disaster area."[65] Amen to that.

When the fierce engagements happened in south Saigon, conveniently close to their downtown offices, American television, radio, and print journalists swarmed to almost every scene of the deadly action. In testimony to the hazards, six reporters perished trying to chronicle Mini-Tet. But they and their colleagues covered the story.[66] The prevailing themes were destruction and death.

Those kind of bleak thoughts occurred to at least one senior officer in country, too. Returning by air to his Tan Son Nhut headquarters after a meeting at II Field Force headquarters at Long Binh Post, deputy MACV commander General Creighton Abrams looked down past the Huey's skid. In June, Abrams would take command from Westmoreland. He had a lot on his mind. Abrams said later:

As I rode back in my helicopter after hearing how well we were doing, smoke was billowing up in Saigon, flames shooting up in the air. I have estimated that we can defend Saigon seven more times, and then we're going to be faced with the embarrassment that there's no *city* left. And I don't know *how* we're going to explain these nine successful defenses of Saigon, but no goddamn city.[67]

The week of Mini-Tet saw more Americans killed than any other during the entire Vietnam War.[68] To what end? For the remaining true believers, men like Ewell and Westmoreland, all that mattered was the scoreboard. But back home, with peace talks beginning and Lyndon Johnson neutered, it all looked like good money after bad, precious American blood down a rat hole. How many more lives, how many more Chuck or Tom Hagels, was this lost war worth?

CHAPTER 8

The River Blindness

Airmobility, dig it, you weren't going anywhere.
It made you feel safe. It made you feel Omni,
but it was only a stunt, technology.

MICHAEL HERR, *Dispatches*[1]

N obody rioted when Bobby Kennedy was shot. No troops in 2-47th Infantry refused to go out on patrol. A gunman from the anxious present, the Cold War, killed John F. Kennedy. A shooter from the sordid past, the American Civil War, murdered Martin Luther King Jr. And now a face from the future, the shape of U.S. wars to come in the Middle East, cut down RFK in the kitchen of the Ambassador Hotel in Los Angeles in the minutes after midnight on June 5, 1968. "It kind of broke everyone's spirit," Chuck Hagel remembered.[2]

But he and the rest just kept going.

It was almost like they were used to it, hardened to it, rendered numb at the rate of loss on both sides of the Pacific. The USS *Pueblo*, Tet, Khe Sanh, Hue; King's killing, the anguished uprisings that burned American cities, Mini-Tet in Saigon, and now RFK's assassination—it just ran on and on, a torrent of pain that bore them all relentlessly downstream, day after day, night after night. Robert Kennedy's death rendered one more tick mark on the long list of things going to hell in 1968 America, one more body to count. And as any rifleman in country knew, there were always more bodies to count.

After Mini-Tet, the VC did what they did best. They seeped into their Mekong Delta haunts, vanishing into midair like tendrils of smoke. *Enemy advances, we retreat.*

Spurred by Major General Julian J. Ewell, the 9th Infantry Division pursued. It sounded decisive to talk of chasing the slippery Cong, but they defied following. The land itself—thick with undergrowth, swollen with shallow mud-choked waterways, and bereft of decent highways—conspired against the weary Americans. The weather went foul, the wet monsoon blowing ashore weeks late but full of fury. Rice paddies filled, the forest floors went sloppy, and the dirt roads turned to strips of mud. For M113s in 2-47th, most of the region became "no go" terrain.[3] The tracks had to stay on the better roads. And Charlie knew exactly where those ran. He didn't go there.

Ewell did not back off. Driven by his will, 2-47th stayed at it. They took the roadways to dismount points, then pushed off into the lush vegetation, hunting Charlie. The intelligence people thought the VC battalions banged up in Mini-Tet moved to regroup, pulling into the villages and jungles of Long An Province, southwest of Saigon. Some 334,000 Vietnamese lived in Long An. And in the Maoist idiom, in this sea of humanity swam four enemy battalions. The Phu Loi II, 5th Nha Be, and 506th regrouped after Mini-Tet, integrating new arrivals from the north. An NVA outfit fresh off the Ho Chi Minh Trail, the 294th, provided a shield for this rebuilding effort.[4] When the 9th Infantry Division G-2 guys explained it in their clean office huts, it all made perfect sense, nice and crisp and neat, red dots precisely located in the green forested swaths on the map. Out in the wilds of Long An, finding the VC proved as difficult as ever. Nevertheless, Lieutenant Colonel John Tower's men of the 2-47th stayed at it.

Operations in Long An stretched the battalion. Camp Martin Cox at Bear Cat, east of Saigon, remained the 2-47th base, with headquarters, supply, and motor pool facilities. But Long An Province lay on the southwestern side of Saigon. To go there, 2-47th units had to traverse the South Vietnamese capital, a distance of fifty miles on dangerous highways and bypasses. And the battalion still had to carry out roadrunner duties to keep routes open, guard the key sites at distant Gia Ray, and keep VC rocket teams away from the division base camp at Bear Cat. The company, sometimes two, sent to Long An had to stay there for weeks. The company left behind had to carry out tasks that before Mini-Tet wore out the entire battalion. It ran the men ragged. And it took a toll.

On May 27, Company C lost a ten-year veteran staff sergeant and a young corporal, both killed by a mine while trying to secure an engineer road-clearing team.[5] The staff people at the division head-quarters discounted these kinds of tasks—not good for running up the score. But the two men were just as dead as if they'd been killed storming the beach at Normandy on D-Day in 1944.

Two days later, on a similar mission near Bear Cat, in the only too familiar jungle on the outskirts of the Binh Son rubber plantation, Chuck Hagel's squad held a stretch of a small circular platoon perimeter, right on the edge of a small clearing. It was midday, a hot one, with the skies already clouding up for the afternoon monsoon rain. The humidity, as usual, matched the 90°-plus temperature. No VC had been seen for days. Sergeant First Class William Edward Smith moved slowly from soldier to soldier, making sure guys were drinking from their canteens. The rest of the day promised more walking, more looking, and not much finding.

Hagel recalled: "We'd taken a water break. And they opened up on us as we were sitting there." The Americans rolled prone and re-turned fire. As usual, nobody saw Charlie. But the AK bullets kept sizzling overhead. Hagel saw Smith shift position, probably to get the pig gunner going. "And I was just a couple of guys away from him," Chuck Hagel said. "He was just coming up out of a tree, and a sniper shot him in the head."[6] The Americans drove off the VC. No enemy bodies turned up, just blood drops on the foliage.

Losing William Edward Smith hurt a lot. With him gone, Chuck Hagel became acting platoon sergeant. Chuck had just advanced to Specialist 4. Now, with about a year in service, he had to replace a senior NCO, an eighteen-year U.S. Army veteran. Hagel had to run the rifle platoon, evacuate Smith, and finish the day's mission. The morrow would bring more of the same, as would every day to come. Tom took over Chuck's squad. To an outsider, it seemed like some kind of children's crusade, eighteen-year-olds led by a nineteen-year-old and a twenty-one-year-old.

And yet, even by the standards of the world wars, both Hagels had been through a lifetime of combat: Tet, patrols, ambushes, road-runner ops, calling in artillery, arranging medevacs, twice wounded, and then Mini-Tet. They knew their jobs quite well, better than some Fort Benning ninety-day-wonder officer candidate could ever absorb from a field manual or a blank-fire game of bang-bang in the Georgia pine woods. It was that Darwinian impulse once more, survival of the fittest. "And both of us were *very, very good at killing*," [emphasis in original] Tom recalled. "We were amazingly proficient at it all."[7]

For a month, the Hagels kept their platoon going. Above them in the chain of command, nobody felt sorry or backed off. Far from it. Ewell kept bringing the heat. "That was the deal, body count," Chuck Hagel said. "You used that body count, commanding officers did, as the metric and measurement [of] how successful you were."[8]

On June 10, the 2-47th scout platoon went out at night. Their lead track ran into another road mine. Two sergeants died hard. To secure the site, the Hagels' platoon rolled up the next morning.

When he saw the dead men, Tom Hagel immediately recognized Sergeant Arthur John Enquist, the scout platoon medic, from Columbus, Nebraska. Enquist, aged twenty, had been in country a few days longer than Chuck. In Hollywood, actors in war movies die with a little red spot and some dramatics. But Enquist didn't go out in any way suitable for family viewing. He would have to go home to Columbus in a closed casket. "He didn't suffer," Tom summarized grimly.[9]

It fell to Tom Hagel to pack up Enquist's things and send them back home. There wasn't much to send. Like the Hagels, like all of them, Enquist didn't have much of his own in his dusty tent at Bear Cat. Tom told himself that when he got home, he'd go see the Enquist family. He never did.[10] Anyone who'd never been in combat would wonder why not. Anyone who had been under fire, like brother Chuck or father Charles Dean . . . well, they'd understand immediately. When you're already carrying the crushing weight of all those you lost, and all those you killed, you don't volunteer to add another.

Tom Hagel did mention it in a letter home, another example of both brothers' tendency to share difficult thoughts with their mother and brothers. After mentioning Enquist, Tom wrote: "Well, last night I was talking to him and messin' around until they had to go on patrol." He continued: "Last night some VC snuck up on them and killed four and wounded four. Bad! Enquist was killed."[11] Tom didn't get the casualty count right—although badly wounded, two scouts he thought dead made it out alive. But it served as a reminder of the steady attrition.

Tom also broke the news of the brothers' second set of Purple Hearts. Here, he softened the blow as Chuck had in his letter about their first wounds. He described Chuck as burned but "completely healed and no scars." Tom spared his mother the details of his brother's post-wound agony. "I had never felt such pain before in my life," Chuck wrote, although not to his family in Nebraska. It would be decades before Chuck Hagel could shave the left half of his face with a nonelectric razor. In later life, an attempt to grow a beard produced a wild patchwork akin to the surface of the Dakota badlands.[12] Not a bit of that made it into Tom's writing to his family.

Tom tiptoed around his own condition, too. He briefly mentioned his own scorched arms and his head concussion, "which is *completely* healed." No more was said, nor could it be. "So no sweat when you get the next set of Purple Hearts," he wrote.[13]

But Betty Hagel did sweat. She loved getting the letters. "She lived for the mail," her son Mike remembered. But she worried, too. What she didn't know could hurt her, all right. When the phone rang one day in May, her son Mike answered. A distant, static-filled military voice asked for "Mrs. Betty Hagel." Mike told her it sounded like the U.S. Army. She began crying, fearing the worst. But it wasn't that. Instead, after Mini-Tet, Chuck and Tom made it to the Bear Cat MARS (Military Auxiliary Radio System) station and phoned home, a bit late for Mother's Day, but close enough.[14] The brothers wanted to give her a surprise. They did.

There weren't any good surprises in the 2-47th those days, only more of the same. The month after Mini-Tet ended badly, just the way it started. In a major firefight with the 294th NVA Battalion on June 25–26, Company A and Company B joined in an attempted encirclement by parts of five U.S. battalions. The piling on went as well as ever—which meant it didn't quite work. Charlie ate a great many artillery rounds, helicopter rockets, and aerial bombs. A lot got away. When the gunfire subsided, the Americans claimed 166 foes killed, one captured, and eighty-two weapons found. It cost twenty U.S. dead and eighty-one wounded. The division hailed it as a great success, a worthy next achievement after Mini-Tet.[15] You wondered if anybody had whispered to Ewell that after LBJ's retrenchment of March 31, only the U.S. losses counted. And twenty were twenty too many.

Among those killed were seven men from Company A, including two platoon sergeants. Company B suffered two killed, PFC Dominic Ungaro Jr. and Specialist 5 Phillip "Doc" Rogers, one of the stalwarts of the outfit.[16] The doc's wound in Mini-Tet turned out to be just enough to get him evacuated from South Saigon but not enough to send him home. It was probably the only diagnosis the senior medic ever missed. The VC did not miss. The deaths just added up, one after another.

At the 9th Infantry Division, the bookkeepers didn't think about William Smith or Arthur Enquist or Doc Rogers, all numbers at that level. It's not that the staffers didn't care. They did. But they didn't know these 2-47th soldiers, any more than they knew Senator Robert Kennedy. What the guys at division headquarters did know was that 2-47th had the worst ratio of American to VC dead in the entire command.[17] And that had to change.

On June 15, just before the big operation that took the life of Doc Rogers, a new commander took over 2-47th Infantry. Lieutenant Colonel Frederick French "Fritz" Van Deusen came with a pedigree and a half: son of an army colonel, West Point Class of 1953, veteran of post-war Korean duty and the 1965–66 Dominican Republic incursion. He owned a reputation as a hard-charger. He was also General

William C. Westmoreland's brother-in-law.[18] Van Deusen had something to prove. He had never failed at anything in his life.

But as Americans learned over and over in Vietnam, there's always
a first time.

HELICOPTERS! They'd carry Fritz Van Deusen and his hard-luck
2-47th to victory. Choppers could zip right across Saigon, from Bear
Cat into the Mekong Delta. Forget about those bulky 12-ton M113s.
In rural Long An, even a mediocre VC leader could guess which few
routes American mechanized forces must use in the wet season. But
with aviation, the possibilities for getting out and about mushroomed
exponentially. Speed, surprise, flexibility—every tactical buzzword
seemed right there for the taking.

Helicopters solved it all in Vietnam. Jungles, mountains, and rivers
could be crossed at will. Moreover, choppers landed and took off not
from long, prepared runways but out of any reasonable patch of open
ground. Whereas World War II parachute drops scattered troops all
over the place and gliders of that era delivered key heavy weapons
and small troop elements almost on the X (admittedly often by crash-
ing there), by the 1960s, rotary wing aircraft placed formed units together smack atop isolated wilderness locales. Leg infantry slogged
at two and a half miles an hour, and M113s on flat hard ground might
roll along at ten times that speed. But helicopters raced above it all
at a hundred miles an hour. Even guerrillas couldn't outrun American sky cavalry. The army called it breaking free of "the tyranny of
terrain."[19] For a society in love with technology, the helicopter sure
looked to be an answer, and probably *the* answer, to the challenges
of finding and killing Cong in the backcountry of South Vietnam.

The enduring image of the Vietnam War must certainly be the
bulbous-nosed UH-1 helicopter, skids up, flaring to land on a flattened
billow of elephant grass. The army labeled the UH-1 "Iroquois," ad-
hering to the service's tradition of naming aircraft for Indian tribes.
Nobody but a few purists ever used the official title. Everybody
called it "Huey."

The Huey came in four basic variants. UH-1C "Hog" gunships carried rockets and mini-guns. UH-1 D "slick" troop transports flew riflemen into battle; those had an M60 machine gun swinging free in each open side door, and so the onboard gunners could stitch a hostile treeline as their Huey came in to land. UH-1H "Dust Off" medevac helicopters pulled out the wounded. Finally, the UH-1D and H model "C&C" or "Charlie-Charlie" birds allowed commanders to get up in the air to direct operations.

In addition, the 9th Infantry Division also used little bubble-top OH-23 Raven choppers for C&C and reconnaissance, and the armed AH-1G Cobra (a heavily modified Huey derivative) for rocket and mini-gun missions. Now and then, higher headquarters allocated larger CH-47 Chinook and CH-54 Tarhe cargo craft to move artillery howitzers and other heavy cargo. Those types could even sling a stripped-down M113 on their cargo hooks, one of the reasons the tracks featured lightweight aluminum armor.[20] Given a choice, most 2-47th soldiers would have preferred heavier M113 armor and the hell with the mech battalion's infrequent resort to heliborne mobility. But, of course, none of the weapons developers asked the infantry privates.

The M113's armor might have been inadequate to stop a .50-caliber machine gun bullet, let alone an RPG, but a track could shrug off the smaller stuff, like AK rounds. Helicopters could not. For all their many advantages, rotary wing aircraft had no armor. If struck in one of their many, many vulnerable spots—engine, transmission, cockpit—helicopters tended to stop running and come apart. It's probably an indicator that the key connector between the rotor shaft and the main blade assembly went by the name of the "Jesus nut."[21] Only He could save you if that thing got hit. Worse, once the main rotor disk quit spinning, or the tail blades failed, a Huey possessed the aerodynamic qualities of a brick. Army aviators told each other, and their human cargo, that a damaged bird could "auto-rotate" to the ground, the big main blades spinning without power until the thing safely touched down. Nobody wanted to try that, especially with Mr. Charles blazing away during the entire lazy downward spiral.

During the entire war, during 36,145,000 separate helicopter sorties, the enemy, bad weather, mechanical failures, and aviator errors combined to knock down 4,642 aircraft. That number amounted to more than the total number of army helicopters in country in 1968, and far exceeds today's entire U.S. Army rotary wing fleet.[22] If you sifted the statistics like an insurance actuary, comfortably ensconced in an air-conditioned office, the probabilities didn't sound that dire. About one flight in eight thousand ended in an unpleasant way, not all fatal, and not all nonrecoverable. Many cracked-up helicopters underwent repairs and flew again. So there.

To say that only one in eight thousand crashed might seem pretty acceptable, until you considered that amounted to twice the rate of incidents in nonhostile military helicopter flights. It also mattered what the choppers were doing. Carting Bob Hope and a USO troupe from one U.S. camp to another didn't risk much. But going into a hot landing zone (LZ) sure magnified the hazard; 57 percent of all helicopters lost went down trying to land or take off under fire. And, of course, if you happened to be aboard unlucky number eight thousand, well . . . all bad. Army aviators, largely young warrant officers with a bit more time in service than the Hagel brothers, flew these dangerous missions. Almost one in ten Americans killed in Vietnam died during helicopter operations. [23]

Most aviation missions in Vietnam occurred in daylight. Two decades later, evolving night-vision technology allowed helicopter operations to benefit from the concealment of night. But in Vietnam, those were unusual. Pushed by Ewell, the 9th Infantry Division carried out more night flights than most, although still less than a fifth of all missions.[24] By 1968, though, any novelty in Vietnam helicopter warfare had long worn thin. Airmobility might be new for 2-47th. But Charlie sure knew the deal.

The warrant officers did, too. Faced by often alerted opponents richly endowed with machine guns, automatic rifles, and RPGs, the aviators argued for strong preparatory airstrikes and artillery fires, cover by helicopter gunships, very careful selection of LZs, and quick dismounting by infantry to permit the most rapid possible trips in and out. If ground commanders tried to get cute, or even worse, if all the pre-assault fires fell flat, experienced flight warrants knew what came next. "We went in there one afternoon," one account read, "and I never seen such shit thrown at us, from both sides of the mountains and below." That from below was more lethal. "You get the River Blindness out there," the speaker said. "It's when you go down to the river and get your *eyes* shot out."[25]

DOWN TO THE RIVER—that's where 2-47th went on July 3, 1968. Lieutenant Colonel Fritz Van Deusen read the tea leaves from higher. The G-2 estimates placed a company, maybe less, of the 294th Battalion (supposedly VC, but really NVA) near Hoang Hon Tren, a gaggle of thatched-roof hootches right on the west bank of the meandering, muddy, rain-swollen Vam Co Dong River. Encouraged by his innovative, fire-breathing brigade commander, Colonel Henry E "Gunfighter" Emerson—Ewell's favorite, but legitimately gifted as a tactician—Van Deusen planned to try a new method called "jitterbugging."[26]

In essence, jitterbugging took advantage of the flat terrain in Long An, a mix of open rice paddies, small settlements, waterways, and irregular patches of thick forests. In the jitterbug approach, a battalion gathered every scrap of intelligence: aerial photographs, radio intercepts, airborne radar readouts, agent reports, the ARVN rumor mill, and even the findings of a Huey rigged with an XM-2 "people sniffer" that smelled human body odors (urine and sweat) in remote areas.[27] The U.S. battalion staff pieced it all together, a mosaic of suspected enemy positions in woods and villages surrounded by an array of small open rice paddies. Then the commander would pick where to get started, the most likely VC hideout, as well as a series of alternates. Working with the aviators, the Americans then selected the nearest possible LZs.

Rather than rely on company-scale or even battalion-strength lifts into big LZs, jitterbugging went small, at least to begin. The infantry battalion used five Hueys to insert a rifle platoon in the rice paddy closest to the suspected enemy positions—in a village, an overgrown river bank, or a wooded area. If the first spot turned out to be a dry hole, the Hueys came right back and the platoon reboarded and flew to the next location, then the next, until the troops struck pay dirt.

Sometimes the intel really came together, and the Americans plopped down within fifteen yards of Charlie. That got interesting fast. When the bad guys reacted, other platoons would be put in by helicopter, one after another, forming a cordon to keep the enemy trapped in the trees or village. Usually those reinforcements came from the U.S. battalion itself, but they could also be thrown into the fray from other nearby friendly outfits. In one really energetic battalion, the troops carried out sixteen separate jitterbug combat assaults in a single day, often into the teeth of VC fire. Once the blocks were set, the Americans poured in the firepower: artillery, helicopter rockets, napalm, and high explosives.[28] It was the field and stream version of what happened in south Saigon during Mini-Tet.

Jitterbugging shocked the Cong in Long An. They were not used to seeing such direct assaults. And it ran up the opposition body count, all right. But it wasn't free of cost. As Ewell later noted: "This was pushing the balance of the risk of a hot landing zone against the achievement of total surprise to its limit."[29] Well, like the guys in Third Army used to say about George Patton, his guts, our blood.

At the user level, among the sergeants and acting sergeants, hopping right on Mr. Charles didn't resonate all that well. Asked for his thoughts by an interviewer enthusiastic about Emerson's jitterbug tactics, Chuck Hagel replied with: "Mm-hmm."[30] His laconic recollection says it all. The bugs were not happy.

Happy or not, first light on July 3 saw 2-47th jitterbugging away. Lieutenant Colonel Van Deusen inserted his lead platoon not long after sunup. They landed a hundred yards west of Hoang Hon Tren, in a rice paddy filled ankle deep with brown water and God knows what else. Mr. Charles welcomed them immediately with AK-47 rifle fire and at least one RPD machine gun. Some guerrilla loosed an RPG, but the Hueys got out okay and headed back to pick up the next platoon. Meanwhile, UH-1C Hog gunships rocketed the hostile treeline.[31] Pile on.

The 9th Infantry Division's massive base at Bear Cat served as the pickup zone for 2-47th. On the helipad waited a single rifle platoon, the next to launch. The riflemen had a new lieutenant, a young guy just in country, and a new platoon sergeant, too. They formed in six-man squads. Each group knelt on the edge of the airstrip, awaiting the inbound Hueys. On paper, a UH-1D could move eleven troops. But in the hot, humid Mekong Delta, ferrying soldiers laden with eighty pounds of gear, water, and ammunition, six about did it, with seven in a pinch.[32] That worked out well, as five Hueys could handily pick up one of the 2-47th understrength rifle platoons.

Specialist 4 Chuck Hagel wasn't with them. He remained on the other side of the huge camp at Bear Cat. Chuck had orders to attend the Reliable NCO Academy, a two-week course that would qualify him for promotion to sergeant. First Sergeant Garcia assigned Chuck to supervise Company B's detail assigned to the local defense team on the Bear Cat base perimeter. That would allow Chuck to report on time to the training.[33] Frankly, with two Purple Hearts already, it was a break. Garcia knew it, and despite the blizzard of orders descending from division about getting a maximum number of infantrymen out into the rice paddies, the first sergeant did it anyway.

Specialist 4 Tom Hagel also received orders to go to the Reliable NCO Academy, and was supposed to be on duty at Bear Cat, too. To allow him to prepare, Tom had been temporarily assigned to the battalion headquarters as an "information specialist," a nebulous position that envisioned him hanging around inside the wire taking photographs and talking to visiting Vietnamese villagers. But with a big portion of the 2-47th chasing Charlie through the Long An wetlands, Tom redefined his new role. He didn't have any intention of staying inside the fence line back at Bear Cat. On the busy morning of July 3, Tom made his way to the base pickup zone intending to snap pictures of the troops preparing for the combat assault. But when he recognized riflemen he'd served with during the last few tough weeks, Tom reinterpreted his duties. After Mini-Tet, Tom Hagel had no illusions about the misbegotten nature of the U.S. war effort, dismissing much of the official line as "propaganda." But for a Specialist

4 and acting NCO, policy and strategy mattered not one whit. "My sole commitment was to my people," he recalled.[34] And although on temporary detached duty, Tom Hagel saw those men as his guys, if only for this day.

He lined up at the tail end of one of the rows of riflemen awaiting the Hueys. Tom carried a cheap camera and a .45 automatic pistol, not exactly the right load-out for a combat assault into a hot LZ.[35] At about 8:30 a.m., he went anyway.

THE HUEYS DESCENDED swiftly to the open rice paddy surface, throwing a light spray of dirty water as the birds flared to land. The left-door gunner pounded away with his M60 machine gun; the right guy held fire, as a ragged rank of prone American troops huddled off to that side, using the shelter of a paddy dike. Beyond them to the east stood the *ville*. Smoke from rocket fire rose in the bright-green trees on either side of the huts of Hoang Hon Tren. If there were Vietnamese civilians still in there, they'd better get into their little scrape-outs and start praying. Charlie wasn't backing off today.

The UH-1D's skids barely touched and Tom Hagel and the other men tumbled out into the wet brown mud. Tom described the scene as "absolute chaos."[36] Enemy fire raised spouts in the paddy puddles. The VC popped bullets into the thin-skinned Hueys, even as the choppers barely touched and then sprang up. At least one lift helicopter looked to be in bad shape, but it got out somehow. Americans on the ground fired back, red tracers versus green tracers, the usual sound and light show. Naturally, nobody saw Mr. Charles. But he sure seemed to see all the Americans. And the VC had no shortage of ammunition.

Hagel and the rest of the platoon, heads down, helmets bobbing, sprinted and sloshed to the paddy dike. There they intermixed with the unit already there. Nobody went forward. Most of the riflemen shot back, especially the M60 pig gunners. Some Americans did not fire at all. One panicked guy even stuck up his M16 rifle and pulled the trigger, a futile gesture at best. Whatever nifty Fort Benning scheme of maneuver had been devised back at Bear Cat went right out the window. "It never seems to happen the way it's supposed to," Tom Hagel said.[37] Pinned along the west flank of the dirt berm, the U.S. troops counted on the armed choppers to suppress Charlie.

A UH-1C Hog gunship came in, mini-guns roaring like berserk chainsaws. A VC machine gunner went right back at the aircraft, green tracers spearing into the Hog's hull. The aviator on the stick pitched violently to shake off the guerrilla shooter. But he didn't let up on the mini-gun. The stream of 7.62mm bullets raked through the paddy dike. The soldier next to Tom Hagel had his rear end blown open, no laughing matter. A sidelong glance showed white pelvic bone in the oozing red gash.[38] Good God.

The gunship's run quelled the VC some. A platoon sergeant urged the Americans to their feet, setting the example. He went down. But the lieutenant, the rah-rah Joe College type leading Hagel's adopted platoon, kept the men going.[39] The Americans slipped past an enemy bunker and reached the edge of the hamlet.

Veteran Hagel, with many firefights as an acting NCO, immediately saw the rookie mistake. That VC bunker hadn't been cleared. It was, Hagel observed, a "cardinal rule" that if you see an enemy position, "you never pass it."[40] In all the confusion, the inexperienced lieutenant did so.

Mr. Charles provided the standard dose of education. From behind the upright U.S. infantrymen, an RPD machine gun rasped, and then an RPG rocket whooshed out of the nearby trees. You could see those coming at you. The thing barely armed before it blew. Hot fragments cut into Tom Hagel's neck, back, and leg. The savvy nineteen-year-old dropped into the corner of a dike to get out of the line of VC fire. He had three rounds left in his pistol. The other Americans had to get shooting.

Except they weren't there.

Tom Hagel watched as the surprised U.S. riflemen ran away. What the hell. In prior firefights, Hagel had sometimes been compelled to make his own guys fire back, to "literally yell and kick at people— start shooting." But these soldiers just skedaddled. Tom had never seen such a thing.[41] Holding only a pistol, all Hagel could do was fold himself into his covered chunk of ground and hope the VC didn't notice him.

Somebody rallied the gun-shy Americans. The continued pounding by the armed helicopters helped, as did the arrival of more troops, more from Company B and more from Company A, too. Charlie had enough. Leaving his dead, the opposing force pulled back to the riverbank. The strengthened U.S. ground force again entered the village. Tom found the men he knew and went with them in among the hovels.[42]

With the shooting over, the Americans set out a security perimeter. Sergeants started redistributing ammunition—they'd gone through a lot. Wounded Americans were moved to the LZ for pickup. A few soldiers began to drag over individual NVA bodies. That's how you usually saw them, dead or captured. But live and shooting—not likely. During all of this, the villagers of Hoang Hon Tren, those few still in town, wisely stayed inside.

In one humble shack, movement flashed in the doorway, a person coming out. Joe College, the lieutenant Hagel labeled "shaky," shot immediately, quick kill, right out of the infantry training course. Shoot at movement. Shoot at a ripple of clothing, the black pajamas. Shoot first. He did, from a few feet away.

The jumpy lieutenant killed a young woman, about twenty years old. To add to the misery, she was pregnant. She held no weapon and wore no web gear. Although Tom Hagel and the other experienced infantrymen had seen more than one female guerrilla, this one wasn't VC. It was a horrible screw-up, face to face. That officer would have to live with it for the rest of his life. Some callous Americans didn't care about Vietnamese casualties, friendly, neutral, or enemy. Not so Tom Hagel. "I could not separate myself from that," he said, "and if I had, I'd really worry."[43]

Hagel and the rest of the platoon finished searching the village. Beyond the one dead civilian, a few enemy corpses—VC, NVA, NVA acting as VC, whatever—and some damaged enemy rifles, gear, and affiliated ammunition, nothing else turned up. By midafternoon, about three o'clock, Tom Hagel and his fellow riflemen made it to the edge of the Vam Co Dong River. The adrenaline rush of the morning clash had long since dissipated. With the searing tropical sun high in the sky, heat left the men "dazed" and "exhausted," as Hagel recalled. The Americans panted, out of water. Although they'd shared their bullets to ensure everybody had some, ammunition had run short.[44] A resupply would be useful.

At about that time, Company A's commander, Captain Richard K. Holoday, reported losing radio communication with one of his rifle platoons. That could mean a battery problem, a failed radio, or VC trouble. A burst of automatic fire to the north indicated that Charlie hadn't left the area yet.

That brought Lieutenant Colonel Van Deusen to the ground. The 2-47th commander had landed his UH-1D C&C chopper a few times during the morning firefight, mostly to place arriving units, but also to assess the situation. Now with Holoday's platoon off the net, Van Deusen touched down. After spending some time with Company A as they traded shots with Mr. Charles, the lieutenant colonel took off again. Holoday and his two radiomen joined the battalion commander inside the aircraft.

Van Deusen told the aviators to circle slowly as Holoday and his two NCOs scanned the rice paddy dikes for the separated platoon. The C&C ship orbited at low level above the river.[45] Numerous radio calls brought no replies. The rifle platoon had seemingly vanished without a trace. That was unlikely, but such friction predominates in combat. Maybe the captain wasn't as sure as he thought of where that platoon really had ended up.

An alert Viet Cong guerrilla took advantage of the low-flying Huey. The enemy had been paying close attention to previous U.S. jitterbug operations. In an order sent to all units in Long An Province, the VC Military Region 2 headquarters directed countertactics. Ideally, communist forces had to avoid getting trapped near obvious landing zones. If found and attacked by a U.S. jitterbug element, a portion of the unit must furiously fire back, tearing up the American aircraft and buying time for the guerrillas to escape. Finally, the VC commander told each of his regiments to select and train several helicopter ambush squads. "The function of the sniping cell will be to shoot down the CP [command post] chopper."[46] In other words, take out the brain of the jitterbug.

Van Deusen probably didn't mean to do it. But by swinging low over the open waterway, trying to locate Company A's orphan platoon, the 2-47th commander made it easy for the enemy. A single marksman with an AK-47 opened up, burping out a series of high-velocity 7.62mm rounds.

The bad guy was right near Tom Hagel and his enervated platoon mates. The AK cracked away, "a very distinct sound," well known to Hagel and the other veterans.[47] A dense wall of greenery hid the busy hostile gunman. The VC quickly ran through a full thirty-round magazine, but not just yanking the trigger. This one was aiming his shots.

From Tom Hagel's vantage point, the Huey suddenly "stopped dead in the air over the river." It almost appeared the helicopter hit an invisible wall in the sky. Then it "fell like a rock," straight down into the river. It belly-flopped into the water and broke apart, a shattered mess. Several misshapen olive-drab pieces sank swiftly. Twenty seconds later, three struggling figures bobbed to the surface. The VC kept methodically banging away, determined to administer the finishing touches of a fatal dose of the river blindness.

Hagel had "never seen anything like it." He described the event as "stunning," which it was, and "incredible" in the absolute sense—not able to be believed. Yet there it was, right in front of him. The gaping troops around Hagel, eyes wide, did nothing. The guerrilla shot again.[48] The Americans in the water, ducking from the AK bullets, had nowhere to go but down.

Yes, there was a lot of undergrowth between that sharp-shooting VC and Hagel's men. Nobody could tell if there were friendlies over on the other side, especially with a platoon from Company A out there somewhere. Tossing grenades or blazing away through the bush might work, but both techniques threatened to rip up any Americans stuck in the line of fire. And unlike on television, real bullets from modern military weapons move with nearly irresistible force.

The slugs keep going and going, even after punching holes in men or foliage. So firing blindly wouldn't work. Meanwhile, the AK guy gave no indication of quitting. "Somebody had to do something."[49]

That somebody was Tom Hagel.

The Specialist 4 picked up a battered Viet Cong M1 carbine, a U.S. World War II surplus weapon taken from the ARVN, used by Charlie, and then repossessed that morning by the Americans. The weapon had a weathered wooden stock and, more importantly, a thirty-round magazine inserted. How many bullets did it still have? Hagel couldn't tell. Hefting it up, the carbine felt like it had some rounds left. It would have to do.

In seconds, although it seemed to unfold in an unreal slow-motion tableau, Hagel plunged through a narrow gap in the lush bushes. The opponent had his back turned. He was still engaging the floaters. Crack. Crack.

The leaves rustled. The VC turned, his powder-smudged AK barrel coming up. He looked right at Tom Hagel, ten feet away. The American squeezed the trigger once. "And I just shot him right in the forehead."[50]

Six other soldiers, two from the 2-47th Infantry battalion headquarters, the pair of radiomen from Company A, and both crew chief/gunners from the 240th Aviation Company, died in the Vam Co Dong River with Lieutenant Colonel Frederick Van Deusen. The two pilots and Captain Holoday survived. When they pulled out the next morning, the Americans claimed a body count of twenty-four VC.[51] Tom Hagel for sure knew of one. Any way you did the arithmetic, it sure didn't feel like a victory.

THERE WAS MORE. It seemed like there was always more misery in Vietnam, especially now, with the war going slowly sour, the homeland in an uproar, and the likes of Julian J. Ewell pressing one and all to stack up more Cong. Thus Charlie had been well and truly slain on July 3. And with Westmoreland's brother-in-law and six more souls fallen into a watery grave, staff officers from the 9th Infantry Division headquarters came down from the clouds like gods to grub among the yeomen. Apparently, they flew out at Ewell's direction to determine what happened. The major general expected plenty of queries from Washington and MACV. As always, Ewell's instincts served him well.

Sweat-stained, bloodied by the RPG blast, thirsty and forlorn, Tom Hagel described what unfolded next. Three Hueys fluttered into the clearing just west of the village. The riflemen watched as "all these sucky-faced colonels with all their shiny shoes and shit got off."[52] Having just been in a big two-way firefight that killed a good number of hostile soldiers and left several Americans dead and badly wounded, seen a village woman cut down by accident, witnessed a horrific helicopter shoot-down, and then drilled a man eye-to-eye, Tom Hagel was in no mood to entertain visitors from on high. Wisely, he stepped aside and kept his mouth shut. A smart specialist 4 knows when to do that.

The staff officers, lieutenant colonels and majors, examined the uneven lineup of dead communists. The headquarters people noticed the relatively fresh khaki uniforms, the new web gear, and the well-maintained AKs, RPDs, and RPG launcher. It all suggested that NVA regulars really were filling in the depleted VC units, just as the division G-2 analysts forecasted. Did these fallen foes come from the 294th Battalion?[53] Nobody could really tell. Such considerations occupied minds up at division.

A few officers stripped watches off the guerrilla corpses. In an odd action, "the only atrocity I ever witnessed," Tom Hagel saw a major tell an ARVN soldier to slice a ring finger off one of the lifeless Cong. The body was already swelling in the heat, and the ring could no longer be yanked free. It's possible these officers needed these items to try to confirm the unit of those killed. But to Hagel and his jaded comrades, it sure appeared to be souvenir hunting.[54]

Of course, no one in authority explained anything to the riflemen. Their interests satisfied, the well-scrubbed staff officers departed in a flurry of Huey rotor blades. Soon afterward, those on the ground also boarded helicopters, but not to leave. Instead, they executed another jitterbug move. The aircraft moved the soldiers across the river, near where the C&C Huey splashed down. The riflemen spent the night in an ambush position. Fortunately, Charlie wasn't interested. Although sore and smarting from embedded RPG fragments, Tom Hagel stayed with his adopted platoon. At long last, he'd gotten something that put him ahead of his high-achieving brother Chuck: a third Purple Heart. When the lift birds came in the next morning, Tom Hagel went out the way he'd gone in—with his guys.[55] He'd seen some things Chuck had not. And it stuck with him, a stain that never washed out.

VAN DEUSEN'S DEATH made the papers. For William C. Westmoreland and his wife, Katherine Van Deusen Westmoreland, July 3 had been set aside for the general's swearing in as U.S. Army chief of staff. The ceremony happened as an afterthought as the devastated Westmoreland household absorbed the tragic message from Vietnam.[56] Six other American families received that same dreaded news. You could leave the war, but it followed you home.

The 9th Infantry Division kept right on jitterbugging, even as Charlie wised up. The division's canny adversaries took down thirty-one helicopters in July and August of 1968; seventy-four other aircraft sustained substantial damage from hostile gunfire. Put another way, jitterbugging pretty much erased an entire army aviation battalion. Mr. Charles killed another battalion commander on the ground and on August 26 nearly finished off Colonel Emerson himself in another successful Huey shoot-down. The division recorded a body count of 563 NVA/VC, plus 37 captured. The Americans secured only 166 rifles and 14 crew-served weapons, generating some concern among those inclined to take an interest in such details. (Exactly how many actual guerrillas, rather than unlucky civilians, had been killed in Long An Province?) In any event, chest-thumping 10:1 kill ratio aside, it all cost way too many Americans: 58 killed and 263 wounded, effectively the field strength of a U.S. infantry battalion.[57] That kind of trade-off might have been acceptable in the trench-line abattoir of World War I. But in post-Tet Vietnam, on the ground and at home, it led to only one question, the one without an answer: Why?

In Fritz Van Deusen's brief tenure (June 15 to July 3), 2-47th registered eighteen U.S. killed. Even by generous accounting, during that period the battalion got credit for fifty-seven dead opponents, two dozen of them in the extended July 3 firefight. For his bravery, the fallen commander earned the Distinguished Service Cross, America's second-highest award for valor. [58] It was something. But no award, not matter how prestigious, could ameliorate the sorrow in the Van Deusen home. Just because he was a long-serving professional didn't make his passing any easier.

Lieutenant Colonel James L. Scovel took over 2-47th Infantry not long after Van Deusen died.[59] The army didn't like to leave a major in command of a battalion, especially in the high-energy 9th Infantry Division. Scovel became the fourth 2-47th Infantry commander in a bit more than fourteen months. Two—Van Deusen and William B. Cronin in late April of 1967—fell by the enemy's hand. Add that to the turnover at the company level, such as the six commanders (one killed, one badly wounded) in Company B since January, not to mention the revolving door of lieutenants and the steady churn of killed and wounded NCOs, and it's no wonder young men like Tom Hagel grew up fast out in the bush.

In the aftermath of the July 3 action, at least one senior officer recommended Tom for the Silver Star, third in precedence among U.S. valor awards, to go with his third Purple Heart. He eventually received the Bronze Star with "V" (valor) device, the nation's fourth most prestigious medal for bravery, which he certainly deserved.[60] For that matter, Tom had more than met the criteria for the Silver Star. For what it was worth, both brothers also rated official commendation for their gutsy effort, although wounded, to lead the company out of the VC-infested jungle back on March 28, but that water had long ago passed under the orderly room bridge. Given the haphazard nature of awards procedures in Vietnam, even Tom's Bronze Star for July 3 came as a welcome surprise.

Infantry units in country were notoriously poor on paperwork. If rifle company leaders liked to fill out forms, they'd have gone into the Adjutant General's Corps. As a result, relatively noncontentious matters, like Purple Hearts and Combat Infantryman Badges, went right through. But valor awards required a carefully worded, properly typed citation and supporting statements. Overworked officers and sergeants didn't always get around to the write-ups. The company clerks had to peck it all out, along with administrative directives, promotion orders, personnel evaluations, supply forms, combat plans, periodic reports, and a thousand other demands of the official U.S. Army. Shooting war or not, the paper chase never let up. Maybe it could have worked out at Fort Bliss or Fort Ord. But at Bear Cat, let alone at forward firebases with a twelfth of the outfit changing out monthly? Forget it.

As a result, all too many times, awards in MACV somehow struck the exact wrong note. As one 9th Infantry Division officer put it: "The awards system was an atrocity." Not in the same league as cutting off a finger to get a ring, but the harsh accusation rang true enough. The officer went on: "It was used more as a morale builder and for other political reasons than to reward true valor in combat."[61] Overly ambitious officers and even some careerist sergeants wrote up their own narratives, citations, and even witness statements, which they pleaded with privates to sign. Draftees were overlooked, as few of those temporary troops cared all that much about such army formalities. But the junior soldiers knew what really went down in firefights. When the younger enlisted men saw the deserving ignored and the undeserving feted, it grated. Over time, the entire awards drill built resentment between draftee riflemen, including acting NCOs like the Hagels, and the lifers.

The Bronze Star marked a critical day in Tom Hagel's evolution as a soldier. On July 3, he killed a foe, a fellow human being, one on one. Even in a rifle company, and despite the high volume of gunfire traded in the claustrophobic jungles and villages of Vietnam, few men on either side dealt that brand of close-quarters death. Movies and television love to portray personal combat, especially hand-to-hand encounters, punching, wrestling, stabbing, and so forth. While quite exciting, such jarring events are also extraordinarily unusual. Most enemy troops in Vietnam died under the stand-off flensing of aerial bombardment, helicopter gun runs, and artillery barrages. Almost all of the rest fell to infantry machine gun engagements and rifle fire at midrange, often through heavy foliage. American riflemen aligned on motion, muzzle flashes, or spots of colored cloth near or far, but definitely not close enough to see a face. The average U.S. infantry soldier met his opponent in person only when the VC lay dead or stood mute in hang-dog captivity.[62] When American troops saw slain enemies, lots of the riflemen had just squeezed their triggers. But who knew whose bullet did the final deed? That had been Chuck Hagel's experience—plenty bad, certainly unnerving, but still allowing for the barest wisp of a distance, and so a thankful degree of impersonality.

Yet after July 3, Tom Hagel had been denied that slim comfort. He saw the man he shot through the head. Certainly it had been him or Tom, shoot or die, the classic showdown. Tom Hagel did just what the drill sergeants taught him to do, that ultimate feat so often discussed and so rarely executed. When lesser men might have frozen and paid with their lives, and those of other Americans, Tom acted like a soldier.

Still, he did it, he alone, eyeball to eyeball, and no rationalization would ever alter that stark fact. Moreover, scant hours earlier, Tom had stood a few steps away when a keyed-up lieutenant blew away an unarmed young female civilian. What a day—a twofer from hell. Now and again, always unbidden, never wholly forgotten, and never really forgiven, those extremely disturbing images came swimming up from the depths.[63] A true psychopath or a person of limited intellect might have let it go. Tom Hagel could not. It changed him for the rest of his days.

SPECIALIST 4 TOM HAGEL'S SAFE RETURN, even if a bit worse for the wear, calmed Chuck. At one point, the rumor mill at Bear Cat listed Tom as missing in action. Given the days it took to extract the waterlogged remains of those killed in the helicopter crash, not to mention the distance to Long An Province and Tom's rather unusual role as a

self-motivated supernumerary—and one with boundless tactical initiative—it took a few days to shake out. Chuck wisely chose not to
pass any of that anxiety back to Nebraska.[64]

From the modest home in Columbus came news from brother
Mike. Eager to do his part like Chuck and Tom, Mike had notified
the draft board he wanted to go, too. When he went for the medical screening, the doctors flunked him, 4F, medically unfit, due to a
knee problem incurred while playing high school football. The result
greatly frustrated Mike, who very much hoped to join his brothers
in uniform, although even the most speeded-up timeline wouldn't
get him to Vietnam until well into 1969. For her part, Betty Hagel
breathed a sigh of relief.[65]

So did Tom. He had seen enough. In a letter to Mike, written not
long after the searing events of July 3, Tom Hagel pulled no punches.
"It is just that joining the Army at the time of the Vietnam crisis is
rather foolish," he wrote. "*This war is completely immoral. We are
losing more every day.*" Tom added a postscript: "You don't have
to go into the Army to have my respect. To the day I die, I will be
ashamed I fought in this war."[66]

Chuck wouldn't agree, and Tom knew it. Ever the All-American
big brother, Chuck nursed his own reservations. But he kept them
to himself. In Vietnam, and back home in America, even in the crazy,
awful year of 1968, Chuck retained his optimism. With two Purple
Hearts already and many more patrols to come, the alternative was
too grim to consider. Like any rifle platoon NCO hopeful to stay on
his feet, Chuck saw the glass as half full.

For his part, Tom wouldn't say the glass was half empty. No, when
you looked into the unblinking eyes of the dead—"river blindness"
indeed—the body counts and the body bags, the upheaval at home
with King, the riots, RFK, and all the rest, the level of the water ceased
to mean anything. In the high summer of 1968, America's glass sure as
hell wasn't half full, or even half empty. It was broken.

CHAPTER 9

Constant Pressure

Every night when you're sleepin'
Charlie Cong comes a'creepin'.

TIM O'BRIEN
If I Die in a Combat Zone, Box Me Up and Ship Me Home[1]

The most pivotal battle in the summer of 1968 didn't occur in the Mekong Delta, the Central Highlands, or the A Shau Valley. No, the big one happened on August 28, 1968, in Grant Park, in the city of Chicago. Not one U.S. citizen died. But because a bunch of enraged American police officers beat the hell out of a number of outraged American protestors, everybody lost. Repercussions rippled into the headquarters in Saigon, the politburo in Hanoi, and the glacial peace talks in Paris. Over time, slowly but surely, the fateful consequences made it all the way down to 2-47th Infantry, busy running roads and setting ambushes in the monsoon-soaked backcountry of Long An Province. The Johnson administration's shell-shocked reaction to the January 1968 Tet Offensive ensured the United States would not win the war. One hot, bloody night in Chicago did much to chart the course to final American defeat.[2]

In embattled Chicago, as nearly ten thousand unruly young dissidents milled in the streets, the fractious Democratic Party nominated their candidate for the 1968 election, Vice President Hubert Horatio Humphrey (HHH) of Minnesota, a well-known liberal trapped in the giant shadow of LBJ. Johnson sneered that he had Hubert's "pecker in my pocket." So it appeared. Regardless of his strong personal misgivings, Humphrey accepted LBJ's war policy right along with the Democratic Party's bid for president.[3] Johnson's bankrupt Vietnam strategy hung around Humphrey's neck like the rotting carcass of an albatross.

Beaming HHH, the self-described "Happy Warrior," gave his acceptance speech as shrewd dissidents goaded the police outside the Hilton Hotel. Like the North Vietnamese generals planning Tet and Mini-Tet, the chief Chicago activists were willing to trade their blood (well, a bit of it) for maximum psychological impact. Chanting "The whole world's watching," the peaceniks and a smattering (a very small one at that) of Black Panthers pelted the Chicago police officers with taunts, insults, profanities, and obscenities. Next came food, garbage, plastic bags of urine, and even feces. Sticks, rocks, bricks, and cement chunks followed.[4] The police held their line, but the taut lawmen, many of them military veterans, chafed and leaned forward.

No communist propagandist in Hanoi could have better arranged matters. Of course, they had nothing to do with it. This violent showdown sprang right from the broken heart of the American nation. Having endured enough gabbing, jabbing, and grabbing, Chicago's men in blue went into action. Squads of helmeted police officers waded into the mob. Truncheons rose and fell. The crowd broke apart. Some supposed ringleaders ended up in paddy wagons. A lot of people on Michigan Avenue found their faces bloodied and their hands cuffed. Members of the news media felt the blows, too. Later, investigators reported 192 law officers hurt, 425 injured demonstrators, and 668 arrests. Tear gas drifted into the posh lobby of the Hilton.[5]

The so-called police riot appalled and horrified average Americans. The country seemed to be coming unglued. Angry and self-righteous, Chicago mayor Richard J. Daley chose to meet the press. He strode to the podium like Westmoreland in the U.S. embassy courtyard after Tet. It turned out about as poorly. In a malapropism that said it all,

Daley summarized: "The policeman isn't there to create disorder; the policeman is there to preserve disorder."[6]

Beyond the debacle in Chicago, other candidates made their case. For the Republicans, Richard Nixon led the ticket. He'd come out of the gate running well, courtesy of a well-organized, traditional convention held in relatively sedate Miami, Florida. The "new Nixon" certainly surprised many, maybe even himself. To many Americans, the old Nixon, "Tricky Dick," conjured up memories of shiftiness, Red-baiting, and defeats in the 1960 presidential contest and the 1962 California gubernatorial election. But for 1968, he did his homework, big time, as only he could. Character questions aside, nobody doubted Nixon's brainpower or will. The reinvented Nixon put his finger directly on the twin, intertwined problems of the day: disorder at home and failure in Vietnam.[7] By simply acknowledging both impressions—something Humphrey could hardly do without parroting the discredited LBJ or breaking with him in public, both unthinkable—Nixon had done enough. Solutions were left purposely vague.

To deal with the campus uprisings and urban unrest, Nixon borrowed the phrase "law and order" from George Wallace. As his running mate, Nixon chose a tough figure from the April Baltimore riot, Governor Spiro Agnew of Maryland.[8] And he left it undefined beyond that. Race wasn't addressed, and by not saying much there, he said a lot. The implication came through. Forget Great Society handouts or reconciliation. Lower the boom on longhairs and arsonists, white, black, brown, whatever. Period.

As for Vietnam, Nixon also played coy. Speaking to audiences, he emphasized the need for a new strategy. The doves heard withdrawal. The hawks heard victory. And all opposed to LBJ's approach, a majority of Americans by mid-1968, understood that Nixon intended to proceed differently. When he talked in public, Nixon tapped his breast pocket, as if the Vietnam plan rested right there.[9] Indeed it did. The pocket was empty.

The third candidate for president left no doubts where he stood. George Wallace wanted to turn back the clock, before hippies, before urban insurrections, and before no-win conflicts in small third-world countries. Wallace didn't bother with policy prescriptions. He threw out the red meat, telling free-loving, foul-mouthed youngsters he had two four-letter words for them: "work" and "soap." "We need some meanness," he thundered, and he wasn't advocating material want. His downscale white audiences, urban ethnics and rural old stock, ate it up. Pollsters estimated that Wallace might earn 20 percent of the vote, carry up to ten states, and throw the election into the House of Representatives.[10] Now that could sure bring on a constitutional crisis, and then . . . well, who knew? Race versus race. Class versus class. Young versus old. Doves versus hawks. The visceral hatred hung out there like a pallid specter, just past the fingertips. And nobody could make it go away.

IN VIETNAM THOSE busy enough lost track of the social insanity back home. From glances at the *Stars and Stripes* and snatches of bulletins caught on Armed Forces Radio, both Hagel brothers knew things in the United States had gotten pretty bad. But after the horrendous spring rioting and the King and Kennedy assassinations, the rest amounted to more of the same, additional blows to an already punch-drunk national psyche. The street brawl in Chicago made far less of an impact in the ranks of 2-47th Infantry. Soldiers in country knew and they didn't know. After all, the Hagels and the rest had their own concerns, not least among them staying alive.

Still, news garnered some interest. In the months heading toward the November election back in America, Specialist 4 Chuck Hagel found time to wager a case of beer with First Sergeant Martin Garcia, tough, smart, and glib. From East Texas and "all the way with LBJ," Garcia dismissed Nixon as "washed up" and "a has-been." The regular army NCO went with Humphrey. Chuck bet that the Republican would win.[11] Neither thought anything of George Wallace. The fiery Alabama populist didn't have many followers among lifers or conscripts.

WHILE THE STORM CLOUDS built up over Chicago in late July, the Hagels went to Honolulu, Hawaii. There the brothers enjoyed five days of rest and recreation. In theory, they should have already gotten a week off at the Vung Tau center in country. But combat operations took priority, and the trip didn't happen.

That said, the battalion's leadership made sure soldiers went on their out of country R&R. As Chuck said, "Once you were on the manifest, you were there." Although 2-47th stayed active, the two Hagels departed on schedule. Tom was still healing up from his shrapnel wounds suffered on July 3. But he felt good enough to board an airliner with his brother and go to Hawaii.[12]

In Honolulu, the brothers met mother Betty, brothers Mike and Jim, and their five aunts, too. "They'd all told their husbands that America would not win the war unless they went to Hawaii and made sure that Chuck and Tom had the kind of support they needed," Chuck joked.[13] For five days, all present enjoyed the amenities of a beachfront hotel. They forgot about the war.

At least they tried to do so. The aunts enjoyed Hawaii. The brothers, both the duo from Vietnam as well as Mike and Jim, soaked up the sun and luxuriated in the surf and sand in the lee of Diamondhead. But Betty noticed something. She kept it to herself—why ruin the vacation? But it gnawed at her.

"I had five sisters," she recalled, "and none of their sons were in." Betty knew nobody else from Columbus whose sons deployed to Vietnam, other than the Enquists, whose son Arthur John paid the full freight as a scout sergeant in 2-47th Infantry. But what about the rest of the young men of Columbus, Nebraska? As far as Betty could tell, they didn't go. She knew no other mothers with a son in combat, let alone two. This sure wasn't World War II, all for one and one for all. This one came down to hooray for me and the hell with you. Those young men who avoided the draft might get some sidelong looks in Nebraska towns. But their mothers slept soundly every night. Betty told herself something she couldn't yet tell her soldier sons: "I *hated* the war."[14]

The five days passed like summer lightning. Chuck and Tom put on their uniforms, said goodbye, and boarded the westbound jet. They'd be home in a few months. Fear not. Brave faces all round—but after the parting came the waterworks.

The plane cabin on the ride back to Vietnam was as silent as the tomb.

CHUCK AND TOM returned to find First Sergeant Garcia with orders in his hand. They had been supposed to go to the Reliable Academy for NCOs back in June. But then had come the split-base Bear Cat–Long An missions, followed by the jitterbug operations, the major July 3 firefights, and then R&R. The Hagels had been acting NCOs, and good ones, for months. The first sergeant wanted to promote them to real sergeants. But that required two weeks of training at division. Off they went.[15]

The course mixed classroom lectures with practical exercises. "There wasn't much they were going to teach us about jungle warfare," Chuck commented. The division apparently agreed. Most of the course focused on the stuff the brothers and the other young combat veterans did not learn under fire: traditions of the service, key regulations, how to resolve personnel issues for subordinates, how the supply system functioned, and the "big picture" of the division's structure and function in country. Said differently, the NCO academy taught the Hagels how the army should run.[16] Practice in Vietnam sure deviated a lot from theory. And there was a message there, all right.

The brothers later joked that they finished first and second in the course. They certainly performed well enough. Promotion, though, necessitated another step, and not an easy one. Within a week after returning, Chuck cleaned himself up and went before a board of senior NCOs headed by Sergeant Major James W. Beam, the august, forbidding long-term professional who served as the battalion commander's strong right arm. After reporting to the board, Chuck froze completely. An acting NCO who faced down Charlie daily found his throat dried up as he looked at that lineup of craggy old senior sergeants. After being allowed to regroup, Chuck nailed it. He typically excelled at public speaking, going all the way back to Nebraska days. But not this time, a good reminder for a new sergeant about to go back out on patrol. Take nothing for granted.

A week later, Tom sailed right through his interview. Naturally skeptical, and increasingly disgruntled with both the war and the army fighting it, Tom found himself considerably less overawed by the highly experienced panel. Both men became sergeants, Chuck a week ahead of Tom.[17] Age mattered, even in the army.

While the Hagels went to relax in Hawaii and then went on to learn the fundamental ways of the army at the NCO academy, the war went on. At MACV, General Abrams took command. A superb tank commander from World War II, praised by General George S. Patton himself, Abrams came across as the anti-Westmoreland: rumpled, candid, and unimpressed by himself or others.[18] He knew on June 11, 1968, the day he took over, that there'd be no more major influxes of U.S. troops, and no real attempt to change the downward trajectory of the American war effort. The Chicago fiasco only underlined that trend. The next significant troop movements would be outbound, regardless of whether Humphrey or Nixon won the U.S. presidency. Wallace's ravings were ignored.

Perceptive and wise behind his cigar and blunt speech, Abrams shouldered the unwelcome task of losing the Vietnam War as slowly as possible, perhaps salvaging something resembling a draw. He ratcheted back large-scale operations and emphasized day-to-day patrolling. After the excesses of Mini-Tet, Abrams also personally approved use of airstrikes and artillery in cities; he didn't okay these measures too often. MACV's maneuver battalions still hunted Charlie—it's what they did, and a new four-star in Saigon didn't alter the army's innate tendencies tracing all the way back to slaying redcoats and tracking Plains Indians. But breaking down into lesser elements did something to meter the pain on South Vietnam's civil communities. And the small-unit approach might just reduce U.S. casualties, a humane act in a faltering war.[19]

The NVA and their VC affiliates backed off, too. They'd been beaten up badly in Tet, Mini-Tet, Khe Sanh, Hue, A Shau, and all the rest, not anywhere near the astronomical totals pronounced in Westmoreland's final days, but crippling losses nonetheless. Time to bring in recruits, reorganize, reequip, and retrain surely made sense.[20] And like Chuck and Tom Hagel, the elderly men in Hanoi also read the newspapers. Divided, impatient America in the 1960s paralleled the path of fractured, distracted colonial France in the 1950s. The MACV battalions would be leaving, maybe not in months, but certainly in years, and not many of those either. The U.S. military knew it, and Charlie knew it. So the communists checked the guerrilla handbook. *Enemy halts, we harass.*

Westmoreland to Abrams marked an adjustment at the MACV level. In the 9th Infantry Division, Major General Julian J. Ewell changed nothing. Rather, he doubled down. Abrams wanted more small-unit operations? Good enough. Jitterbugging filled the bill. A variant, called "checkerboard," put out individual rifle squads to make contact. Another idea, "night hunter," used armed helicopters to troll across suspected VC strongholds in darkness. The choppers tried to draw fire. In all of these methods, when the opposition showed himself, the Americans unloaded a world of hurt. Ewell demanded day patrols and night ambushes, "constant pressure," "tremendous pressure," "excruciating pressure."[21]

Ewell weighed 2-47th Infantry and found the battalion wanting. Sure, 2-47th did great things in Tet and Mini-Tet, roaring into action in and around the built-up districts of Saigon. But how much more of that looked likely? The 9th Infantry Division's campaign now focused on the wet, overgrown Mekong Delta, an area distinctly lacking in roads. Tower, Van Deusen, and now Scovel—it didn't matter who commanded. The mech guys lacked some indefinable "it." It's one reason the general happily traded out 5-60th Mech for a leg battalion, suitably renumbered to keep the 9th Infantry Division's books straight. Paratrooper Ewell saw the M113s as the problem. Reliance on tracks curbed the battalion's mentality. They didn't like to leave their "horses" behind, and weren't as able when they did. Not that it mattered. When Ewell ran the numbers—and he did so daily—it made little difference. On M113s, on helicopters, and on foot, 2-47th just could not close the deal with Charlie Cong.[22] So Ewell quit asking them to do so.

With the 9th Infantry Division concentrating its forces in the upper Mekong Delta, and moving its main base camp from Bear Cat to Dong Tam southwest of Saigon, it fell to 2-47th to escort the many heavily laden supply truck convoys carrying key equipment and supplies through Saigon down to the new site. The Black Panther battalion also inherited the mundane duty of handing over Camp Martin Cox to the Royal Thai Army. Come September 9, 2-47th relocated permanently and completely into Long An Province.[23]

There, Ewell assigned the battalion not to a combat brigade, but to the Division Support Command (DISCOM), the service support guys. The supply and maintenance people used 2-47th to secure Dong Tam Base Camp (Bear Cat revisited) and to run the roads, notably Route 4. Emblematic of DISCOM's rather humdrum sense of itself, 2-47th inherited not some inspirationally named ongoing operation but a routine effort called Kudzu, after the fast-growing nuisance weed found splayed all over roadsides in the American south.[24] From the division's fast, hard-hitting reaction force to gate guards, berm squatters, and truck protectors—how low the mighty had fallen.

For their new role, 2-47th occupied the former 5-60th Infantry camp at Binh Phuoc. That put them just east of the vital Route 4 and within a few miles of the division's main base at Dong Tam. The troops immediately rechristened their new digs "Been Fucked," which about summarized the prevailing view of the battalion's unglamorous realignment under supervision of the herbivores of DISCOM.[25] The DISCOM commander worked with Lieutenant Colonel Scovel to figure out the right mix of roadrunning, fence bunker guards, day patrols, and night ambushes to protect Dong Tam and Route 4. As much as they could, 2-47th adopted the approved Ewell tactics: jitterbug, checkerboard, and night hunter. Rueful troops characterized all of these schemes more bluntly: "bait."[26]

As a trusted, experienced NCO, finally wearing the stripes he'd earned many times over, Chuck Hagel drew one of the first night ambushes in the new area. When out at night near the Binh Son rubber groves, 2-47th preferred to go in squad or even platoon strength. This one, though, followed Ewell's new dictates. Chuck took only three other riflemen. And a radio—to call down the heavens if Charlie showed up.

Night operations in Vietnam juxtaposed each side's essential ways of war. The guerrillas learned to love darkness. Rightly fearing ubiquitous U.S. jets and helicopters, necessity compelled Charlie to move, resupply, and try to attack in the black hours, which hobbled the pitiless Yankee airpower. To do anything at all, the NVA and VC had to go by night. Habit built experience, and repetition honed skills. Nutritionists argued that the American diet, strong on vitamin A, gave U.S. troops an advantage in seeing things in low light.[27] That may well have been. But in terms of learning by doing, all the edge went to Mr. Charles. If he wanted to live, let alone win, he had no other option. That's why night belonged to Charlie.

For their part, the Americans turned to their preferred solutions. Technologies, some experimental, others tried and true, proliferated: night vision scopes, infrared detectors, ground radars, and people sniffers all played parts. With the high-speed gear humming along, the U.S. then used numbers, dozens and dozens of small foot patrols, to flood the zone. Men with radios linked together orbiting aircraft, ground patrols, and artillery ready to fire.[28] When working as advertised, each night saw the upper Mekong Delta arrayed like a pinball machine, with scores of well-positioned ambushes as bumpers, armed helicopters as flappers, and artillery and airstrikes ready to tilt the table in MACV's direction. Every time Charlie rolled through, he hit something. Then the whole thing lit up, ding-ding-ding, and the scoreboard rang up, body after body. Goodbye, Charlie Cong. Game over.

Well, so went the idea. But it depended on quality ambush work. Picking soldiers for a night patrol drew on those army-preferred alpha male talents Chuck had shown since day one at Fort Bliss. At this phase of the war, with duties onerous and repetitive, contacts infrequent, and way too much alcohol and marijuana available, privates found ways out of missions. Going out in the dark required stealth. So irresponsible soldiers drank too much, or smoked too much, and then bellowed or giggled or screamed like banshees. Those guys could not be used.[29]

Sometimes Chuck and Tom resorted to their fists to tame such miscreants. One time, Chuck pulled a big soldier away who had belted a smaller man. In the ensuing fisticuffs, they crashed through a screen door. But Chuck prevailed. When it came to that, Tom did too. Bigger and smarter still counted for a lot in the world of aggressive young males.[30] By the book, the two sergeants should have written up the misbehaving privates. In Vietnam, though, threatening someone with minor punishments such as the loss of his meager pay or his nonexistent liberty went nowhere. Court-martial took forever to arrange and in the end, more than a few riflemen preferred the secure austerity of Long Binh Jail (three hots and a cot) to the filth and fear of war on foot. So a hard belt to the head sufficed. The officers and senior NCOs made sure not to be around.

Whacking a belligerent, a smart-ass, or a loafer only took it so far. Most guys straightened up and played the game. The outright slackers . . . well, you didn't want them outside the wire with you. The war's hard truth applied. In the end, men volunteered to fight. Chuck knew the reliable ones. He chose three for the night ambush.

The men tied down their gear to dampen any metal-on-metal rattles or squeaks. Each soldier carried his M16 rifle and the usual twenty magazines, each of twenty 5.56mm M16 rounds. They didn't bring all the extra ammunition and additional water typical for daylight missions. And they certainly left behind their ungainly flak vests. Hagel intended to move handily this night.

Along with his rifle, each man carried two M18A1 Claymore mines, wicked little curved rectangular plates made up of 3.5 pounds of C4 explosive and seven hundred packed steel ball bearings. The mine could be rigged with a trip line, but more often was detonated using an electrical hand-switch, which troops called the clacker, attached

by a hundred-foot wire. Squeeze the clacker—"command detonation" in army-speak—and the Claymore, like its Scottish blade namesake, cut quite a swath from about one to six feet above ground level.
In open ground, the deadly BBs might zip out fifty yards.[31] In thick
jungle, ten would be a miracle. But that would work. The Claymores
gave Hagel's team a lot of options.

One capability not available, the five-pound AN/PVS-2 starlight
scope, gathered ambient light from the moon, stars, distant manmade illumination, or even bioluminescence. The battery-powered
starlight scope could be mounted on a rifle or carried like a tele-
scope. When you looked through it, akin to peering through a toilet
paper tube, you saw a narrow circle of the world lit in shades of
green. The imagery resembled what you saw when you opened your
eyes underwater in a pond rich with algae. Stateside technical engineers estimated a soldier could detect an enemy figure out to four
hundred yards.[32] Of course, in Vietnamese underbrush at night, seeing anything four hundred yards away seemed pretty unlikely. The
AN/PVS-2 wasn't much. But compared to inky nothing, it made a difference. Decades later, the U.S. military made wide use of many such
devices to see, drive, fly, and shoot at night. Hagel's men could have
used a starlight scope. But they didn't get one. These gizmos were
hard to come by in 2-47th. The few on hand went to the battalion
scouts and snipers.

As the leader, Chuck shouldered the PRC-25 backpack radio, the
23.5-pound lifeline to higher headquarters, supporting firepower,
medevac, and help.[33] In essence, the entire ambush revolved around
placing a pair of eyeballs and a working radio near Charlie. Everything else—the other three riflemen, the Claymores, the careful
preparations—existed to make that single event happen. If it did, the
9th Infantry Division's constant pressure notched another night success. If not, okay. Coming back in one piece might be nice, too.

The battalion's intelligence section pinpointed a supposed VC trail
for Hagel's team to watch. It didn't seem promising. The intel guys
predicted a hundred out of every ten enemy routes. Hagel figured
this one would go like most—slip out at 10 p.m., work into position,

routine radio check-ins, no action, pick up, return around six after sunup, and lose a night's sleep. Thanks to Ewell's constant pressure mantra, the next day would see work as usual. Plus, night belonged to Charlie. What the hell. But Chuck Hagel cut no corners. That's why the officers and senior NCOs trusted him.

The foursome filed out of the wire in complete blackness. No moon shone. Just as well. It concealed the team, and staying hidden equaled staying alive. Lieutenant colonels and majors up at division headquarters joked about live bait.[34] The bait weren't laughing.

Hagel led, navigating and walking point. Before he left, Hagel planned his route on a map, working around the edges of cultivated fields. He kept the team off trails, but he also avoided going with the machete to hew out a path cross-country. At night, that kind of raucous movement sounded like an elephant walk. The officers back at Binh Phuoc discouraged it; they worried about scaring off Charlie. Hagel thought a lot more about the risks of attracting the VC. No sense doing so. He skirted woodlines, staying just inside the trees. Experience paid off. Within an hour and a half, after a final thirty yards or so of slowly working through vines and branches, the team found the designated trail.

It looked like it had once been a lane in a rubber plantation. Looking right and left, Hagel saw straight rows of trees. Thank the French, he figured. With practiced hands, the men set up their Claymore mines, snuggling each against the base of a tree. The army helpfully printed "front toward enemy" in raised letters on the convex side. Well, okay. To keep it idiot proof, and accommodate some of that ever-brewing battlefield entropy, Hagel learned long ago to put Claymores on the likely bad guy side of a wooden tree trunk. That way, if Charlie turned the weapons around (and the sneaky VC did that), you shredded some timber, not your head and shoulders.[35]

The quartet then backed off, paying out the thin electrical wires. Soldiers allowed the requisite fifteen yards and added a few more. Better safe than sorry. From that far back, prone in the thick vegetation, the team could hear anything on the trail but only barely see it. Hagel gathered the clackers right in front of his arms. He faced the trail, a dark smudge almost seen twenty yards away. The sergeant arranged his men boot to boot. From above, had anyone been looking down from the jungle canopy, the riflemen formed a cross, feet in, heads out. With the radio receiver tight to his ear, Hagel okayed the other guys to sleep—no snoring.[36] He'd nudge them if something happened.

The black-plastic radio handset looked like a six-inch-long doll's telephone. It received as long as the battery remained viable and the sender tuned to the proper frequency. The handset transmitted when you pressed a rubber-covered bar on the side. To avoid yabbering—sound really carried at night—sergeants learned to push the transmit bar to send a message. When depressed, even if no words were said, a rush of white noise followed. The military called it breaking squelch.

Once every thirty minutes, on the half hour and top of the hour, Hagel pressed once. That told the base camp all remained quiet and well, no VC, no trouble. At any time, two quick pushes meant "danger nearby." Three announced "coming in, don't shoot." Four equaled "pinned down, unable to move, hostiles all around."[37] Chuck Hagel hoped very much for a one-push night.

Every thirty minutes, Hagel broke squelch. His head drooped some, but he did not sleep. The trio with him seemed to doze. But not the sergeant. He'd seen what happened when everyone bagged out. Get too comfortable and Mr. Charles might very well help you sleep forever.

The minutes crawled. Midnight. Thirty minutes after. One a.m. One-thirty. Nothing. Various critters, mostly insects, whirred and chirrupped and snapped. Fat warm drops fell now and then, leftovers from the day's monsoon shower.

Two a.m.

And then, a faint clang.

Clang.

It sounded like a cowbell in a Nebraska pasture. Hagel instantly alerted.

The team leader didn't wake his mates. He feared a startled reaction, a panicked gunshot, and then . . .

Well, if Charlie really approached, and came in strength, Claymores or not, four Americans would constitute short work. And for God's sake, don't break squelch twice. That would get the duty people at Binh Phuoc all spun up. They'd start asking questions and blabbing away, and worse, insisting Hagel do likewise. Better to listen and let this play out. So Hagel waited. Experienced military professionals called it "tactical patience." It sounded like a fine idea in a Fort Ord classroom. In a Mekong Delta jungle, in a night so dark you could barely see your hand in front of you, it took everything a man had to stay in place, ears attentive.

The clang became regular, and close, maybe a wobbling wheel on some kind of larger crew-served weapon. Charlie owned big machine guns, mortars, and rocket launchers with wheels.[38] Hagel thought he heard footfalls, too. He certainly smelled something, or someone. A lot of someones—way more than four.

In the movies, Hagel might have hollered "Geronimo!," blown the Claymores, and come up with his M16 blazing: very exciting, highly exuberant, and most certainly terminal. But the young sergeant knew enough to realize that such a gesture probably defined futility. The enemy might not be in front of the Claymores. And how many VC were there? Had any enemy flankers spread out?

Hagel waited some more. When the clangs and swishing and odors got really close, he squinted through the lower leaves. Was that a shadow on the trail? Charlie?

The sergeant slowly, very slowly, rolled over and up, facing his three belly-down mates. He tapped each in turn, fingers on a boot, firm but silent. As he did so, he placed a hand over each man's mouth—gently, a gesture, not a threat. No need to get the guys all cranky. Hagel made his intentions clear. Don't talk.

Out on the trail, half-heard whispers carried through the still air.[39] The metallic tone rang softly, rhythmic, deliberate, possibly a stripped tire going around. Steady shuffling noises grew louder. Someone out there—some VC—just barely coughed.

Hagel touched each of his men. Then the sergeant slid slowly to his belly, M16 in hand. The riflemen figured it out. They, too, flattened onto their stomachs. Chuck slowly, very slowly, crawled away from the trail. Like a human snake, left hand extended to graze the foot of the man in front, the quartet wriggled through the brush. They carried their rifles resting on their right hands, muzzles up out of the dirt. They left the Claymores behind, clackers, wires, and all the rest.[40]

Hagel made a quick but conscious decision to abandon the PRC-25 radio. He just couldn't figure out how to heft it back onto his back, or drag it like a boat anchor, without rustling so much foliage that they'd hear it all the way up in Hanoi. The choice greatly aided the foursome's concealment.[41] But it also ensured mission failure—no artillery, helicopters, or air support. And no medevac, reinforcements, or transmissions to get back through the U.S. barbed wire without getting blown into the next province. Military schools often feature classroom debates on life and death decisions. That night, Chuck Hagel made one.

Once they slithered for over an hour, a hundred yards or more by Hagel's guess, the team stopped in a thicket. The four men sat up back to back, rifles facing out. Nobody slept, or even thought about sleeping. The Americans waited for the sun. Once it became light, Charlie would be long gone. More importantly, in daytime the U.S. guys manning the firebase berm asked questions before opening fire. Chuck Hagel just had to hope the radio watch at Binh Phuoc didn't do something dumb, like send out a reaction force or vector helicopters overhead. People sniffers didn't discriminate all that well between U.S. and VC bodies.

The sun came up not long after six-thirty. Charlie's march column seemed long gone, its noises disappearing more than an hour before the first graying of dawn. Hagel and his wrung-out, stiff soldiers stood up and stretched. Taking point, he led them back to the ambush site. The sergeant checked the map coordinates carefully. He saw the impressions made by his team, and the markings on the trail that many people and something on tires had passed. But no radio, no Claymores—all had been taken. Hagel's knee trembled uncontrollably as he looked at the spot. As he put it: "Everything was gone."[42]

When the tired quartet came into the U.S. base that morning, the officers asked questions. Weak NCOs at times "sandbagged" patrols, going out a few hundred yards and sacking out while pretending to be in the assigned ambush site. Chuck Hagel, though, wasn't that kind of sergeant. He'd made his decision and that was that. And to their credit, the 2-47th chain of command deferred to the tactical leader. The senior people were disappointed. But they didn't second-guess, at least in Hagel's presence. The intel guys at battalion tried to determine which VC outfit Hagel's men encountered. Naturally, they had no idea.[43]

The experienced NCOs and officers, the ones who had been out and about with Charlie enough times to matter, knew the deal. Any night ambush had three possible outcomes. If the pinball machine lit and rang, the VC died by the gross and the Americans walked home in triumph. That hardly ever happened, but when it did, it made all the dry holes seem worthwhile. Second, nothing happened and everybody came home tired—the usual result. Third, something very bad occurred.[44] Hagel and his men achieved a version of number two. Not the best, they thought, but not the worst.

The worst came not long afterward. Up at division, Ewell and his brain trust tweaked the knobs and directed larger ambush elements. The general thought it encouraged his infantrymen to stand their ground and take more risk.[45] On the night of October 3–4 outside Binh Phuoc, a reinforced Company B rifle squad, eleven strong, moved out to a night ambush position. They followed a good route and got into their site without any trouble. The first few radio checks came in loud and clear: one push.

Then nothing.[46]

All that long night at Binh Phuoc, nobody on duty heard any distant gunfire. Maybe the radio failed. The heat and humidity chewed through batteries, and it had been especially warm and muggy. Perhaps the squad ran into a larger VC force, took a page from Chuck Hagel's experience, and just laid low. The company commander worried. Well he should. At sunrise, Company B sent out a mounted reaction force, two platoons and the company headquarters. Chuck and

Tom Hagel rolled out with this force. The M113s roared to the vicinity of the ambush location.

On the side of a rice paddy off Route 4, three bedraggled figures appeared. PFC Eddie Bivens and PFC John Hodges stood together, both hit, but upright, helping each other. Near them, Sergeant Charles N. Peace, the squad leader, leaned into a tree. He'd also been wounded. With his good arm he waved a strobe light, the perfect means to attract a medevac chopper in darkness. But it was broad daylight. Peace's eyes had that thousand-yard stare.[47] Not good at all.

Mr. Charles made a house call on the U.S. ambush. Eight men lay scattered in the trees, shot to death: PFC Robert J. Bergeron, PFC George M. Clayton Jr., PFC Daniel J. Czajak, PFC Donald R. Gise, PFC Gary G. La Chapelle, Corporal Charles N. Schall, PFC John P. Stepp, and Specialist 4 Danny Williams. In all of that bloody year of 1968, Company B, 2-47th Infantry never suffered a worse blow.[48] All the company could do was to pick up the pieces.

The company and battalion officers and senior NCOs tried to put together what transpired. They never could. Possibly the men conked out, run ragged by too many daily iterations of jitterbug and checkerboard and too many nightly ambushes. Or it could be they ran the patrol to standard, and Mr. Charles got lucky. Peace, Bivens, and Hodges offered nothing. What could they say? For the rest of their lives, they'd see those final muzzle flashes. And they'd wonder why they lived, and eight died.

The Hagel brothers had rolled the same dice day after day and night after night. After five Purple Hearts between them, they knew that war, like football, was a game of inches. God or fate or a cosmic random number generator—it mattered not. You could do everything right and lean forward at the wrong instant, or peek around a blind corner, or zig when you should have zagged, and then: "The Secretary of the Army regrets to inform you . . ."[49] That same awful October 4, Chuck Hagel marked his twenty-second birthday. He didn't feel much like celebrating.

THE REST OF October didn't go much better for 2-47th Infantry. Both Hagels stayed out in the field, doing their bit to generate Ewell's constant pressure. The smart guys at DISCOM and Lieutenant Colonel Scovel came up with a brainstorm that placed six ambush patrols out in contested ground every night. By the end of October, the battalion's exertions ran off most VC mortar and rocket crews, sparing the Dong Tam Base Camp, and thus accomplishing one important goal of Operation Kudzu. Division accounting teams recorded 120 VC killed and 26 captured, but only eighteen individual weapons taken (a disturbing discrepancy shrugged aside), plus twenty-six "structures" destroyed. To do all this cost 2-47th Infantry another seven American lives on top of the eight from October 4 and another soldier lost back in August, a total of sixteen killed in action. The battalion sustained 255 wounded.[50] Once more, 2-47th Infantry basically traded its entire field strength to hold Charlie at bay for a couple months. In some MACV circles, that evidently counted as a win.

And speaking of winning, the 1968 presidential campaign limped to its finish line. George Wallace faded into the background, irate to the end. In a salute to his wartime B-29 service, on October 3, Wallace tagged General Curtis LeMay as his number two. It turned out to be a disaster. As a political candidate, LeMay came across as a bellicose crackpot, opining that "there are many times when it would be most efficient to use nuclear weapons."[51] Hiroshima or Hanoi—for the old air force general, a target was a target and a weapon was a weapon. Bombs away. That kind of loose talk might go over fine in an air force bomber crew's ready room. But it scared the hell out of middle-class families in America. LeMay managed the seemingly impossible feat of making George Wallace sound reasonable by comparison. But not reasonable enough.

In the end, Wallace carried five southern states and almost 10 million votes, about 13.5 percent. Most observers thought he damaged the already staggering Humphrey. Even with that, and allowing for the mess in Chicago, Nixon barely edged HHH. The Republican prevailed by a half million, although that narrow popular vote translated to a decent 301 electoral votes.[52] Thus Dick Nixon would have his chance to ride the tiger.

First Sergeant Martin Garcia duly delivered a case of Budweiser beer to Sergeant Chuck Hagel. By election day, November 5, Chuck had been given a cushy job in the base camp, running the small enlisted men's club. He didn't go to the field anymore. That violated both the letter and the spirit of Julian J. Ewell's draconic dictates to put every rifleman in the bush. But Garcia just did it.[53] He thought it was right. And in the infantry, the word of the first sergeant is final.

Chuck had a month to go. Tom had three. Even though he arrived only six weeks behind his brother, the younger Hagel had to extend two weeks to be sure he could get out as soon as he made it home. The army let draftees leave the service if they had 150 days or less left in service. When Chuck departed on December 4, he'd make it just under that five-month wire. But Tom needed an extra two weeks in Vietnam to be sure.[54] It seemed crazy. Yet in the words of the troops in country: there it is.

Chuck considered extending to stay with Tom. But his brother refused to permit it. He stood up to his fellow sergeant in no uncertain terms. "No," Tom said. "That's the wrong thing to do. Our mother is expecting you home. You need to do that. I'll be fine."[55] So Chuck left on schedule.

But Tom Hagel would not be fine.

CHAPTER 10

Children of Nyx

And Night [Nyx] bore hateful Doom and black Fate
and Death and Sleep and the brood of Dreams.

HESIOD, *Theogony*[1]

They thought they were doing a favor for Tom Hagel. With three Purple Hearts and his older brother on the way home, the battalion sergeant major and the first sergeants assigned Tom to run the little post exchange (PX) at Binh Phuoc.[2] Somebody had to do it. It promised an end to day patrols and night ambushes. Now and then, in emergencies or near emergencies, Tom had to report to the berm line and take charge of a bunker. But chasing Charlie fell to others, the newer troops. Mrs. Hagel's second son would most likely make it back to Nebraska in one piece.

In taking Tom Hagel away from line infantry duties, the 2-47th leadership gave credence to a set of dismal facts about combat riflemen. Extensive studies in World War II charted a trajectory: becoming "battlewise," "maximum efficiency," "overconfidence/hyperreactivity," "emotional exhaustion," and then a "vegetative stage." Timing varied by individual. People with preexisting problems might go immediately to the wrong end of the scale. Those better educated, physically stronger, and well grounded in their families endured longer—those old army preferences at work once more. Unit teamwork and especially good officers and NCOs also helped keep things together. Most infantrymen made it under fire from 200 to 240 days (six and two-thirds to eight months) before cracking. As one study summarized, at the eight-month mark: "Practically all men in rifle battalions who are not otherwise disabled ultimately become psychiatric casualties."[3] The pace varied. The eventual progression did not.

As veterans of World War II and Korea, the U.S. Army and Marine Corps generals in Vietnam well understood this grim sequence. Yet for reasons attributable only to the same kind of unhealthy institutional inertia seen in the trenches of the Great War, the senior commanders adopted personnel policies tailor-made to accelerate combat soldier and unit disintegration. Individual replacements created steady coming and going, and that atop the steady drain of casualties. Scheduled swap-outs of key officers, typically in as little as six months, really spun the cycle. Twelve-month (army) and thirteen-month (Marine Corps) assignments applied to riflemen and rear-area clerks alike—very fair, but guaranteed to outrun that historic six- to eight-month breaking point. Well, the old guys told each other, that limit didn't really apply. Vietnam wasn't thought to be much of a war, not like Bastogne or Iwo Jima.[4] From a hovering helicopter or a quiet office, it may have been so. Neither Chuck nor Tom Hagel saw things that way.

Objective post-war assessments explained why the generals pictured a rather low-intensity conflict (except high points such as Tet or Mini-Tet) and the junior soldiers believed they had been run ragged. Like any smart guerrilla, Charlie refused combat except in those rare situations where VC victory looked likely. That caused the Americans, determined to make contact, to increase patrols and ambushes, to substitute volume of activity in hopes of forcing engagements. Ewell's 9th Infantry Division epitomized this mentality. Yet even under the scourge of a most unyielding commanding general, urging day and night constant pressure, the division never compelled the VC to fight in more than 9 percent of all their many operations.[5] For the riflemen out beating the bush, and the aviators loitering above, those numbers offered no comfort. Any trip outside the wire could devolve into "the big one." And each one chipped away at a soldier's finite reservoir of battle resilience.

Sergeant Chuck Hagel explained how it added up. "I don't know how many firefights I was in," he said. "I don't know how much combat—I mean, the actual day-to-day people shooting at you and you shoot at them." In the long, monotonous stretches in between, patrol followed patrol, day after day and night after night, all wrapped in stifling heat and dripping humidity, and all affected by chronic lack of sleep. "Maybe you go for a week and not have anything," Hagel said. "Maybe you go for two weeks and just not have anything." But you never knew when it would go upside down. It could happen any day, any time. "The intensity of that pressure," Hagel summarized, "does make an individual break.[6]

Chuck Hagel never reached his breaking point. Tom Hagel didn't either. But when 2-47th shifted Tom to look after the PX hut, they inadvertently did the Nebraskan a disservice. He still endured just enough risk, from mortar rounds and odd angry shots, to keep him anxious, and yet not enough to keep him busy. In war, idle minds wander, and perceptive ones, more so. In that last month of 1968, Armed Forces Radio in Saigon took a lot of requests for the late great Otis Redding's "(Sittin' On) The Dock of the Bay."[7] Tom Hagel could relate to lyrics about hanging around, watching the sun go up and down, wasting time. He faced two months with the exact twosome he most hoped to avoid: the war he loathed . . . and himself.

THE MORE TOM or any Vietnam combat veteran thought about it, the more obvious it became. The problem with the U.S. campaign in Vietnam went beyond strategy, the objection of learned war college faculties. It eclipsed morality, the favored talking point of passionate anti-war agitators. And it certainly had very little do with the news media, or long hair, or hippies, or drugs, or the Age of Aquarius. Those ideas found audiences because they implied that the war's conundrum could be solved. Americans love to fix things.

Vietnam defied vaunted Yankee ingenuity. In essence, America endeavored to use the wrong tool, the conventional U.S. Armed Forces, for the wrong job, counterinsurgency. A force manned, organized, equipped, and trained to close with and defeat the German *Wehrmacht*, or perhaps the Soviet army, found itself scrabbling through pigpens trying to figure out which guy in black pajamas to kill. The inability to do so ensured that no matter how many Charlie Cong died, too many local villagers went with them, and the rest became refugees disillusioned with the weak Saigon regime and its U.S. allies. It all resembled exterminating termites by running a family out of their house, shooting at the bugs (and laggard children) with a machine gun, then setting fire to the edifice to finish the job. As a U.S. officer said of the Mekong Delta city of Ben Tre during Tet: "It became necessary to destroy the town to save it."[8] There it is.

Just as form follows function, so the GI slang of the era very much reflected this ugly truth at the core of America's ill-fated venture in Vietnam.[9] The military lexicon of any epoch brims with acronyms, abbreviations, nicknames, and euphemisms. It has ever been so. You can find the like chiseled onto Roman monuments. Learning the appropriate martial lingo, understanding it, and employing it correctly differentiates civilians from soldiers, outsiders from insiders, and those with questions from those with answers, or at least better questions.

In Vietnam, the ground combat troops called themselves "grunts." That terse animalistic term came from the guttural sound that welled up from an overloaded soldier laboring through a morass of vines and branches. Slip in the mud. Knock a knee. Bang a sweat-stained head under a cloth-covered steel pot helmet as it slow-cooked the brain underneath. Shift the rucksack straps digging into shoulders. Heft up that long, black M60 machine gun. Look right, then left, then ahead. Keep going. Discipline and exhaustion strangled speech. Men moving through the bathwater-warm air and dank undergrowth strode step by step, swaying, stumbling, their passage marked by the chopping of the machete, the swishing of leaves—and grunts. They became what they did.

"REMFs," rear-echelon motherfuckers, comprised the majority of MACV's hundreds of thousands, safe in base camps. Where REMFs started depended on where you served. Nobody assigned to 2-47th Infantry, even the clerks puttering around Binh Phuoc, considered themselves REMFs. But in the rifle squads, sometimes guys joked about the bastards back at platoon headquarters. In essence, a REMF could be anybody routinely safer than you. To grunts, gradations of REMF-dom didn't mean much. You either went outside the wire all the time or you didn't. You were either a grunt or you weren't.

Lieutenants and captains and lifer NCOs certainly qualified if they went out on missions day after day. Men like Robert Keats, Jim Craig, Skip Johnson, William Smith, and Doc Rogers might be regular army types. Still, they certainly lived and fought, and sometimes died, as grunts. The battalion and brigade commanders, not to mention the various generals, did not count. Flying overhead in a helicopter or popping out as a guest patroller impressed none of those sweating and bleeding on the ground. Soldiers credited "Gunfighter" Emerson as crazy-tough, swooping down in his chopper to chase VC, and sometimes loping along on foot in the dirt, out with rifle platoons. The grunts saw old Ewell mix it up, too, now and again. But those two were the exception. Most senior officers sent out grunts. They didn't lead them. As a rule, the top guys lived up in the ether, orbiting in their C&C birds, out of sight, out of mind. "You just didn't ever see those people," recalled Chuck Hagel. "They didn't make much of an impact or difference."[10] The braver and smarter higher commanders earned some credibility. But not enough.

Grunts "humped." Humping bore two connotations. The obvious one referred to camels, beasts of burden. A rifleman lugging eighty pounds of ammunition, water, and gear through the hot, humid Mekong Delta certainly sympathized with the erstwhile ships of the desert.[11] The less obvious idea, a bit crude, tied to sex, not in the sense of anything pleasurable, but in the way it drained you, took it all out of you, left you limp and gasping. Given the utter absence of satisfaction in laboring cross-country under a bulging rucksack, perhaps humping might have been better rendered as dry-humping. But nothing stayed dry for long in Vietnam.

Moist and warm as an overgrown greenhouse, the "boonies" hosted the grunts. Boonies derived from boondocks, the hinterlands, the countryside, the pastiche of jungles, hamlets, and Mekong tributaries that characterized the Delta. In Tet and Mini-Tet, 2-47th fought in and around Saigon. The marines up north, reinforced by army battalions, did likewise in Hue city. But those were unusual occurrences. Most of the grunt war happened in the great outdoors. Riflemen also called it the bush or the field. Or Indian country.[12] They called it that, too. By whatever name, although green and savagely beautiful, it was anything but inviting or pleasant. The bad guys saw to that.

The opposition went by "Charlie," of course. To be precise, that referred to the true guerrillas, the VC, Victor Charlie in the military phonetic alphabet. The NVA regulars never rated their own nickname. When especially able, Charlie earned promotion to Mr. Charles or even, in exceptional cases, Sir Charles. Sergeant Tom Hagel, for all his doubts about the war, judged the VC cause "absolutely evil."[13] The opposition brutalized the Vietnamese villagers in the most personal ways, opting for retail hut by hut murder by AK-47 bullet and knife edge as compared to wholesale U.S. attempts to blow away entire square acres with artillery shells and high-explosive bombs. In the end, though, Charlie's harsh methods suited the war he fought.

Runty, slight, and often young, Charlie displayed endless ingenuity, courage, and endurance. He could also be obstinate, suicidal, and predictable. But for sure, Charlie fought, and fought hard. While U.S. body counts tended to be inflated, undoubtedly the enemy suffered high casualties. Somehow, though, enough of them always seemed to slip away and the hostile battalions reappeared as consistently as weeds on the lawn. The communists fought so hard that, despite their many reasons to think otherwise, the U.S. riflemen respected their foe. Tom Hagel certainly did, referring to his opponents as "incredible soldiers." Senior officers discouraged such "Charlie worship."[14] But the grunts believed.

As guerrillas, Charlie swam in the sea of the local people. The fighting fish impressed U.S. infantrymen. The sea—the Vietnamese population—did not. Although neither Chuck nor Tom Hagel resorted to
the common terminology, they certainly heard it constantly. Americans called the Vietnamese "gooks," "slopes," and "dinks" as a matter
of course.[15] Even in the much more tin-eared American society of
1968, one in which the most offensive racial monikers could be heard
daily on radio, television, and in street conversation, calling a human
a gook, slope, or dink consigned the already put-upon citizenry of
South Vietnam into a subdungeon all their own.

The cultural contempt extended into the pidgin dialect used by
U.S. soldiers in their interactions with the Vietnamese. The residents
of the south ranked so lowly that the men from across the Pacific
did not often deign to address the locals in their own vernacular, a
delicate tonal language that remained almost wholly unintelligible
to pretty much all Americans. Instead, impatient grunts employed
an amalgam of words borrowed from previous wars and other
countries, plus a very few choice snatches of Vietnamese. From the
French era came *beaucoup* (many) and *fini* (the end); most rural
Vietnamese understood neither. Out of occupied Japan Americans
appropriated "hootch" (from *uchi*, house), "papa-san," "mama-san,"
and "baby-san," all nonsense even in the Tokyo *ginza*, let alone in
the hamlets of Long An Province. The Korean War contributed the
callous epithet gook (literally people, but most often applied to an
individual), which meant nothing to the populace of the Mekong
Delta.[16] The usual remedy to U.S. linguistic incoherence involved
yelling louder, gesticulating forcefully, and waving firearms around.
It all got responses. But most replies made as little sense as the gib-
berish shouted by frustrated American troops.

As for Vietnamese phrases, the real business terms were few. *Di di
mau* (move out). *Dung lai* (halt). As a villager, get those wrong and it
might earn a burst of M16 rounds. Whatever happened, good, bad, or
indifferent, the Americans shrugged and offered the all-purpose conversation closer: *xin loi* (sorry about that). That one came not from
the traditions of the region, but from the U.S. television spy comedy

Get Smart.[17] When a zany character caught his nose in a fast-closing elevator door or the unwieldy cone of silence clunked on unwitting heads, "sorry about that" made it all better. Raised on television, sardonic American grunts favored the phrase, courteously translated into Vietnamese. Shoot the family hog? Burn the hut? Kill the daughter? *Xin loi,* mama-san. They were only dinks.

Sweeping racist generalizations also included ARVN and the national police, the White Mice. Those often inept organizations lived down to their reputations. All the committed, brave Vietnamese appeared to have signed up for the VC. Our side got the leftovers. Tom Hagel contemptuously recalled moving out on dangerous M113 roadrunner missions and passing ARVN soldiers "swinging in their hammocks" on the roadside, taking their ease. It might be their country, but a great number seemed ready to sit this one out. [18] After all, they had the best army in the world—the Americans—fighting on their behalf. From their South Vietnamese allies, grunts expected very little.

With regard to the village inhabitants, the Americans thought even less. Dirt poor and alien to the grunts, the average Vietnamese hardly ranked as humans. Some actively supported the Viet Cong. Others strongly opposed the communists. Most seemed to blow with the wind, "GI Number One" by day, "GI Number Ten" by night. The locals sold everything: smokes, soft drinks, beer, black-market post exchange goods, marijuana, hard drugs, their daughters, you name it. And the prices stayed low, low, low. The grunts figured that being so desperately indigent, the Vietnamese would do anything for money, to include selling out a neighbor. And the locals just didn't appear to care about much of anything, even each other. Life seemed cheap. Even well-educated senior U.S. officers sometimes echoed such stereotypical sentiments.[19] They were, of course, horribly wrong. But the language and cultural barriers, combined with the incredibly tortuous need to figure out which guy sowed rice and which one buried land mines—and which Vietnamese planted both—well, it demanded the patience of Job. American grunts just didn't have it.

And impatience, rashness, anger—those impulses led directly to the short, blunt, single-syllable words, the ugly ones. Bust caps. Fuck 'em up. Light 'em up. Nape and snake. Rock and roll. Zap. Waste.[20] "Kill" and "dead" and "body" were three other four-letter words, but grunts tended to use them only in reference to Charlie or other Vietnamese. The telling term, *le mot juste* (with a nod to the French who'd gone before), had to be "waste." It served as a verb. It worked as a noun. It summarized the whole damn war.

DURING THE DAY, Tom Hagel found things to do. As those who placed him there expected, the lanky sergeant determined to operate the best possible small PX in Vietnam. The big bases, like Dong Tam, overflowed with creature comforts: a swimming pool, clubs (officer, NCO, junior enlisted), USO shows, intramural sports leagues, and even a Red Cross club-mobile, staffed by young female American civilian volunteers.[21] Dong Tam hosted a large PX full of televisions, radios, and other consumer goodies. The quality beer like Ballantine, Budweiser, Michelob, and Miller High Life remained cold and ready in bulk at Dong Tam.

Binh Phuoc had almost none of this beyond tiny club huts and Hagel's miniscule PX. Out at the 2-47th firebase, the suds stayed warm and inferior: Carling's Black Label, Falstaff, Pabst Blue Ribbon, Schlitz, and even Vietnamese 33 brand. In later wars, American soldiers didn't drink alcohol.[22] In Vietnam, they did.

Officially, each man received an okay to drink two beers a day. Unofficially, the cans accumulated while troops carried out missions. Some units drank in the field—tracks with coolers were not an uncommon sight, and one wiseass battalion commander even told Ewell that his M113's basic load included six cases of beer. Old campaigner Ewell, product of a much more rough-hewn army than today's more tightly wound bunch, laughed it off. The general had been known to quaff a few cold ones when mingling with his men, Chuck Hagel among them.[23] Sergeant Tom Hagel inherited the responsibility of feeding this habit. He decided to improve the stockage.

That necessitated a shopping expedition. Hagel approached the major and master sergeant at battalion S-3, the operations section, the 2-47th planners and command post team. Drawing on his reservoir of good will as a veteran NCO with three Purple Hearts and a valor award, Hagel asked to borrow the major's jeep and trailer. The dutiful PX supervisor intended to make a trip to Dong Tam. He knew "contacts" there. He'd bring back the good stuff. The major agreed immediately. He liked decent brews, too.[24]

So on a clear December morning—the dry season had returned—Hagel set off as part of a supply convoy en route to Dong Tam Base Camp. He drew on all his M113 mission experience as he planned and executed the movement. Hagel drove northwest on Route 207 into the overcrowded town of Tan An. Had he turned north, he'd run into the same Vam Co Dong River where Lieutenant Colonel Van Deusen's helicopter crashed on July 3. Bad vibes for sure—and no Budweiser waited up that way. Instead, Hagel motored south on Route 4, entering Dinh Tuong Province. After creeping through the refugee-swollen city of My Tho (about 63,000 people), Hagel turned his jeep onto Route 25 and proceeded west to Dong Tam Base Camp. The twenty-two-mile trip took a few hours, with most of the delays brought on by dodging bicycles, pull carts, and scooters in Tan An and My Tho.[25]

Bustling Dong Tam Base Camp brimmed with some 10,000 U.S. troops. The major combat forces included the 2nd Brigade (the riverine outfit) and some of their partners in the U.S. Navy task force. The majority of Dong Tam housed the 9th Infantry Division headquarters, the DISCOM logistics battalions, the 9th Aviation Battalion, and various smaller support and service units.[26] The place looked like Fort Bliss, only with more tents, corrugated metal roofing, and plywood huts. The riverine guys and aviators certainly sallied forth to fight. The rest? Not so much.

A wily peasant in the imperial capital, Tom Hagel found his way to the right provisioning centers. He backed up his jeep and trailer. Over the next few hours, he loaded up "cases of beer, cigarettes, toothpaste, you know, the essentials." Being Tom Hagel, he thought it ironic that 2-47th depended on him to get their beer, and yet by law, he couldn't pop a cold one back in the United States. Tom had just passed his twentieth birthday in November. Well, he gave himself a dispensation. If he could zap Charlie for America, he could certainly see fit to knock back a few.[27] Or more than a few, he figured. He owed it to himself.

It took until late afternoon for Hagel and the rest of the convoy to finish their business, such as it was, at Dong Tam. They rolled out not long after three o'clock, heading back to Binh Phuoc. Every uniformed American in country knew the deal. Get to a safe space by nightfall, just before seven. In this potentially terminal version of musical chairs, if the tune ended and the trucks were still out, well . . . between the ill will of Charlie and the various 9th Infantry Division night hunters in the sky and ambushes on the ground, nothing pleasant would result.[28] Sergeant Hagel had no intention of testing that folk wisdom.

About 4 p.m., north of My Tho on Route 4, barely across the Long An provincial boundary, that friction so common in battle showed up right on schedule. Civilian traffic disappeared, which always raised antenna among veteran grunts like Hagel. The locals always seemed to know where not to be. Near the highway, 2nd Battalion, 3rd Infantry, on loan from the 199th Light Infantry Brigade, had been chasing VC rocket teams.[29] Evidently one of Charlie's elements elected to do something about it. Some kind of desultory firefight developed. The distant smoke puffs of unseen shell bursts crumped among the trees a mile or so out from the road, well across a flat expanse of open rice paddies. Not his issue, and far away, Sergeant Hagel thought. He kept right on going.

As Hagel's jeep and a 2-47th Infantry 2.5-ton (universally nicknamed "deuce-and-a-half") cargo truck rumbled north, a VC mortarman overshot his target. An 82mm projectile popped in a hot gray spray right at the roadside. The chance impact riddled Hagel's trailer. Both tires went flat. Holes appeared in the metal sides. Beer began spraying out in random golden streamers. Unwilling to wait around for more 82mm encouragement, Hagel gunned it. The cargo truck's driver did, too.

A few miles north, though, Hagel had to stop. The trailer's wheels, reduced to shaky, creaky rims, sparked on the pavement.[30] They'd outrun Charlie's mortar range. But the trailer was finished.

Hagel went to work. Working with the men from the deuce-and-a-half, Hagel chucked out the leaking cans. Lady Bird Johnson might be keeping America beautiful on the far side of the Pacific. In Long An, Hagel and the other soldiers dumped their damaged goods. Wet cardboard, torn-up cans, busted wooden pallet slats went into the roadside ditch. The locals would eventually pick through the detritus. Charlie might, too. But with the trailer pretty well chewed into junk, there wasn't much of an alternative. Hagel crammed the intact cases atop the rest of the boxes and crates in the already laden jeep. Then he and the other troops wrestled the trashed trailer up into the deuce-and-a-half's cargo bed.[31] Fortunately, the 2-47th men in a large truck had already delivered their load at Dong Tam. Well, now they had something to carry back.

The jeep and the bigger truck got through the gate into Binh Phuoc about dusk. Hagel expected a less than welcome reception from the S-3 major and master sergeant. "Oh God, I'm in trouble now," he thought. The major raised some hell, and at least one staff officer mentioned court-martial charges. But in the end, with Hagel weeks from going home—and those three Purple Hearts—nothing came of it. When one of the higher-ups mentioned that Tom Hagel sure went the extra mile to take care of his fellow grunts, the sergeant nodded. "Nobody else would."[32]

STAYING BUSY IN the sunshine, even in such dubious exploits, checked off the days on the calendar. But nights proved to be a different matter. Battery B, 2nd Battalion, 4th Field Artillery pounded away the dark hours, its six 105mm howitzers engaging "harassment and interdiction" targets all over Long An. Together, the half dozen cannons fired an average of 150 rounds a night, and more on many occasions. The nearby 2-47th Infantry heavy mortar platoon pumped out big illumination rounds. The golden glow lit up the dark spots across the fence line. "Plenty of juice up there," Tom recalled.[33] The sound and light show went on all night, every night.

Under the thunder of the outgoing shells, 2-47th soldiers guarded Binh Phuoc's roughly rectangular defensive wall. At each corner, a squat tower featured a .50-caliber machine gun. Fired from a dozen feet above ground, the big rounds were effective to about a mile, but could keep right on zipping out to four miles.[34] On the wide packed-dirt wall, the berm, a succession of sandbagged bunkers also included M60 machine guns. In between, other bunkers allowed riflemen to shelter under cover and shoot back. At night, 2-47th manned the four corners and some of the berm line. Until the alarm sounded, and then all on the firebase took their posts, most of the bunkers stood empty. Well, not totally empty—on more than one occasion, both Chuck and Tom met the bunkers' full-time inhabitants, feisty rats the size of raccoons.[35]

Inside the berm, the Americans crowded together in some seventy-three temporary buildings. In one of the few open stretches, artillery and U.S. heavy mortar crews set up in sandbagged firing spots at the south end of the base. At the northeast end, a bare field—mud in the wet times, dust in the dry—served as the motor pool, with the battalion's M113s aligned in company ranks, fueled, armed, and set to roll out the gate. The battalion command post was in the northwest, just across from where the tracks parked. Between those two key areas stood the main gate and a "battalion street" that ran all the way to the big guns in the South. On either side of the dirt main artery, a tight clutch of metal-roofed barracks alternated with a mess hall, company orderly rooms, an aid station, and Tom Hagel's little PX.[36] If you lived inside the dirt wall, you lived in very close quarters.

Beyond the berm, cleared flat ground, much of it flooded former rice paddies, spread all around. About ten yards out, the 2-47th had emplaced and staked down the first of three rows of razor-rimmed, head-high concertina wire. Another such ring ran ten more yards out. And the third one stood ten yards beyond that. Dozens of Claymore mines dotted the open space between the concertina rolls. Any attackers, even skilled NVA sappers, had a rough time ahead of them if they tried to penetrate Binh Phuoc.[37]

Charlie, being Charlie, avoided such strength. An infantry assault would be suicidal, unless for some reason 2-47th disarmed themselves. The Black Panther battalion leadership knew way better than that. No matter what else went on, the lieutenant colonel always kept enough defenders around to protect Binh Phuoc. Charlie made a few feints, but never mounted a serious attack. But as Chuck Hagel mentioned, at Binh Phuoc: "A regular evening was to get rocketed, mortared."[38] Both brothers had been out of the congested firebase most nights. Now Tom was on the inside, at the receiving end. What if things really got out of control? If you thought about it too much, it reminded you of Bernard Fall's disturbing history of Dien Bien Phu, *Hell in a Very Small Place.*

Usually, the VC favored 82mm mortars. As Binh Phuoc had been there for years, and many Vietnamese had gone in and out of the camp for official and unofficial reasons, the VC benefited from a very good lay-down of key facilities. Skilled hostile gunners knew how to "walk 'em across the compound," Tom remembered. Unwilling to share the bunkers with the active colony of rats, Tom and the other base types sat atop the berm. When they saw flashes in the distant darkness, they knew those were Charlie's mortar projectiles leaving the tubes. The grunts then had thirty seconds to slide into the bunkers, rats or not.[39] During Tom's two months there, the VC mortar gunners never killed anyone. But it wasn't from lack of trying.

Before and after the 82mm rounds each night, Tom drank. He tried every type of beer, the good ones and the bad ones. From some Australians, he learned to squeeze a lime into his brew. That added a new taste. Still, after a while, the sergeant didn't much care, as long as the cans had alcohol.

He also smoked marijuana. Vietnam's tropical climate produced quality dope, and a lot of it. The lifer NCOs did not approve, but Tom didn't ask for their okay. He toked up out of their sight. They didn't ask. He didn't tell. Tom Hagel had never smoked grass on operations, nor permitted it. As he noted later, "peer pressure" kept men straight in the bush. But as the PX guy, well, dope was like the beer. He owed it to himself.

One dull day in late December, with his neat PX hut all in order, and having watched enough of the time slip away à la Otis Redding, Tom decided to adjust his nightly routine. The bored sergeant got tired of playing games with the rats and Cong mortars. He chose to build his own bunker. Hagel went to the artillery cannoneers and asked for dozens of their old wooden ammunition boxes, each about the size of two window planting containers side by side. He spent the rest of the day, and a good part of the next, filling the boxes with ruddy dirt. When he'd completed a little hideaway, he nestled a green army cot inside and rigged up a mosquito net. There he planned to stay each night until he left Vietnam.[40]

Had the VC stuck to the customary mortar and rocket barrages, with rounds landing here and there but mostly nowhere important, Tom might have enjoyed his new rat-free digs. But a few nights later, Charlie made one of his rare ground efforts. They staged in the little village—really just a row of huts—to the north. A few furtive guerrillas, erstwhile sappers, actually messed around at the outer ring of concertina wire. If they ever got through the wire . . .

Confronted with this kind of probe, the American defenders opened up with the entire repertoire. Tracers from machine guns lanced into the nondescript shanties. The battalion heavy mortars coughed up one brilliant illumination round after another. Those drifting parachute flares lit up the darkness.[41] With a potential infantry breach under way, the 2-47th Infantry command post duty officer summoned all hands. Along with the other base people, Tom Hagel reported to the berm with his M16 in hand. Was this the long-feared big one?

An hour or so of shooting and shouting ensued. Green tracers crossed the berm line, reflecting continued interest from the VC. The Americans returned a hundred, maybe even a thousand, for every bullet received. Men in the towers reported shadows flitting in the *ville*. Helicopters came on station overhead, but the aviators radioed that they didn't really see much. The howitzer battery couldn't engage, as the enemy had gotten too close. But if Charlie got over the wall and came running into the base, the artillerymen prepared to level their tubes, set fuze zero, and shoot straight into the enemy infantry. The big 105mm shells would blow right at the muzzle, gouts of white-hot shrapnel, six giant shotguns scything 'em down.[42] It never got that bad. Having stirred up enough trouble, way more than he bargained for, Charlie backed away.

When he returned to his home-made bunker, Tom found that a sharp-edged shell fragment—theirs, ours, who knew—had pierced right through the wood and dirt. Had his head been on the cot, it would have gone through him, too. Tom looked at the holes. Then he just laid down and crashed into a black, boozy sleep. "In the shape I was in, I didn't care."[43] For the first time in his life, he felt he was definitely his father's son.

FOR MOST OF WORLD WAR II, the fliers of the 42nd Bombardment Squadron never really saw what happened after they dropped their deadly bombs. Sergeant Charles Hagel saw the dead and wounded Americans who came back in shattered airplanes. And he watched comrades spiral downward in smoking hulks with wings gone. Sometimes parachutes blossomed. Often they did not. In that last horrible summer over the home islands of Japan, Hagel and his buddies flew low enough to see and smell the residue of their handiwork. He never forgot any of it. It came home with him. And although his 1962 death certificate read heart attack, what he witnessed in combat, and what he could not put aside, probably did much to put him in an early grave.

Now his son Tom faced the same, in the quiet hours of darkness gifted to him by distracted superiors at Binh Phuoc. The best thing in war is to stay busy as hell. The old sweats—Curtis LeMay, Julian Ewell, Martin Garcia, Creighton Abrams, William Joyce—certainly agreed heartily. Most of them remained on the go long after their war years ended, hyperactive, doing this and doing that, anything to run out each day to exhaustion. The key was not to remember the faces, ours or theirs. Keep it vague, generic, and impersonal.

Yet Tom saw the faces, a parade of them, night after night. The alcohol and dope made them go away for a few hours. But nothing ingested erased the vivid memories. "Half the time you didn't see anything," he said. Even in nightmares, old Mr. Charles hardly ever showed his hand. "Until you'd find the bodies."[44] And all too many wore civilian clothes. How many carried weapons? And if they didn't, were they VC? Concerned citizens? The wrong guys in the wrong place? What about the women? The children?

Up at 9th Infantry Division, Major General Julian J. Ewell dealt with the same issue. He saw those killed not as subhuman gooks, or dinks, or slopes to be slaughtered at will. Nor did he visualize them as individual NVA soldiers, sons and husbands with homes and families near Vinh or outside Haiphong, fellow military men separated only by team colors. No, Ewell slept soundly because he'd reduced the division's foes to numbers. When the jitterbug juked by day or the choppers hunted by night, the statistics piled up. At almost the same time twenty-year-old Sergeant Tom Hagel wondered what the hell he'd done to himself and to others, Ewell added up and sifted the numbers. He found comfort there. Tom Hagel did not.

In the six months after Mini-Tet in May, the 9th Infantry Division claimed to have killed 5,574 NVA/VC and captured 677. Sweeps recovered 1,291 individual enemy firearms and 273 crew-served weapons. Very impressive—until you realized, as Ewell and his staff did, that even this result still left 44,777 hostile troops in the field: twenty-one battalions and ninety-seven separate companies. By the MACV estimate, built around metrics furnished by the 9th Infantry Division, three-quarters of the countryside in Ewell's area of operations remained under Hanoi's effective control.[45] Ewell only saw the count of enemies killed in action. We wiped them out. For Ewell, that defined success.

To ring up these "achievements," the Mekong Delta home had been well and truly smashed up, the family members run off, cowed, or accidentally finished off—and the termites remained in the rubble, numerous as ever. Moreover, three-quarters of those slain were unarmed.[46] That's why Tom Hagel and plenty of others at the user end would spend the rest of their lives seeing faces they didn't ever want to see.

Some tried to jog the hard-bitten general from his complacency. Staff officers raised the gap between assessed enemy dead and number of weapons captured. Ewell and his brigade commanders waved it off. The VC did great work pulling out their dead and their arms. (Yet, if so, why were so many corpses left behind to be tallied? Or were those figures just nighttime "guesstimates"?) The heavy use of air strikes and artillery incinerated the enemy AKs and RPDs. And that marshy, flooded Delta no doubt swallowed abandoned armaments by the dozen.[47] You could talk yourself into it.

Ewell believed that he did the best he could with the blunt instruments at hand: rifle squads, helicopters, howitzer batteries, and jet fighter-bombers, all manned and run by an ever-shifting team of individuals rotating in and out every twelve months. He assessed his battalion and brigade commanders as about 25 percent effective and the rest merely good for following orders, if that. The general knew he lacked quality, veteran NCOs. He thought a lot of the troops and the front-line officers, the real grunts, but he knew they could only do so much, shackled as they were by rampant inexperience, not to mention wildly inapplicable conventional army doctrine and training.[48] His division's uniquely lethal arcade laydown every night—sniff 'em and stiff 'em—anticipated the twenty-first-century sensor-to-shooter battlefield of all-seeing 24/7 overhead surveillance and roving armed drones.[49] Had he been able to do so, Ewell would have leaned even more heavily on things, not humans. But the technology didn't yet exist.

Because Ewell was doing surgery with a chainsaw, chips flew. He just could not discriminate. "You know at night we had a curfew," he said later, "and anybody that was out there was fair game. So you'd have five VC and twenty peasants carrying mortar ammunition. You'd knock off five or six." Ewell continued: "It's true that probably two were VC and four were peasants but they weren't supposed to be out there. So that's tough luck."[50] It sure was.

Thus anyone out at night became VC. In the sunshine, anyone who looked up when a helicopter flew over also might count as VC. Those who did not look up—well they were probably VC, too. If they ran away from helicopters or ground patrols, they must be VC. And if they gave you a defiant look, well, you know that deal. Plus, the Cong all wore black pajamas. So anyone dressed like that must be enemy.[51] All VC were Vietnamese, and all Vietnamese in the Mekong Delta might well be VC. Or sympathizers. Hell, three-quarters of the villages had thrown in with Hanoi. The bottom line seemingly followed naturally. Dead equaled VC.

Now MACV didn't just declare open season. Far from it. Many officers, including other generals, roundly criticized Ewell's heavy-handed approach, especially after LBJ moved toward peace talks, Abrams took command, and domestic support for the war cratered. The old paratrooper dismissed these complaints as a preference for "toe-dancing," "fan dancing," and "Maypole celebrations" over finding and killing Cong.[52] Yet he had to follow orders. Despite some fairly lurid allegations, then and later, the 9th Infantry Division did not defoliate, burn, and slaughter their way across the entire Mekong Delta. Ewell stretched the U.S. tactics as far as he could. He took a very hard line, putting paid to many opposing forces and not a few unfortunate civilians caught in the backblast. But this wasn't World War II. And the Mekong Delta wasn't Dresden or Nagasaki.

As 2-47th Infantry learned during Mini-Tet, use of heavy firepower took time-consuming approval. Chuck Hagel correctly observed that the United States "went well beyond" the customary laws of land warfare in not torching villages, slaughtering cattle, and wiping out villagers, even as those locales hosted (willingly or unwillingly) scores of enemy troops. Nobody in 2-47th Infantry perpetrated a My Lai massacre, the horrendous crime committed up north in the Americal Division on March 16, 1968. Chuck Hagel acknowledged "mistakes" and even "atrocities," but also noted that American restraint "cost us lives."[53]

That said, something jagged and hurtful was keeping Tom Hagel up at night. He tried. But he couldn't exorcise these unquiet ghosts.

THE UNIFORMED ENEMIES bothered him less. He understood those guys, even the nameless AK-47 shooter he encountered close up on July 3 at the riverbank. They were soldiers like him. They took their chances. The man he shot face to face returned now and then to pay his respects. In certain dark hours, Tom Hagel again saw that stunned visage, neat bullet hole drilled in the forehead.[54] But it didn't eat at Hagel.

The bodies of the NVA and VC also didn't linger long in Hagel's nightmares. He'd found them gnarled and rigid, cut down by machine gun bullets, cooked by napalm, cut up by shell fragments, laid low by helicopter rocketry. Charlie lacked airpower and heavy weaponry—he wouldn't trundle out that stuff until 1972, as the Americans folded their tents. But as with the individual Tom had killed, the hostile fighters seemed like equals, even the women found with gear. Too bad the bad guys had to ply their trade with hand weapons. If they chose to go at it, they, too, understood the risks.

"But there were all the others," Tom said. "Women and children," he went on, "and they didn't have guns—because we saw them after."[55] The supporting fires, artillery and air, blotted out big areas. But sometimes the deaths came more directly. He thought about the pregnant woman killed on July 3 by the jumpy lieutenant in that sad riverside *ville*. Tom Hagel couldn't just write off these people as collateral damage or rounding errors or by-catch from America's relentless culling of the Mekong Delta Viet Cong. He personally didn't do any of it. But he didn't stop it, either.

Another scene, a bad one, flashed up now and then. On a night mission near a village, Tom's platoon took a lot of fire. An NCO, reeling with liquor, swung up into an M113 commander's cupola. The unsteady sergeant settled behind the .50-caliber machine and ran through a few belts, pouring tracer slugs into the Vietnamese hovels. One was an orphanage. The crazed sergeant finally ceased fire. Did he wipe out any children? Nobody knew. "None of us went in to check," Tom remembered. Chuck had been there, too.[56] The older Hagel blamed the drunken NCO. Tom blamed himself.

There was more. On New Year's Eve at Binh Phuoc, a good many Americans partook of Tom Hagel's stacked cases of PX beer. The recent VC mortar attack and lunge at the outer wire had encouraged the 2-47th leadership to clear out those hootches on the northwest corner. The Vietnamese rumor mill buzzed that before the action, Charlie evicted families and used the shacks to get close. In the next few days, 2-47th officers expected to arrange to remove the nearby structures. On December 31, as part of celebratory fun, well-lubricated grunts decided to get a head start.

Well after dark, unprovoked by any hostile gesture, the boisterous team up in the corner tower near the *ville* opened up with the big .50-caliber heavy machine gun. They'd loaded up a long belt of armor-piercing incendiary, a sort of supertracer that set aflame what it struck. After pouring in a few belts of those deadly 12.7mm rounds, the troops had a few low-ceilinged shacks burning merrily. If there were any noncombatants in there, nobody much cared. Instead, guys took turns cranking off more rounds.[57]

Tom Hagel never doubted that the Vietnamese buildings needed to go. The U.S. firebase couldn't be secured if enemy sappers enjoyed a concealed route right to the barbed wire near the main gate. "You don't have any options," he admitted much later.[58] But that night, all he saw were civilian homes blazing and fellow soldiers spraying slugs into the bonfire—and laughing like demons. *Xin loi*, mama-san.

It was past time to go home.

THEY CALLED IT the "Freedom Bird" and of all the welcome things that dropped out of the sky in Vietnam, the grunts wanted this one most of all. As they waited to board the contracted airliner, outbound soldiers at Tan Son Nhut looked across the steamy parking apron. An uncertain group of fresh troops stood there, uncomfortable in their clean uniforms. Many departing soldiers razzed the newly arrived privates. "You'll be sorry." "Charlie's gonna love you." "They're going to cut your ears off." Other comments were unprintable.[59] The same thing happened every day, inbound meeting outbound, the doomed passing the saved.

Tom Hagel chose not to say anything. He sympathized with the rookies. Had it only been a year and two weeks? It seemed like a lifetime. For twenty-eight men of Company B, 2-47th Infantry, it had been.[60] Tom's rifle company took more casualties, killed and wounded, than any other in the battalion. Three of those wounded were him. Two were Chuck. And to what end? *Xin loi*, grunt.

Tom went home the way he came over, with a hundred-odd uniformed strangers, guys whose departure date matched his. The troops shuffled into assigned seats, no thought given to former divisions or the like, the military's bureaucratic widget and screw drill maintained right to the end. When the jet took off, those aboard cheered and clapped. Then most just zoned out. The lucky ones drifted off to sleep. Most of them didn't have bad memories. Or at least they didn't think they did.

Once he arrived at Travis Air Force Base, California, the U.S. Army owned Sergeant Hagel for three more days. Out-processing at the Oakland Army Terminal emphasized form over substance.[61] An anonymous major welcomed all of them back to America. A sergeant major got up and growled at them, reminding the soldiers to shut up, follow the out-processing checklist, and move with a purpose from station to station. The senior NCO made sure to mention that the Uniform Code of Military Justice still applied. In plain English, screw up, face a court-martial. The smarter draftees, like Tom Hagel, would be out of the army when this final purgatory passed. A good number hadn't watched their timeline to be sure to get down to the magic 150 days. Others had enlisted voluntarily for more than the two-year conscription period. All of those soldiers received orders for stateside posts.

Once more, as he'd done so many times since that first long day at Fort Bliss, Tom Hagel made the rounds. Dutiful finance clerks settled up back pay. A doctor went over Tom's medical records, gave him a most cursory medical examination, and pronounced all well. A chaplain talked to him. A psychological interviewer—not a doctor, just some guy—questioned Tom, too.[62] Apparently, Tom gave the right answers. The fellow initialed Tom Hagel's checklist. Not crazy. He now had the paperwork to prove it.

At the final stop on the line, a careful personnel specialist typed up Department of Defense Form 214, the military version of that infamous permanent record you'd always heard about in grade school. But a DD 214 was quite real. If you ever hoped to merit anything from the Veterans Administration, you needed that key document.[63] To get it right, the typist checked each line of Tom's records, verifying his rank, his training, his assignments, his combat awards, and his campaign ribbons. The three Purple Hearts got attention. Well they should.

And then it ended. For the last time, Sergeant Thomas Leo Hagel walked out of a U.S. Army headquarters. He had a wallet full of money, a government-paid ticket back to Nebraska, and a long way to go. No hippies spit on him. And nobody turned out for a dress parade, either. He left the army as he entered it. Alone.

On the way out, Tom heard a voice. He never saw the person who spoke. "Thank you for your service, young man," someone said. "Now go have a good life."[64]

CHAPTER 11

Ashes

Our poor children. There seemed to be no middle crowd
or ground. They were either violently for or violently opposed.

KATHERINE VAN DEUSEN WESTMORELAND[1]

S tay out of the middle of the street, the veteran sergeants warned
the privates. The NCOS had been in this dangerous neighborhood before, and knew the deal. Even in darkness, it wasn't
safe out there. Flickering light from burning storefronts cast long
shadows, but also served to silhouette men who didn't watch where
they walked. Snipers loved to pick off guys who wandered out in the
open. So the wise heads spread the word. Use the buildings as cover.
Move near them. And watch the roofs. Shooters lurked up there.

Even under concealment of night, hugging the first-floor walls
didn't work too well, either. The file of rifle-armed troops worked
deliberately from doorway to doorway. But they had to be careful.
Bright flames licked out of gaping window frames.[2] Avoid the light,
men. The sergeants kept saying it. So the privates tried to thread
the needle, near the structures, but not too near. Wary soldiers hop-
scotched in slow motion from one dim spot to another. None hesitated in front of the lit-up stretches.

Oily smoke lingered at ground level, making it tough to breathe.
The book told troops to don gas masks, but as usual in the oppressive
summer, it was way too hot for that. Plus, who could see anything

from inside the rubber mask? Rifles up, eyes raised, the soldiers coughed and stepped slowly, placing their boots with care. Smashed wood, garbage, and glass chips covered the broken sidewalks. Who knew what other unpleasant surprises waited underfoot? Experienced NCOs cautioned all. Take your time. Stay alert.

Along both sides of the street, a long row of riflemen, a company of them, worked west. Here and there, dotted along the street, bashed automobiles squatted on flattened tires. Some of the wrecks flared up, too. Other cars sat askew on the cracked pavement, gutted and blackened, stinking of burnt gasoline.[3] Like napalm. It smelled just like napalm.

Overhead, a pair of helicopters kept watch. They wove between the columns of smoke as their crews looked down into the maelstrom of choking soot lit by golden spots of fire. Aviators called out sightings on the radio.[4] Two men moving together one block south, paralleling the dismounted infantry column. One unidentified person on the next corner to the west—can't tell if he's armed. With the gloom of night and all the obscuration drifting in the summer evening air, any aerial reports at all amounted to a miracle.

This wasn't south Saigon, but Twenty-fourth Street in Omaha, Nebraska, on the evening of Tuesday, June 24, 1969. A month later to the day, three Americans returned from space. During their eight-day voyage, two walked on the moon for the first time in human history. The *Apollo* 11 astronauts thought they'd seen "magnificent desolation" and left it behind, a quarter million miles away from earth.[5] But they were wrong. Just ask the citizens of ravaged North Omaha.

IN THE WORDS of Chuck Hagel: "I knew what America had just gone through in 1968 when we were in Vietnam: the assassination of Martin Luther King and Bobby Kennedy, the riots and upheaval." But Omaha? The long hot summer of 1966 came first, then the in-your-face Wallace visit of 1968, the violence after King's assassination, and now this. Times in Nebraska had changed, all right, and in the worst possible way. "It was a different place," offered Chuck.[6]

Yet in too many ways, North Omaha wasn't different enough, and therein lay the true problem. National Guard sergeants knew exactly what to instruct their men to do because the older guys had been there in 1966 and in 1968. The riots came and went. People died. Shops and homes burned. Yet underlying conditions of poverty and discrimination persisted. In 1969, another dreadful incident sparked violence.

Heat, overcrowding, and indigence characterized the Logan Fontenelle public housing complex, which crammed more than two thousand people into 550 small units. But after fifty-one years of hard use, the cookie-cutter brick housing and its neat grid of streets had long since degenerated into a trash-strewn hellhole. Plagued by criminals, dejected residents named it "Little Vietnam."[7]

In an alley in Little Vietnam on the warm afternoon of June 24, 1969, a nervous white Omaha police officer mistakenly shot and killed fourteen-year-old African American resident Vivian Strong.[8] Word went around right away. A white cop shot a young woman. People gathered, and few argued for restraint. Instead, things escalated, and fast. Within an hour, neighborhood rabble-rousers smashed open liquor store windows. White-owned shops on Twenty-fourth Street ignited. Gunfire echoed across a ten-block area. For hours, unchecked mayhem ensued.[9] As usual in these terrifying episodes, innocent law-abiding citizens found themselves caught up in the violence. No reasonable person in North Omaha or anywhere else condoned the death of Vivian Strong. But burning, looting, and shooting up the neighborhood only added to the pain. Yet it went on.

The National Guard mobilized. Along with the Omaha police, the guardsmen had only too much experience in the Twenty-fourth Street community. It took three days to quell all the unrest. When the last fires flickered down to ashes, eighty-eight residents had been injured, sixty-six arrested, and fifty businesses torched, just under a million dollars in property damage.[10] Looking up and down the ransacked streets of the business district, distraught citizens stared at the charred remnants of hardware stores, groceries, dry cleaners, restaurants, gas stations—all gone. Like Ben Tre in the Mekong

Delta, and with some unwelcome "help" from uniformed Americans, North Omaha destroyed itself. Whether or not it would be saved remained to be seen.

BY 1969, THOUGHTFUL OBSERVERS of the American urban scene believed that the worst had passed.[11] Compared to the height of inner-city disorders in 1965–68, culminating in the nationwide swath of arson and bloodshed after the death of Dr. King, the Omaha disturbance of June 1969 barely registered. But people in Washington paid attention. As long as the headquarters of Strategic Air Command, mighty SAC, remained at Offutt Air Force Base, any dissension in Omaha topped the agenda at the FBI and the Pentagon. If the high tide of America's racial strife had subsided, why did discontent endure in Nebraska?

The standard excuse by municipal authorities pinned rioting on the usual suspects, which is to say the infamous "outside agitators." From Watts 1965 to Chicago 1968, self-assured mayors and chiefs of police told themselves and their worried citizens that the local African American communities could be trusted, but imported activists showed up with money, guns, and bad attitudes. And then hell followed.

In Omaha, right on cue, newly elected mayor Eugene E. Leahy invoked the traditional culprits.[12] Of course, that argument allowed city officials to avoid the more intractable conditions that brought on violence. In this case, an Omaha police officer's fatal error set off long-building passions. If any distant manipulators could arrange such a thing, their powers bordered on the supernatural.

Yet Omaha was tied so closely to the direction of America's nuclear forces that those paid to think about the unthinkable had little choice but to consider the worst. FBI director J. Edgar Hoover recognized that Soviet KGB and GRU intelligence officers enjoyed unique skills and resources. They could well be behind the Omaha riot. Hoover studied reports of uniformed, armed Black Panther Party members standing guard in North Omaha during the June 1969 disturbance. Since the Wallace imbroglio in March of 1968, Hoover had ordered special interest in the Black Panthers of Omaha.[13] The FBI chief suspected a Russian link, tied to designs on Offutt Air Force Base.

Accordingly, Hoover promoted FBI efforts in Omaha to the top of the clandestine, quasi-legal domestic surveillance and preemption enterprise called COINTELPRO (Counterintelligence Program). This high-priority undertaking originated back in the Eisenhower administration. Along with full use of lawful investigatory measures, the FBI's COINTELPRO relied all too often on warrantless searches, illicit wiretapping of telephones, interception of U.S. mail, and recruitment of undercover informants. When dealing with perceived threats to national security, the Fourth Amendment of the U.S. Constitution evidently could be honored in the breach. For J. Edgar Hoover and a number of U.S. presidents, the Cold War nuclear stand-off justified it all. By the 1960s, the Bureau paid special interest to student anti-war groups and militant elements like the Black Panthers.[14]

Active as COINTELPRO had been under LBJ, things really took off under President Richard M. Nixon. When FBI director Hoover pointed out the hazards of possible Soviet-backed anti-government conspiracies, he found a very willing listener in Nixon. Both men displayed morbid suspicion of all entities with any trace of communist ties. They also had no love for white supremacist groups like the Ku Klux Klan, but in the hothouse of 1969, the KKK carried little weight.[15] But the Black Panthers? Those self-proclaimed revolutionaries deserved a long, hard look, and the most vigorous application of law enforcement.

The disorder in North Omaha, right on SAC's doorstep, seemed ripe for quashing. In his 1968 presidential campaign, Nixon ran on putting an end to this kind of rioting. He talked of providing "law and order," a phrase lifted from the rhetoric of the odious George Wallace, but certainly in line with what almost all Americans, black or white, hoped to see.[16] Nixon, buttressed by Hoover's FBI, did a great deal for domestic order. Law sometimes suffered in the pursuit of public calm.

The Black Panthers of North Omaha didn't hide themselves. In the street clashes after the killing of Vivian Strong, the Panthers protected key locations, including the office of the *Omaha Star*, the

African American community newspaper. Photographer Rudy Smith took their picture. Eddie Bolden carried a rifle with a bandolier of ammunition across his chest. David Rice and Edward Poindexter also stood there. All three men offered forbidding scowls and wore black berets. "They served a valuable community service that night," said Smith.[17] The *Omaha Star* sustained no damage.

After the fires went out and calm returned, the Panthers moved to consolidate their role in the North Omaha community. They organized the Vivian Strong Liberation School.[18] The little gathering, held in the group's headquarters, aimed to raise consciousness among the youth. It attracted some interest from the neighborhood teenagers and a lot of notice from the FBI and the Omaha police.

One instructor at the school, David Rice, described himself as a "blippy," a black hippie who often spent time with a white girlfriend. Back in March of 1968, Rice found himself swept up in the unrest spurred by George Wallace's visit. Rice earned some money working for the government-funded Greater Community Action organization, a product of President Lyndon Johnson's anti-poverty legislation. But that kind of job training and self-esteem building only went so far. Rice thought it to be a dead end. A poet, performance artist, and free spirit, the small, slight Rice didn't match the typical profile of a menacing Black Panther. But he believed in the struggle for revolutionary justice at the expense of the Man. He concentrated on developing propaganda flyers, exhorting potential sympathizers, spreading the latest party line in the community, and maybe changing some minds.[19]

Another teacher at the Vivian Strong Liberation School, Edward Poindexter, made a more immediate impression. Six feet, five inches tall, Poindexter exerted a presence, all right. Despite his imposing frame, he was soft spoken, and worked days as a post office letter carrier. A six-year U.S. Army veteran, Poindexter served in Germany, Vietnam, and then Fort Benning, Georgia. He believed racial discrimination denied him promotions. The Black Panthers gave him an outlet to go after such institutional injustice.[20]

The FBI Omaha special agent in charge, Paul Young, took note of Rice, Poindexter, and the other Black Panthers.[21] Running a small discussion circle grandiosely labeled as a liberation school didn't mean much by itself. But if these guys tried anything else—sabotage, shootings, bombings—then the FBI would move. In the meantime, the Bureau fed information to the Omaha police. The men in blue had enough to keep busy already.

THE OMAHA POLICE paid a call on Chuck and Tom Hagel one night. The brothers had nothing to do with the Black Panthers, but they did live together in a modest rental home in North Omaha, not too far (but far enough) from the squalid Logan Fontenelle housing project. They both attended the nearby University of Nebraska-Omaha, an institution that welcomed veterans. Chuck majored in history. Tom chose a pre-law curriculum, aiming to become an attorney. The GI Bill paid for college, but with no family largesse, both men worked. Chuck tended bar. Tom, like Ed Poindexter, worked as a mailman. And after a long day, the Hagel brothers liked to relax with a drink or two.[22] Or more.

One evening, the alcohol pulled the brothers over the dam. Well along in his cups, Tom started ranting about Vietnam. He pulled the pins and flung the loaded words like grenades. Foolish. Losing. False. Chuck tried to argue that the U.S. policy made sense, that South Vietnam deserved a chance to be free of communism, but the military strategy had been flawed. Tom went right back at his brother. Senseless. Immoral. Murder. Face to face, voices raised, hands clenched . . .

Then came the punches. Chuck carried more muscle. Tom was taller and had the reach. And both hit hard. "We were in a fistfight," Tom recalled, "smashing beds, knocking doors off."[23] They didn't stop.

The tumult alarmed a neighbor. An older person living nearby apparently didn't care for indoor boxing. "Someone called the cops," Tom said. Not long after, two taciturn Omaha police officers showed up at the front door, fortuitously still on its hinges.

That sobered up the two Hagels. "We were immediately all buddy-buddy," Tom remembered.[24] Their hard-learned military courtesy shone through. Yes, sir. No, sir. Just a misunderstanding, officers. The police left. No harm, no foul—and no formal citation was issued.

After the run-in with the law, the Hagel brothers learned not to talk about the war with each other. Mother Betty, remarried to E. J. Breeding, moved with Mike and Jimmy to Hastings, Nebraska. She categorically forbade any Vietnam fireworks when the two college students came home to visit. "Enough of this," she commanded.[25] Her word held. No first sergeant ever spoke with more authority.

On campus, Chuck paid no attention to the student rebels clamoring about Vietnam. Tom agreed with many of the sentiments of the peace movement, but found the anti-war people to be ridiculous. He guessed that 10 percent really cared. "The rest, some dressed in their 'regulation' hippie uniform, were far too busy in the social-recreational activities," said Tom. "I was particularly impressed by the individuals who verbally attacked 'this filthy, capitalist system'—and then got into their Corvettes and drove off to rage in their fraternity houses."[26] Compared to the height of 1960s college activism, the shenanigans at University of Nebraska-Omaha hardly wiggled the needle.

The university students lost interest in the war for a good reason. As with the dissipation of urban disturbances in response to the carrots of civil rights legislation and LBJ's Great Society programs and the sticks of Nixonian "law and order," plus the likes of COINTELPRO, so conscious government actions gradually reduced, and then removed, the major issue that made American campuses seethe. Nixon rose to the presidency promising to end the war in Vietnam and, coincidentally, the unfair and unpopular military draft.[27] Upon inauguration, he acted immediately on both points.

With regard to the Vietnam War, Nixon began troop withdrawals in the same summer that saw Americans walk the moon and Vivian Strong die in North Omaha. The first increment of 15,712 came from the 1st and 2nd Brigades of the 9th Infantry Division. Officially, regiments of ARVN soldiers took over security across the Mekong Delta.[28] In reality, the communists continued to hold the countryside. Except for all those killed and wounded, ours and theirs, it was as if the Americans never showed up at all. You had to wonder what Chuck and Tom Hagel thought. But they didn't dare discuss the war anymore.

Nixon justified the pull out of the 9th Infantry Division as the opening round of "Vietnamization," in which reequipped South Vietnamese forces backed by U.S. air and naval support would hold the line in country.[29] Could the South do it? Nobody knew. But the pattern had been set. Every few months, another division's worth of Americans departed. Each reduction lessened the need for draftees.

As draft calls decreased, slowly at first, but faster over time, Nixon pressed the U.S. Armed Forces to transition back to volunteer recruiting, the usual method for most of American history. Nixon announced the plan to end the draft within the next few years. He also sharply curtailed almost all deferments, substituting a birth-date lottery for the vagaries of local Selective Service boards. The call-up numbers ramped down, nearly halving each year: 283,586 in 1969, 162,746 in 1970, 94,092 in 1971, 49,514 in 1972, and a final 646 in 1973.[30] Except for those still being inducted, the draft ceased to be a huge bogeyman for many American males. Although most students still decried the war, the incentive to pour blood on military records, burn draft cards, or flee to Canada dwindled proportionately.

The war in Vietnam limped on. The North Vietnamese backed down, checked their calendars, and awaited the final U.S. farewell. Bombs still dropped. Men still died. Nixon allowed shallow cross-border incursions into Cambodia in 1970 and Laos in 1971. Neither worked. By 1972, the refurbished North Vietnamese, to include tanks and heavy artillery, charged south in force, took terrain, and held it. ARVN could not eject the communists. And America lacked the stomach to do anything that stuck. Nixon tried overtures to the Soviet Union. He broke decades of strict American sanctions and visited Mao Zedong's Red China. He unleashed B-52s full of conventional munitions to rain death on Hanoi at Christmas of 1972.[31] None of it mattered. Only the U.S. withdrawal clicker counted. Both Hanoi and Washington knew it. Vietnam would soon be in the rearview mirror, a screw-up, a fiasco, a horrific mistake, never to be repeated.

One-time B-24 bomber pilot Senator George McGovern ran against Nixon in 1972 and lost—did he ever, humiliated in a forty-nine-state rout. The South Dakotan ran on the slogan "Come Home America."[32] But for all his foreign policy intrigues, Nixon was already there. A country that had dared to go to the moon, declare war on poverty, and bear any burden in the Mekong Delta gave up on every bit of it. Come home America.

But as the Hagel brothers learned in Omaha, home wasn't what it used to be.

THE TELEPHONE RANG at 5:30 a.m. on Sunday, November 16, 1969. Both Hagels rose early, but not on Sunday. This couldn't be good.

It wasn't. E. J. Breeding sounded gruff, choked up. Jimmy Hagel had died in a car crash. Breeding asked Chuck and Tom to come to Fullerton, Nebraska, to identify the body.

James Joseph Hagel dead? It didn't make sense. "It seemed so bizarre," Chuck said. "Tom and I went through what we did, and came back in good shape." Now this. Their youngest brother, only sixteen, achieved top grades and quarterbacked the football team at St. Cecilia Catholic high school.[33] But if Vietnam taught the brothers anything, they'd learned that it could all go in an instant. For Jimmy, it had.

After the sad trip to Fullerton, the brothers and their stepfather talked to Nance County sheriff Richard Shepoka. His police report covered the facts. After midnight, Jimmy Hagel drove his vehicle through a country road junction. The sixteen-year-old missed the turn and piled into a ditch. The automobile flipped. Three other high schoolers, one from Hastings and two from Columbus, suffered whiplash and abrasions, but made it out okay.[34] Just like a bad night near Binh Phuoc: there it is.

Betty didn't take it well. After the funeral, she began drinking, rivaling Tom on intake. It went on for a few months, but after a while her religious faith won out. "Maybe God's testing me," she thought. She checked into rehabilitation and never touched another glass of alcohol. In admiration, son Chuck wrote proudly: "She hit things straight up."[35]

Chuck took after his mother. Jimmy's death might have made anyone rethink the last few years, especially that long twelve months with 2-47th Infantry. Not Chuck Hagel: "I never regretted it, never looked back, never thought about it." Like his mom, Betty, he'd made his choice and lived with it. "Once you made the decision, you go forward."[36]

Tom, however, followed his father's less sure route. Like Charles Dean Hagel, Tom never missed a day of school or work. And like his father, in the evening, Tom often found himself sitting in a tavern and pounding 'em down. "If anyone said anything to me, I'd just go crazy," he said.[37] Dad Charles at least had the American Legion, and other men who understood, even though few words passed between them. Tom lacked even that.

Anyone who sees combat—not just hanging around in the theater of operations, but real fighting—will experience post-traumatic stress. It's baked into the cake. Gruesome wounds, arbitrary cruelty, and chance encounters with mortality all combine to generate an inordinate degree of psychological pressure.[38] Whether that stress manifests itself as a disorder, PTSD, depends on the individual, the immediate group (family or unit), and society as a whole.

In Tom's case, he took his battle experiences very hard. Jimmy's shocking accident only underscored the dark forebodings of horrid things half glimpsed, searing macabre scenes, and unrelenting survivor's guilt. Even with a pretty strong upbringing, those last few empty weeks in Vietnam did Tom no good at all. The Hagel family, Chuck in particular, had no desire to hear about combat or talk about it. Tom's older brother shared almost all of Tom's most awful moments in country. Yet Chuck didn't want to discuss those disquieting matters. He would have to reach a reckoning with his own hard memories in the decades to come. But in the years right after Vietnam, Tom's older brother settled on denial. He homed in on school, on work, and, as he put it, moved forward, not looking back, but "all about tomorrow."[39]

And the army? Well, the random individual assignment policy tor-pedoed unit cohesion, atomizing the band of brothers. Coming and going to war alone bred PTSD like the Mekong Delta rice paddies bred mosquitoes. The U.S. Army of that era, run at the highest levels by World War II veterans who should have known better, took no ownership of this psychological wasteland.[40] The military saw it as an individual weakness, not an institutional challenge, even as the era's prevalent personnel policies sped the evil plow.

As for American society, most turned their backs on Vietnam veterans like Tom. Neither Hagel dealt with outright hostility in Nebraska, even on the university grounds where some self-styled peaceniks abided. But indifference did its own harm. At a university social gathering, when a faculty member asked if he had served in combat, Tom answered. From those around Hagel, "there was just, simply, *silence*. Everyone got real uncomfortable."[41] People looked off into the distance. They refused to go there. But Tom had done so, whether or not these students cared to acknowledge it.

In the end, Tom sorted himself out. He drew on enough innate character to do it. He took up veteran counseling, helping guys se-cure benefits. Next came working with the mentally challenged. Leaning left politically, Tom took his convictions well beyond words. He consistently worked with and represented the downtrodden, the powerless, and the forgotten. Tom started law school in Lincoln. The booze dried up. And the nightmares grew less frequent.[42] The terrible visions never wholly disappeared. But the inner angst faded the more Tom Hagel looked out.

Chuck Hagel, for his part, also faced outward. He drew on his ed-ucation at Brown Institute of Radio and Television and applied for a job at Omaha radio station KBON. Chuck became an on-air host. When management switched to call letters KLNG and tried a new all-talk format, his long interests in history and politics made Chuck the natural choice to handle the current events show. "It was a great experiment," Hagel said.[43] And it paid, too.

Talk radio in 1970–71 hadn't yet degenerated into today's all-too-common swamp of sharp-edged, opinionated hooting and hollering.

Although on the conservative end himself, Chuck interviewed people from across the political spectrum. He let them talk, and allowed callers time to express themselves, too. Among those Chuck interviewed, former governor Frank B. Morrison, a Democrat, made a strong impression.[44] It intrigued Chuck that after losing a senatorial bid in November of 1970, the former governor had chosen to serve as the Douglas County public defender. Morrison sure as hell didn't do it for the meager salary. The three-term governor's dedication to public service also impressed Tom Hagel, who saw the self-effacing pragmatic liberal as a role model.[45]

As it happened, Frank Morrison's tenure as public defender would begin with a bang. The calendar indicated that the turbulent 1960s had ended. But from the disheartened populace of racially divided Omaha, the cruel decade demanded one more blood sacrifice. Frank Morrison would be right in the middle of it. And this time, white society in Omaha, the Hagels among them, could not avert its gaze.

NORTH OMAHA AGAIN—2:23 a.m., August 17, 1970, and few warm fuzzy things unfolded in that sullen area at that unholy hour. The dispatcher notified a unit to respond to trouble at an empty house. Three other police cruisers in the area closed in, too. On a summer night in a crime-ridden community, numbers mattered.

When four policemen entered the abandoned structure, a bomb detonated. Officer Larry D. Minard died; the other three were injured.[46] Anguished people from up and down the block, many in pajamas, gathered to offer condolences, prayers, and tears. None of the residents had any inkling who emplaced the fatal device.[47]

The city cops had no clues, no tips, and no idea of how to find Minard's killer. But the FBI knew. Thanks to COINTELPRO, the Bureau had a human source inside the North Omaha Black Panther cell. "We have excellent informer coverage of the Panthers," the FBI man said. So the Panthers did it. That tracked with trends seen in other cities. The FBI had seen a very similar dynamite bombing on May 13 at a police station in Des Moines, Iowa.[48]

But then the FBI representative threw a curve ball. "And our key source advises us that two white males were observed running from the scene shortly before the blast."[49] Two white males? Student radicals? Russians?[50] The Omaha police superiors took it all down.

Despite the otherwise uncorroborated lead about two white men, the balance of the FBI's information, some of it gathered by highly questionable methods, pointed right to the Panthers. The militants had bomb-making expertise—the device was pretty elementary— and access to materials, and the national Black Panther Party included many belligerent elements with track records of similar attacks. The local Omaha chapter alleged it had quit the Black Panther Party, and in mid-1969 rebranded itself as the National Committee to Combat Fascism. That fooled nobody, not even the members. Key figures in the chapter remained Ed Poindexter, deputy chairman, and David Rice, deputy minister of information, both well known to the FBI and Omaha police.[51] On the morning of August 17, 1970, law enforcement officials agreed that Poindexter and Rice must be part of the bombing.

If they hoped to avoid suspicion, the two Panthers said and did all the wrong things. Although Poindexter and Rice held government jobs, as a postal carrier and anti-poverty counselor respectively, each spent hours regaling various North Omaha citizens, expressing utter contempt for the United States, Nebraska, and city governments. Law-abiding neighbors all heard the usual Panther slogans. "Freedom by any means necessary!" "The power of the people is found in the gun." "Off the pigs!"[52] That last one sure didn't help when Omaha police started questioning people in the neighborhood.

It took almost six days to unearth a witness willing to finger Rice. Once that occurred, the police raided Rice's home, which also served as the headquarters for the National Committee to Combat Fascism, complete with a large identification plaque helpfully mounted over the door. The law enforcement team recovered fourteen sticks of dynamite, four blasting caps, a six-volt battery, and pliers. Forensic examiners tied the pliers to residue from the bomb that killed Officer Minard. In addition, when the police arrested Rice, then Poindexter, they found dynamite residue on their clothing, although none on their skin.[53] Game. Set. Match. The police assumed they had their bombers.

The pair's trial began with ill portents. Proceedings started on an incongruous date, April 1, 1971, and at an unfortunate place, the venerable Douglas County courthouse, site of Omaha's first major race riot in 1919. The senior Douglas County public defender, former governor Frank Morrison, assessed the judge as fair and the jury of eleven whites and one black as about the best possible in Omaha at the time. But he also would have preferred a change of venue. "I'm convinced they just set out to get some evidence on Rice and Poindexter 'cause they didn't like the way they talked," Morrison observed.[54] Much of the city, white and black, followed the proceedings. Those interested included KLNG talk-show host Chuck Hagel, who covered the trial for his station. Pre-law student Tom Hagel also followed the proceedings with interest. "We were very aware of it," Chuck said later.[55] So were most people in Omaha, black and white.

Both Rice and Poindexter pled innocent and insisted they did not construct, plant, or direct setting the bomb. Defense attorney Frank Morrison didn't know about the FBI informant's supposed sighting of two white guys. All evidence from COINTELPRO remained unacknowledged. The physical evidence and some witness statements proved very compelling. Former governor Morrison did what he could. But the outcome was never really in doubt.

The jury deliberated four days. They found both Poindexter and Rice guilty of first-degree murder. The judge sentenced both men to life in prison. Rice (who renamed himself Mondo we Langa) died in the penitentiary in 2016. Poindexter continues to serve his time and maintain his innocence.[56]

Frank Morrison stayed at it, filing appeals that emphasized technical failings. In support of the Douglas County public defender, the Nebraska chapter of the American Civil Liberties Union (including Tom Hagel) and even Amnesty International all took up the cause of the pair they titled the "Omaha Two." When other events in the 1970s revealed the extensive scope of COINTELPRO, subsequent Freedom of Information Act petitions exposed some of the FBI's machinations surrounding the case.[57] For those convinced the system is rigged and the Man will always find a way, the Rice-Poindexter case offers an object lesson.

From the perspective of the local citizenry, black and white, the case ended the cycle of riots and violence in North Omaha. The Black Panthers disbanded. Former members drifted into oblivion, remembered, if at all, as the grainy subjects in stark photos from another era. Racism didn't go away, but outright segregation did. While there's been undeniable progress, North Omaha today remains less affluent and more violent than other neighborhoods in the city.[58]

The Rice-Poindexter trial affected both Hagel brothers. As he finished law school, Tom followed the course charted by former governor Frank Morrison, standing up for those unable to stand up for themselves. While offering no excuse for cop killings, he strongly believed that those accused deserved a fair trial. As a public defender in Lancaster County, Tom decided to do his part even when it got really sticky. "He had these real toughies that people just felt like hanging," his mother recalled.[59] Not on Tom Hagel's watch—he spoke up for them all with passion and skill. By his lights, America demanded equality before the law and due process. As he'd done in Vietnam, Tom waded right in there.

As for Chuck, although he embraced the Nixon-era law and order ethos more fully than his brother, he also believed in fairness. People in America were innocent until proven guilty, and had a right to an impartial trial. Many years later, as a U.S. Senator Chuck Hagel took action to release to the public more than a thousand pages of FBI documents related to the Rice-Poindexter investigation.[60] Political pundits, especially those on the right end of the table, wondered why a conservative Republican legislator would get embroiled in such a mess. But anybody who really knew Chuck Hagel wasn't surprised at all.

"LOOK WHAT'S FLYING OVER IT NOW."

Tom pointed to the Binh Phuoc pole, the same one that stood there in 1968. Chuck glanced up. A red banner with a yellow star fluttered in the warm breeze.[61] The flag belonged to the Socialist Republic of Vietnam.

That standard did not get there by accident. The North's tank battalions and infantry regiments stormed Saigon one fine spring only six years after Tom Hagel departed Binh Phuoc. Those victorious NVA troops didn't wear black pajamas or skulk in the underbrush. They brushed aside the ARVN, hapless to the last, and rolled right down Highway 1 like they owned the place. As of May Day, 1975, they did.[62]

On that sunshine-drenched, humid afternoon of August 14, 1999, professor of law Tom Hagel and his brother, U.S. senator Chuck Hagel, walked their former firebase. They did so as guests of the politburo in Hanoi. The next day, Senator Hagel represented the United States at a ceremony at the new American consulate in Ho Chi Minh City. Except for some Vietnamese Communist Party hacks and the authors of official correspondence, the population still referred to their city as Saigon.[63] They always would. All the reeducation in the world couldn't erase that traditional name.

For three days, the Hagels visited their old haunts. With them went some escort officers from the U.S. Army, a Vietnamese "minder" (after all, they were communists), and Brad Penner and his able video production team from Nebraska Educational Television Network. Cameras and microphones captured hours of discussion, as well as a few staged interviews and ceremonial events. Thirty-one years on, the sights, sounds, and smells of Vietnam brought back many memories. When edited and aired on Nebraska public television as *Echoes of War*, the half-hour documentary told quite a story.[64]

In the film, both brothers seemed relaxed and happy: Tom the self-deprecating academic with his trimmed salt and pepper beard, Chuck the optimistic political leader, husky and smiling, shaking hands all around. Although the two men were in their fifties, they exuded health. Tall, forceful, alert, and vigorous in short-sleeve shirts, they both looked like they could shoulder up M60 pig machine guns and go tramping off through the bush. When accompanying U.S. Army officers pulled out maps, operational reports, and unit radio logs, both Hagels lapsed immediately into grunt-speak. The two former sergeants knew their business, and the Hagels' depth of recall caught a few of the young officers by surprise. The earnest active-duty types hadn't seen enough combat, if any, to grasp just how deeply ingrained those searing experiences can be.

Aboard a tidy Vietnamese minibus, Chuck and Tom traveled all across the 9th Infantry Division's former area of operations. At one halt, they walked through a village on the edge of the Binh Son rubber plantation, not far from where they were wounded in both the March and April 1968 firefights. The blue-trimmed white motor transport carried them around the perimeter of Long Binh Post, converted by the not-so-communist Vietnamese to a commercial warehouse complex. In south Saigon, they went right down bustling Route 320, to the Y-bridge, through Xom Ong Doi, to the Y-bridge, and on to Xom Cau Mat, all heavily contested during Mini-Tet. In south Saigon, the brothers dismounted and noticed how little had changed in those once deadly streets. Tom pointed to former sniper posts on the roofs. Chuck nodded knowingly. And finally, they stopped at Binh Phuoc.[65]

While the rust-red dust hung in the afternoon sun, the brothers stood together, quiet. It's uncertain if the brisk military escorts or the busy television team, let alone the Vietnamese communist chaperone, picked up Tom's distant gaze or noticed the tinge of mist in Chuck's eyes. But the unblinking camera saw it all, a shadow over the pair, like a cloud crossing the sun. Then it passed, and the brothers let it go. The ghosts faded away. Tom and Chuck moved on.

The Old Sergeant

Only the dead are safe;
only the dead have seen the end of war.

GEORGE SANTAYANA, *"Tipperary"*[1]

C huck Hagel wanted to see for himself. And thus in March of 2013, the newly appointed U.S. secretary of defense flew out to Afghanistan to see the sausage made. He intended to get a grip on what the Americans, the other NATO troops, and especially the Afghans were doing now and could do in the future. He asked the four-star U.S. commander to maximize the time in country: get out on the ground, meet the key actors, and gain a sense of the war effort.[2]

Of course, the American four-star's staff took that guidance, shoved it into the standard template for Very Important Person visits, and gave birth to an itinerary that underwhelmed. Two and a half days on the ground and this was the best the general could do? Same old, same old. The force headquarters scheduled a PowerPoint briefing. The corps headquarters listed another slide presentation. Even at Jalalabad, at the American Forward Operating Base Fenty, the division and brigade proposed to flog Hagel through a welter of computerized charts. Hell, he could stay in the Pentagon and scroll through a deck of bullet points and statistics. But the generals and colonels loved their formal pitches. If the American secretary of defense took the time to fly all the way to Afghanistan, he deserved a chance to meet some actual humans, walk around a few real places, and sniff some local smells.

The Afghans chose not to show slides, but then again, that wasn't their style. At least traveling by ground to the ministry buildings in Kabul promised to let the American secretary see something interesting on the way. The street markets teemed with life, and even from behind the tinted, bullet-proof windows of an armored sport utility vehicle, you could get a notion of the mood on the city streets. So there was that.

Yet the drive never happened. Hours before the scheduled appointment at the Afghan ministry of defense, a determined Taliban bicycle bomber wormed his way through the facility's barrier maze, reached the front gate, and blew his load. Nine Afghan civilians died and fourteen more Kabul residents were wounded, a real mess. To cap it off, once the suicide assailant exploded, frantic ministry guards gratuitously sprayed the area with bullets, maybe to ward off evil spirits or the like.[3] None of it engendered confidence in Afghan security measures.

The secretary's personal protection team and nervous U.S. generals reacted, or perhaps overreacted, in a predictable way. They convinced the secretary to relocate his meeting with the Afghan defense minister, and later the interior minister (the police chief), too, inside the well-defended American compound. The Afghan ministers received notifications, not requests, to travel to the secure U.S. facility if they still wanted to talk to the American secretary of defense.[4] So much for deference to the host country—America's clients knew who they were. Both Afghan officials swallowed their pride and showed up on schedule. They needed U.S. advisers, U.S. equipment, and, especially, U.S. funding.

Bad as it was, the bike-bombing posed no real threat to the visiting American dignitary. The press people, however, hyped it up anyway. They often did. Asked about the explosion, Chuck Hagel waved it off. "I was in a briefing," he said, "but we're in a war zone. I've been in a war. So you shouldn't be surprised when a bomb goes off."[5] He was not.

The hastily repositioned discussions with his Afghan counterparts sent all the wrong messages, and Hagel knew it. Take precautions, sure, but the Afghan ministers did their duties out and about. An American secretary of defense couldn't lead his troops from a steel-plated desk or some subterranean bunker. Hagel had an itch to see the Afghan troops and their NATO advisers at Kabul Military Training Center. Thankfully, the U.S. three-star out there, an old infantryman himself, hated slide shows. This visit would be all about meeting Afghans in training. No PowerPoint.

Hagel loved it. His personal security detail hated it. Too risky—potential mortars or snipers, maybe a rocket into the helicopter, and only the unreliable Afghans holding the ring at Kabul Military Training Center, a venue teeming with thousands of unvetted, armed local soldiers. What about a traitor? How about a hidden bomb? After the blast at the Afghan ministry of defense, why take a chance? Hagel listened, but then made his decision.[6]

Go.

Sergeant Mohammed Amin finished his operation order with a flourish, to include a British-style open-palm salute that would have done credit to the Coldstream Guards. The other Afghan sergeants in the class burst into thunderous applause. The ovation stepped on the patter of the interpreter, who waited until after the clapping to finish his translation from Dari into English.

Chuck Hagel, seated in a place of honor next to Brigadier General Aminullah Patyani, sprang to his feet. For a few seconds, he moved like a lithe rifle squad sergeant. Hagel stood tall, an infantryman still despite his dark wool coat, khaki trousers, and a little too much gray hair. Well, the Vietnam generation always pushed the GI haircut regulations. The years melted away. Hagel's eyes gleamed. He spoke with authority, soldier to soldier.

"I've been a sergeant. My brother was a sergeant. Wars are won by sergeants."

The translator picked it up, word for word.

"Your country, your families, depend on you."

Again, the conversion to Dari rolled out, steady and strong.

"I thank you. And I salute you."

And the secretary delivered a crisp salute worthy of George Patton in his heyday.[7] Somewhere in drill sergeant heaven, William Joyce nodded. His top Fort Bliss trainee, the one on whom people relied, and would always rely, did not forget what really counted.

What would become of the Afghan sergeants? For that matter, what of the Americans, the NATO troops, and all the rest? The final outcome of the long, brutal war in Afghanistan would not be determined by anything or anyone at the Kabul Military Training Center on that fine Sunday morning of March 10, 2013. Probably, it was already lost, yet another Vietnam on top of the shambles in Iraq. The old sergeant knew. The younger ones would learn. Maybe someday, America would, too.

Acknowledgments

This book reflects the contributions and wisdom of many, most notably Chuck and Tom Hagel, the central figures of this narrative. They are American heroes. Both made available their time, interviews, photographs, papers, and related archives, to include fine collections at the Dr. C. C. and Mabel L. Criss Library of the University of Nebraska at Omaha and the U.S. Library of Congress. The Hagel brothers' willingness to share their stories reflects a degree of moral courage equivalent to the bravery they showed time and time again under fire in Vietnam.

Special thanks go to my very patient agent, E. J. McCarthy. This book was his idea, and it was a good one. I must also salute the great team at Da Capo. Robert Pigeon and his associates, especially Lissa Warren, all deserve gratitude. Gifted project editor Christine Marra and her able team skillfully sorted out my draft. My colleagues at North Carolina State University have also been immensely supportive. This book reflects their collective wise counsel.

I must particularly recognize the late Keith Nolan, the dean of Vietnam combat historians. His many books covered all of the major operations of the war, drawing on extensive and thoughtful use of official sources, personal accounts, and a relentless quest for what the great British historian John Keegan once labeled the face of battle. Through Keith Nolan, readers learned what really happened in action after action that flared in the jungles and villages of South Vietnam. Had Keith lived, I am sure he would have done justice to the story of Chuck and Tom Hagel. I hope this book approaches what he would certainly have accomplished.

There have been many able journalists and authors who have taken up portions of the stories of the Hagel brothers. Among these, Myra MacPherson stands foremost. Her wonderful, haunting *Long*

Time Passing (1984), a definitive collection of voices of that era, introduced readers to the Hagels long before Tom became a professor of law or Chuck entered the U.S. Senate. Charlyne Berens in *Chuck Hagel: Moving Forward* (2006) offered a superb single-volume political biography of the senator, to include a brief consideration of his military service. And Chuck Hagel himself, with coauthor Peter Kaminsky, wrote *America: Our Next Chapter* (2008), a candid and useful look at his background and beliefs. There are many other fine articles available that address aspects of the Hagels' history. These have been cited in the notes.

In considering the brothers' wartime service, I am grateful to both Chuck and Tom for all they have shared. The U.S. Senator Chuck Hagel Archives at the University of Nebraska at Omaha offer wonderful insights into the rich life of the Hagel family. The photo collection is especially impressive. In 1968, Mike Hagel carefully preserved the photos sent home by his brothers. We are all in his debt.

Particularly valuable insights can be found in the hours of unedited interview footage captured by Brad Penner for a half-hour Nebraska Educational Television documentary on the 1999 visit by Chuck and Tom Hagel to Vietnam. The brothers donated these recordings to the Library of Congress. This is a first-rate resource, amounting to a tour of the sites of key Vietnam engagements from 1968, with the brothers as guides. Chuck and Tom spoke with candor and conviction, and that shines through.

This book is neither an authorized biography nor a comprehensive life and times of the Hagel brothers. Rather, it is an infantryman's account of two infantry sergeants at war. There's a broader story told because there's always more to war than fighting. The heroism and achievements belong to Chuck and Tom Hagel and their fellow Vietnam veterans. Any errors are on me.

Notes

PROLOGUE. LIGHT

1. Bernard Fall, *Hell in a Very Small Place: The Siege of Dien Bien Phu* (New York: Da Capo Press, 1966), 28. General Henri Eugène Navarre commanded the French forces during their disastrous defeat at the hands of the Viet Minh in the valley of Dien Bien Phu in 1954.

2. Thomas L. Hagel, telephone interview by Daniel P. Bolger, October 4, 2016.

3. Charles T. Hagel, telephone interview by Daniel P. Bolger, September 12, 2016.

4. General William C. Westmoreland, U.S. Army, "Progress Report on the War in Vietnam," *State Department Bulletin* (Department of State: Washington, DC, December 11, 1967), 785.

5. I know that handshake. I met General Westmoreland quite by accident in the summer of 1986 on the day my wife and I moved into our quarters at West Point. I was just another captain joining the faculty. Westmoreland was the guest of a colonel who lived nearby. As I walked out to meet the moving van, the general strode up to me, stuck out his hand, and said, "I'm General Westmoreland." Indeed he was.

6. Edward B. Furguson, *Westmoreland: The Inevitable General* (Boston: Little, Brown, 1968) and Lewis S. Sorley, *Westmoreland: The General Who Lost Vietnam* (New York: Houghton Mifflin Harcourt, 2011).

7. Sorley, *Westmoreland*, 18. Otto Kerner Jr. later served as the governor of Illinois (1961–68).

8. This comes from a Bill Moyers account quoted in Sorley, *Westmoreland*, 69.

9. Harry G. Summers Jr., *On Strategy: The Vietnam War in Context* (Carlisle, PA: U.S. Army War College, 1981), 55. Colonel Harry Summers served in Vietnam. His trenchant critique of the U.S. war effort pulled no punches.

10. For Westmoreland's early doubts about Rolling Thunder, see William C. Westmoreland, *A Soldier Reports* (Garden City, NY: Doubleday, 1976), 141. For an assessment of the bombing campaign in both North and South Vietnam, as well as Laos and Cambodia, see John Morocco, *Rain of Fire, The Vietnam Experience* (Boston: Boston Publishing, 1985), 177, 179. For comparisons to World War II bombing, see Micheal Clodfelter, *Vietnam in Military Statistics* (Jefferson, NC: McFarland, 1995), 225. Of 7,662,000 tons of bombs dropped in the Vietnam War, just over a million fell on North Vietnam. In World War II, the United States dropped 623,418 tons on Germany and 160,800 tons on Japan, including all the incendiary raids and the two atomic bombs.

11. *Westmoreland, A Soldier Reports*, 185. Westmoreland went on to add that "since the World War I battles of the Somme and Verdun, that has been a strategy in disrepute, one that to many appeared particularly unsuited for a war in Asia with Asia's legendary hordes of manpower." That sentence speaks for itself.

The names Viet Cong and North Vietnamese Army were American terms. Viet Cong comes from *Viet Nam Cong-san*, "Vietnamese Communists," a pejorative label applied by the Saigon authorities. The Hanoi government called these guerrillas the People's Liberation Armed Forces of South Vietnam, the military arm of the National Liberation Front. The North Vietnamese Army called itself the People's Army of Vietnam. As this is an American account, for clarity, Viet Cong and North Vietnamese Army will be used.

12. *Westmoreland, A Soldier Reports*, 172. The phrases in quotation marks are written in the same way in Westmoreland's memoirs. It's unclear what document or message the general is quoting.

13. Ibid., 160–61, 171–72.

14. Shelby L. Stanton, *Vietnam Order of Battle* (Washington, DC: U.S. News Books, 1981), 333.

15. Mao Zedong, *Strategic Problems of China's Revolution* (Beijing: Foreign Languages Press, 1954), 96.

16. Andrew F. Krepinevich Jr., *The Army and Vietnam* (Baltimore: Johns Hopkins University Press, 1986), 188. A West Point graduate who completed his military service as a lieutenant colonel, Krepinevich earned his doctorate from Harvard and remains a well-known defense analyst. He later headed the Center for Strategic and Budgetary Assessments. Krepinevich's book is considered a key work in evaluating the U.S. Army's inability to defeat the communist insurgency in Vietnam.

17. Phillip B. Davidson, *Vietnam at War: The History 1946–1975* (Novato, CA: Presidio Press, 1988), 364. Davidson retired as a U.S. Army lieutenant general. He served in MACV in 1967–69 as the intelligence chief for General William C. Westmoreland and then General Creighton B. Abrams.

18. Ibid. Page 360 has the VC/NVA number. For the U.S. casualties, see U.S. National Archives, "DCAS Vietnam Conflict Extract File Record Counts by ncident or Death Date (Year) as of April 29, 2008" in *Military Records* at http://www.archives.gov/research/military/vietnam-war/casualty-statistics.html, accessed May 4, 2016.

19. For the crossover point, see Davidson, *Vietnam at War*, 390. As the MACV intelligence chief, Davidson kept the books on assessed enemy losses. For counting enemy forces, see Davidson, *Vietnam at War*, 360–61. See also Sorley, *Westmoreland*, 163.

20. Sorley, *Westmoreland*, 154. General Fred Weyand admitted he was the source after both Apple and Westmoreland were dead.

21. Clark Dougan and Stephen Weiss, *Nineteen Sixty-Eight, The Vietnam Experience* (Boston: Boston Publishing, 1983), 69.

22. Samuel Zaffiri, *Westmoreland* (New York: William Morrow, 1994), 5.

23. Westmoreland, "Progress Report on the War in Vietnam," 785–88.

CHAPTER 1. THE HOLE IN THE PRAIRIE

1. *Unforgiven*, directed by Clint Eastwood, Warner Brothers Studios, 1992. Sheriff Little Bill Daggett, portrayed by Gene Hackman, was the cruel antagonist in this classic western. Hackman served as a U.S. marine in China in the late 1940s, during the concluding years of that country's long civil war. Director Clint Eastwood, who played protagonist Will Munny, served as a draftee in the U.S. Army at Fort Ord, California, from 1951 to 1953.

2. For the origin of the name Sioux, see Evan S. Connell, *Son of the Morning Star: Custer and the Little Big Horn* (New York: North Point Press, 1984), 87. For Nebraska, see John E. Koontz, "Etymology," Siouan Languages at http://spot.colorado.edu/~koontz/faq/etymology.htm, accessed May 7, 2016. Borrowing from the Indians, early French explorers and fur traders named the major waterway Rivière Plate (Flat River), anglicized as the Platte River. In addition, zoologists remind us that the well-known American buffalo is, in fact, a bison, not to be confused with the true African and Asian variants. The more common designation "buffalo" was used by both the Indians and the European peoples who displaced them, and remains the common name today.

3. U.S. Congress, An Act to Secure Homesteads to Actual Settlers on the Public Domain, 37th Congress, 2d Session, May 20, 1862.

4. Robert Utley, *Frontier Regulars: The United States Army and the Indian, 1866–1890* (New York: Macmillan, 1973), 3, 99, 100.

5. For the number of engagements, see Russell F. Weigley, *History of the United States Army* (Bloomington, IN: Indiana University Press, 1984), 267. For the details on reported losses, see Utley, *Frontier Regulars*, note 19, 423. Utley compiled these numbers from U.S. Army adjutant general casualty records. Of 948 U.S. Army soldiers killed in the 1865–1891 Indian campaigns, 258 (27 percent) of them died at the Little Big Horn on June 25–26, 1876.

6. Don Russell, "How Many Indians Were Killed?," *American West* (July 1973), 43–44. The U.S. Census of 1890 recorded 248,253 Indians. The 1910 census reported 265,683.

7. Utley, *Frontier Regulars*, note 20, 423.

8. Connell, *Son of the Morning Star*, 13.

9. Nebraska includes all or part of six Indian reservations. Four are wholly in Nebraska: the Omaha (established 1854), the Ponca (est. 1858), the Winnebago (est. 1863), and the Santee Sioux/Dakota (est. 1863). Parts of two other reservations also extend from Kansas into Nebraska: the Ioway (1861) and the Sac/Fox (1836). All predate the Plains Indian campaigns after the Civil War, and all six were there before Nebraska became a state. The estimated Indian population of Nebraska as of 2015 is 26,547 (1.4 percent) of 1,896,190 total population. See https://

www.census.gov/quickfacts/table/PST045215/31, accessed May 14, 2016. For the connection between Vietnam and the Indian conflicts, see Davidson, *Vietnam at War,* 319. Davidson noted that defeating the Indians required "grinding attrition" in a military sense, but more so in the economic and demographic spheres.

10. L. Douglas Keeney, 15 *Minutes: General Curtis LeMay and the Countdown to Nuclear Annihilation* (New York: St. Martin's Press, 2011), 49.

11. U.S. Department of the Interior geological survey, *Geographical Centers of the United States* (Washington, DC: Department of the Interior, 1964), 2.

12. For the naming of Offutt Air Force Base see A. I. Hansen, *OAFBP 210-2: The History of Fort Crook (1888)/Offutt Air Force Base (1976)* (Offutt Air Force Base, NE: 3902nd Air Base Wing, 1981), 1. The base was originally the U.S. Army's Fort Crook, named for Indian-fighting Major General George Crook.

13. U.S. Department of the Interior, *Historic American Engineering Record: Offutt Air Force Base,* Glenn L. Martin-Nebraska Bomber Plant (Washington, DC: Department of the Interior, 2002), 37–38, 40–41. The United States produced 3,760 B-29s in World War II.

14. Keeney, 15 *Minutes,* 174, addresses nuclear bombs and targets, and page 118 includes the quote regarding the planned destruction of the USSR. For bomber numbers, see Phillip S. Meilinger, *Bomber: The Formation and Early Years of Strategic Air Command* (Maxwell Air Force Base, AL: Air University Press, 2012), 339.

15. Keeney, 15 *Minutes,* 250.

16. Omaha reported a population of 251,117 in 1950. See http://www.biggestus cities.com/1950, accessed May 13, 2016.

17. The KGB (*Komitet Gosudarstvennoy Bezopasnosti,* Committee of State Security) was the Soviet Union's national foreign intelligence service, and also carried out a major role in providing domestic surveillance and repression. The GRU (*Glavnoe Razvedyvatelnoe Upravlenie,* "Main Intelligence Directorate") was the military intelligence organization of the Soviet Armed Forces. During the Cold War, the KGB's American counterparts were the Central Intelligence Agency (CIA, foreign intelligence) and Federal Bureau of Investigation (FBI, internal security), although the KGB employed much more ruthless measures abroad and at home. For KGB and GRU surveillance in and around Offutt Air Force Base, see Loch K. Johnson, ed., *Strategic Intelligence: Understanding the Hidden Side of Government* (Westport, CT: Praeger Security International, 2007), 3; and Scott D. Sagan, "SIOP 62: Nuclear War Plan Briefing to President Kennedy," *International Security* (Summer 1987), 31.

18. Walter Kozak, *LeMay: The Life and Wars of General Curtis LeMay* (Washington, DC: Regnery Publishing, 2009), 280.

19. James Carroll, *House of War* (Boston: Houghton Mifflin, 2006), 17–21. Carroll knew General Curtis LeMay. His father, Lieutenant General Joseph F. Carroll, U.S. Air Force, served under LeMay.

20. Ibid., 19–20.

21. Eric Larrabee, *Commander in Chief: Franklin Delano Roosevelt, His Lieutenants, and Their War* (New York: Simon and Schuster, 1987), 597, 592–93.

22. Ibid., 599. For LeMay's words, see Carroll, *House of War*, 19.

23. Kozak, *LeMay*, 197.

24. Larrabee, *Commander in Chief*, 617.

25. Ibid., 619–20.

26. Ibid., 620.

27. Marshall is quoted in Dan Reiter and Allan C. Stam, *Democracies at War* (Princeton, NJ: Princeton University Press, 2002), 164. The Seven Years' War of 1756–1763 pitted Great Britain and Prussia against France, Austria, and (for most of the war) Russia. The American phase was called the French and Indian War (1754–63). Battles also occurred in India and the Caribbean Sea.

28. Carroll, *House of War*, 94–95. Carroll's prose is sobering.

29. Chuck Hagel with Peter Kaminsky, *America: Our Next Chapter* (New York: HarperCollins, 2008), 3–4, 218.

30. U.S., Headquarters, 42nd Bombardment Squadron, *History of the 42nd Bombardment Squadron (Heavy)* (Fort Shafter, HI: 42nd Bombardment Squadron, April 1944), 3–4. For an account of the attack on Hickam Field on December 7, 1941, by a soldier of the 42nd Bombardment Squadron, see Barbara Belt, interviewer, and Evelyn Kriek, transcriber, *Oral History Interview Attilio F. Caporiccio*, Douglas County Libraries, Denver, CO, September 14, 2004, 28–31. Charles Dean Hagel arrived in Hawaii after the Pearl Harbor attack.

31. Ibid., 7–11.

32. U.S., Headquarters, Army Air Forces, *AAF Manual 50-12: Pilot Training Manual for the Liberator* (Washington, DC: Headquarters, Army Air Forces, May 1, 1945), 4, 7, 20. The B-24 featured a unique double bomb bay, each segment covered by two metal tambour-panel doors. These panels looked like the cover of a roll-top desk. When opened, the four doors rolled up into the aircraft. This design reduced aerodynamic drag and thus permitted more speed during a bombing run.

33. Ibid., 9–12.

34. The Mitsubishi A6M Type Zero navy carrier fighter was the most well-known and widely produced Japanese interceptor. Officially, the United States referred to the plane as a "Zeke," following a pattern that gave male names to fighters and female names to bombers. American fliers, army or navy, routinely called the plane a Zero. There were other similar single-engine Japanese fighters, such as the imperial army's Nakajima Ki-43 Type 1 *Hayabusa* (Peregrine Falcon) fighter (code name "Oscar") and the Nakajima Ki-84 Type 4 *Hayate* (Gale) fighter (code name "Frank"). The capable Type 4 Frank proved a menace to B-29s at high altitude. With some modifications, it served as a night fighter, too. All of these single-engine types were often misidentified as Zeros, too. See Jonathan Parshall and Anthony Tully, *Shattered Sword: The Untold Story of the Battle of Midway* (Dulles, VA: Potomac Books, 2005), 78–79, 89–90, 479–80.

35. HQ, 42nd Bombardment Squadron, *History of the 42nd Bombardment Squadron (Heavy)*, 13–16. For the crash of U.S. Olympian Louis Zamperini and his crew, see Lauren Hillenbrand, *Unbroken: A World War II Story of Survival, Resilience, and Redemption* (New York: Random House, 2010), 125–26. Zamperini's story was made into the movie *Unbroken*, released in 2015.

36. HQ, 42nd Bombardment Squadron, *History of the 42nd Bombardment Squadron (Heavy)*, 19–20.

37. U.S., Headquarters, 42nd Bombardment Squadron, *October Monthly Summary* (Apana Airfield, Guam: 42nd Bombardment Squadron, November 1, 1944), 1–9; U.S., Headquarters, 42nd Bombardment Squadron, *November Monthly Summary* (Apana Airfield, Guam: 42nd Bombardment Squadron, December 1, 1944), 1–8; U.S., Headquarters, 42nd Bombardment Squadron, *December Monthly Summary* (Apana Airfield, Guam: 42nd Bombardment Squadron, January 1, 1945), 1–9; U.S., Headquarters, 42nd Bombardment Squadron, *January Monthly Summary* (Apana Airfield, Guam: 42nd Bombardment Squadron, February 1, 1945), 1–4; U.S., Headquarters, 42nd Bombardment Squadron, *February Monthly Summary* (Apana Airfield, Guam: 42nd Bombardment Squadron, March 1, 1945), 1–10; U.S., Headquarters, 42nd Bombardment Squadron, *March Monthly Summary* (Apana Airfield, Guam: 42nd Bombardment Squadron, April 1, 1945), 1–3; U.S., Headquarters, 42nd Bombardment Squadron, *April Monthly Summary* (Apana Airfield, Guam: 42nd Bombardment Squadron, May 1, 1945), 1–3; U.S., Headquarters, 42nd Bombardment Squadron, *May Monthly Summary* (Apana Airfield, Guam: 42nd Bombardment Squadron, June 1, 1945), 1–3; U.S., Headquarters, 42nd Bombardment Squadron, *June Monthly Summary* (Apana Airfield, Guam: 42nd Bombardment Squadron, July 4, 1945), 1–3.

38. U.S., Headquarters, 42nd Bombardment Squadron, *July Monthly Summary* (Okinawa: 42nd Bombardment Squadron, August 6, 1945), 1–2.

39. George Lauby, "From the Platte to the Potomac: Hagel Recalls His Roots," *North Platte Bulletin*, January 16, 2013.

40. Bolger interview with Charles T. Hagel; Bolger interview with Thomas L. Hagel.

41. Bolger interview with Charles T. Hagel; Bolger interview with Thomas L. Hagel. See also Myra MacPherson, *Long Time Passing* (Garden City, NY: Doubleday, 1984), 13. In addition, see Myra MacPherson, "The Private War of Chuck and Tom Hagel," Salon.com, April 30, 2007, accessed May 15, 2016. Chuck Hagel recalled that he began paying into Social Security at age eight.

42. Charlyne Berens, *Chuck Hagel: Moving Forward* (Lincoln, NE: University of Nebraska Press, 2006), 11–13. See also Bolger interview with Charles T. Hagel and Bolger interview with Thomas L. Hagel.

43. MacPherson, *Long Time Passing*, 14. For the Hagel lumber company and its several locations, see http://www.centurylumbercenter.com/locations.aspx ?location=Ainsworth, accessed May 16, 2016. The company began in 1883. In 1972, the firm took the name Century Lumber.

44. Berens, *Chuck Hagel*, 15–16. For Charles Dean Hagel's employers, see Lauby, "From the Platte to the Potomac: Hagel Recalls His Roots," 1.

45. Berens, *Chuck Hagel*, 15; Bolger interview with Thomas L. Hagel.

46. MacPherson, "The Private War of Chuck and Tom Hagel." Chuck Hagel in his book *America: Our Next Chapter*, 251, attributes his father's death to a heart attack. Charlyne Berens in Chuck Hagel, 19, describes the death as the result of a brain aneurysm. The two causes are not mutually exclusive.

47. Berens, *Chuck Hagel*, 20–23; MacPherson, *Long Time Passing*, 13–14; Bolger interview with Thomas L. Hagel.

48. Berens, *Chuck Hagel*, 23–24. See also Bolger interview with Charles T. Hagel.

49. Bolger interview with Charles T. Hagel; Bolger interview with Thomas L. Hagel; MacPherson, *Long Time Passing*, 13–14; Hagel, *America: Our Next Chapter*, 153.

50. Bolger interview with Thomas L. Hagel. See also MacPherson, *Long Time Passing*, 13; Berens, *Chuck Hagel*, 16–17, 24–25. By volunteering for the draft, both Hagel brothers kept their service obligation to two years. Had they enlisted, they would have had to sign up for a minimum of three years.

CHAPTER 2. THIS MAN'S ARMY

1. Peter Tauber, *The Sunshine Soldiers: A True Journal of Basic Training* (New York: Ballantine, 1971), 243. An army reservist, Tauber completed his basic training at Fort Bliss, Texas. He did not deploy overseas.

2. Lawrence H. Suid, *Guts and Glory: The Making of the American Military Image in Film* (Lexington KY: University Press of Kentucky, 2002), 118–23, 129, 136, 424. Suid's book is the classic study of how the military has worked to present itself through movies. All the examples listed were in circulation in 1967. Richard Widmark played a Fort Bliss training sergeant in *Take the High Ground* (1953), filmed at the installation.

3. Berens, *Chuck Hagel*, 24–25. For Hagel's own account, see Mike Perry, interviewer, "Interview with Senator Charles Hagel," Experiencing War: Stories from the Veterans History Project (Washington, DC: Library of Congress, August 2002) at http://memory.loc.gov/diglib/vhp-stories/loc.natlib.afc2001001.02230/transcript?ID=mv0001, accessed May 27, 2016.

4. Terrence Maitland and Peter McInerney, *A Contagion of War, The Vietnam Experience* (Boston: Boston Publishing, 1983), 27.

5. Perry, "Interview with Senator Chuck Hagel"; Hagel, *America: Our Next Chapter*, 151.

6. For more on Sergeant First Class William Joyce of Alabama, see Hagel, *America: Our Next Chapter*, 151–53. See also Perry, "Interview with Senator Charles Hagel" and Bolger interview with Charles T. Hagel.

7. John M. Collins, "Basic Combat Training: Flashbacks and Forecasts," Army (August 2004), 47–48. Collins entered the U.S. Army as a private in 1942

and retired as a colonel after wartime service in World War II, Korea, and Vietnam. For the history of basic training in the U.S. Army, see Weigley, *History of the United States Army*, 371–77 (World War I), 400–3 (1918–1940), 428–30, 436–39 (World War II), 503–4, 528, (1945–1963).

8. For the location of the U.S. Army training centers during the Vietnam War, see Stanton, *Vietnam Order of Battle*, 361. For more on training centers, to include both draftee and voluntary enlistment numbers, see also Ellen R. Hartman, Susan I. Enscore, and Alan D. Smith, Vietnam and the Home Front: How DoD Installations Adapted, 1962–1975 (Champaign, IL: U.S. Army Engineer Research and Development Center, December 2014), 41, 60–61. For the number of voluntary enlistments, see Clark Dougan and Samuel Lipsman, *A Nation Divided, The Vietnam Experience* (Boston: Boston Publishing, 1984), 76. A half million young men enlisted from June 1965 to June 1966. For the number of draftees trained, see U.S. Selective Service System, "Inductions," at https://www.sss.gov/About/History-And-Records/Induction-Statistics, accessed May 27, 2016. Inductions totaled 382,010 in 1966, 228,263 in 1967, and 296,406 in 1968, the height of the draft calls. Depending on the month and year, draftees made up from 40 to 60 percent of all army inductions. Of note, like Chuck and Tom Hagel, about 10 percent of draftees volunteered to be drafted.

9. Perry, "Interview with Senator Charles Hagel."

10. Hartman, Enscore, and Smith, *Vietnam and the Home Front*, 54–57.

11. Bolger interview with Charles T. Hagel.

12. For excellent, if hilariously cynical, descriptions of the first day or so at Basic Combat Training at Fort Bliss, see Tauber, *The Sunshine Soldiers*, 29–35. For a useful half-hour video summary of Basic Combat Training, see U.S. Department of the Army, *The Big Picture: The Men from the Boys, The First Eight Weeks* (Washington, DC: Office of the Chief of Information, 1967). Actor and U.S. Army Air Forces World War II veteran Gary Merrill narrated this program. For Chuck Hagel's role as a peer leader, sometimes by force of threat thereof, see Perry, "Interview with Senator Charles Hagel." Hagel recalled: "So it was kind of just like you'd pick out the biggest, toughest, smartest guy in the bunch. And you say, 'Okay. You're in charge. Now do something with it.' And I remember in basic training—it didn't ever happen in AIT [Advanced Individual training], but I had a couple of guys come at me with shovels and—guys in my own unit."

13. Herman Wouk, *The Caine Mutiny* (New York: Dell, 1951), 116.

14. Berens, *Chuck Hagel*, 25.

15. Perry, "Interview with Senator Charles Hagel."

16. For marching and running rates, see U.S. Department of the Army, *Field Manual 22-5: Drill and Ceremonies* (Washington, DC: Department of the Army, November 30, 1966), 11. For the M14 rifle, see Stanton, *Vietnam Order of Battle*, 276.

17. R. P. Carver and F. R. Winsmann, "Analysis of the Army Physical Proficiency Test in Terms of the Fleishman Basic Fitness Tests" in *Perceptual and Motor Skills* (April, 1968), 203–8; Whitfield B. East, *A Historical Review of Phys-*

ical Training Readiness and Assessment (Fort Leavenworth, KS: Combat Studies Institute, March 2013), 129.

18. For an entertaining summary of M14 rifle training, see Tauber, *The Sunshine Soldiers*, 48, 113–14, 153–54. See also Department of the Army, *The Big Picture*.

19. Department of the Army, *The Big Picture: The Men from the Boys*.

20. Tauber, *The Sunshine Soldiers*, 191–93. Even anti-war satirist Tauber found the night infiltration course exhilarating and challenging.

21. Ibid., 248–49; Department of the Army, *The Big Picture: The Men from the Boys*.

22. Perry, "Interview with Senator Charles Hagel." For a more cleanly edited version of this quotation, see Tom Weiner, ed., *Voices of War: Stories of Service from the Home Front and the Front Line* (Washington, DC: National Geographic Society, 2012), 19.

23. Berens, *Chuck Hagel*, 25–26; Hagel, *America: Our Next Chapter*, 152; Bolger interview with Charles T. Hagel.

24. Todd Gitlin, *The Sixties: Years of Hope, Days of Rage* (New York: Bantam, 1993), 212–16. Gitlin was a leader of the anti-war movement as well as one of its most articulate chroniclers.

25. Dave Grossman, *On Killing* (New York: Back Bay Books, 1995), 253–57. Grossman, a former U.S. Army infantry officer and former West Point instructor, looked closely at the psychology behind military training and its relationship to actual combat. See also Hartman, Enscore, and Smith, *Vietnam and the Home Front*, 59. Tom Hagel noted that the E and F targets depicted men with Asian faces wearing conical straw hats.

26. Maitland and McInerney, *A Contagion of War*, 30; Hartman, Enscore, and Smith, Vietnam and the Home Front, 66. For a very readable account of infantry Advanced Individual Training at Fort Dix, New Jersey, see John Sack, *M* (New York: Signet, 1967), 9–71. In 1968, infantry Advanced Individual Training was extended to nine weeks to accommodate additional Vietnam War techniques.

27. Berens, *Chuck Hagel*, 28. For Officer Candidate School policies, see Ron Milam, *Not a Gentleman's War: An Inside View of Junior Officers in the Vietnam War* (Chapel Hill, NC: University of North Carolina Press, 2009), 18–23. Milam served as an officer in Vietnam.

28. Berens, *Chuck Hagel*, 28. For the Redeye, see Mary T. Cagle, *History of the Redeye Weapon System* (Redstone Arsenal, AL: U.S. Army Missile Command, May 23, 1974), 146, 192–94.

29. Bolger interview with Thomas L. Hagel; Berens, *Chuck Hagel*, 33.

30. Berens, *Chuck Hagel*, 28–29, 33.

31. Gitlin, *The Sixties*, 255; Carroll, *House of War*, 293–97. Both authors were active protestors in the 1960s. Carroll was present at the Pentagon on October 21, 1967.

32. Weigley, *History of the United States Army*, 431–40; Dougan and Lipsman, *A Nation Divided*, 72–76.

33. B. G. Burkett and Glenna Whitley, *Stolen Valor: How the Vietnam Generation Was Robbed of Its Heroes and Its History* (Dallas, TX: Verity Press, 1998), 51–52. Burkett served as an officer in Vietnam with the 199th Light Infantry Brigade. Whitley is a prominent Texas journalist. This book is controversial, as Burkett aggressively exposes numerous phonies claiming to be Vietnam veterans. That aspect aside, the book contains some authoritative and thought-provoking demographic data derived from reliable, annotated sources. For corroborating data, see Committee to Review the Health Effects in Vietnam Veterans of Exposure to Herbicides, *Veterans and Agent Orange: Health Effects of Herbicides Used in Vietnam* (Washington, DC: National Academy Press, 1994), 74–79.

34. Dougan and Lipsman, *A Nation Divided*, 76. Those who served expressed particular respect for the conscientious objectors who served in Vietnam without carrying weapons. Most were medics, and many earned decorations for valor. Corporal Thomas W. Bennett and Specialist 4 Joseph G. LaPointe Jr. both earned the Medal of Honor. Both were killed in action.

35. Gitlin, *The Sixties*, 291.

36. Ibid. Among those who chose a religious vocation was James Carroll, son of a U.S. Air Force lieutenant general. The younger Carroll left air force ROTC at Georgetown University to pursue the Catholic priesthood. Carroll resigned as a priest in 1974. The draft ended in 1973. See Carroll, *House of War*, 336–40.

37. Ibid., 291–93; Dougan and Lipsman, *A Nation Divided*, 76.

38. Ibid. For Johnson's unwillingness to call up the National Guard and the service reserves, see H. R. McMaster, *Dereliction of Duty: Johnson, McNamara, the Joint Chiefs of Staff, and the Lies That Led to Vietnam* (New York: Harper-Collins, 1998), 316–17. West Point graduate and armor/cavalry officer Lieutenant General H. R. McMaster served in Iraq I, Iraq II, and Afghanistan. His book is a very damning indictment of the senior U.S. military leadership of the 1960s. Although no significant mobilization of the National Guard and U.S. Army Reserve occurred, a call-up in 1968 sent 7,040 guardsmen to Vietnam. See John D. Stuckey and Joseph H. Pistorius, "Mobilization for the Vietnam War: A Political and Military Catastrophe," *Parameters* (Spring 1985), 35–36.

39. Stanton, *Vietnam Order of Battle*, 346–47; Morocco, *Rain of Fire*, 179; John S. Bowman, ed., *The Vietnam War: An Almanac* (New York: World Almanac, 1985), 358. The navy lost 628 air crewmen; the air force sustained 1,472 dead fliers. Those who opted for the navy sometimes ended up under fire on the ground in Vietnam. Martin J. Mayer, a Rutgers graduate, joined the navy to avoid carrying an M16 as a soldier in country. Selected for Officer Candidate School, he ended up on a riverine patrol boat (one played a key part in the film *Apocalypse Now*) and, yes, he carried an M16. Mayer eventually advanced to command the USS *Enterprise* Carrier Battle Group and, after thirty-seven years of service, retired as a vice admiral (three stars) in 2003.

40. Burkett and Whitley, *Stolen Valor*, 48, 52. Some 7,000 U.S. women served in Vietnam. Eight nurses were killed in action. See Committee to Review the

Health Effects in Vietnam Veterans of Exposure to Herbicides, *Veterans and Agent Orange*, 83. For the draftees in combat arms, see also Dougan and Lipsman, *A Nation Divided*, 78.

41. Colin L. Powell with Joseph E. Persico, *My American Journey* (New York: Ballantine, 1995), 99, 135. Powell advised a South Vietnamese unit in his 1962–63 deployment; he was wounded in action. He then served as G-3 (operations officer) for the 23rd Infantry (Americal) Division in 1968–69.

42. MacPherson, *Long Time Passing*, 28.

43. Committee to Review the Health Effects in Vietnam Veterans of Exposure to Herbicides, *Veterans and Agent Orange*, 82; Burkett and Whitley, *Stolen Valor*, 47–48. Of the 101 eighteen-year-olds killed in Vietnam, 7 were African Americans.

44. Arnold Barnett, Timothy Stanley, and Michael Shore, "America's Vietnam Casualties: Victims of a Class War?" *Operations Research* (September–October 1992), 856–66. Among Yale graduates who served off the Vietnam coast aboard the destroyer USS Fox was navy officer and future *Washington Post* investigative reporter Bob Woodward.

45. Burkett and Whitley, *Stolen Valor*, 55–56; Milam, *Not a Gentleman's War*, 18–23.

46. Burkett and Whitley, *Stolen Valor*, 454; Committee to Review the Health Effects in Vietnam Veterans of Exposure to Herbicides, *Veterans and Agent Orange*, 83; Dougan and Lipsman, *A Nation Divided*, 78. Hispanic ethnic groups were not well tracked during the Vietnam era, and their numbers appear to be split between the white, black, and other categories. The usual number offered is that Hispanics totaled at least 5 percent of all casualties.

47. Tom Wolfe, "Art Disputes War: The Battle of the Vietnam Memorial," *Washington Post*, October 13, 1982.

CHAPTER 3. WIDOWS VILLAGE

1. Ron Marks, . . . *Of Bags, Counts, and Nightmares* (Bloomington, IN: Xlibris, 2013), 532. Marks served in Vietnam in both the 173rd Airborne Brigade and the 1st Infantry Division.

2. Keith W. Nolan, *The Battle for Saigon: Tet 1968* (Novato, CA: Presidio Press, 1996), xii–xiii (map), 199–205. The late Keith Nolan wrote numerous superb tactical histories of key engagements in the Vietnam War. His work set the standard, interweaving personal accounts with relevant documents.

3. Berens, *Chuck Hagel*, 29.

4. John E. Gross, "One Rifle Company's Wild Ride: The Battles of Bien Hoa and Long Binh," *Vietnam*, February 2008, 50. John Gross commanded Company C, 2-47th Infantry during the Tet Offensive. He completed his military service as a lieutenant colonel. For a map of 2-47th Infantry's movements on January 30–31, 1968, see Donn A. Starry, *Vietnam Studies: Mounted Combat in Vietnam* (Washington, DC: U.S. Government Printing Office, 1978), 120–21. Starry served in J-3

Plans in MACV headquarters and then commanded the 11th Armored Cavalry Regiment in 1969–70, to include service in the Cambodia operation. He retired in 1983 as a general (four stars).

5. Davidson, *Vietnam at War*, 396. Davidson, the MACV intelligence chief, noted that Giap strongly advised against launching the Tet Offensive in 1968. The North Vietnamese military leader did not think it would work; he considered the United States too strong, and recommended reversion to classic guerrilla tactics. For the number of targets attacked, see Clark Dougan and Stephen Weiss, *Nineteen Sixty-Eight, The Vietnam Experience* (Boston: Boston Publishing, 1983), 8.

6. Davidson, *Vietnam at War*, 396–99, 419–21, explains the North's planning and preliminary operations for Tet. Giap's quote, as well as an overall pre-Tet strategic assessment, can be found in Krepinevich, *The Army in Vietnam*, 238–39. For a graphic depiction of MACV and ARVN battalion-level positions on the eve of Tet, see Stanton, *Vietnam Order of Battle*, 385.

7. Davidson, *Vietnam at War*, 425–26; Dougan and Weiss, *Nineteen Sixty-Eight*, 8–11, 184.

8. For General Erich Ludendorff's quote, see Keith Neilson and Greg Kennedy, *The British Way in Warfare: Power and the International System, 1856–1956* (London: Routledge, 2010), 139.

9. Stanley Karnow, *Vietnam: A History* (New York: Viking, 1983), 545. Lieutenant General Tran Do, a key VC commander during the war, died in 2002. He fell out of favor with the Hanoi party leaders in 1999.

10. Westmoreland, *A Soldier Reports*, 392; Davidson, *Vietnam at War*, 426.

11. Neil Sheehan, *A Bright Shining Lie: John Paul Vann and America in Vietnam* (New York: Vantage, 1989), 707–9. For examples of later arguments that MACV anticipated the Tet Offensive, see Westmoreland, *A Soldier Reports*, 393, and Davidson, *Vietnam at War*, 430–31. Westmoreland claims "no surprise." To his credit, Davidson admitted that while he and his intelligence staff discerned that the NVA would strike, "much more unexpected were the assaults on the many cities and towns."

12. Gross, "One Rifle Company's Wild Ride," 50; Nolan, *The Battle for Saigon*, 200–1.

13. Perry, "Interview with Senator Charles Hagel"; Berens, *Chuck Hagel*, 29–30. For a video summary of the introductory training at Camp Martin Cox (Bear Cat), see U.S. Department of the Army, Headquarters, 9th Infantry Division, *Reliable Academy* (Bear Cat, Republic of Vietnam: Headquarters, 9th Infantry Division, 1967) at https://www.youtube.com/watch?v=90SmIUVepdo, accessed June 4, 2016.

14. Weigley, *History of the United States Army*, 436–38.

15. Ibid., 510.

16. Westmoreland, *A Soldier Reports*, 358.

17. Krepinevich, *The Army in Vietnam*, 205–10.

18. Russell F. Weigley, *Eisenhower's Lieutenants: The Campaign of France and Germany 1944–1945* (Bloomington, IN: Indiana University Press, 1981), 13.

19. Perry, "Interview with Senator Charles Hagel."

20. Stanton, *Vietnam Order of Battle*, 77.

21. John Sloan Brown, *Kevlar Legions: The Transformation of the U.S. Army 1989–2005* (Washington, DC: U.S. Army Center for Military History, 2011), 253–57. A 1971 West Point graduate, Brown commanded a tank battalion in the 1990–91 Iraq War and completed his U.S. Army service as a brigadier general. His son served in Iraq in 2003–04.

22. John E. Gross, *Our Time: Training, Deploying, and Combat with Company C, 2nd Battalion, 47th Infantry* (Bloomington, IN: iUniverse, 2013), 80–81.

23. *Forrest Gump*, directed by Robert Zemeckis, Paramount, 1994. Forrest Gump and Bubba Blue walk past a wooden sign with the words ALPHA COMPANY, 2ND/47TH INFANTRY, 9TH INFANTRY DIV. "OLD RELIABLES." The latter is the nickname of the 9th infantry Division.

24. Starry, *Mounted Combat in Vietnam*, 60, 106–7; Perry, "Interview with Senator Charles Hagel." For more on the M113, UH-1D, and numbers of maneuver battalions in MACV, see Stanton, *Vietnam Order of Battle*, 260–61, 280, 282, 333.

25. Perry, "Interview with Senator Charles Hagel."

26. Ibid.; Hagel, *America: Our Next Chapter*, 154. The AK-47, Avtomat Kalashnikova Model 1947, took its name from its inventor, Mikhail Timofeyevich Kalashnikov.

27. U.S. Department of the Army, Headquarters, 2nd Battalion (Mechanized), 47th Infantry, *Significant Activities for Calendar Year of 1968* (APO San Francisco, CA: Headquarters, 2nd Battalion (Mechanized), 47th Infantry, March 31, 1969), 1. The mortar might have been a Russian-made 82mm, but the VC used captured U.S. and ARVN 81mm mortars, too.

28. Starry, *Mounted Combat in Vietnam*, 120–21, 123–24; Gross, "One Rifle Company's Wild Ride," 50; Perry, "Interview with Senator Charles Hagel." For the contemporary record of orders and movements, see U.S. Department of the Army, Headquarters, 2nd Battalion (Mechanized), 47th Infantry, *DA Form 1594: Daily Staff Journal* (Bien Hoa, Republic of Vietnam: Headquarters, 2nd Battalion (Mechanized, 47th Infantry), 0001–2400, January 31, 1968, 1–2.

29. Bolger interview with Charles T. Hagel.

30. Perry, "Interview with Senator Charles Hagel"; Nolan, *The Battle for Saigon*, 206; Starry, *Mounted Combat in Vietnam*, 124; Headquarters, 2nd Battalion (Mechanized), 47th Infantry, *DA Form 1594: Daily Staff Journal*, 2–3. For video of the ammunition supply point explosion, see U.S. Department of the Army, 221st Signal Company (Pictorial), Attack at Long Binh and Widow's Village (Long Binh Post, Republic of Vietnam: 221st Signal Company (Pictorial), January 31, 1968) at https://www.youtube.com/watch?v=GZhPUVDCZHo, accessed June 4, 2016. Some sources refer to the town as Widow's Village, but the official accounts clearly refer to Widows Village (plural, not possessive).

31. Nolan, *The Battle for Saigon*, 210; Headquarters, 2nd Battalion (Mechanized), 47th Infantry, DA Form 1594: Daily Staff Journal, 3.

32. Headquarters, 9th Infantry Division Public Affairs, "Widows Village: VC Graveyard Tet 1968," *Octofoil*, April–May–June 1968, 1. The *Octofoil* was the division's quarterly magazine. Some sources identify Robert Andrew Huie as a private or private first class, but the record of casualties lists him as a corporal, the most junior NCO rank. Given his role as a track commander, that was clearly his duty position on January 31, 1968.

33. Nolan, *The Battle for Saigon*, 210–11. For additional details by a soldier present at the firefight, see John Driessler, *Widow's Village—The True Story* at http://www.angelfire.com/ny2/SGTFATS/WidowsVillageTruth.html, accessed June 3, 2016. Sergeant First Class William N. Butler earned the Silver Star at Widows Village. See Headquarters, 2nd Battalion (Mechanized), 47th Infantry, *Significant Activities for Calendar Year of 1968*, 2. The RPD, ruchnoy pulemyot Degtyaryova, the standard VC light machine gun, was designed by Vasiliy Alekseyevich Degtaryov.

34. Headquarters, 2nd Battalion (Mechanized), 47th Infantry, *DA Form 1594: Daily Staff Journal*, 3; Perry, "Interview with Senator Charles Hagel." See also 221st Signal Company (Pictorial), *Attack at Long Binh and Widow's Village*.

35. 221st Signal Company (Pictorial), *Attack at Long Binh and Widow's Village*. For additional video of the U.S. attack on Widows Village, see U.S. Department of the Army, Armed Forces Vietnam Network, *Contact with Vietcong During Tet, 2nd Battalion, 47th Infantry, 9th Infantry Division*, 01/31/1968 (Saigon, Republic of Vietnam: Armed Forces Radio and Television Service, January 31, 1968) at https://archive.org/details/ContactWIthVietcongDuringTet, accessed June 4, 1968.

36. Headquarters, 2nd Battalion (Mechanized), 47th Infantry, *DA Form 1594: Daily Staff Journal*, 3–6; Nolan, *The Battle for Saigon*, 212–19. For 2-47th Infantry, two additional Americans (one scout and another from Company A) were killed in action, making a total of five dead for January 31, 1968. The battalion's wounded totaled forty-five. For the day, the battalion reported 213 VC killed and 17 enemy prisoners. The number of prisoners was listed as 32 in the U.S. Army Valorous Unit Award earned for the actions on January 31, 1968.

37. Perry, "Interview with Senator Charles Hagel"; Bolger interview with Charles T. Hagel. Captain Robert George Keats graduated from West Point in the Class of 1965. See Chris Carroll, "Hagel Pays Tribute to Fallen Commander," *Stars and Stripes*, May 24, 2013. See also A Classmate (anonymous member of the U.S. Military Academy Class of 1965), "Robert George Keats" at http://www.west-point.org/users/usma1965/25736/, accessed June 29, 2016. Keats earned the Silver Star during the Tet Offensive. He was buried in the West Point cemetery.

38. Yuri Beckers, "The Octofoil Shoulder Patch," at https://9thinfantrydivision.net/9th-infantry-division-history/the-octofoil-shoulder-patch/, accessed June 5, 2016.

39. Michael Casey, Clark Dougan, Denis Kennedy and Shelby Stanton, *The Army at War, The Vietnam Experience* (Boston: Boston Publishing, 1987), 145–46.

40. James Hinds, *3rd Squadron, 5th Cavalry*, Third Squadron, 5th Cavalry

in Vietnam: Part I (CONUS and III Corps) (Self-published, 1992), 72–79. CONUS refers to the continental United States. III Corps was the Vietnamese designation for headquarters assigned to the provinces around Saigon. In the month before Tet, the squadron lost seventeen killed, three missing, and sixty-three wounded. On December 31, 1967, on Route 2, Troop C, 3-5th Cavalry had been ambushed. The U.S. lost ten troopers killed, three missing in action, and twenty-nine wounded. Two tanks and six armored personnel carriers had been damaged too badly to move. No Viet Cong casualties were reported. A month later during Tet, Troop A fought in Bien Hoa, suffering six killed and twenty-four wounded. Troop B secured Route 2, but despite three straight nights of contact, sustained no casualties. Troop C fought in Xuan Loc and lost one killed and ten wounded.

41. Bolger interview with Thomas L. Hagel. The letter is quoted in MacPherson, *Long Time Passing*, 10. Tom Hagel and Chuck Hagel correctly recalled that the 11th Armored Cavalry Regiment was commanded by Colonel George S. Patton III, son of the famous World War II general, who took over on July 15, 1968. The younger Patton looked, talked, and fought like his illustrious father. As commander of the 11th Armored Cavalry Regiment, Patton earned two Distinguished Service Crosses, the Silver Star, and the Purple Heart, rare distinctions for a full colonel. Because 3-5th Cavalry went north in mid-February of 1968, it detached from the 11th Armored Cavalry Regiment. Tom Hagel never served under Patton's command. For a summary of the younger Patton's service in Vietnam, see Brian M. Sobel, *The Fighting Pattons* (Westport, CT: Praeger, 1997), 137–59. The younger Patton completed his service in 1980 as a major general. Like his famous father, he commanded the 2nd Armored Division.

42. Hinds, *3rd Squadron, 5th Cavalry in Vietnam: Part I (CONUS and III Corps)*, 79; Bolger interview with Thomas L. Hagel.

43. Westmoreland's quotes come from Associated Press, "Recapture U.S. Embassy," *Chicago Tribune*, January 31, 1968; Sorley, *Westmoreland*, 177–78.

44. Westmoreland's quote comes from Associated Press, "Recapture U.S. Embassy." For the situation in Saigon and across South Vietnam, see Lewis Sorley, *Thunderbolt: From the Battle of the Bulge to Vietnam and Beyond: Creighton Abrams and the Army of His Times* (New York: Simon & Schuster, 1992), 211–18.

45. Davidson, *Vietnam at War*, 434. For the best examination of the role of the press in Tet, written by an experienced Saigon journalist who reported from Saigon during the war, see Peter Braestrup. *Big Story*, 2 vol. (Boulder, CO: Westview Press, 1977).

46. Westmoreland, *A Soldier Reports*, 406; Davidson, *Vietnam at War*, 434.

47. Westmoreland, *A Soldier Reports*, 404.

CHAPTER 4. THE BUTCHER OF THE DELTA

1. Alan Clark, *The Donkeys* (London: Hutchinson, 1961), 9. Clark served very briefly in the Household Cavalry and then as a long-time member of Parliament.

He wrote several military history books. With regard to the quotation, General Erich Ludendorff and Major General Max Hoffman served in the Imperial German Army in World War I. After earlier duty on both the western and eastern fronts, by 1916 Ludendorff was the chief staff deputy in the German national high command. Hoffman spent the entire war in the east. In his bitter, controversial, influential, and eminently readable book *The Donkeys*, Clark attributed this exchange to the memoirs of General Erich von Falkenhayn, chief of the German general staff in 1914–16. No book written by Falkenhayn contained the quotation. It can be found, attributed to Ludendorff and an unnamed officer in the German general staff, in Evelyn, Princess Blucher (Evelyn Fuerstin Blucher von Wahlstatt), *An English Wife in Berlin* (London: Constable, 1921), 211. It's unclear why Clark did not properly attribute the sentences, as they are central to his book's strong argument. If nothing else, he offered an easy opening to his many critics. John Terraine, *The Smoke and the Fire: Myths & Anti-Myths of War 1861–1945* (London: Leo Cooper, 1980), 170–71, offers one of many attempts to sort out the veracity of the quote. Terraine (1921–2003) was a well-known apologist for the British senior leaders in World War I with little time for Clark. British historians of the era split over the entire matter. The majority dismissed Clark's sloppy research, although Great War veterans Basil Liddell Hart and Field Marshal Bernard Law Montgomery both praised the book. Given all of that, I think all we can do is credit Clark himself. Whatever the source of the quote, the sentiment rang only too true.

2. Ted Gittinger, *Interview with Lieutenant General Julian J. Ewell* (Austin, TX: Lyndon Baines Johnson Library, November 7, 1985), 41. This interview occurred in Ewell's home in McLean, Virginia.

3. John Keegan, *The Mask of Command* (New York: Viking, 1987), 208–10, 214.

4. Terraine, *The Smoke and the Fire*, 43–47, 148–57. Terraine strongly supports Haig's performance, but as a good historian, reflects contrary facts and opinions as well.

5. Josiah Bunting III, *The Lionheads* (New York: George Braziller, 1972), 15. Bunting served in Vietnam as an infantry officer in the 9th Infantry Division under Ewell's command. A former enlisted marine and Rhodes Scholar, Bunting consciously made reference to British Great War literature, and his use of the term "Lions" in depicting American soldiers reflected that connection. The novel fictionalized the division as the 12th Infantry Division ("the "Lionheads" with a "Young Lion Academy" to train new arrivals and a "River Lion" riverine brigade). In Bunting's narrative, "George Lemming" commanded. The outfit was clearly the 9th and the character was unmistakably Julian J. Ewell. Bunting, a graduate of the Virginia Military Institute, made Lemming a product of The Citadel, the military college in Charleston, South Carolina, and a friendly rival of Bunting's alma mater. Westmoreland spent a year at The Citadel before going to West Point. Ewell was a West Point alumnus.

6. Allen C. Guelzo, *Gettysburg: The Last Invasion* (New York: Vintage, 2013), 22–23.

7. For the Offutt family history, see http://offutt-history.tripod.com/id14.html, accessed June 9, 2016.

8. Patricia Gates Lynch Ewell and Ira A. Hunt Jr., "Julian J. Ewell 1939," at http://apps.westpointaog.org/Memorials/Article/11388/, accessed June 9, 2016.

9. Clay Blair, *Ridgway's Paratroopers: The American Airborne in World War II* (Garden City, NY: Dial Press, 1985), 30–38.

10. Ibid., 42.

11. Ibid., 413, 611.

12. Ibid., 491, note, 611. For the defense of Bastogne, see Major Gary F. Evans and Specialist 5 Michael R. Fischer, U.S. Army, *The 501st Parachute Infantry Regiment at Bastogne, Belgium, December 1944* (Bozeman, MT: 50th Military History Detachment, June 22, 1972), 1–10.

13. Larrabee, Commander in Chief, 153. King sometimes denied the quote, but he certainly embraced its intent.

14. For the importance of Kien Hoa Province to the Viet Cong, see Lieutenant General Julian J. Ewell and Major General Ira A. Hunt Jr., U.S. Army, *Vietnam Studies: Sharpening the Combat Edge: The Use of Analysis to Reinforce Combat Judgments* (Washington, D.C.: U.S. Government Printing Office, 1974), 188. For pacification status of the Mekong Delta in 1968, see Ira A. Hunt Jr., *The 9th Infantry Division: Unparalleled and Unequalled* (Lexington, KY: University Press of Kentucky, 2010), 141–42. Hunt served as both chief of staff and a brigade commander during Ewell's tenure. He strongly supported Ewell's approach. For a graphic depiction of the security situation in the ARVN IV Corps Tactical Zones, see Martin G. Clemis, "The Control War: Communist Revolutionary Warfare, Pacification, and the Struggle for South Vietnam, 1968–1973" (PhD dissertation, Temple University, May 2015), 475. In Vietnamese, the Mekong River is sometimes called the Nine Dragons River (*Song Cuu Long*), and thus the Delta is the Mouth of the Dragon.

15. Julius Caesar, *The Gallic War*, trans. H. J. Edwards (Cambridge, MA: Dover 2009), 1. The famous first line is *Gallia est omnis divisa in partes tres.* All Gaul is divided into three parts.

16. For province populations, see U.S. Agency for International Development, *Economic and Engineering Study Grain Storage and Marketing System Vietnam* (Toledo, OH: Wildman Agricultural Research, March 1970), 25. For unit locations, see Stanton, *Vietnam Order of Battle*, 274, 371.

17. Stanton, *Vietnam Order of Battle*, 6, 77–78.

18. Ewell and Hunt, *Sharpening the Combat Edge*, 16; Casey, Dougan, Kennedy, and Stanton, *The Army at War*, 145, 155; Stanton, *Vietnam Order of Battle*, 142, 153. In September 1968, as brokered by II Field Force, the 9th Infantry Division sent the mechanized 5-60th Infantry to the 1st Infantry Division and received back the 1-16th Infantry, a foot battalion. The units switched names, so the 1st Infantry Division ended up with the 1st Battalion (Mechanized), 16th Infantry and the 9th Infantry Division had a new leg 5-60th Infantry.

19. Hunt, *The 9th Infantry Division*, 11. Bunting's novel *The Lionheads* turns on the known tactical shortcomings of the Mobile Riverine Force. During their counterinsurgency of 1945–54, the French employed similar *dinassaut* (*Division Navale d'Assaut*, Naval Assault Division) riverine units.

20. The 9th Infantry Division study is cited in Lieutenant General John J. Tolson, U.S. Army, *Vietnam Studies: Airmobility 1961–1971* (Washington, DC: U.S. Government Printing Office, 1973), 181.

21. Gittinger, *Interview with Lieutenant General Julian J. Ewell*, 6, 11.

22. Westmoreland, *A Soldier Reports*, 99–100, 184; Ewell and Hunt, *Sharpening the Combat Edge*, 78.

23. Krepinevich, *The Army and Vietnam*, 6. He quotes the idea as "it is better to send a bullet than a man."

24. For the number of artillery shells to kill an enemy at Anzio, in Korea, and in Vietnam, see Edgar C. Doleman Jr., *Tools of War, The Vietnam Experience* (Boston: Boston Publishing, 1984), 48. For the 25th Infantry Division, see Eric M. Bergerud, *Red Thunder, Tropic Lightning: The World of a Combat Division in Vietnam* (Boulder, CO; Westview Press, 1993), 77. In the first quarter of 1967, the 25th Infantry Division shot 207,000 artillery rounds and claimed 231 enemy killed by those fires.

25. Major Robert A. Doughty, U.S. Army, *The Leavenworth Papers Number 1: The Evolution of U.S. Army Tactical Doctrine, 1946–76* (Fort Leavenworth, KS: Combat Studies Institute, August 1979), 38–39. Doughty served as an adviser in Vietnam, later headed the Department of History at West Point, and completed his service as a brigadier general.

26. Bergerud, *Red Thunder, Tropic Lightning*, 73.

27. Patton was quoted in Doughty, *The Leavenworth Papers Number 1: The Evolution of U.S. Army Tactical Doctrine, 1946–76*, 36.

28. Hunt, *The 9th Infantry Division*, 22; Ewell and Hunt, *Sharpening the Combat Edge*, 19–24.

29. Bergerud, *Red Thunder, Tropic Lightning*, 40. Bergerud interviewed numerous 25th Infantry Division veterans. Lieutenant Richard Blanks described his schedule, which matched that found in the 9th Infantry Division before Ewell took command.

30. Gittinger, *Interview with Lieutenant General Julian J. Ewell*, 24, 32.

31. Perry, "Interview with Senator Charles Hagel." Chuck Hagel noted that his unit was understrength and usually short on NCOs as well as riflemen. He saw no real change from the Ewell policies.

32. Gittinger, *Interview with Lieutenant General Julian J. Ewell*, 13 ; Ewell and Hunt, *Sharpening the Combat Edge*, 83. The authors stated: "We then began to realize that the supermarket approach of large turnover with small unit profit paid off much more than the old neighborhood grocery approach of small turnover with a large markup."

33. Ewell and Hunt, *Sharpening the Combat Edge*, 16, 38–39.

34. For helicopter combat contributions and increased aviation availability, see Ewell and Hunt, *Sharpening the Combat Edge*, 44–46, 56–57.

35. For Ewell's constant pressure quote, see Gittinger, *Interview with Lieutenant General Julian J. Ewell*, 24.

36. Ewell and Hunt, *Sharpening the Combat Edge*, 38–39; Hunt, *The 9th Infantry Division*, 32–33; Agency for International Development, *Economic and Engineering Study Grain Storage and Marketing System Vietnam*, 25.

37. Ewell and Hunt, *Sharpening the Combat Edge*, 186; Hunt, *The 9th Infantry Division*, 26.

38. Gittinger, *Interview with Lieutenant General Julian J. Ewell*, 15; Ewell and Hunt, *Sharpening the Combat Edge*, 186.

39. Both of these quotes can be found in Nick Turse, *Kill Anything That Moves: The Real American War in Vietnam* (New York: Picador, 2013), 206–7. Turse argues that the entire American way of war in Vietnam constituted a war crime. Leaving aside his extreme claims, he drew on excellent sources, including previously unreleased official investigations. The 9th Infantry Division under Major General Julian J. Ewell comes in for particular criticism. For the casualty totals, see Ewell and Hunt, *Sharpening the Combat Edge*, 185. The 9th Infantry Division reported over three thousand enemy killed in February, March, and April of 1969, but never exceeded those numbers before or after that period. In April of 1969, the 9th alone, one of eight army divisions in country, accounted for one-third of all VC/NVA killed.

40. Bunting, *The Lionheads*, 17.

41. Krepinevich, *The Army and Vietnam*, 240–41; Westmoreland, *A Soldier Reports*, 431–32.

42. Krepinevich, *The Army and Vietnam*, 240–41; Halberstam, *The Best and the Brightest*, 793, 798; Davidson, *Vietnam at War*, 452; Sorley, *Westmoreland*, 191.

43. Sorley, *Westmoreland*, 194.

44. Krepinevich, *The Army and Vietnam*, 240.

45. Halberstam *The Best and the Brightest*, 794–95.

46. MacPherson, *Long Time Passing*, 11; Bolger interview with Thomas L. Hagel.

47. Bolger interview with Thomas L. Hagel; U.S., Fleet Marine Force Pacific, *WestPac SitRep #1066 through #1071* (Camp H.M. Smith, Hawaii: Fleet Marine Force, Pacific, February 27 through March 3, 1968), 3–9. See also Jack Shulimson; Lieutenant Colonel Leonard A. Blasiol, USMC; Charles R. Smith; Captain David A. Dawson, USMC, *U.S. Marines in Vietnam: The Defining Year, 1968* (Washington, DC: Headquarters, U.S. Marine Corps, History and Museums Division, 1997), 248. The marines later assessed a total of thirty-five enemy dead, although that exceeds the counts reflected in the contemporary records.

48. Perry, "Interview with Senator Charles Hagel."

49. Bolger interview with Thomas L. Hagel; Berens, *Chuck Hagel*, 33.

50. Richard B. Frank, *Guadalcanal: The Definitive Account of the Landmark Battle* (New York: Penguin, 1990), 457–59, 489–90. The 1944 movie was *The Fighting Sullivans*. The destroyer USS *The Sullivans* (DD-537) served in both World War II and Korea. A new guided missile destroyer, USS *The Sullivans* (DDG-68), served in the global war on terrorism. The Sullivans were not the only family so affected. Another famous case involved Fritz, Bob, Preston, and Edward Niland of Tonawanda, New York. Wartime reporting convinced the authorities in Washington that all but Fritz had been killed in action, with both Bob and Preston killed in the 1944 Normandy invasion and Edward dead in Burma. Fritz was evacuated to the United States as the sole survivor. After the war, Edward emerged alive from a Japanese prison camp. The Niland family's story became the basis for the 1998 movie *Saving Private Ryan*.

51. U.S. Department of Defense, *Department of Defense Instruction Number 1315.15: Special Separation Policies for Survivorship* (Washington, D.C.: Department of Defense, with Change 1 of June 1, 2012), 1–4.

52. Perry, "Interview with Senator Charles Hagel."

53. MacPherson, *Long Time Passing*, 11; Berens, *Chuck Hagel*, 33.

54. Perry, "Interview with Senator Charles Hagel"; Bolger interview with Charles T. Hagel; Bolger interview with Thomas L. Hagel. See also MacPherson, *Long Time Passing*, 11.

55. Perry, "Interview with Senator Charles Hagel"; MacPherson, *Long Time Passing*, 11. For Chuck Hagel's quote, see Patricia Sullivan, "A Vietnam War That Never Ends," *Washington Post, Post Mortem* blog (August 5, 2009) at http:// voices.washingtonpost.com/postmortem/2009/08/vietnam_still_resonates_in_ the.html, accessed June 11, 2016.

56. Bolger interview with Thomas L. Hagel.

57. Berens, *Chuck Hagel*, 34, 36. For Betty Hagel's quotes, see MacPherson, *Long Time Passing*, 419.

CHAPTER 5. BLAST

1. James Jones, *WWII* (New York: Ballantine, 1975), 86. Author of the novels *From Here to Eternity* and *The Thin Red Line*, James Jones served as a rifleman in the 25th Infantry Division in World War II. He earned the Purple Heart when wounded during combat on Guadalcanal in January of 1943.

2. U.S. Department of the Army, *FM 7-15: Rifle Platoon and Squads, Infantry, Airborne, and Mechanized* (Washington, DC: Headquarters, Department of the Army, April 1965), 4–6, 192–95. Although the U.S. Army in World War II used yards to mark distances, by Vietnam, most measurements were metric. Altitudes and elevations continued to be counted in feet. For consistency and reader understanding, measurements have been converted to standard units, with the exception of weapons (5.56mm, for example).

3. Perry, "Interview with Senator Charles Hagel"; Krepinevich, *The Army and Vietnam*, 188.

4. Eric Brandner, "Just as in Vietnam, Hagel Still Navigates the Road Less Traveled, *On Patrol: The Magazine of the USO*, Summer 2014, 30. For an example of a three-man point element, see Bergerud, *Red Thunder, Tropic Lightning*, 108.

5. Perry, "Interview with Senator Charles Hagel."

6. Department of the Army, *FM 7-15: Rifle Platoon and Squads, Infantry, Airborne, and Mechanized*, 207; Bergerud, *Red Thunder, Tropic Lightning*, 108.

7. Department of the Army, *FM 7-15: Rifle Platoon and Squads, Infantry, Airborne, and Mechanized*, 254–55.

8. Perry, "Interview with Senator Charles Hagel."

9. U.S., Headquarters, 9th Infantry Division, *Operational Report of 9th Infantry Division for Period Ending 30 April 1968* (Camp Martin Cox, Republic of Vietnam: Headquarters, 9th Infantry Division, May 12, 1968), 7. For casualties on February 28, 1968, see David L. Argabright, ed., *9th Infantry Division "The Old Reliables" Those who Gave Their Lives in Southeast Asia 1966–1970* (St. Charles, IL: 2nd Battalion, 60th Infantry Southeast Asia Vietnam Association, September 18, 2000), 6, 7, 9, 23, 36, 38, 43, 46. In addition to those killed in the rocket attack, two others were killed in action elsewhere on February 28, 1968.

10. 9th Infantry Division, *Operational Report of 9th Infantry Division for Period Ending 30 April 1968*, 29–30; Perry, "Interview with Senator Charles Hagel."

11. Casey, Dougan, Kennedy, and Stanton, *The Army at War*, 153, 155. For more on this event, see Ray Funderburk, "Mekong: Memoirs of Ray Funderburk, PIO [public information officer], 9th Infantry Division, 1967–68," at www.mrfa.org/pdf/Funderburk.Memoirs.pdf, accessed June 14, 2016. The Hagel brothers recalled the incident in Brad Penner, producer, writer, reporter, "Interview with Charles Timothy Hagel and Thomas Leo Hagel, Part 14 of 21," Nebraska Educational Television, August 15, 1999. Penner created a half-hour documentary from his many hours of file footage. Most of the interviews occurred on site in Vietnam as the brothers visited the locations of their key 1968 experiences. The raw video can be reviewed at http://memory.loc.gov/diglib/vhp/story/loc.natlib.afc2001001.88134/, accessed June 26, 2016. For the 25th Infantry Division's base camp and the Cu Chi tunnels, see Bergerud, *Red Thunder, Tropic Lightning*, 29–33.

12. Perry, "Interview with Senator Charles Hagel."

13. Rudyard Kipling, "Gunga Din," in M. M. Kaye, ed., *Rudyard Kipling: The Complete Verse* (London: Kyle Cathie, 1990), 323.

14. Bergerud, *Red Thunder, Tropic Lightning*, 24, 114.

15. Department of the Army, *FM 7-15: Rifle Platoon and Squads, Infantry, Airborne, and Mechanized*, 207.

16. Hagel, *America: Our Next Chapter*, 154–55.

17. Bolger interview with Thomas L. Hagel. Specialist 5 Phillip Rogers held a rank no longer used in the contemporary U.S. Army. For those with responsibilities but not leadership authority, the army designated specialist ranks 4 through 7, and briefly even an 8 and 9 level. In World War II, these were known

as technical ranks and marked by a "T" inside the soldier's chevrons. Except for Specialist 4, all these designations were eliminated by 1985. Despite common usage, to include some official documents, the ranks were never formally titled as specialist fourth class, fifth class, and so on.

18. Myra MacPherson, *Long Time Passing*, 8–9.

19. Bergerud, *Red Thunder, Tropic Lightning*, 200.

20. Ronald J. Glasser, *365 Days* (New York: Bantam, 1971), 4–6. During the Vietnam War, Dr. Ronald Glasser served as a U.S. Army major at Camp Zama, Japan. In addition to his own experiences, Glasser collected accounts of those in country. See also Bergerud, *Red Thunder, Tropic Lightning*, 200–5; Doleman, *Tools of War*, 68, 70–71. For triage, see Peter Dorland and James Nanney, *Dust Off: Army Aeromedical Evacuation in Vietnam* (Washington, DC: U.S. Government Printing Office, 2008), 5.

21. Sam McGowan, "Herculean Ordnance," *Air Force*, March 2016, 58–62. The M121 went into service in the spring of 1969. A year later, the 15,000-pound BLU-82 became available. It remained in use through the 2001 Afghanistan campaign. Since then, the BLU-82 has been replaced by the GPS-guided 21,600-pound GBU-43/B Massive Ordnance Air Blast (MOAB, "mother of all bombs").

22. Dorland and Nanney, *Dust Off*, 71–72; Hagel, *America: Our Next Chapter*, 155.

23. MacPherson, *Long Time Passing*, 8; Penner, "Interview with Charles Timothy Hagel and Thomas Leo Hagel, Part 14 of 21."

24. Dorland and Nanney, *Dust Off*, 68–69.

25. Stanton, *Vietnam Order of Battle*, 212, 214, 215, 217. Bear Cat did not have a full-fledged hospital, only a clearing (emergency treatment and stabilization) facility run by the 50th Medical Company and the 9th Medical Battalion. The 3rd Surgical Hospital was in Dong Tam in May of 1967, and would eventually support the bulk of the 9th Infantry Division by the second half of 1968.

26. MacPherson, *Long Time Passing*, 9.

27. Perry, "Interview with Senator Charles Hagel"; Bolger interview with Charles T. Hagel; Bolger interview with Thomas L. Hagel.

28. Stanton, *Vietnam Order of Battle*, 53.

29. Weigley, *History of the United States Army*, 533–35.

30. Sorley, *Thunderbolt*, 184.

31. Weigley, *History of the United States Army*, 533–35. See also Lewis Sorley, *A Better War: The Unexamined Victories and Final Tragedy of America's Last Years in Vietnam* (Orlando, FL: Harvest Books, 1999), 288.

32. Perry, "Interview with Senator Charles Hagel."

33. Sorley, *A Better War*, 288. In an extreme case, General Creighton Abrams found a rifle company in which only the captain, one platoon sergeant, and one squad leader had more than two years in the army.

34. MacPherson, *Long Time Passing*, 11; Bolger interview with Thomas L. Hagel.

35. Berens, *Chuck Hagel*, 32. For more on both brothers in Vietnam, see Charles P. Pierce, "'Before This Is Over, You Might See Calls for His Impeachment,'" *Esquire*, April 2007, 143.

36. Bolger interview with Thomas L. Hagel.

37. Brad Penner, producer, writer, reporter, "Interview with Charles Timothy Hagel and Thomas Leo Hagel, Part 15 of 21" (Lincoln, NE: Nebraska Educational Television, August 15, 1999) at http://memory.loc.gov/diglib/vhp/story/loc.natlib .afc2001001.88134/, accessed June 26, 2016.

38. MacPherson, *Long Time Passing*, 9.

39. Ewell and Hunt, *Sharpening the Combat Edge*, 65–66.

40. *Paddy Griffith, Forward into Battle: Fighting Tactics from Waterloo to Vietnam* (Strettington, UK: Antony Bird Publications, 1981), 124–25.

41. 9th Infantry Division, *Operational Report of 9th Infantry Division for Period Ending 30 April 1968*, 10, 38, 110.

42. MacPherson, *Long Time Passing*, 19.

43. Perry, "Interview with Senator Charles Hagel."

44. Ibid.

45. Myra MacPherson, *Long Time Passing*, 18.

46. Ibid, 19.

47. Ibid, 19.

48. Ibid., 9; Berens, *Chuck Hagel*, 35; Perry, "Interview with Senator Charles Hagel."

49. Jones, *WWII*, 88.

50. Perry, "Interview with Senator Charles Hagel." For the *Stars and Stripes*, see http://www.stripes.com/customer-service/about-us/about-stars-and-stripes -1.101084, accessed June 17, 2016.

51. Associated Press, "Youth Slain as Wallace Visit Ignites Violence in Omaha," *Stars and Stripes*, Pacific edition, March 7, 1968.

CHAPTER 6. KILLSHOTS

1. Dr. Martin Luther King Jr., "A Time to Break the Silence," delivered at Riverside Church in Manhattan, New York, April 4, 1967, at http://www.ameican rhetoric.com/speeches/mlkatimetobreaksilence.htm, accessed June 17, 2016. The original speech included this ellipsis. After the pause, King went on to say ". . . and if we ignore this sobering reality, we will find ourselves organizing 'clergy and laymen concerned' committees for the next generation." King was assassinated exactly one year later in Memphis, Tennessee.

2. George Wallace's crew flew to Tinian aboard a new B-29 they named *Sentimental Journey*, after the hit tune by Les Brown and his Band of Renown. When the crew arrived, the 794th Bombardment Squadron took the new aircraft and reassigned the men to the older *Li'l Yutz*. See Robert W. Bushouse, "Ray Crew," in *B-29 Crews, 794th–795th Bombardment Squadrons, 468th Bombardment Group*

(Windsor Locks, CT: New England Air Museum, 2010), 1–2. Captain Jack Ray headed the eleven-man crew that included Wallace. Sergeant Robert Bushouse was the senior fire control NCO (the B-29's chief gunner).

3. Dan T. Carter, *The Politics of Rage: George Wallace, the Origins of the New Conservatism, and the Transformation of American Politics* (Baton Rouge, LA: LSU Press, 2000), 109, 137. See also Stephen Lesher, *George Wallace, American Populist* (Boston: Da Capo Press, 1995), 56–57.

4. Rick Perlstein, *Nixonland: The Rise of a President and the Fracturing of America* (New York: Scribner, 2008), 223–24.

5. U.S. Bureau of the Census, 1970 *Census, Volume I: Characteristics of the Population, Part 29: Nebraska* (Washington, DC: U.S. Government Printing Office, January 1973), 29–6, 29–13, 29–33, 29–40. For African American population numbers, see U.S. Bureau of the Census, 1970 *Census of Population, Supplementary Reports, PC (S1), Negro and Total Population of the United States: 1970* (Washington, DC: U.S. Government Printing Office, June 1971), Table 1.

6. Adam Fletcher Sasse, "A History of the North Omaha Riots," North Omaha History blog at http://northomaha.blogspot.com/2013/07/the-north-omaha-riots.html, accessed June 22, 2016.

7. "Mob in Omaha Lynches Negro; Attempts to Hang Mayor Smith," *Omaha Morning World-Herald,* September 29, 1919. Nebraska State Historical Society, *We the People: The 1919 Riot* at http://nebraskahistory.org/exhibits/we_the_people/1919_riot.htm, accessed June 22, 2016.

8. Gitlin, *The Sixties,* 146. Malcolm X (*né* Little) only lived very briefly in Omaha after his 1925 birth. The post-1919 situation wasn't good for African Americans in the city. The Littles moved to Milwaukee, Wisconsin, and then Lansing, Michigan.

9. Jessica Fargen, "King's Legacy Continues in Lincolnites' Lives," *Daily Nebraskan,* January 14, 1999, 1. Doctor Martin Luther King Jr. graduated from Morehouse College in Atlanta and earned his doctorate at Boston University.

10. Paul J. Scheips, *The Role of Federal Military Forces in Civil Disorders 1945–1992* (Washington, DC: U.S. Government Printing Office, 2005), 169. The 1965 Watts riot saw thirty-four killed and about a thousand injured, as well as 950 buildings looted and 200 burned or otherwise damaged.

11. Perlstein, *Nixonland,* 103–4.

12. Sasse, "A History of the North Omaha Riots."

13. Christopher Andrew and Vasili Mitrokhin, *The Sword and the Shield: The Mitrokhin Archive and the Secret History of the KGB* (New York; Basic Books, 1999), 290. Mitrokhin defected from Russia in 1992, after the collapse of the USSR. For the KGB role with the Black Panthers, see Yuri V. Andropov, "#1128A, Committee for State Security to Central Committee of the Communist Party of the Soviet Union, 28 April 1970" in Vladimir Bukovsky, *Soviet Archives Collected by Vladimir Bukovsky,* at https://matiane.wordpress.com/2010/02/08/soviet-archives-collected-by-vladimir-bukovsky/, accessed June 22, 2016. Andropov headed the KGB from 1967 until 1982. Bukovsky, a prominent Soviet dissident,

was forcibly deported in 1976. He smuggled out a large number of government documents. For Soviet intelligence collection versus the Strategic Air Command, see Loch K. Johnson, ed., *Strategic Intelligence: Understanding the Hidden Side of Government* (Westport, CT: Praeger Security International, 2007), 37. For the GRU role, see Viktor Suvorov, *Spetsnaz: The Inside Story of the Soviet Special Forces* (New York: W.W. Norton, 1987), 158–59. Suvorov is a pseudonym for Vladimir B. Rezun, a former GRU officer who defected in 1978.

14. Walter C. Jersey, director, *A Time for Burning* (San Francisco: Quest Productions, 1967).

15. Michael Richardson, "George Wallace Rally in Omaha Triggered Riot After Demonstrators Were Beaten," Examiner.com, March 12, 2011, at http://www.examiner.com/article/george-wallace-rally-omaha-triggered-riot-after-demonstrators-were-beaten, accessed June 22, 2016.

16. Ibid. David Rice later took the name Mondo we Langa.

17. Associated Press, "Negro Youth Shot in Omaha Looting," *La Crosse Tribune*, March 5, 1968. Some sources give Stevenson's age as twenty-three. The FBI Omaha Field Office account listed him as sixteen years old. Officer Abbott was not charged.

18. Erin Duffy, "1968 Visit by George Wallace, Riots, State Tourney Loss Left Lasting Marks on Central High," *Omaha.com*, March 21, 2014, at http://www.omaha.com/news/visit-by-george-wallace-riots-state-tourney-loss-left-lasting/article_fbdf0f1f-f7a7-5b2e-bac1-7f7492bb3117.html, accessed June 22, 2016. Omaha Central High School lost to Lincoln Northeast High School 54–50.

19. Associated Press, "Youth Slain as Wallace Visit Ignites Violence in Omaha."

20. The FBI memorandum is quoted in Richardson, "George Wallace Rally in Omaha Triggered Riot After Demonstrators Were Beaten."

21. Lyndon B. Johnson, *The Vantage Point: Perspectives of the Presidency, 1963–1969* (New York: Holt, Rinehart, and Winston, 1971), 533.

22. The Kerner Commission, *Report of the National Advisory Committee on Civil Disorders* (New York: Bantam, 1968), 1. The members were I. W. Abel of the United Steelworkers of America, Senator Edward Brooke of Massachusetts, Representative James Corman of California, Senator Fred Harris of Oklahoma, Atlanta police chief Herbert Turner Jenkins, Mayor John Lindsay of New York, Representative William McCullough of Ohio, Commerce Commissioner Katherine Graham Peden of Kentucky, Charles Thornton of Litton Industries, and Roy Wilkins of the National Association for the Advancement of Colored People.

23. King, "A Time to Break the Silence."

24. Tom Buckley, "Westmoreland Requests 206,000 More Men, Stirring Debate in Administration," *New York Times*, March 10, 1968.

25. Perlstein, *Nixonland*, 228–32.

26. Ibid., 241.

27. Dougan and Weiss, *Nineteen Sixty-Eight*, 69.

28. Westmoreland, *A Soldier Reports*, 439.

29. Sorley, *Thunderbolt*, 224–27.

30. U.S., Office of the President, "President Lyndon Baines Johnson's Address to the Nation Announcing Steps to Limit the War in Vietnam and Reporting His Decision Not to Seek Reelection," March 31, 1968, at http://www.lbjlib.utexas.edu /johnson/archives.hom/speeches.hom/680331.asp, accessed June 22,2016.

31. Andrew and Mitrokhin, *The Sword and the Shield*, 291.

32. Gerald Posner, *Killing the Dream: James Earl Ray and the Assassination of Martin Luther King, Jr.* (New York: Mariner Books, 1999), 39–41, 93–95, 200. Ray served in the U.S. Army as part of the occupation forces in Germany from 1946 to 1948. A poor soldier, he committed minor offenses and received a general discharge. The U.S. Marine Corps often says once a marine, always a marine. Older veterans may merit the title former marines. There is but one ex-marine: Lee Harvey Oswald, the assassin of President John F. Kennedy. James Earl Ray was an ex-soldier.

33. Scheips, *The Role of Federal Military Forces in Civil Disorders 1945–1992*, 271. James Earl Ray confessed, then recanted. In later life, he spun imaginative tales of who really killed King. Although rumors continue, the weight of evidence has long implicated Ray.

34. Ibid., 272, 287, 288–89, 308, 325, 329. The U.S. Army sent the 1st Armored Division and a brigade of the 5th Infantry Division into Chicago. The 82nd Airborne Division sent a brigade to Baltimore and another brigade to Washington, joining local marine and army ceremonial troops committed for security. When the 82nd needed another brigade in the District of Columbia, it came from the 5th Infantry Division. The 82nd's third brigade had already left for Vietnam, one of the post-Tet reinforcements.

35. Nebraska State Historical Society, *We the People: Separate but Not Equal*, at http://nebraskahistory.org/exhibits/we_the_people/separate_not_equal.htm, accessed June 23, 2016.

36. Scheips, *The Role of Federal Military Forces in Civil Disorders 1945–1992*, 337, 440–41. Aside from the North Omaha riot of 1969, the only significant urban unrest over the next few decades occurred in the Liberty City neighborhood of Miami, Florida, (1980) and the disturbances in Los Angeles, California, (1992) in the wake of not-guilty verdicts for police officers accused of beating African American Rodney King. The 2014 racial confrontation in Ferguson, Missouri, also came after the death of an African American youth shot by a white police officer. This episode catalyzed the Black Lives Matter movement to highlight similar allegations across the country.

37. Perlstein, *Nixonland*, 267.

38. Dougan and Lipsman, *A Nation Divided*, 78, 80; Burkett and Whitley, *Stolen Valor*, 54–55.

39. Perry, "Interview with Senator Charles Hagel."

40. Richard Sisk, "Hagel Remembers Martin Luther King," *DoD Buzz*, January 20, 2014, at http://www.dodbuzz.com/2014/01/20/defense-secretary-hagel

-remembers-martin-luther-king/, accessed June 23, 2016. See also Bolger interview with Charles T. Hagel.

41. Milam, *Not a Gentleman's War*, 154. Ron Milam served as a junior officer in Vietnam. He quoted one African American soldier stating: "Black soldiers should not have to serve under the Confederate flag or with it. We are serving under the American flag and the American flag only." For another example of the routine display of the Confederate flag, see Bunting, *The Lionheads*, 113. Bunting referred to the flag's use on air-cushioned vehicles in the Mekong Delta. For racist epithets in Vietnam, see James William Gibson, *The Perfect War: Technowar in Vietnam* (New York: Atlantic Monthly Press, 1996), 217–18. Gibson's book has a strong polemic slant, but his citations and cited evidence speak for themselves.

42. For a typical example of the reliance on photographs of white soldiers in one of the army's most widely distributed field manuals, see U.S. Department of the Army, *FM 22-5 Drill and Ceremonies* (Washington, DC: Department of the Army, August 1968). See also Samuel Lipsman and Edward Doyle, *Fighting for Time, The Vietnam Experience* (Boston: Boston Publishing, 1983), 101–102. James Marshall "Jimi" Hendrix served in the 101st Airborne Division before the Vietnam War.

43. Milam, *Not a Gentleman's War*, 27–28.

44. Ibid., 28. In the U.S. Armed Forces as a whole in the Vietnam era, African American officers totaled 2 percent.

45. Scheips, *The Role of Federal Military Forces in Civil Disorders 1945–1992*, 332.

46. Perry, "Interview with Senator Charles Hagel"; Bolger interview with Thomas L. Hagel.

47. David Martin, "Defense Secretary Hagel Finds Long-Lost 'Brother.'" CBS News, February 17, 2014, at http://www.cbsnews.com/news/defense-secretary-hagel-finds-long-lost-brother/, accessed June 23, 2016; Bolger interview with Charles T. Hagel; Bolger interview with Thomas L. Hagel. Tom Hagel noted that Johnson was serving outside his assigned armor branch but did just fine.

48. Claudette Roulo, "Hagel 'Quintessentially American' Obama says at Farewell Tribute," DoD News, Defense Media Activity, January 28, 2015. President Barack H. Obama met both Jerome Johnson and Secretary of Defense Chuck Hagel in the Oval Office in 2014. In his farewell to Hagel, Obama quoted Johnson. Johnson's comment about his personal order comes from Martin, "Defense Secretary Hagel Finds Long-Lost 'Brother.'"

49. Davidson, *Vietnam at War*, 486–87.

50. With regard to the shortcomings of MACV's body counting formula for victory, in Halberstam, *The Best and the Brightest*, 794, the author included a devastating exchange that occurred during the deliberation of LBJ's wise men. U.S. ambassador to the United Nations Arthur Goldberg asked the military briefer the hostile strength as of February 1, 1968. The answer came back: 160,000 to 175,000. How many did we kill? Forty-five thousand. And for every NVA/VC death, how

many were wounded? Three. At that, Goldberg did the mental arithmetic. He remarked that using MACV math, there were no enemy left in the field.

51. 9th Infantry Division, *Operational Report of 9th Infantry Division for Period Ending 30 April 1968*, 12.

CHAPTER 7. HEAT

1. John Ellis, *The Sharp End: The Fighting Man in World War II* (New York: Charles Scribner's Sons, 1980) 130. Private Stephen Bagnall served as an infantryman in the British army with Company C, 5th East Lancashire Regiment during the extended battle at Caen in Normandy in the summer of 1944. His 1947 novel, *The Attack*, drew from his experiences.

2. Starry, *Mounted Combat in Vietnam*, 9–10. The northern part of South Vietnam experiences opposite seasons. So it was wet, foggy, and muddy up north near Khe Sanh and Hue during Tet and the following weeks, with consequent degradation of U.S. and ARVN operations.

3. James A. Warren, *Giap: The General Who Defeated America in Vietnam* (New York: St. Martin's Press, 2013), 157. For the relationship between the one-slow, four-quick tactics and the Mao Zedong approach to guerrilla warfare, see Starry, *Mounted Combat in Vietnam*, 14.

4. Ewell and Hunt, *Sharpening the Combat Edge*, 15–16.

5. U.S. Department of the Army, Headquarters, 9th Infantry Division, *Ground Force Commander's Situation Report 22001H to 222400H April* (Camp Martin Cox, Bearcat, Republic of Vietnam: Headquarters, 9th Infantry Division), April 23, 1968, 1.

6. Perry, "Interview with Senator Charles Hagel."

7. For Tom Hagel's description, see Penner, "Interview with Charles Timothy Hagel and Thomas Leo Hagel, Part 14 of 21." For details of the chemical defoliation program, see Committee to Review the Health Effects in Vietnam Veterans of Exposure to Herbicides, *Veterans and Agent Orange*, 89–90. The three principal defoliants were Agent Orange (dichlorophenoxyacetic and trichlorophenoxyacetic acid, 11,261,429 gallons), White (picloram, 5,246,502 gallons), and Blue (cacodylic acid, an arsenic derivative, 1,124,307 gallons). Orange wiped out broad-leaf forests. White lasted longest and proved useful around base camps, including Bear Cat. Blue worked well on rice crops. Prior to 1964, compounds known as Purple, Pink, and Green were also used, but the total amounted to less than a quarter million gallons. When Chuck Hagel served as an official with the Veterans Administration in 1981–82, he tabbed brother Tom to assist in the study of the long-term effects of Agent Orange on those who served in Vietnam.

8. Penner, "Interview with Charles Timothy Hagel and Thomas Leo Hagel, Part 14 of 21."

9. For an example of a cordon and search using mechanized infantry, see Starry, *Mounted Combat in Vietnam*, 103–6.

10. Although often done in Vietnam, carrying exposed linked machine gun ammunition "bandit style" can be a problem. If the gunner goes prone, dirt usually encrusts the ammunition, leading directly to stoppages. Experienced soldiers prefer to carry the ammunition coiled in a slung pouch. A gas mask carrier (minus the mask) works well. By the time of the Afghanistan (2001–14) and Iraq (2003–11) campaigns, the military issued pouches to carry belts of linked machine gun rounds.

11. Penner, "Interview with Charles Timothy Hagel and Thomas Leo Hagel, Part 14 of 21."

12. Ibid.

13. Bergerud, *Red Thunder, Tropic Lightning*, 188–93.

14. Penner, "Interview with Charles Timothy Hagel and Thomas Leo Hagel, Part 14 of 21."

15. 9th Infantry Division, *Operational Report of 9th Infantry Division for Period Ending 30 April 1968*, 13, 43.

16. Perry, "Interview with Senator Charles Hagel."

17. U.S. Department of the Army, *Technical Manual 9-2350-261-10 Operator's Manual for Carrier, Full-Tracked, Armored M-113A2* (Washington, DC: Headquarters, Department of the Army, August 2005), section 028.00. Although the manual is new, the basic driving method for an M113 has not changed.

18. Brad Penner, producer, writer, reporter, "Interview with Charles Timothy Hagel and Thomas Leo Hagel, Part 2 of 21," Nebraska Educational Television, August 14, 1999 at http://memory.loc.gov/diglib/vhp/story/loc.natlib.afc2001 001.88134/, accessed June 29, 2016.

19. Bolger interview with Thomas L. Hagel.

20. Brad Penner, producer, writer, reporter, "Interview with Charles Timothy Hagel and Thomas Leo Hagel, Part 5 of 21," Nebraska Educational Television, August 14, 1999, at http://memory.loc.gov/diglib/vhp/story/loc.natlib.afc2001 001.88134/, accessed June 29, 2016.

21. Ibid.; Hagel, *America: Our Next Chapter*, 155–56; Berens, *Chuck Hagel*, 42; Bolger interview with Thomas L. Hagel; Bolger interview with Charles T. Hagel.

22. U.S. Department of Defense, Defense and Veterans Brain Injury Center, "TBI & the Military" (Washington, DC: Defense Centers of Excellence for Psychological Health and Traumatic Brain Injury, 2016) at http://dvbic.dcoe.mil/ about/tbi-military, accessed June 29, 2016.

23. Penner, "Interview with Charles Timothy Hagel and Thomas Leo Hagel, Part 2 of 21."

24. 9th Infantry Division, *Operational Report of 9th Infantry Division for Period Ending 30 April 1968*, 34; Keith W. Nolan, *House to House: Playing the Enemy's Game in Saigon*, May 1968 (St. Paul, MN: Zenith Press, 2006), 216.

25. Nolan, *House to House*, 210.

26. For participating enemy units, see 9th Infantry Division, *Operational Report of 9th Infantry Division for Period Ending 30 April 1968*, 7–11. Sorley, *Thunderbolt*, 230, summarized Mini-Tet's bombardment, including 450 attacks

by 122mm and 107mm rockets and various mortars directed at targets across Saigon's eight districts.

27. Davidson, *Vietnam at War*, 487, claimed MACV intelligence derived "almost complete knowledge of the details of the enemy's plans" for the May 1968 Mini-Tet offensive. For the name of the offensive, see Starry, *Mounted Combat in Vietnam*, 129.

28. John A. Cash, "Gunship Mission" in John A. Cash, John Albright, and Allan W. Sandstrum, *Seven Firefights in Vietnam* (Washington, DC: U.S. Government Printing Office, 1970), 139–52. During a major engagement near the Phu Tho Racetrack, the 120th Aviation Company flew attack missions on May 5, 1968, in support of the 30th Ranger Battalion.

29. 9th Infantry Division, *Operational Report of 9th Infantry Division for Period Ending 30 April 1968*, 19–21.

30. Ibid., 20; Nolan, *House to House*, 215–16; Brad Penner, producer, writer, reporter, "Interview with Charles Timothy Hagel and Thomas Leo Hagel, Part 6 of 21," Nebraska Educational Television, August 14, 1999, at http://memory.loc .gov/diglib/vhp/story/loc.natlib.afc2001001.88134/, accessed June 29, 2016.

31. Bolger interview with Thomas L. Hagel.

32. 31st Infantry Association, "Chapter 18: 6th Battalion, Fort Lewis and Vietnam, 1967–1970" in *America's Foreign Legion*, 11–12 at http://www.31stinfantry .org/wp-content/uploads/2014/01/Chapter-18.pdf, accessed July 1, 2016. The 6-31st Infantry history provides an excellent overview of the entire engagements at Xom Ong Doi and Xom Cau Mat. See also Nolan, *House to House*, 216–17.

33. Penner, "Interview with Charles Timothy Hagel and Thomas Leo Hagel, Part 6 of 21"; Perry, "Interview with Senator Charles Hagel"; Bolger interview with Thomas L. Hagel.

34. Nolan, *House to House*, 216–17.

35. Argabright, *The 9th Infantry Division "The Old Reliables" Those Who Gave Their Lives in Southeast Asia 1966–1970*, 17, 21.

36. Ibid.

37. Penner, "Interview with Charles Timothy Hagel and Thomas Leo Hagel, Part 6 of 21."

38. Nolan, *House to House*, 218–19.

39. Bolger interview with Charles T. Hagel; Bolger interview with Thomas L. Hagel.

40. 31st Infantry Association, "Chapter 18: 6th Battalion, Fort Lewis and Vietnam, 1967–1970," 11–13.

41. Nolan, *House to House*, 221.

42. 31st Infantry Association, "Chapter 18: 6th Battalion, Fort Lewis and Vietnam, 1967–1970," 15; Nolan, *House to House*, 225.

43. Sorley, *A Better War*, 27–28. Both Hagels were aware of these restrictions and commented on their effects on the ground. See Penner, "Interview with Charles Timothy Hagel and Thomas Leo Hagel, Part 6 of 21."

44. 31st Infantry Association, "Chapter 18: 6th Battalion, Fort Lewis and Vietnam, 1967–1970," 11–13.

45. Nolan, *House to House*, 225–29.

46. 31st Infantry Association, "Chapter 18: 6th Battalion, Fort Lewis and Vietnam, 1967–1970," 11, 13–14; Nolan, *House to House*, 238–39.

47. Bolger interview with Thomas L. Hagel; "Penner, "Interview with Charles Timothy Hagel and Thomas Leo Hagel, Part 6 of 21." For the tendency to call all hostile marksmen snipers, see Bergerud, *Red Thunder, Tropic Lightning*, 252–58.

48. John Morocco, *Thunder from Above, The Vietnam Experience* (Boston: Boston Publishing, 1984), 46–47, 66, 79. The Mark 81 250-pound Snakeye had a set of big tail brakes that slowed its descent and allowed for on-target drops near troops. The Mark 47 500-pound napalm canister mixed gelling aluminum salts and petroleum. It exploded in a nasty fireball and stuck to people and things. The F-4D Phantoms carried their 20mm rotary cannon in an attached gun pod.

49. Nolan, *House to House*, 230–31; Argabright, *9th Infantry Division "The Old Reliables" Those Who Gave Their Lives in Southeast Asia 1966–1970*, 49.

50. 9th Infantry Division, *Operational Report of 9th Infantry Division for Period Ending 30 April 1968*, 19–22; 31st Infantry Association, "Chapter 18: 6th Battalion, Fort Lewis and Vietnam, 1967–1970," 14; Nolan, *House to House*, 242–43. Of note, the single VC prisoner stated that his female unit commander took his weapon for her own use.

51. 9th Infantry Division, *Operational Report of 9th Infantry Division for Period Ending 30 April 1968*, 21.

52. Stephen E. Atkins, *Writing the War: My Ten Months in the Jungles, Streets and Paddies of Vietnam, 1968* (Jefferson, NC: McFarland, 2010), 163–64. Atkins served with Company C, 6-31st Infantry; Bolger interview with Charles T. Hagel; Bolger interview with Thomas L. Hagel.

53. Nolan, *House to House*, 301.

54. Perry, "Interview with Senator Charles Hagel."

55. Penner, "Interview with Charles Timothy Hagel and Thomas Leo Hagel, Part 6 of 21." In this segment, both Chuck and Tom Hagel actually walked the Route 320 areas of the May 9 and May 11, 1968, firefights.

56. Nolan, *House to House*, 304–5.

57. Ibid., 316–19.

58. Penner, "Interview with Charles Timothy Hagel and Thomas Leo Hagel, Part 6 of 21."

59. 31st Infantry Association, "Chapter 18: 6th Battalion, Fort Lewis and Vietnam, 1967–1970," 28–32. See also Nolan, *House to House*, 320–21.

60. 9th Infantry Division, *Operational Report of 9th Infantry Division for Period Ending 30 April 1968*, 18–22; Nolan, *House to House*, 339; Gittinger, *Interview with Lieutenant General Julian J. Ewell*, 13.

61. Westmoreland, *A Soldier Reports*, 439. For MACV's claim of 40,000 enemy dead, see Sorley, *A Better War*, 97.

62. Westmoreland, *A Soldier Reports*, 422–24, 437. For the 101st Airborne Division's operations in the A Shau Valley, see Tolson, *Airmobility*, 182–92. The A Shau Valley operation recorded 869 NVA dead for the cost of 142 Americans killed.

63. 9th Infantry Division, *Operational Report of 9th Infantry Division for Period Ending 30 April 1968*, 10–11, 22. In assessing the enemy losses, the 9th Infantry Division's intelligence section judged the Phu Loi II Battalion (strength 300) as "combat effective," 5th Nha Be Battalion (strength 60) as "not combat effective," and 506th Battalion (strength 270) as "marginally combat effective." All three battalions escaped from the south Saigon neighborhoods.

64. 9th Infantry Division, *Operational Report of 9th Infantry Division for Period Ending 30 April 1968*, Inclosure 6 "Summary of Rounds Fired."

65. Ibid., 31; Nolan, *House to House*, 312–14, describes U.S. embassy efforts to estimate civilian casualties in Saigon during Mini-Tet. See also Sorley, *A Better War*, 77.

66. Nolan, *House to House*, 349–51, lists the six journalists killed. See also Herr, *Dispatches*, 231.

67. Sorley, *A Better War*, 29. Sorley transcribed the quote from a 1968 tape recording. He added the italics to depict words emphasized by General Abrams in his comments. The first two defenses Abrams mentioned were Tet (January–February) and Mini-Tet (May).

68. The United States lost 616 troops in the week of May 5 through 11, 1968. This is noted in Herr, *Dispatches*, 230, and explained in Ronald Spector, *After Tet: The Bloodiest Year of the Vietnam War* (New York: Vintage, 1993), 319.

CHAPTER 8. THE RIVER BLINDNESS

1. Herr, *Dispatches*, 13. Among his many other accomplishments. Michael Herr wrote much of the narration for the 1979 film *Apocalypse Now*.

2. Berens, *Chuck Hagel*, 36. Senator Robert F. Kennedy won the California presidential primary just before his assassination by Sirhan Sirhan, a Palestinian Christian from Jordan. Sirhan was not a U.S. citizen and said he shot Kennedy due to the senator's support of Israel.

3. Starry, *Mounted Combat in Vietnam*, 11–13.

4. 9th Infantry Division, *Operational Report of 9th Infantry Division for Period Ending 30 April 1968*, 8, 11.

5. Argabright, *9th Infantry Division "The Old Reliables" Those Who Gave Their Lives in Southeast Asia 1966–1970*, 51, 53.

6. Perry, "Interview with Senator Charles Hagel."

7. MacPherson, *Long Time Passing*, 22. The words "infantry" and "infant" share a common root. In addition, the U.S. Army infantry's branch color is baby blue, the traditional color associated with male children. That's an interesting but apparently unintentional coincidence. The U.S. Army's choice of blue

probably had more to do with finding a contrast between the Continental Army's uniforms and the red coats of British infantry regiments during the Revolutionary War (1775–83).

8. Sullivan, "A Vietnam War That Never Ends," 1.

9. Brad Penner, producer, writer, reporter, "Interview with Charles Timothy Hagel and Thomas Leo Hagel, Part 7 of 21," Nebraska Educational Television, August 14, 1999, at http://memory.loc.gov/diglib/vhp/story/loc.natlib.afc2001001 .88134/, accessed July 4, 2016.

10. Ibid.

11. MacPherson, *Long Time Passing*, 19.

12. Hagel, *America: Our Next Chapter*, 156; Penner, "Interview with Charles Timothy Hagel and Thomas Leo Hagel, Part 2 of 21"; Berens, *Chuck Hagel*, 35.

13. MacPherson, *Long Time Passing*, 19. Emphasis in original.

14. Berens, *Chuck Hagel*, 35–36. The Military Auxiliary Radio System allowed civilian ham radio volunteers to assist the U.S Armed Forces in tying field radio traffic into commercial phone lines. The radio-wire interface allowed soldiers in Vietnam to "phone home," although connections could be spotty and both sides had to use radio procedures, such as "over" to end a sentence and "out" to end the transmission.

15. 9th Infantry Division, *Operational Report of 9th Infantry Division for Period Ending 30 April 1968*, 21.

16. Argabright, *9th Infantry Division "The Old Reliables" Those Who Gave Their Lives in Southeast Asia 1966–1970*, 49, 57.

17. 9th Infantry Division, *Operational Report of 9th Infantry Division for Period Ending 30 April 1968*, Inclosure 8, "Division Operations Data." During the reporting period, the 2-47th Infantry lost thirty-one killed (plus two attached aviation soldiers) and claimed thirty-one VC killed and two prisoners taken.

18. Carolyn S. Van Deusen, "Frederick F. Van Deusen, Class of 1953" at http:// apps.westpointaog.org/Memorials/Article/19460/, accessed July 4, 2016.

19. Tolson, *Airmobility*, 14.

20. Ibid., 264–65, 269, 272–74; Dorland and Nanney, *Dust Off*, 66, 69; Ewell and Hunt, *Sharpening the Combat Edge*, 46, 116. The OH-23 Raven was an exception to the usual use of Indian names for U.S. Army aircraft. The model was a variant of the UH-12, already named by the U.S. Navy.

21. Robert Mason, *Chickenhawk* (New York: Viking Penguin, 1983), 97, 209. As a warrant officer, Mason flew Hueys in Vietnam in 1965–66, to include duty with the 1st Cavalry Division (Airmobile). He flew during the vicious combat in the Ia Drang Valley in November of 1965.

22. U.S. Department of Defense, Office of the Comptroller, *Air War in Indochina* (Washington, DC: Office of the Secretary of Defense, 1972), 267–72, 283. For current U.S. Army numbers, see U.S. Congressional Budget Office *Modernizing the Army's Rotary-Wing Aviation Fleet* (Washington, DC: Congressional Budget Office, November 2007), ix, 24.

23. For overall accident rates of the Vietnam era, see U.S. Department of the Army, U.S. Army Board for Aviation Accident Research, *Rotary Wing Sortie Study by Phase of Operation for FY 69* (Fort Rucker, AL: U.S. Army Board for Aviation Accident Research, 1970), 6, 8. Helicopter-related casualties are summarized in Stanton, *Vietnam Order of Battle*, 346. Two-thirds of those killed in helicopter operations were aviators, the soldiers flying the aircraft.

24. Ewell and Hunt, *Sharpening the Combat Edge*, 49, 69.

25. Emphasis in original. Winston Groom, *Better Times Than These* (New York: Berkley Books, 1978), 68. Groom, also the author of the novel *Forrest Gump* that became the basis for the movie, served in Vietnam with the 4th Infantry Division. Groom's earlier novel *Better Times Than These* is a fictionalized version of the experiences of the 1st Cavalry Division in the Central Highlands in 1966–67. The sentences quoted are from a character speaking of his experiences as a helicopter aviator in the Ia Drang Valley, scene of fierce fighting in November of 1965.

26. Lieutenant Colonel Jonathan R. Jackson, U.S. Army, interviewer, and Colonel John R. Dabrowski, U.S. Army, ed., *An Oral History of Lieutenant General Henry E, Emerson* (Carlisle, PA: U.S. Army Military History Institute, 2004), 27. Emerson developed the jitterbug tactic during his time as the commander of the 2nd Battalion (Airborne) 502nd Infantry, 101st Airborne Division in the Central Highlands in 1965–66. Ewell referred to Emerson as "a genuine genius" [emphasis in original] in Gittinger, *Interview with Lieutenant General Julian J. Ewell*, 35. A graduate of West Point (Class of 1947), Emerson completed his thirty years of service as a lieutenant general in command of XVIII Airborne Corps. As commander of the 2nd Infantry Division in the Republic of Korea in 1973–75, he had a strong positive influence on then-Lieutenant Colonel Colin Powell, who commanded the 1st Battalion, 32nd Infantry during that time.

27. 9th Infantry Division, *Operational Report of 9th Infantry Division for Period Ending 30 April 1968*, 41. The XM-2 was also called an E63 man-pack personnel detector. It was supposed to be employed by a soldier on foot, but the 9th Aviation Battalion figured out how to emplace it on a UH-1 helicopter. The XM-3 device, introduced later, was specifically designed for use aboard a rotary wing aircraft.

28. Hunt, *The 9th Infantry Division*, 58–61.

29. Ewell and Hunt, *Sharpening the Combat Edge*, 107–10.

30. Perry, "Interview with Senator Charles Hagel."

31. Tribune Wire Services, "Van Deusen, Westmoreland's Brother-in-Law, Dies in Viet," *Chicago Tribune*, July 6, 2016; U.S. Department of the Army, Headquarters, U.S. Army Vietnam, *General Orders No. 3240: Citation for the Distinguished Service Cross: Lieutenant Colonel Frederick French Van Deusen* (Long Binh Post, Republic of Vietnam: Headquarters, U.S. Army, Vietnam, July 9, 1968).

32. Tolson, *Airmobility*, 35–36, 272.

33. Perry, "Interview with Senator Charles Hagel."

34. Bolger interview with Thomas L. Hagel; see also Brad Penner, producer, writer, reporter, "Interview with Charles Timothy Hagel and Thomas Leo Hagel, Part 5 of 21," Nebraska Educational Television, August 14, 1999, at http://memory .loc.gov/diglib/vhp/story/loc.natlib.afc2001001.88134/, accessed July 7, 2016.

35. Bolger interview with Thomas L. Hagel; MacPherson, *Long Time Passing*, 16.

36. Bolger interview with Thomas L. Hagel.

37. Penner, "Interview with Charles Timothy Hagel and Thomas Leo Hagel, Part 5 of 21."

38. Bolger interview with Thomas L. Hagel.

39. MacPherson, *Long Time Passing*, 16.

40. Bolger interview with Thomas L. Hagel; Penner, "Interview with Charles Timothy Hagel and Thomas Leo Hagel, Part 5 of 21."

41. Ibid.

42. MacPherson, *Long Time Passing*, 16.

43. Penner, "Interview with Charles Timothy Hagel and Thomas Leo Hagel, Part 5 of 21." The Vam Co River has two branches: Dong (east) and Tay (west).

44. Ibid.; Bolger interview with Thomas L. Hagel.

45. Headquarters, U.S. Army Vietnam, *General Orders No. 3240: Citation for the Distinguished Service Cross: Lieutenant Colonel Frederick French Van Deusen.*

46. Hunt, *The 9th Infantry Division*, 46–48.

47. Bolger interview with Thomas L. Hagel.

48. For the details of the shoot-down, to include a modern perspective of the terrain, see Army Air Crews, *UH-1 Crews: UH-1 Vietnam Losses 1968* at http:// www.armyaircrews.com/huey_nam_68.html, accessed July 7, 1968. For Tom Hagel's recollections, see Penner, "Interview with Charles Timothy Hagel and Thomas Leo Hagel, Part 5 of 21."

49. Penner, "Interview with Charles Timothy Hagel and Thomas Leo Hagel, Part 5 of 21."

50. Bolger interview with Thomas L. Hagel; see also MacPherson, *Long Time Passing*, 16–17.

51. Tribune Wire Services, "Van Deusen, Westmoreland's Brother-in-Law, Dies in Viet"; Headquarters, U.S. Army Vietnam, *General Orders No. 3240: Citation for the Distinguished Service Cross: Lieutenant Colonel Frederick French Van Deusen.*

52. MacPherson, *Long Time Passing*, 17; Bolger interview with Thomas L. Hagel.

53. 9th Infantry Division, *Operational Report of 9th Infantry Division for Period Ending 30 April 1968*, 8, 11; U.S. Army Vietnam, General Orders No. 3240: Citation for the Distinguished Service Cross: Lieutenant Colonel Frederick French Van Deusen. Van Deusen's award citation noted the search for an enemy battalion command post.

54. MacPherson, *Long Time Passing*, 17.

55. Bolger interview with Thomas L. Hagel; Penner, "Interview with Charles Timothy Hagel and Thomas Leo Hagel, Part 5 of 21."

56. Westmoreland, *A Soldier Reports*, 321.

57. 9th Infantry Division, *Operational Report of 9th Infantry Division for Period Ending 30 April 1968*, 2, 22, Inclosure 8 "Division Operations Data"; Hunt, *The 9th Infantry Division*, 101–2. Lieutenant Colonel William Edward Berzinec of 4-39th Infantry was killed in action by an enemy land mine on July 30, 1968.

58. 9th Infantry Division, *Operational Report of 9th Infantry Division for Period Ending 30 April 1968*, 21, Inclosure 8 "Division Operations Data"; U.S. Army Vietnam, *General Orders No. 3240: Citation for the Distinguished Service Cross: Lieutenant Colonel Frederick French Van Deusen.*

59. Starry, *Mounted Combat in Vietnam*, 235. Lieutenant Colonel William Bernard Cronin was killed in action on April 27, 1967.

60. Perry, "Interview with Senator Charles Hagel"; MacPherson, *Long Time Passing*, 20; Bolger interview with Thomas L. Hagel. Tom Hagel received the Purple Heart, the Bronze Star with "V" (valor device), and the Army Commendation Medal with "V" for his various actions on July 3, 1968. Years later, when his brother was a senator, a review of Tom's records caused some officious bureaucrat to rescind the Bronze Star under the theory that only one award could be given for each engagement, as if heroism can be quantified. Tom Hagel kept another Bronze Star and another Army Commendation Medal with "V" given for other actions.

61. Nolan, *House to House*, 277. The speaker was First Lieutenant Ronald P. Garver, who served during Mini-Tet with Company C, 5-60th Infantry. See also 9th Infantry Division, *Operational Report of 9th Infantry Division for Period Ending 30 April 1968*, 82. From May 1 to July 31, 1968, 2-47th Infantry soldiers earned eighty-six Purple Hearts, to include thirty-one men killed in action. Soldiers received eighty-one valor awards (one Distinguished Service Cross, thirteen Silvers Stars, forty Bronze Stars with "V," and twenty-seven Army Commendation Medals with "V"). Compared to other 9th Infantry Division battalions, 2-47th Infantry processed fewer awards.

62. Grossman, *On Killing*, 97–119.

63. Bolger interview with Thomas L. Hagel.

64. Perry, "Interview with Senator Charles Hagel"; Penner, "Interview with Charles Timothy Hagel and Thomas Leo Hagel, Part 5 of 21."

65. Berens, *Chuck Hagel*, 37.

66. MacPherson, *Long Time Passing*, 17–18. Emphasis in original.

CHAPTER 9. CONSTANT PRESSURE

1. Tim O'Brien, *If I Die in a Combat Zone, Box Me Up and Ship Me Home* (New York: Laurel, 1979), 91–92. An acclaimed writer, O'Brien wrote this book about his year (1969–70) in Vietnam. The short book originally came out in 1973.

The title comes from a cadence call used in basic training. The epigraph about Charlie Cong was also a cadence call and another drill sergeant favorite. The first part was sometimes rendered "Late at night when you're sleepin'." In addition to the nonfiction account *If I Die in a Combat Zone*, O'Brien also wrote the novel *Going After Cacciato* (1978) and a short story collection, *The Things They Carried* (1990). Both of these well-regarded books offer more of O'Brien's views on the Vietnam War. He served in Company A, 5th Battalion 46th Infantry in the 23rd Infantry Division (Americal) in northern South Vietnam during 1969. Like the Hagel brothers, draftee O'Brien advanced to sergeant in country. He earned one Purple Heart.

2. Gitlin, *The Sixties*, 331. Todd Gitlin was in Chicago as a participant in the unrest.

3. For crowd estimates, see Scheips, *The Role of Federal Military Forces in Civil Disorders 1945–1992*, 358; and Dougan and Weiss, *Nineteen Sixty-Eight*, 164. For Lyndon Johnson's crude remark, see Perlstein, *Nixonland*, 267. For the nomination of Humphrey as street clashes escalated, see Tom Wicker, "Humphrey Nominated on the First Ballot After His Plank on Vietnam Is Approved; Police Battle Protestors in Streets," *New York Times*, August 29, 1968, 1. Humphrey chose as his running mate the colorless Senator Edmund Muskie of Maine. He delivered his state's four electoral votes and not much else.

4. Dougan and Weiss, *Nineteen Sixty-Eight*, 168.

5. Gitlin, *The Sixties*, 331–34. Gitlin was there.

6. Carl D. Rostow and Robert D. Davis, *A Handbook for Psychological Fitness-for-Duty Evaluations in Law Enforcement* (Binghamton, NY: Haworth Press, 2004), 18.

7. Richard M. Nixon, "What Has Happened to America?" *Reader's Digest*, October 1967, 49–54. Conservative writer Patrick Buchanan assisted Nixon in drafting this article.

8. Ibid., 302–4; Scheips, *The Role of Federal Military Forces in Civil Disorders 1945–1992*, 320–22.

9. Dougan and Weiss, *Nineteen Sixty-Eight*, 176.

10. Lessing, *The Politics of Rage*, 343, 364; Lesher, *George Wallace*, 399, 416. For "work" and "soap," see Marianne Worthington, "The Campaign Rhetoric of George Wallace in the 1968 Presidential Election" at http://www.ucumberlands.edu/downloads/academics/history/vol4/MarianneWorthington92.html, accessed July 12, 2016. For the meanness quotation, see Perlstein, *Nixonland*, 340.

11. Perry, "Interview with Senator Charles Hagel"; Berens, *Chuck Hagel*, 36–37.

12. Perry, "Interview with Senator Charles Hagel."

13. Ibid.

14. MacPherson, *Long Time Passing*, 419. Emphasis in original.

15. U.S., Headquarters, 9th Infantry Division, *Operational Report of 9th Infantry Division for Period Ending 31 October 1968* (Dong Tam, Republic of Vietnam: Headquarters, 9th Infantry Division, November 15, 1968), 24.

16. Perry, "Interview with Senator Charles Hagel"; Penner, "Interview with Charles Timothy Hagel and Thomas Leo Hagel, Part 7 of 21."

17. Penner, "Interview with Charles Timothy Hagel and Thomas Leo Hagel, Part 7 of 21."

18. Sobel, *The Fighting Pattons*, 39; Sorley, *Thunderbolt*, 57. Abrams, like Westmoreland, hailed from the West Point Class of 1936.

19. Sorley, *A Better War*, 17–30.

20. Davidson, *Vietnam at War*, 512–13. Davidson's intelligence analysts recognized that the NVA and VC shifted to guerrilla activities by mid-1968.

21. Ewell and Hunt, *Sharpening the Combat Edge*, 118–20, 129–30; Gittinger, *Interview with Lieutenant General Julian J. Ewell*, 22–23, 25, 32.

22. Hunt, *The 9th Infantry Division*, 23–25.

23. Headquarters, 2nd Battalion (Mechanized), *47th Infantry, Significant Activities for Calendar Year of 1968*, 4. Binh Phuoc is in Long An province.

24. 9th Infantry Division, *Operational Report of 9th Infantry Division for Period Ending 31 October 1968*, 21. A small segment of Route 25 near Dong Tam also had to be secured.

25. Stanton, *Vietnam Order of Battle*, 150–53; Bolger interview with Charles T. Hagel.

26. Perry, "Interview with Senator Charles Hagel."

27. Bergerud, *Red Thunder, Tropic Lightning*, 109. For a detailed examination, see Jean L. Dyer, Kimberli Gaillard, Nancy R. McClure, and Suzanne M. Osborne, *Evaluation of an Unaided Night Vision Instructional Program for Ground Forces* (Alexandria, VA: U.S. Army Research Institute, October 1995), 2–4, B-1, B-2.

28. Hunt, *The 9th Infantry Division*, 64–77; Bolger interview with Charles T. Hagel. Hagel said he led "a lot of ambush patrols."

29. Perry, "Interview with Senator Charles Hagel."

30. Penner, "Interview with Charles Timothy Hagel and Thomas Leo Hagel, Part 7 of 21."

31. Stanton, *Vietnam Order of Battle*, 277.

32. Doleman, *Tools of War*, 40–41.

33. Ibid., 305.

34. Bunting, *The Lionheads*, 47, 54–58. Bunting's novel reflects many of the attitudes he witnessed during his time serving under Major General Ewell's command with the 9th Infantry Division in Vietnam.

35. For a good description of setting up a Claymore mine in a night ambush, see O'Brien, *If I Die in a Combat Zone*, 93–94.

36. Perry, "Interview with Senator Charles Hagel."

37. Berens, *Chuck Hagel*, 31.

38. David C. Isby, *Weapons and Tactics of the Soviet Army* (London: Jane's Publishing, 1988), 251–52, 284–85, 331–33, 419–21. The Soviets and Chinese shipped towed mortars, towed rocket launchers, and towed heavy machine

guns to the North Vietnamese. All of these came mounted on rubber tires, to be pulled by trucks. In Vietnam, the VC and NVA often dragged these weapons by hand.

39. Berens, *Chuck Hagel*, 31.

40. Perry, "Interview with Senator Charles Hagel."

41. Berens, *Chuck Hagel*, 32.

42. Perry, "Interview with Senator Charles Hagel."

43. 9th Infantry Division, *Operational Report of 9th Infantry Division for Period Ending 31 October 1968*, 6–8, 21.

44. Bergerud, *Red Thunder, Tropic Lightning*, 109–10.

45. Gittinger, *Interview with Lieutenant General Julian J. Ewell*, 34.

46. John "Fats" Spizzirri, "One Day in Nam (For Chuck)," at http://www.angel fire.com/ny2/SGTFATS/page10A.html, accessed July 13, 2016. John Spizzirri served in 2nd Platoon, Company B, 2-47th Infantry in 1968–69. Like Chuck and Tom Hagel, he advanced to sergeant and spent most of his time as an acting NCO. He knew the men on the patrol of October 3–4, 1968, and participated in the morning reaction force mission.

47. Ibid.; Bolger interview with Thomas L. Hagel. Tom Hagel was part of the reaction force. For his additional recollections, see Brad Penner, producer, writer, reporter, "Interview with Charles Timothy Hagel and Thomas Leo Hagel, Part 9 of 21," Nebraska Educational Television, August 14, 1999, at http://memory .loc.gov/diglib/vhp/story/loc.natlib.afc2001001.88134/, accessed July 14, 2016.

48. Argabright, *The 9th Infantry Division "The Old Reliables" Those Who Gave Their Lives in Southeast Asia 1966–1970*, 3, 9, 11, 17, 26, 41, 44, 50; Bolger interview with Charles T. Hagel.

49. The words of a Vietnam-era military death notification message are noted in Harold G. Moore and Joseph L. Galloway, *We Were Soldiers Once . . . And Young: Ia Drang—The Battle That Changed the War in Vietnam* (New York: Presidio Press, 1992), 345.

50. 9th Infantry Division, *Operational Report of 9th Infantry Division for Period Ending 31 October 1968*, 16, 21.

51. Carroll, *House of War*, 320; Carter, *The Politics of Rage*, 359–61; Lessing, *George Wallace*, 425–26.

52. Perlstein, *Nixonland*, 354. Wallace won Alabama, Arkansas, Georgia, Mississippi, and Louisiana. He was the last third-party candidate to earn an electoral vote in a U.S. presidential election.

53. Perry, "Interview with Senator Charles Hagel"; Berens, *Chuck Hagel*, 37; Roger L. Vance, "Chuck Hagel Nomination: An Interview with Senator Hagel on His Vietnam War Experience and Vision for the War's Commemoration," *Vietnam*, December 2012, 30.

54. Perry, "Interview with Senator Charles Hagel", Bolger interview with Thomas L. Hagel.

55. Perry, "Interview with Senator Charles Hagel."

CHAPTER 10. CHILDREN OF NYX

1. Hesiod, *Theogony*, Stanley Lombardo, trans. (Indianapolis, IN: Hackett Classics, 1993), 67. A Greek contemporary of Homer, Hesiod wrote his *Theogony*, the genealogy of the gods, sometime between 750 and 650 B.C. Among her many progeny, the primordial goddess Night (*Nyx*) gave birth to Doom (*Moros*), Fate (*Ker*), Death (*Thanatos*), Sleep (*Hypnos*), and Dreams (*Oneiroi*).

2. Bolger interview with Thomas L. Hagel; see also Vance, "Chuck Hagel Nomination," 31.

3. For the phases of breakdown, see Roy L. Swank and Walter E. Marchand, "Combat Neuroses: Development of Combat Exhaustion," *American Medical Association: Archives of Neurology and Psychology*, March, 1946, 236–43. For the official military findings, see Robert R. Palmer, Bell I. Wiley, and William R. Keast, *U.S. Army in World War II: The Army Ground Forces, Vol. 2: The Procurement and Training of Ground Combat Troops* (Washington, DC: U.S. Government Printing Office, 1991), 228.

4. Gittinger, *Interview with Lieutenant General Julian J. Ewell*, 5–6.

5. Ewell and Hunt, *Sharpening the Combat Edge*, 102, 127.

6. Perry, "Interview with Senator Charles Hagel."

7. MacPherson, *Long Time Passing*, 181.

8. Sheehan, *A Bright Shining Lie*, 719. Reporter Peter Arnett, a longtime Vietnam hand, secured this evocative quote for a story published on February 8, 1968. Like the "lions led by donkeys" line in World War I, it has been much disputed. Colleagues Neil Sheehan and David Halberstam, two award-winning journalists and historians of the Vietnam War, supported the integrity of Arnett's reporting. Both Major Phil Cannella, U.S. Army, and Major Chester L. Brown, U.S. Air Force, have been named as the sources. Arnett interviewed four officers that day in Ben Tre and could not recall who said it.

9. Westmoreland, *A Soldier Reports*, 369–70. While there are many dictionaries of Vietnam War slang, the thoughts of the longtime MACV commander are rather interesting. He certainly heard the words and knew their definitions. Whether he understood what it all really meant is another matter.

10. Perry, "Interview with Senator Charles Hagel," offers thoughts on the battalion and brigade commanders, including Emerson. For Chuck Hagel's positive view of Ewell's field leadership, see Sullivan, "A Vietnam War That Never Ends."

11. Bergerud, *Red Thunder, Tropic Lightning*, 112.

12. Philip Caputo, *Indian Country* (New York: Vintage, 1987), vi. Caputo served in Vietnam as a U.S. marine lieutenant in 1965–66, to include service as a rifle platoon commander. This novel is one of several books he wrote based on his experiences in combat and subsequent role as a journalist.

13. Penner, "Interview with Charles Timothy Hagel and Thomas Leo Hagel, Part 5 of 21."

14. Penner, "Interview with Charles Timothy Hagel and Thomas Leo Hagel, Part 9 of 21." For "Charlie worship," see Bergerud, *Red Thunder, Tropic Lightning*, 255.

15. Herr, *Dispatches*, 178, recounts a colonel calmly discussing the etymology of "dinks."

16. Westmoreland, *A Soldier Reports*, 369–70. With regard to "gook," the Korean language makes broad use of the word. Koreans are Hanguk. Americans are Miguk, literally "the beautiful people." The Chinese are Chunguk. English are Anguk.

17. *Get Smart*, CBS Studios, 1965–70. This comic look at spies and espionage followed the adventures of Maxwell Smart, Agent 86, and his female partner, known only as Agent 99. World War II veteran and noted comedian Mel Brooks joined with Buck Henry to develop the show.

18. Penner, "Interview with Charles Timothy Hagel and Thomas Leo Hagel, Part 9 of 21."

19. Davidson, *Vietnam at War*, 390; Gittinger, *Interview with Lieutenant General Julian J. Ewell*, 2–3, 32.

20. Bunting, *The Lionheads*, 67.

21. 9th Infantry Division, *Operational Report of 9th Infantry Division for Period Ending 31 July 1968*, 81–82, 84.

22. The no alcohol rule, known as General Order Number One, originated in the 1990–91 war with Iraq. Vietnam veteran General H. Norman Schwarzkopf Jr. banned beer and hard liquor in deference to the customs of Saudi Arabia, the country where American troops staged. Whatever the Saudis made of it—and despite their ostensible religious views, most Saudis liked a drink as much as anyone—the lack of alcohol greatly reduced disciplinary problems. Every subsequent U.S. overseas operation has followed that example. See H. Norman Schwarzkopf Jr. and Peter Petre, *It Doesn't Take a Hero: The Autobiography of General H. Norman Schwarzkopf* (New York: Bantam, 1992), 360, 384.

23. Nolan, *House to House*, 59. Lieutenant Colonel Eric F. Antila of 5-60th Infantry offered that statement. For Ewell drinking beer with 2-47th Infantry troops, see Chuck Hagel's comments in Sullivan, "A Vietnam War That Never Ends."

24. Penner, "Interview with Charles Timothy Hagel and Thomas Leo Hagel, Part 8 of 21"; Bolger interview with Thomas L. Hagel.

25. Jeffrey Race, *War Comes to Long An: Revolutionary Conflict in a Vietnamese Province* (Berkeley, CA: University of California Press, 2010), i, 330–31.

26. Lieutenant General Carroll H. Dunn, U.S. Army, *Vietnam Studies: Base Development 1965–1970* (Washington, DC: U.S. Government Printing Office, 1991), 135; Stanton, *Vietnam Order of Battle*, 77–78.

27. Penner, "Interview with Charles Timothy Hagel and Thomas Leo Hagel, Part 8 of 21."

28. Hunt, *The 9th Infantry Division*, 72–78.

29. 9th Infantry Division, *Operational Report of 9th Infantry Division for Period Ending 31 July 1968*, 21.

30. Penner, "Interview with Charles Timothy Hagel and Thomas Leo Hagel, Part 8 of 21"; Bolger interview with Thomas L. Hagel.

31. Bolger interview with Thomas L. Hagel.

32. Penner, "Interview with Charles Timothy Hagel and Thomas Leo Hagel, Part 8 of 21."

33. Penner, "Interview with Charles Timothy Hagel and Thomas Leo Hagel, Part 9 of 21." For artillery round counts, see 9th Infantry Division, *Operational Report of 9th Infantry Division for Period Ending 31 October 1968*, 22. About 70 percent of all artillery fired went toward these harassment and interdiction missions, all based on intelligence reports and aerial spottings of varying reliability. See Krepinevich, *The Army and Vietnam*, 201.

34. Stanton, *Vietnam Order of Battle*, 276.

35. Penner, "Interview with Charles Timothy Hagel and Thomas Leo Hagel, Part 9 of 21."

36. For an excellent overhead view of Bien Phuoc, see Bob Pries, *Welcome to Binh Phouc!* at http://www.angelfire.com/ny/binhphouc/, accessed July 15, 2016.

37. Penner, "Interview with Charles Timothy Hagel and Thomas Leo Hagel, Part 9 of 21"; 9th Infantry Division, *Operational Report of 9th Infantry Division for Period Ending 31 October 1968*, 5, 16.

38. Perry, "Interview with Senator Charles Hagel."

39. Brad Penner, producer, writer, reporter, "Interview with Charles Timothy Hagel and Thomas Leo Hagel, Part 10 of 21," Nebraska Educational Television, August 14, 1999, at http://memory.loc.gov/diglib/vhp/story/loc.natlib.afc2001001.88134/, accessed July 15, 2016.

40. Penner, "Interview with Charles Timothy Hagel and Thomas Leo Hagel, Part 9 of 21"; Bolger interview with Thomas L. Hagel.

41. Perry, "Interview with Senator Charles Hagel." Chuck Hagel described a similar enemy attack from his time in country.

42. Bergerud, *Red Thunder, Tropic Lightning*, 159, describes this method of artillery direct fire.

43. Penner, "Interview with Charles Timothy Hagel and Thomas Leo Hagel, Part 9 of 21."

44. MacPherson, *Long Time Passing*, 177; Bolger interview with Thomas L. Hagel.

45. 9th Infantry Division, *Operational Report of 9th Infantry Division for Period Ending 31 July 1968*, 12; 9th Infantry Division, *Operational Report of 9th Infantry Division for Period Ending 31 October 1968*, 11; Hunt, *The 9th Infantry Division*, 109–10; Clemis, "The Control War," 475–77. See also Race, *War Comes to Long An*, 417, 419. In that province, enemy force strength increased from 2,180 to 3,100 and 79.7 percent of villages remained outside of Saigon's authority.

46. In a later operation named Speedy Express (December 1, 1968 to June 1, 1969), the 9th Infantry Division reported 10,899 enemy killed and 748 weapons taken. See U.S. Headquarters Military Assistance Command Vietnam, *Review of*

Ground Operations (Tan Son Nhut Air Base, Republic of Vietnam: Headquarters, MACV, June 1969), 94.

47. Turse, *Kill Anything That Moves*, 217. Turse quotes from "A Concerned Sergeant" letter sent to the secretary of the army and subject to an extensive investigation. Turse had access to the investigation documents.

48. Gittinger, *Interview with Lieutenant General Julian J. Ewell*, 33–36, 39–40.

49. Doleman, *Tools of War*, 164–76.

50. Ibid., 27–28.

51. Turse, *Kill Anything That Moves*, 211–12. Major Bill Taylor reported these rationalizations after he witnessed a UH-1 Huey door gunner engage Vietnamese in race paddies.

52. Gittinger, *Interview with Lieutenant General Julian J. Ewell*, 11, 38.

53. Penner, "Interview with Charles Timothy Hagel and Thomas Leo Hagel, Part 10 of 21." At My Lai, Quang Ngai Province, on March 16, 1968, U.S. soldiers of Company C, 1st Battalion, 20th Infantry, killed hundreds of unarmed Vietnamese villagers in an unprovoked atrocity. See Westmoreland, *A Soldier Reports*, 456–62.

54. Bolger interview with Thomas L. Hagel.

55. MacPherson, *Long Time Passing*, 22.

56. Toby Harnden, "Chuck Hagel, Obama's Pick for Pentagon, Was 'Very, Very Good at Killing' in Vietnam," *Sunday Times* (UK), January 27, 2013.

57. Penner, "Interview with Charles Timothy Hagel and Thomas Leo Hagel, Part 10 of 21."

58. Ibid.; MacPherson, *Long Time Passing*, 21.

59. Perry, "Interview with Senator Charles Hagel."

60. Argabright, *The 9th Infantry Division "The Old Reliables" Those Who Gave Their Lives in Southeast Asia 1966–1970*, 1–52. During the time the Hagel brothers served in 2-47th Infantry (December 4, 1967 until January 31, 1968), the battalion lost eighty-two soldiers killed in action.

61. Perry, "Interview with Senator Charles Hagel."

62. Ibid.

63. Penner, "Interview with Charles Timothy Hagel and Thomas Leo Hagel, Part 7 of 21."

64. Perry, "Interview with Senator Charles Hagel."

CHAPTER 11. ASHES

1. Sorley, *Westmoreland*, 258.

2. Adam Fletcher Sasse, "A History of North Omaha's June 1969 Riot," North Omaha History blog, August 21, 2015, at http://northomaha.blogspot.com/2015/08/remembering-vivian-strong.html, accessed July 18, 2016.

3. Amy Helene Forss, *Black Print with a White Carnation: Mildred Brown and the* Omaha Star *Newspaper, 1938–1989* (Lincoln, NE: University of Nebraska Press, 2014), 143–44.

4. For the role of helicopters in riot control, see Scheips, *The Role of Federal Military Forces in Civil Disorders 1945–1992*, 76, 321, 347, 389.

5. Andrew Chaikin, *A Man on the Moon: The Voyages of the Apollo Astronauts* (New York: Penguin, 1998), 211, 226. The second American to walk on the moon, Lieutenant Colonel Edwin E. "Buzz" Aldrin Jr., U.S. Air Force, spoke the words "magnificent desolation" as he stepped off the lander.

6. Vance, "Chuck Hagel Nomination," 32.

7. Adam Fletcher Sasse, "A History of the Logan Fontenelle Housing Projects," North Omaha History blog, August 20, 2015, at http://northomaha.blogspot .com/2015/08/a-history-of-logan-fontenelle-housing.html, accessed July 18, 2016. Hall of Fame St. Louis Cardinals pitcher Bob Gibson grew up in this housing area. The project was named for Logan Fontenelle (1825–1855), an Omaha Indian with a French father. Fontenelle acted as an interpreter in early negotiations between the Omaha and arriving settlers.

8. Forss, *Black Print with a White Carnation*, 143.

9. Frederick C. Luebke, *Nebraska: An Illustrated History* (Lincoln, NE: Bison Books, 2005), 336–37.

10. Sasse, "A History of North Omaha's June 1969 Riot"; Forss, *Black Print with a White Carnation*, 144.

11. Scheips, *The Role of Federal Military Forces in Civil Disorders 1945–1992*, 335.

12. United Press International, "Omaha Negroes Urged to End Disorder," *Arizona Republic*, June 27, 1969, 36.

13. For FBI interest in Omaha, Nebraska, see U.S. Federal Bureau of Investigation, Special Agent in Charge, Omaha, *Memorandum for Director, Subject: Counterintelligence Program, Racial Intelligence, Black Nationalist-Hate Groups, Racial Intelligence, Black Panther Party (BPP)* (Omaha, NE: FBI Special Agent in Charge, July 14, 1969), 1. For reference to photographs of Black Panthers guarding a location in North Omaha, see Leo Adam Biga, "A Brief History of Omaha's Civil Rights Struggle Distilled in Back and White by Photographer Rudy Smith," *Leo Adam Biga's My Inside Stories, May 2, 2012*, at https://leo adambiga.com/2012/05/02/a-brief-history-of-omahas-civil-rights-struggle -distilled-in-black-and-white-by-photographer-rudy-smith/, accessed July 18, 2016. Photojournalist Rudy Smith captured key images of the 1969 Omaha riot.

14. Tom Weiner, *Enemies: A History of the FBI* (New York: Random House, 2013), 195–96, 270, 279, 283, 347.

15. For anti-government groups targeted by the FBI Counterintelligence Program, see U.S. Federal Bureau of Investigation, "COINTELPRO," *FBI Records: The Vault* at https://vault.fbi.gov/cointel-pro, accessed July 19, 2016.

16. Perlstein, *Nixonland*, 331, 363.

17. Biga, "A Brief History of Omaha's Civil Rights Struggle Distilled in Back and White by Photographer Rudy Smith."

18. Sasse, "A History of North Omaha's June 1969 Riot."

19. Paul Hammel, "David Rice, Long Known as Mondo we Langa, Maintained His Innocence in 1970 Slaying Until the End," *Omaha World-Herald*, March 16, 2016, at http://www.omaha.com/news/nebraska/david-rice-long-known-as -mondo-we-langa-maintained-his/article_44514dcc-2778-5593-a7ff-23f5dcbad22c .html, accessed July 19, 2016.

20. Elena Carter, "The Forgotten Panthers," *Buzzfeed*, February 11, 2016, at https://www.buzzfeed.com/e6carter/the-omaha-two?utm_term=.wv1El3bY7# .urzqeLv8A, accessed July 19, 2016. Carter's father, Earl Sandy Carter, worked in North Omaha in the early 1970s as a Volunteer in Service to America (VISTA) anti-poverty worker.

21. Michael Richardson, "Omaha FBI Office Sets Up COINTELPRO Unit and J. Edgar Hoover targets Black Panthers," *San Francisco Bay View*, June 25, 2011, at http://sfbayview.com/2011/06/the-story-of-the-omaha-two-2/, accessed July 19, 2016.

22. Vance, "Chuck Hagel Nomination," 32; Bolger interview with Charles T. Hagel; Bolger interview with Thomas L. Hagel.

23. Robert Nelson, "War and Peace," *Omaha Magazine*, July 10, 2014, 60–61.

24. Ibid.

25. Berens, *Chuck Hagel*, 37–38, 46.

26. MacPherson, *Long Time Passing*, 22–23.

27. Westmoreland, *A Soldier Reports*, 455–56.

28. Stanton, *Vietnam Order of Battle*, 274, 334. The ARVN 7th Infantry Division and 9th Infantry Division assumed responsibility for the former U.S. 9th Infantry Division area of operations.

29. Davidson, *Vietnam at War*, 542–47.

30. U.S. Selective Service System, "Induction Statistics" at https://www.sss .gov/About/History-And-Records/Induction-Statistics, accessed July 19, 2016. See also U.S. Selective Service System, "The Vietnam Lotteries," at https://www.sss .gov/About/History-And-Records/lotter1, accessed May 27, 2016.

31. Sorley, *Thunderbolt*, 291, 313–14, 317–18; Davidson, *Vietnam at War*, 653–54.

32. Thomas J. Knock, *The Rise of a Prairie Statesman: The Life and Times of George McGovern* (Princeton, NJ: Princeton University Press, 2016), 429. McGovern earned the Distinguished Flying Cross during a 1944 bombing mission over German-held Czechoslovakia.

33. Berens, *Chuck Hagel*, 45–46; Bolger interview with Charles T. Hagel.

34. Unattributed, "Hastings Youth, 16, Is Victim," *Lincoln Evening Journal*, November 17, 1969.

35. Betty Breeding was quoted in MacPherson, *Long Time Passing*, 420. For Chuck Hagel's quotation, see Hagel, *America: Our Next Chapter*, 279. He offered similar thoughts in the Bolger interview with Charles T. Hagel.

36. Berens, *Chuck Hagel*, 18–19.

37. MacPherson, *Long Time Passing*, 180.

38. Richard Holmes, *Acts of War: The Behavior of Men in Battle* (New York: Free Press, 1985), 213–20.

39. Bolger interview with Charles T. Hagel.

40. Grossman, *On Killing*, 287–89.

41. MacPherson, *Long Time Passing*, 180. Emphasis in original.

42. Ibid., 180; Bolger interview with Thomas L. Hagel; University of Dayton, "School of Law: Thomas Hagel" at https://www.udayton.edu/directory/law/hagel _thomas.php, accessed July 19, 2016.

43. Berens, *Chuck Hagel*, 47.

44. U.S. Senate, Senator Charles T. Hagel, "Governor Frank B. Morrison," 108th Congress, 2nd Session, *Congressional Record* (April 22, 2004), S4288; Bolger interview with Charles T. Hagel.

45. Bolger interview with Thomas L. Hagel.

46. Carter, "The Forgotten Panthers."

47. James Moore, Very Special Agents: *The Inside Story of America's Most Controversial Law Enforcement Agency—The Bureau of Alcohol, Tobacco, and Firearms* (Champaign, IL: University of Illinois Press, 1997), 103–4.

48. The FBI special agent is quoted in ibid., 104 below. For the Des Moines, Iowa, attack, see United Press International, "Des Moines Building Ripped by Explosion," *Chicago Tribune*, June 14, 1970.

49. Ibid., 104.

50. In Operation Pandora, on July 25, 1971, the KGB directed emplacement of bombs "in the Negro section of New York," preferably at a black-majority college. See Andrew and Mitrokhin, *The Sword and the Shield: The Mitrokhin Archive*, 238.

51. Unattributed, "Students, Police to Be Topics of UFAF Confab," *Omaha Sun*, January 1, 1970. This source refers to the United Front Against Fascism, an alternative name for the National Committee to Combat Fascism. That latter name was on the sign in front of David Rice's house.

52. Carter, "The Forgotten Panthers."

53. Ibid.; Moore, *Very Special Agents*, 104.

54. Carter, "The Forgotten Panthers."

55. Bolger interview with Charles T. Hagel.

56. Hammel, "David Rice, Long Known as Mondo we Langa, Maintained His Innocence in 1970 Slaying Until the End."

57. Carter, "The Forgotten Panthers"; Bolger interview with Thomas L. Hagel.

58. Jennifer Mascia, "People Were So Stunned That a 12-Year-Old Could Be Holding a Gun," *Trace*, July 30, 2015, at https://www.thetrace.org/2015/07/omaha -nebraska-urban-gun-violence-city-limits/, accessed July 20, 2016.

59. MacPherson, *Long Time Passing*, 420; Bolger interview with Thomas L. Hagel.

60. Todd Cooper, "After 35 years, Witness Still Says He Was 911 Caller. Duane Peak Holds Firm on the Recording That Led to the Death of an Omaha Officer and the Convictions of Two Men in the 1970s," *Omaha World-Herald*, May 14, 2006. For Chuck Hagel's thoughts on due process, even when it is very unpopular, see Hagel, *America: Our Next Chapter*, 101.

61. Penner, "Interview with Charles Timothy Hagel and Thomas Leo Hagel, Part 10 of 21"; Bolger interview with Charles T. Hagel.

62. Davidson, *Vietnam at War*, 706–10.

63. Edward Doyle and Terrence Maitland, *The Aftermath, 1975–1985, The Vietnam Experience* (Boston: Boston Publishing), 102. For Chuck Hagel's thoughts on the differences between Saigon of 1968 and 1999, see Hagel, *America: Moving Forward*, 8–9. Following his stint as a public defender, Professor Tom Hagel served on the law faculty of Temple University and then the University of Dayton. He also filled in as an acting municipal judge in Dayton, Ohio.

64. Brad Penner, producer, writer, reporter, *Echoes of War*, Nebraska Educational Television, 1999, at http://memory.loc.gov/diglib/vhp/story/loc.natlib.afc 2001001.88134/, accessed July 21, 2016.

65. The complete set of available raw video footage and sound can be found at http://memory.loc.gov/diglib/vhp/story/loc.natlib.afc2001001.88134/, accessed July 20, 2016.

EPILOGUE. THE OLD SERGEANT

1. George Santayana, "Tipperary," *Soliloquies in England and Later Soliloquies* (London: Constable, 1922), 102. Santayana wrote these lines following the armistice of November 11, 1918. The quotation is often attributed to Plato, most notably on the wall of the British Imperial War Museum in London. It was also linked to Plato by General of the Army Douglas A. MacArthur in his famous "Duty, Honor, Country" speech to West Point cadets on 1962. The words appear again as Plato's aphorism at the beginning of the 2001 film *Black Hawk Down*. No extant work of Plato includes this quotation.

2. Karen Parrish, "Hagel Visits Afghanistan to Assess Operations," American Forces Press Service, March 8, 2013, http://archive.defense.gov/news/newsarticle .aspx?id=119473, accessed August 2, 2016.

3. Mirwais Harooni and Phil Stewart, "Suicide Bomber Kills Nine Afghans in Kabul During Hagel Visit," Reuters, March 9, 2013, http://www.reuters.com/ article/us-afghanistan-blast-idUSBRE92804220130309, accessed August 1, 2016.

4. Karen Parrish, "Hagel Offers Observations After Meeting with Karzai," American Forces Press Service, March 10, 2013, at http://archive.defense.gov/ news/newsarticle.aspx?id=119483, accessed August 1, 2016.

5. Karen Parrish, "Suicide Bomber Attacks Nearby During Hagel ISAF Meeting," American Forces Press Service, March 9, 2013, at http://archive.defense .gov/news/newsarticle.aspx?id=119480, accessed August 1, 2016.

6. Chris Carroll, "On Hagel's First Afghan Visit, Karzai Alleges US, Taliban Are Colluding," *Stars and Stripes*, March 11, 2013.

7. Daniel P. Bolger, "Notes on Events of March 10, 2013," NATO Training Mission—Afghanistan commander's journal.

Index

Abbott, James Frank, 142
Abrams, Creighton
  background, 210
  description/traits, 210, 239
  Ewell and, 93
  on military strength, 127
  on Saigon, 178–179
  task of "losing war" and, 210
  Vietnam, 178, 210
Acheson, Dean, 106
Advanced Individual Training/
    Chuck Hagel
  leave/return to Nebraska and
    family, 50
  Officer Candidate School offer
    and, 49
  Redeye antiaircraft missile
    training, 49–50
  training description, 47–49
Afghanistan/fighting, xii, 265–268
Agent Orange, 157
Agnew, Spiro, 206
Ali, Muhammad, 54, 163
American Civil Liberties Union, 261
American Independent Party, 137,
  141
American Spirit Honor Medal, 47
Amin, Mohammed, 267
Amnesty International, 261
Andrews Air Force Base
  description, 17–18
  as target, 17, 18
anti-war movement, 52

anti-war movement/Vietnam
  by 1967 and, 10–11, 51–53
  Chicago riots (1968) and, 204,
    205–206
  college students losing interest
    in, 254
  draft and, 52–53
  march on the Pentagon (1967), 52
  media and, 85–87
  military claims on enemy
    casualties and, 177
  rallies/sayings, 52
  Tet Offensive and, 85–87, 145
  US people/statistics (1967), 10–11,
    145
  See also specific individuals
APC (armored personnel carrier)
  advantages/disadvantages, 70–72
  maintenance and, 102, 117
  movements, 161
  tanks vs., 71
Apollo 11 astronauts, 248
Apple, R.W., Jr. ("Johnny"), 10, 65
Arapaho, 13
Armstrong, Louis, 138
ARVN (Army of the Republic of
    Vietnam)
  Nixon/Vietnamization and, 254,
    255
  role of, 7
  Tet Offensive and, 86
  US military views of, 7, 231
Asterisk, 142